The American Home

Material Culture, Domestic Space, and Family Life

EDITED BY

Eleanor McD. Thompson

Henry Francis du Pont Winterthur Museum
WINTERTHUR, DELAWARE

Distributed by University Press of New England
HANOVER, NEW HAMPSHIRE

Copy Editing and Production: Teresa A. Vivolo

Copyright © 1998 by The Henry Francis du Pont Winterthur Museum, Inc.

Printed in the United States of America.

First edition.

Cover image: John Lewis Krimmel, woman ironing, 1819. Watercolor. (Joseph Downs Collection of Manuscripts and Printed Ephemera, Winterthur Library.)

Library of Congress Cataloging-in-Publication Data

The American home : material culture, domestic space, and family life / edited by
    Eleanor McD. Thompson.
        p.   cm.
    ISBN 0-912724-49-8 (cloth)
    1. Prefabricated houses—United States.   2. Bungalows—United States.
    3. Aladdin Company.   I. Thompson, Eleanor McD.
    NA8480.A63   1998
    392.3'6'0973—dc21   98-21941
                                                                                     CIP

ISBN 0-912724-49-8

Contents

THE INTERIOR AND ITS FURNISHINGS

CONSUMPTION AND LIFE-STYLE

Introduction

Eleanor McD. Thompson

When my co-chair, Charles Hummel, and I sent out our call for papers for the 1992 Winterthur Conference, The American Home: Material Culture, Domestic Space, and Family Life, we were unprepared for the overwhelming interest in this topic and were amazed by the response to our proposal. An avalanche of papers descended upon us. Many weeks and hours of reading and discussion — and many difficult decisions — went into our consideration of this impressive mass of scholarship. This volume holds only a fraction of the many fascinating proposals submitted; and, because of considerations of space, only a portion of those excellent papers delivered at the conference could be included in this final volume. The conference was shaped by the thoughtful responses of every author whose papers we read, and we thank them all.

Aside from the sheer volume of response, equally unanticipated was the *range* of viewpoints centering on the seemingly straightforward topic of the American home. Indeed, one of the revelations of this conference, and one that will strike any reader of the table of contents for this volume, is the breadth of scholarship proffered on the simple concept of home. Many of the homes that are the jumping-off points for the essays included have little in common aside from being grouped here. Some authors have chosen to focus on the home as a building, other on the home as the locus of furnishing choices and imperatives, and still others on the home as the scene for complex family relationships or the necessary backdrop for daily routines and activities. These essays examine an array of homes spanning four centuries and many geographical settings. The cast of characters is equally varied: servants and masters, children and parents, casual visitors and members of extended families. In the end, the range of these papers is heartening witness to the willingness of today's scholars to draw meaning from the everyday activities of ordinary lives and testimony to these researchers' abilities to tease out the facts of these lives from initially unpromising evidence. The response of conference attendees and the scholarly community has demonstrated that these examined lives have great meaning to us today on both personal and theoretical levels.

The home is, of necessity, a building: beyond this, definitions vary. Jan Gilliam's examination of the evolution of the home in early Virginia sets the stage for Marlene Heck's paper on the houses of one great Virginia family in the postrevolutionary period. Indeed, the Chesapeake has been the focus of extensive scholarship in recent years; Dennis Pogue's discussion of the standard of living in this area in the seventeenth century nicely complements John Sprinkle's detailed and somewhat surprising dissection of the material lives of the participants in Bacon's Rebellion. Conover Hunt's account of the relationship between architecture and personal necessity at Montpelier, the Virginia retirement home of James Madison, contrasts with Martha Katz-Hyman's account of the research and results of Colonial Williamsburg's challenging decision to rebuild and refurnish the slave quarters at Carter's Grove: Virginia homes, all of these, but each essay presents vast differences in approach and interpretation.

However, for most of us, homes are neither especially grand nor particularly humble. Two conference papers focused on such houses — those of middle-class, often first-generation, homeowners. Emily Clark describes the career of Chicago promoter S. E. Gross, purveyor of middle- and working-class housing, while Scott Erbes discusses the marketing of modest houses by the Aladdin Company, successful manufacturer of mail-order houses on a national scale. Olive Graffam's description of nineteenth-century kitchen furnishings and technologies is based on firsthand accounts that will be both familiar and revealing to many readers, as will Jane Nylander's description of the daily life of New England housewife Sarah Snell Bryant. Whether from our own family stories or the novels of Louisa May Alcott, we are lulled by the familiarity of these settings only to be suddenly confronted by the unexpected, proving once more that the past *is* a different country.

The house was also the setting for encounters with the outside world. Family life in its more extended domestic setting is the scene of Barbara Carson, Ellen Donald, and Kym Rice's examination of the complex relationships of masters and servants in early Washington, while Marion Winship unearths complexities of a different sort in the early New England household of Samuel Sewall and his wife, Hannah Hull. Sarah Luria's detailed and intriguing look at the Washington home of a very public figure, Frederick Douglass, contrasts with James C. Curtis's dissection of the documentation of African American homes through Farm Security Administration photography.

It is fitting that this volume concludes with Rodris Roth's paper on virtual houses of the late nineteenth and early twentieth centuries: scrapbook houses assembled from Sears catalogues and newspaper advertisements by the little girls who were homeowners of the future. If this volume proves anything, it is that each of us has not only a home of some sort but also an *idea* of home and that this nesting impulse is universal and has been for centuries. That this impulse continues to manifest itself in such varied ways guarantees rich rewards for tomorrow's scholars, who no doubt will be as fascinated by tract housing, beanbag chairs, and take-out Chinese food as we are by coal stoves. Palladian architecture, and the routine of Monday washdays. They should have good hunting.

I would like to thank my co-chair, Charles Hummel, for his help and support throughout the planning, sifting of papers, and chairing of sessions for the 1992 conference for which these papers were written. His experience and advice were essential to the success of the event itself, and I am grateful to him for his willingness to fit this project into his busy schedule. I thank Katharine Martinez, the head of Winterthur Library in 1992, both for suggesting my participation in the conference and for all her help thereafter; and Gary Kulik, presently Deputy Director for Library and Academic Affairs, for his support and advice during the evolution of these published proceedings. Lisa Lock, Teresa Vivolo, and the staff of the Publications Division have been informative and helpful in countless ways. To my colleagues on the staff of the Winterthur Library, a special thank-you: without you, I couldn't have done it!

"*Appearance and Effect Is Everything*"

The James River Houses of Samuel, Joseph, and George Cabell

Marlene Elizabeth Heck

Historians of Virginia's early nineteenth-century architecture must first escape the pull of Thomas Jefferson and his legacy. Captivated by this intriguing figure, few scholars press on to inquire into the remaining riches of Virginia's postrevolutionary landscape. The draw of the great statesman-architect is most strongly felt when questions are raised about Palladian architecture, and so, for nearly a half century, historians have portrayed Jefferson as the principal, even sole, creator of the state's federal-period Palladian tradition.[1]

We are misserved by this myopic deference to Jefferson in at least two ways. First, our determined search for Monticello's smallest remaining secrets blinds us to the region's other remarkable buildings and the histories they embody. While Jefferson's status as the first citizen of the Virginia Piedmont is unquestioned, social, political, and economic interests connected him to a broad, vital regional community. Historians have yet to chart this larger local context, including the architectural settings, in which he moved. Thomas Tileston Waterman's very generous attribution of most things Palladian to Jefferson also misled

The author warmly thanks Kevin "Strong Verb" Reinhart, who seems always to know just the right word.

us and effectively ended all critical thinking about the subject for nearly a half century. American Palladianism found its widest expression in Virginia, and Waterman devoted the bulk of his canonical work, *Mansions of Virginia, 1706–1776*, to the subject. Waterman demonstrated no real link between Jefferson and the late eighteenth-century Palladian houses he so carefully described, but subsequent studies never questioned the veracity of his claims. Once set down, Waterman's assertions about Jefferson's role in the design of Virginia's Palladian dwellings took on the authority of a biblical decree.[2]

This essay offers a fresh perspective on Virginia Palladianism and seeks to remedy the claim of one historian who correctly charged that "the western progress of Palladianism from Vicenza to Richmond County [Va.] has received its full share of textbook pages, leaving us with a few mildly convincing examples and a not very useful view of society." Ironically, one need not look far from Monticello to begin the rewriting of Virginia's Palladian history as a number of exceptional, but largely unknown, Palladian houses are scattered through the landscape surrounding Jefferson's mountaintop retreat. Three dwellings in Nelson County, south of Charlottesville, provide an especially fine group for study. Just above the banks of the James River, near the now-abandoned town of Warminster, evidence remains of the extraordinary architectural activities of Jefferson's neighbors and political colleagues, Samuel, George, and Joseph Cabell. During a three-year building campaign, from 1806 until 1809, these young cousins both contracted for new dwellings and radically altered existing houses. At the end of the decade, three handsome vernacular Palladian dwellings stood overlooking the James River.[3]

The history of the Cabell houses and the circumstances of their construction offer a corrective to standard accounts of Virginia's Palladian architecture. First, this important building tradition has a longer and more complex history than previously acknowledged. Rather than ending with Jefferson's monumental effort, the distinctive form endured as it was remade by a new generation of builders. Moreover, these three houses suggest Virginia's Palladian tradition owed more to transformations in social practices, political activity, and changing concepts of privacy, fashion, and power than to the aesthetic sway of one much-admired designer. For the Cabells, Palladian houses and the furnishings that defined their interior spaces performed important cultural work in reshaping their owners' postrevolutionary social world.

An angry Joseph Carrington Cabell penned away his wrath on a hot summer day in a letter to his cousin, Col. William Cabell. "In truth—nothing is impossible in these times," he began. "The rascal of a miller at the Liberty Hall mill has refused to grind for me, and upon my sending him a decent remonstrance thro' the medium of my overseer, has returned me the most outrageous insolence of language you can possibly imagine. . . . The fellow is really intolerable. I am about to try the law upon him." The indignant author of this note was a wealthy politician from a prominent Virginia family whose members included a United States senator, a Virginia governor, and distinguished physicians. Cabell's felicitous marriage in 1807 to Polly Carter, daughter of the late George Carter, descendent of Robert "King" Carter, and stepdaughter of renowned Williamsburg jurist St. George Tucker, had bound him to one of the state's most prominent families. Marriage brought him the Carter family's famed Corotoman estate, and he received a substantial Piedmont plantation from his father. Cabell, in fact, could not resist a bit of bragging about his comfortable position. "Polly and myself are rich and I shall not live as if we were poor," Joseph announced to his brother soon after his marriage. Certainly Cabell moved comfortably in the company of Virginia's powerful social and political leaders. Yet this same man who was greeted with respect in the parlors and dining rooms of Richmond and Williamsburg and was mentioned for political appointment in Washington was denied service by a miller in his own village. What was happening here?[4]

Joseph Cabell's problems were at home, in Warminster, at the *local* level. In his exchange with the miller, Cabell found his status no longer assured him preferential treatment, and a routine transaction soured when the miller responded with curses rather than the expected show of deference. Such a rewriting of the rules at the Liberty Hall mill clearly stunned Cabell. This small incident reflects the erosion of local privilege and status experienced by many upper-class Virginians after the Revolution. Certainly resistance to gentry authority emerged long before Cabell's unsatisfactory transaction with Liberty Hall's "rascal" miller. Prior to the war with Britain, Virginia's leadership class sustained challenges from religious dissenters, Scottish merchants who siphoned away their economic powers, and an increasingly independent population that fell less and less under their sway.

But historians recently have demonstrated that an accelerated breakdown of Virginia's social hierarchy followed the Revolution. Such changes remade the state's postwar society and profoundly altered its most important institutions; old symbols and rituals of power and privilege were supplanted. While the full story of this social transformation lies outside the scope of this essay, the essential properties of this breakdown can be sketched. Land ownership remained central to wealth and political authority, yet property partition among multiple male heirs meant that few of Cabell's generation possessed the large, valuable parcels that once characterized the region. As property wealth, and thus agricultural fortunes, declined, so did the planter-gentleman status that accompanied it. Economic impairment forced Virginia's young elite males to train for professional careers, and they grudgingly enrolled for legal studies at the College of William and Mary and for medical training at the University of Pennsylvania. And when family name lost its power to provide automatic access to political office, ruling-class Virginians lost their lock on political life. The movement of yeomen and middling farmers into local offices undermined the once-exclusive authority of elites. Eager to exercise recently acquired powers and to assume the privileges of office, these new officials no longer honored old patterns of behavior and social hierarchy. As Cabell discovered, deference ceased to be automatic, and consequently, gentry values were questioned. His William and Mary classmate Peyton Randolph found himself so repelled by the changed local circumstances that he decided to "renounce politics" in favor of continued legal studies. While he observed that "the lawyer does not appear as conspicuous in the eye of the world as the politician. . . . To crawl in the mire of county court practices is too loathsome an idea for a man of spirit."[5]

Virginians also renegotiated the rules that governed relationships among social classes. These changes left many Virginians, especially those like Joseph Cabell, who felt their status threatened, angry and confused. "In our high republican times," the Reverend Devereux Jarratt wrote in 1804, "there is more leveling than ought to be" and "too little regard and reverence paid to magistrates and persons in public office." The social leveling that disturbed Jarratt was a response, he thought, to "the want of a proper distinction, between the various orders of the people." Jarratt's comments were provoked by encounters with people he found dressed beyond their social rank. Styles and types of clothing provided Virginians with the means of structuring encounters, especially with strangers. Once the lower and middle classes seized opportunities to improve their social and political standing—including the appropriation of markers of rank expressed in dress previously available only to elites—social cues blurred. In social situations, just as in political settings, newly empowered Virginians refused to submit to old rules requiring the show of "regard and reverence" to powerful public officials. Jarratt's experience suggests that by the early nineteenth century it was difficult to confidently assess "proper distinctions."[6]

But the three Cabells at the center of this study defied the leveling that attends such social revolutions and aggressively resisted the loss of their position. In an unarticulated but clearly definable response, Joseph Cabell and his cousins shrewdly acknowledged changing political practices, an altered social and economic order, unanticipated career demands, and the distortion of social distinctions. They did so by fashioning a complex adaptive strategy that permitted them to maintain their public eminence. Because land and agricultural investments no longer guaranteed a suitable income, they joined the Commonwealth's other elites in training for professional careers. George Cabell traveled north to Philadelphia for medical school at the University of Pennsylvania, as there were no opportunities for instruction in his home state. But it was law that especially attracted the state's young gentry. Joseph Cabell and his William and Mary classmates elected a legal career even while repelled by the poor character of many of its practitioners and the low esteem in which the public held lawyers. "The mob of the profession get as little money and less respect, than they would by digging the earth," observed Thomas Jefferson, one of law's most reluctant practitioners, who practiced only briefly. Garritt Minor, who studied at William and Mary with Joseph Cabell, confessed, "It has been for a long time a matter of doubt in my mind whether nations which boast of freedom and independence ought to tolerate lawyers." But legal training could be redeemed. Minor described legal studies as disagreeable and laborious but tolerable because of their "intimate connexion with politicks." Joseph Cabell, like his friend Jefferson, would quickly abandon law for a political career.[7]

The political component of this strategy required Joseph and Samuel to abandon to the middling sorts the local arena, which for nearly two centuries had provided the foundation of the family's uncontested political authority. Instead they sought the more powerful and prestigious legislative seats in Richmond and Washington. In one of the most

striking political changes, Joseph and Samuel Cabell actively cam-
paigned for political office. No longer could they wait until election
day to announce their candidacy by "swilling the planters with bumbo,"
or treating the voters with a potent punch, a campaign tactic successfully employed by their fathers and grandfather. They reluctantly took
to the campaign trail—and it was literally a trail—demonstrating that
sound bites, defense of one's military record, and election-year promises
are in no way unique to the late twentieth century. Ironically, once
established at the capitol in Richmond, Joseph did not find the quality
of his fellow politicians much improved over those left behind in Nelson County. The freshman delegate described his new colleagues to
close friend Isaac Coles: "Unfortunately we have many on the stage
who ought to be in the pit. I could not have supposed it possible that
the generality of the members of our assembly should resemble so much
a court house crowd. The republican sein has brought up this year 20
herrings for one shad."[8]

Professional and political adjustments constituted only a portion
of their efforts, and handsome houses filled with fashionable furnishings
also marked and reinforced their prominence. At a time when the
miller denied them service and a hostile electorate threatened to with-
hold their vote, the Cabells turned to the power of material goods and
symbolic acts to provide a "proper distinction" and maintain their ruling-class rank. All three Cabells deftly used fine objects to create new
symbols and practices that distinguished them from those who denied
them their "first-place" status and bound them to those who affirmed
their ambitions. The observation of a young Virginian who wrote, "Appearance and effect is everything, and really between ourselves it would
seem as if every solid virtue was sacrificed to these," perfectly captured
the complexion of the time. In the early nineteenth century, Samuel,
Joseph, and George Cabell used Palladian dwellings, expensive furnishings, fine clothing, and fashionable carriages to maintain the desired
"appearance and effect" and preserve the distinctions that separated
them from the "court house crowd."[9]

Class and rank certainly were not new issues to Joseph Cabell.
Shortly before his wedding Joseph confided to his brother that he would
rather be "the first man in a village, than the second in Rome." To his
confidant, Isaac Coles, Cabell revealed his craving for esteem, writing,
"He who thought himself entitled to the first place, would scarcely be

contented in the second." Guided by the desire for primacy that his rank and nature demanded, Joseph deliberated over the location of his residence for a long period after his marriage. As owner of the Corotoman lands, he considered establishing residence in the Tidewater region so that he could run from there for political office; but he rejected the plan because he found "the place . . . insulated and the society bad." Cabell debated returning to his family's lands near Warminster, an idea he at first dismissed, for he reasoned, "I do not suit the bulk of the people there, nor do they suit me." He would later describe his homeplace as "a miserable little village" and claim that residency there was only a temporary solution; yet Cabell returned to Nelson County when it became clear the district offered his best chance for election to political office. But one thing more was necessary before he could establish himself as a commanding political force. Isaac Coles identified the missing component of his plan: "You have been a wanderer long enough. It is now fit that you should have a home and that you should be the master of it. . . . Until you do this you can have no real weight or influence in society."[10]

While ownership of a gentleman's seat would have ensured Cabell's membership in the leadership class, it would not suffice for preeminence. In his pursuit of status as "first man of the village," Cabell required a more extraordinary architectural presentation, especially since he was not well known and he understood that he did "not suit the bulk of the people there." Joseph Cabell—and his cousins, Samuel and George—called on their houses to do what fine domestic buildings had done for Virginians since the early eighteenth century, namely, to serve as compelling markers of rank and authority.

Like the Cabell dwellings, the state's earliest great houses appeared at a time of social redefinition. When Virginia's nascent gentry class took shape in the 1710s and 1720s, they replaced their flimsy impermanent structures with well-framed or brick dwellings, which they now needed to set themselves apart from the lesser sorts. As Clifford Geertz points out, cultural symbols are particularly necessary "where institutionalized guides for behavior, thought, or feeling are weak or absent." Because fine houses were widely understood in Virginia culture by the turn of the nineteenth century to be instruments of authority, the Cabells were eager to build. Beginning in 1806 and continuing through the end of the decade, all three cousins contracted for new dwellings or

Fig. 1. Soldier's Joy, Nelson County, Va. Early twentieth-century photograph copied from a print in a private collection. (Virginia Department of Historic Resources.)

radically altered existing houses. But to heighten the impact of their
building campaigns, they constructed not the I-houses or three-room
houses or Georgian-plan dwellings of their neighbors but rather vernacular Palladian villas.[11]

Samuel Cabell began the building campaign in 1806 by hiring
Jefferson's workman, James Oldham, to remodel and enlarge Soldier's
Joy, the three-room house built as a wedding gift by his father in 1785
(fig. 1). Oldham transformed the original, sparely detailed house into
a splendid five-part Palladian dwelling. The newly remodeled Soldier's
Joy featured a portico supported by four Doric columns, handsome federal-style details on both the exterior and interior, and an elaborately
detailed west wing that seems to have served as the best entertaining
room. Oldham reinforced the multipart Palladian imagery of the house
by enhancing the facade with three Palladian openings, one into each
hyphen and one set above the portico.[12]

Joseph Cabell conceded to Coles the "impropriety of my trifling
with the people, by offering my services, without having a fixed residence in the county" and decided to enlarge the house he bought from

Fig. 2. Edgewood, Nelson County, Va., 1930s. (Library of Congress; Photo, Frances Benjamin Johnston.)

Samuel Cabell's sister and her husband into a "comfortable box." Perhaps the decision to expand an existing house was principally a financial one, as Joseph explained to his brother, Nicholas, "I am already too much in [debt to] saddle myself with heavy additional obligations." Not far from Samuel Cabell's land, on the same side of the James River, Joseph acquired the three-part house in 1808 and immediately prepared for its expansion into a five-part Palladian dwelling that he renamed Edgewood (fig. 2). Even after arranging for the purchase and renovation of Edgewood, Joseph could not, it seems, bring himself to leave the social life of Williamsburg for the more routine obligations of Warminster, and he depended on his brothers Nicholas and George to oversee the construction executed by his slaves and area workmen. Polly and Joseph Cabell moved to Edgewood in the summer of 1808 as the remodeling continued and immediately filled it with guests.[13]

Joseph's brother, Dr. George Cabell, Jr., began work on his three-part Palladian house, Bon Aire, in 1809. Unlike his brother and cousin, George Cabell built a new dwelling, which he sited on a commanding

Fig. 3. Bon Aire, Nelson County, Va., 1930s. (Library of Congress; Photo, Frances Benjamin Johnston.)

spot at the crest of a hill (fig. 3). Bon Aire shares a similar form and many architectural details with Point of Honor, a house found nearby in Lynchburg that was built for George's cousin, Dr. George Cabell, Sr. Since the younger Dr. Cabell studied with his cousin during the period Point of Honor was under construction, it is likely that the same builder was responsible for both houses. When Bon Aire was completed George Cabell conjoined the new and old professions of status by practicing medicine in one of the two brick dependencies that flanked the house while overseeing tobacco and grain cultivation from his elevated vantage point overlooking the James River.[14]

Undoubtedly the decision to build a Palladian house when other domestic building types were available and widely used was a carefully calculated one. In the early nineteenth century, most of the Cabells' neighbors organized their daily routines into one- and two-room dwellings. Those who could afford better put up I-houses or contracted for three-room houses similar to the original Soldier's Joy. In Nelson Country there were a few, but very few, Georgian-plan dwellings to mark the homeplace of a powerful figure, such as the house of the Cabells' grandfather called Union Hill. When given the opportunity to build, not only did the three Cabells deliberately choose a different house type, but they did so at great expense. Samuel and Joseph acquired multipart dwellings only through costly, extensive remodeling efforts, and the construction of George's Palladian house left him deeply in debt. This intentional shift away from common local building practices suggests the strategic value of the multipart form. The Cabells' willingness to subject themselves to the expense of new building or the inconvenience of extensive remodeling to secure a Palladian house attests to the form's powerful, highly desirable association in the minds of some Virginians. Indeed, by the time Joseph and his relations built their three- and five-part dwellings, some Virginians had communicated their upper-class ranking with Palladian houses for nearly a century.[15]

The celebrated houses of the eighteenth-century gentry were significant markers of status in large measure because they contrasted with the stock of meager, impermanent domestic buildings that dominated Virginia's built landscape. Their scale, form, and handsomely crafted details signaled access to surplus capital and labor and identified their owners as persons of permanence and rank. And so it was some sixty years later with Soldier's Joy, Edgewood, and Bon Aire. By the construction of new substantial dwellings or the elaboration of standing houses, in a setting where such ambitious structures were the exceptions, the Cabells intended to send an identical message. Perceptively, they amplified their message by choosing a house type that had functioned in Virginia as an architectural shorthand for wealth, authority, and status. By the first decade of the nineteenth century, Palladianism had been a feature of Virginia's built landscape for more than a half century. The distinctive form had never disappeared but rather was transformed continuously to suit the changing circumstances and needs of the state's ruling-class builders. This temporal sequence meant the association of the Palladian form with elite status had neither faded nor weakened. Through their houses, which served as instruments of continuity, Joseph, Samuel, and George Cabell linked themselves to the owners of earlier Palladian houses, such as John Tayloe of Mt. Airy and John Bannister of Battersea, and to the attributes of these men—power, affluence, mastery of land, and human labor. Like those who built before them, the Cabells employed the Palladian form to publicly assert their local power and prestige in Nelson County; to mark "the center as center"; in Clifford Geertz's words, to visually establish that they were the leaders—and they led from these houses.[16]

It is true that Soldier's Joy, Bon Aire, and Edgewood are modest in size and detail; no one would mistake them for a Mt. Airy or Battersea. But cultural meaning is locally constituted, and it is "at the local level that social differentiation [is] most critical." Joseph and his cousins needed to direct their message principally to the Nelson County residents upon whom their continued political power and social ranking rested. And because the symbol need not be more sophisticated than the audience for whom it is intended, the Cabells were not required to construct extraordinary architectural examples. Moreover, the style is an allusion, a shorthand, and in its local lexicon it no doubt was sufficient. In a region where most Virginians lived in one- and two-room dwellings, the three Cabell dwellings were powerful statements in Flemish-bond brick and milled timber, and their very construction constituted an act of social presentation. The Cabells extracted the basic three- and five-part Palladian form from earlier examples and updated it with fashionable federal details, including temple fronts and Palladian openings. Resultant dwellings both drew from the authority of the past and spoke of their builder's knowledge of current architectural movements.[17]

While the form of Soldier's Joy, Bon Aire, and Edgewood clearly functioned as a dramatic public marker of their owners' local status, casual access to interiors was not permitted. Surly constituents and bitter political campaigns sapped enthusiasm for public life from ruling-class Virginians and increased the appeal of a separate, private sphere. Seeking escape from a belligerent public world by taking refuge in the secure private world, a weary Jefferson informed a correspondent in 1793, "I am going to Virginia . . . I am then to be liberated from the hated occupation of politics, and to remain in the bosom of my family, my farm and my books." The Cabells were among the many Virginians of rank who withdrew into their homes, seeking asylum in the company of their wives, children, and trusted companions. Virginia's elite now craved control and separation in their social exchanges. William Brockenbrough cautioned his friend Joseph Cabell on the dangers of "intermixture with society at large." He counseled Cabell to seek "partial Solitude, and a select society." One visitor to Monticello recorded her impressions of Jefferson's need "to secure himself the pleasure of a select and refined society." In the hurly-burly of class competition, restriction spoke of status more forcefully than indiscriminate mixing.[18]

The same Palladian facades that showed all and sundry that the Cabells were figures to be reckoned with also encased carefully partitioned interiors. Rooms were designated either public or private, and those located in the public sphere were stages for controlled social interaction. Handsomely decorated passages held unbidden visitors until their dismissal while hinting at the fine settings to be found on the other side of secured doors. Specific circulation sequences dictated the paths of those who gained entry, as at Soldier's Joy, where the linear, five-part plan divided at the passage, dictating a sharp demarcation of public and private domains. The western half of the house consists of a series of entertainment rooms, which increase in levels of finish until they terminate at the highly decorated west-wing room. Across the passage, in the eastern portion, arches, hyphens, and closed doors kept prying eyes from progressively private quarters.

But seclusion behind passages and doors did not mean dour isolation and inactivity. As they retreated from the public arena, the Cabells drew family and friends with them. Joseph Cabell reported to Coles that his father- and mother-in-law had just departed for Williamsburg, good friend John Hartwell Cocke and his family had spent a week at Edgewood, and one of their William and Mary classmates also had been a recent guest. Cabell later declined an invitation from Coles to visit, explaining, "I have friends with me now, and some new ones promise to arrive here the very day I have fixed on for leaving home." Hospitality, however, as the Brockenbrough admonishment informs, now was reserved for the likes of the Tuckers and Cockes, that is, those who were well known to the Cabells and of similar rank. Elites felt at ease only in the company of other upper-class Virginians. In such society one found security and acted with an assurance not possible in the competitive public world. Private tranquility and reciprocal cordiality forged a bond among these embattled ruling-class Virginians.[19]

In the same way, familiar social rituals enacted in their houses reinforced the Cabells' rank in the eyes of their equals and fostered social solidarity among all present. At Soldier's Joy, the west-wing room's exceptional detail—now installed at the Cincinnati Art Museum—provided a grand backdrop for social gatherings, and it joined to the hyphen, parlor, passage, and dining room to create an impressive suite of entertaining rooms. Handsomely appointed rooms at both Bon Aire and Edgewood also were set aside for the entertainment of guests. Because rules of hospitality demanded that visiting family and friends be properly feted and entertained, the Cabells equipped these specialized rooms for evenings of music, dance, games, and multicourse dining.

Cabell family correspondence, purchase receipts, probate inventories, and tax records document the trio's enthusiastic acquisition of fashionable goods used in such restricted social performances. The Cabells furnished the public rooms of their Palladian houses with mahogany pieces; set their tables with engraved silver; padded pine floors with carpets; and enlivened the walls of dining rooms, passages, parlors, and libraries with mirrors, paintings, and prints. Family documents disclose the high standard of living enjoyed by this third generation of Cabells, who owned silver coffee-, tea-, and chocolate pots; guitars and a pianoforte; backgammon tables and chess boards; hundreds of books; dining and card and sewing tables; wineglasses, china cups, engraved spoons, silver platters, and pewter plates. These accumulated furnishings distinguished the three cousins among their exclusive company in the same manner as their Palladian facades publicly elevated them to all passersby. Fine objects, handsomely displayed and expertly used, were essential components in the creation and maintenance of a genteel culture. This elaborate material spectacle laid out by the Cabells silently signaled their position and implicitly confirmed the rank of their guests.[20]

Mere possession of these objects would have been impressive, but the Cabells competed in quantity as well as quality: they simply owned more than anyone else in the county. A personal property evaluation taken in 1815 catalogued the extraordinary range of possessions amassed by the Cabells. This county-wide assessment revealed that family members owned the largest and most valuable dwellings, the greatest number of slaves, and a spectacular collection of fine furniture, silver, musical instruments, and luxury items. Of the thirty-seven houses in Nelson County that were valued above $300, eight belonged to the Cabells or their relations.[21]

Soldier's Joy, assessed at $15,000, received the highest valuation of any house in the county. Samuel Cabell also possessed the most costly and largest variety of objects, including two clocks, three mahogany dining tables, more than a dozen chairs ornamented with gold or silver leaf, eleven pictures or engravings, and one of only two pianos listed in the entire evaluation. An extensive silver collection substantially increased he estate's worth. In addition to silver flatware and silver coffeepots and teapots, eighteen of the twenty-three large silver pitchers, tankards, and serving pieces owned by Nelson County residents were at Soldier's Joy.[22]

At $3,000, Edgewood ranked fourth in the appraisal. While the value of his estate was surpassed by Samuel's extraordinary holdings, Joseph Cabell too had assembled an impressive collection of furnishings. He owned one of the eight venetian blinds recorded (the remaining seven belonged to a relation) and three of the four portraits assessors cited; and he decorated the rooms of Edgewood with thirty-six pictures, prints, or engravings. Two of the four carpets in the county belonged to Joseph, as did four mahogany dining tables, three mahogany bedsteads, a single mahogany chest of drawers, and eight pieces listed as "bureaus, secretaries or bookcases in whole or in part mahogany."[23]

Although enumerators assessed the value of Dr. George Cabell, Jr.'s, Bon Aire at $5,000, which made it the county's third-most valuable dwelling, the $1,707 tally of his possessions was far lower than that of his two relations. His rather modest showing simply points up the Cabell family's substantial fortunes, for his assets were not meager. Bon Aire's assessors noted fourteen prints or engravings, a mirror and clock, and a selection of mahogany furnishings, including three dining tables, sideboards, tea tables, card tables, and a sofa.[24]

Houses could not be moved, however, and mahogany tables were anchored to their rooms. Entry into a world where others might be unfamiliar with their status also required portable objects that spoke of the Cabells' position. The large collection of receipts that survive for great coats, buckles, gold jewelry, yards of ribbon and fine material, and multiple pairs of leather boots and shoes evince the Cabells' use of these items to stand apart from their social inferiors and to mix in a poised and refined manner with their peers. Family members used carriages in a similar way to publicly demonstrate their privileged status. To succeed as a truly effective statement, the coach, like the chair and coat, had to be the most stylish and recently offered version. In 1807 Joseph asked his brother William, who had contacts in Philadelphia, to order a new carriage for him. In correspondence to Thomas Ogle, a Philadelphia coachmaker, William stipulated that the carriage was "to be made on the same scale as [Mr.] Randolph's" but ordered that "the [shape was] to be more in the present fashion." Shortly after placing the order, William wrote to assure his brother of his close attention to the matter, guaranteeing, "I shall direct the color to be black (as it is very fashionable and handsome)." Clearly Joseph wished to make his rounds through Nelson Country in an expensive, fine coach and to move smartly through the streets of Richmond and Williamsburg.[25]

The episode with the carriage recalls Joseph Cabell's boast to his brother that "Polly and myself are rich and I shall not live as if we were poor." For the next several years Cabell—and his cousins—engaged in a frenzy of buying and building. Traveling about in new carriages, perhaps pulling gold watches from pockets of stylish coats, Samuel, Joseph, and George Cabell must have been striking figures as they crossed the Virginia countryside. Vernacular Palladian villas, silver collections, and mahogany furnishings provided additional sure and impressive means of publicizing their status. With their political, economic, and social communities in a state of flux, such prestigious markers were more essential than ever.[26]

But maintaining "appearance and effect" drained their resources, which turned out to be more limited than they might have wished, and the three Cabells found themselves perpetually in debt. One confided that "the times are so hard that I am actually unable to pay my debts, much less to move with a family thro' the scenes of fashion." James Oldham complained in a number of letters to Jefferson that Samuel Cabell repeatedly ignored his requests to pay for the work at Soldier's Joy. Dr. George Cabell, Jr., struggled to earn a living from his medical practice, and the lack of steady income slowed the completion of Bon Aire. Dire circumstances forced George to write to his brother Joseph, who was then in Richmond, to ask for assistance in settling accounts that were due to him. He explained, "I cannot get one cent here . . . my inability to attend to practice, short collections, low prices, family charges, and expenses of building have (as Mother says) put Moll Thomson's hand in my pockets."[27]

Joseph Cabell, despite his otherwise clever strategies, could not preserve the preeminence he sought so resolutely. Only two years after the order was placed for the carriage, Cabell wrote his friend John Hartwell Cocke of Bremo, urging him to take the stylish vehicle off his hands. "Why should you not buy my carriage, as you want one," Cabell wrote, plaintively adding, "I am too much in want of money to keep it."[28]

---

[1] Since 1993, the 250th anniversary of his birth, Jefferson's architectural activities have again come under considerable review. A sampling of perspectives can be found in Mark R. Wenger, "Thomas Jefferson, Tenant," *Winterthur Portfolio* 26, no. 4 (Winter 1991): 249–65; Charles Brownell, "Laying the Groundwork: The Classical Tradition and Virginia Architecture, 1770–1870," in Charles E. Brownell, Calder Loth, William M. S. Rasmussen, and Richard Guy Wilson, *The Making of Virginia Architecture* (Richmond: Virginia Museum of Fine Arts, 1992), pp. 46–53; Susan R. Stein, *The Worlds of Thomas Jefferson at Monticello* (New York: Harry N. Abrams/Thomas Jefferson Memorial Fndn., 1993); Rhys Isaac, "The First Monticello," in Peter Onuf, ed., *Jeffersonian Legacies* (Charlottesville: University Press of Virginia, 1993), pp. 77–108; Gary Wills, "The Aesthete," *New York Review of Books* (August 12, 1993): 6–10; and Joyce Henri Robinson, "An American Cabinet of Curiosities: Thomas Jefferson's Indian Hall at Monticello," *Winterthur Portfolio* 30, no. 1 (Spring 1995): 41–58.

[2] Thomas Tileston Waterman, *The Mansions of Virginia, 1706–1776* (Chapel Hill: University of North Carolina Press, 1946). Virginia has an abundantly rich architectural past, yet so strong is the association between Jefferson and Virginia's architecture that 3 recent publications on Virginia's architecture have all used Jefferson buildings as cover illustrations; see Mills Lane, *Architecture of the Old South: Virginia* (New York: Abbeville Press, 1989); Brownell et al., *Making of Virginia Architecture*; and Calder Loth, ed., *Virginia Landmarks Register* (3d ed.; Charlottesville: University Press of Virginia, 1986).

[3] Edward Chappell, "Looking at Buildings," *Fresh Advices* (November 1984), p. i. The topic of the Cabell houses and their place in the history of American Palladian architecture is discussed in Marlene Elizabeth Heck, "Building Status: Pavilioned Dwellings in Virginia," in Carter L. Hudgins and Elizabeth Collins Cromley, eds., *Shaping Communities: Perspectives in Vernacular Architecture VI* (Knoxville: University of Tennessee Press, 1997), pp. 46–59.

[4] The history of the Cabell family is set down in great detail in Alexander Brown, *The Cabells and Their Kin* (Richmond: Garrett and Massie, 1939). Joseph C. Cabell to William H. Cabell, August 17, 1811, Cabell Family Papers, box 5:5, Swem Library, College of William and Mary; Joseph C. Cabell to William H. Cabell, November 1806, Cabell Papers, Campbell Deposit, 38-111, box 4, Alderman Library, University of Virginia, Charlottesville (hereafter, cited as Cabell Papers).

[5] Peyton Randolph to Joseph C. Cabell, December 28, 1800, Cabell Papers, box 2.

[6] Historians have detailed the eighteenth-century use of fine clothing as the "most obvious, the most socially visible" means of "displaying [pecuniary] strength, and thereby retaining or enhancing one's social standing." In those situations where one was in the company of many stranger who were unfamiliar with their status, the "temptation to dress above one's rank was especially acute" (Neil McKendrick, John Brewer, and J. H. Plumb, *Birth of a Consumer Society: The Commercialization of Eighteenth-Century England* [Bloomington: Indiana University Press, 1987], p. 52). Also, see Karin Calvert, "The Function of Fashion in Eighteenth-Century America," in *Of Consuming Interests: The Style of Life in the Eighteenth Century*, Cary Carson, Ronald Hoffman, and Peter J. Albert, eds. (Charlottesville: University Press of Virginia, 1994), pp. 252–83.

[7] Frank L. Dewey, *Thomas Jefferson, Lawyer* (Charlottesville: University Press of Virginia, 1986), p. 112; Garritt Minor to Joseph C. Cabell, July 8, 1800, Cabell Papers, box 1; Garritt Minor to Joseph C. Cabell, May 20, 1800, Cabell Papers, box 2.

[8] Joseph C. Cabell to Isaac Coles, January 18, 1809, Cabell Papers, box 6. For an instructive record of Joseph C. Cabell's campaign strategies and political setbacks, see Cabell Papers, boxes 5, 6, and 7.

[9] Letter to Elizabeth Ambler, 1780, Elizabeth Barbour Ambler Papers, Alderman Library, University of Virginia, Charlottesville.

[10] Joseph C. Cabell to William H. Cabell, November 1806, Cabell Papers, box 4; Joseph C. Cabell to Isaac Coles, January 18, 1809, Cabell Papers, box 6; Joseph C. Cabell to Isaac Coles, November 6, 1807, Cabell Papers, box 5.

[11] In his recent work on the creation of gentility in America from the seventeenth through the nineteenth centuries, social historian Richard Bushman writes, "Nineteenth-century gentry and people with newly acquired wealth were as determined to present themselves as refined members of polite society as their eighteenth-century predecessors, and as before the great house was the most forthright statement of person's cultural condition" (Richard Bushman, *Refinement of America: Persons, Houses, Cities* [New York: Alfred A. Knopf, 1992], p. 239). The transformation from impermanent to permanent dwellings in Virginia is chronicled in Cary Carson et al., "Impermanent Architecture in the Southern American Colonies," *Winterthur Portfolio* 16, nos. 2/3 (Summer/Autumn 1981): 135–96. Fraser Neiman details the use of finely detailed Georgian houses to establish social rank in "Domestic Architecture at the Clifts Plantation: The Social Context of Early Virginia Building," in Dell Upton and John Vlach, eds., *Common Places: Readings in American Vernacular Architecture* (Athens: University of Georgia Press, 1986) pp. 292–314. Clifford Geertz, *The Interpretation of Cultures* (New York: Basic Books, 1973), p. 218.

[12] A more detailed description and complete history is available in the National Register of Historic Places nomination for Soldier's Joy and associated documents, Virginia Division of Historic Landmarks, Richmond.

[13] A more detailed description and complete history is available in the National Register of Historic Places nomination for Edgewood and associated documents, Virginia Division of Historic Landmarks, Richmond. Joseph C. Cabell to Isaac Coles, January 22, 1808, Cabell Papers, box 5; Joseph C. Cabell to Isaac Coles, March 2, 1808, Cabell Papers, box 5; Joseph C. Cabell to Nicholas Cabell, Jr., January 7, 1808, Bremo Recess Papers, box 6, Alderman Library, University of Virginia, Charlottesville. Edgewood burned in the 1950s, and its appearance is documented by nineteenth-century insurance policies and a few photographs taken in the 1930s by Frances Benjamin Johnson.

[14] A more detailed description and complete history is available in the National Register of Historic Places nomination for Bon Aire and associated documents, Virginia Division of Historic Landmarks, Richmond.

[15] For a discussion of the way builders like the Cabells maintained traditional plans and spatial organizations in the Palladian house type, see Heck, "Building Status," pp. 46–59, and Marlene Elizabeth Heck, "Palladianism: An American Story," unpublished manuscript.

[16] Clifford Geertz, *Local Knowledge: Further Essays in Interpretive Anthropology* (New York: Basic Books, 1983), p. 124.

[17] Dell Upton, *Holy Things and Profane: Anglican Parish Churches in Colonial Virginia* (New York: Architectural History Fndn., 1986), p. 220.

[18] William Brockenbrough to Joseph C. Cabell, April 29, 1798, Cabell Papers, box 1; Margaret Bayard Smith, *The First Forty Years of Washington Society*, ed. Gaillard Hunt (New York: Scribner, 1906), p. 68.

[19] Joseph C. Cabell to Isaac Coles, October 26, 1808, Cabell Papers, box 5; Joseph C. Cabell to Isaac Coles, September 12, 1809, Cabell Papers, box 7.

[20] The Cabell Family Papers at Swem Library, College of William and Mary, are a valuable record of business records and receipts. Inventory for Samuel Cabell of Soldier's Joy, Nelson County Will Book C. Virginia State Library, Richmond (hereafter cited as VSL); and Nelson County Personal Property Tax Records, 1815, VSL. For an extended account of the creation and maintenance of a genteel culture during the period under discussion, see Bushman, *Refinement of America*.

[21] Nelson County Personal Property Tax Records, 1815, VSL.

[22] Nelson County Personal Property Tax Records, 1815, VSL.

[23] Nelson County Personal Property Tax Records, 1815, VSL.

[24] Nelson County Personal Property Tax Records, 1815, VSL.

[25] William H. Cabell to Thomas Ogle, March 21, 1807, Cabell Papers, box 4; William H. Cabell to Joseph C. Cabell, April 2, 1807, Cabell Papers, box 4.

[26] Joseph C. Cabell to William H. Cabell, November 1806, Cabell Papers, box 4.

[27] Joseph C. Cabell to Isaac Coles, January 18, 1809, Cabell Papers, box 6; James Oldham to Thomas Jefferson, March 9, 1806, Massachusetts Historical Society Papers (microfilm, University of Virginia); James Oldham to Thomas Jefferson, August 25, 1807, Massachusetts Historical Society Papers (microfilm, University of Virginia); Dr. George Cabell, Jr., to Joseph C. Cabell, February 5, 1809, Bremo Recess Papers, box 2, Alderman Library, University of Virginia, Charlottesville.

[28] Joseph C. Cabell to John Hartwell Cocke, November 31, 1809, Cabell Papers, box 6.

Racial Equality Begins at Home

Frederick Douglass's Challenge to American Domesticity

Sarah Luria

During his extensive travels on behalf of the abolitionist cause, Frederick Douglass noted that while his white colleagues were ready to associate with him in public spaces, some were uneasy about having him in their homes; they could not bring themselves to offer Douglass a much-needed bed for the night. Douglass attributed his colleagues' reluctance to their being only "half-cured" of color prejudice; such a person indeed "is sometimes driven to awkward straits, especially if he happens to get a genuine specimen of the race into his house." In his autobiography, Douglass tells how he rid one "half-cured" abolitionist from his disease.[1]

He was traveling and lecturing in 1843 in Indiana with a friend, William White (who was in fact white):

At the close of one of our meetings, we were invited home with a kindly-disposed old farmer, who, in the generous enthusiasm of the moment, seemed to

The author thanks Carnell Poole, Cathy Ingram, and Douglass Stover of the Frederick Douglass National Historic Site for their invaluable and generous assistance. Bill Clark of the National Park Service generously lent his photographs of the Douglass estate for reproduction here. George Dekker, Jay Fliegelman, and Thomas Schwarz offered many helpful comments on earlier drafts of the essay.

have forgotten that he had but one spare bed, and that his guests were an ill-matched pair. All went on pretty well, till near bed time, when signs of uneasiness began to show themselves, among the unsophisticated sons and daughters. White is remarkably fine looking, and very evidently a born gentleman; the idea of putting us in the same bed was hardly to be tolerated; and yet, there we were, and but the one bed for us, and that, by the way, was in the same room occupied by the other members of the family. . . . Who should have this bed, was the puzzling question. There was some whispering between the old folks, some confused looks among the young, as the time for going to bed approached. After witnessing the confusion as long as I liked, I relieved the kindly-disposed family by playfully saying, "Friend White, having got entirely rid of my prejudice against color, I think, as a proof of it, I must allow you to sleep with me to-night." White kept up the joke, by seeming to esteem himself the favored party, and thus the difficulty was removed.

Imbedded in this humorous incident is Douglass's suggestion that it is only when different races can share without qualms the most intimate spaces that "colorphobia" is fully cured. When we think of civil rights movements, we think of gaining access to public spaces—to railway cars, buses, lunch counters, schools—but for Douglass the center of the struggle for racial equality was the home. Douglass would not settle for being applauded in public by an audience who hid their convictions of his racial inferiority in their segregated homes. The home was the heart and inner mind of America. One might legislate equal access to public space, but without a corresponding change of heart the law would be little more than a "dead letter." This essay examines Douglass's emphasis on domestic space in the larger context of the public debate on civil rights during Reconstruction. Douglass's use of domestic space to project a fully integrated society culminates in his last and most impressive home. The bulk of this essay analyzes that property in detail as it subverts the American creed of racial difference.[2]

In his writings and speeches, Douglass portrays the home as a space of activism rather than retreat, a place to surface and challenge prejudice rather than hide and nurture it. Douglass wins his way into the bedroom of the Indiana family by bringing the cause of the difficulty out in the open and meeting it head-on. In a signature move, exemplified often in his own home, Douglass disarms color prejudice by reversing its assumptions. It is not Douglass's black skin but his friend's white skin that is the problem, and therefore it is Douglass who must overcome his color prejudice and permit his white friend to share a bed with him. By turning the problem on its head, Douglass shows how arbitrary and illogical color prejudice is and, by doing so, takes control of the situation: "After witnessing the confusion as long as I liked," Douglass decides to "relieve" his hosts. Douglass's status no longer depends on his acceptance by his hosts; he is their equal, their superior even, because of his rhetorical brilliance and ingenious sense of humor.

Convinced of the home's crucial role in the life or death of color prejudice, Douglass urged African Americans to acquire homes of their own. A house provided a second skin by which African Americans could define themselves by class, taste, and morality rather than by their skin color. A respectable home did more than any speech or law to establish one's social equality. If blacks could acquire middle-class homes, then the chances for social contact with one's white neighbors would be improved greatly and so too the chance for lasting social change. After all, if Douglass had not been invited into the Indiana home, the abolitionist's lingering colorphobia would have gone undetected and uncured. Further, private property offered African Americans the one spot in American life where they might exert significant control. Douglass used his own homes to further the liberation of his people (his home in Rochester, New York, was a station on the Underground Railroad) and to present his vision of domestic and national life no longer divided along arbitrary lines of race.

The home as a contested site of racial equality was underscored when, in 1872, Douglass's house in Rochester—his family home of twenty-five years—was burned to the ground by arsonists. Douglass contended that "even in one of the most liberal of northern cities . . . that Ku Klux spirit . . . makes anything owned by a colored man a little less respected and secure than when owned by a white citizen." Nevertheless, Douglass moved to Washington, D.C., ready to build again.[3]

In 1877, as Reconstruction was officially abandoned and segregation moved from social convention to law, Douglass bought a large white house on a hilltop high above the Capitol Building and the Washington Monument. Overlooking the capital city, Douglass staged his most visible challenge to the increasing "Ku Klux spirit" of the nation. Douglass lived there until his death in 1895. His home enjoyed a constant flow of visitors (publicized by the press) of both races and of high and low rank. Further, after the death of his first wife in 1882, Douglass fell in love with his neighbor's niece, a white woman named Helen Pitts. The two were married in 1884. Through his estate, Douglass offered a prominent and irreproachable example of an integrated home.

Douglass's rather exceptional marriage to a white woman fed right into the deepest fears of the segregationists—that increased social contact between the races would lead to "social intermixture." In Washington, D.C., debate about integration of public spaces quickly turned into a debate about integration of the home. In 1872 Douglass's son Lewis, who sat on the Washington City Council, successfully introduced a groundbreaking local civil rights bill that prevented restaurants, bars, and hotels from denying service due to a person's "race, color, or previous condition of servitude." The law was tested by African Americans who pressed charges against those establishments that refused to serve them. The first rulings upheld the law. But on appeal, the judge ruled in the proprietors' favor, reasoning that "the proprietor of a hotel, or a restaurant was the proper judge of who should have either refreshments or lodgings in his house, and no one could dispute his authority in that matter." The judge's ruling made Douglass's point: a civil rights bill cannot survive among a racist population; social change has to begin in the home. By pointedly terming restaurants and hotels "houses," the ruling placed them beyond the reach of the law. The Bill of Rights insures the sanctity of private property—"a man's home is his castle"—beyond the reach of the government or legislation. The government can force a white person to share a trolley with a black person, but it cannot force a white person to permit a black person into his home. Segregationists found a loophole by which to curtail civil rights laws—any distinction between public and private space was arbitrary and could be contested. What civil rights activists termed *public spaces*, because they were "theoretically open to the public," opponents of civil rights termed *houses* and hence eliminated them from legislative intervention.[4]

With or without the support of the law, segregationists attempted to privatize public space. When legislation was passed in Washington granting African Americans equal access to theaters, a white editorialist wrote: "We doubt if many colored people will avail themselves of the privileges given them by the law. . . . What they would probably ask is that they may be admitted to equally eligible seats with the whites, but probably they would prefer to have their own quarter in each part of the house—for instance, a portion of the parquette, the dress circle, the orchestra, etc." Not only is the theater a "house," but the "colored" section is referred to as a "quarter." Segregation replaced the explicit racial hierarchy established by slavery. The plantation paradigm, where the "big house" and the slave quarters stood side by side, interdependent but separated, became a model for the national landscape. Not only would theaters adopt this model but so too would more obvious examples of public space, such as railway station waiting rooms, railway cars, and buses. It was as if these spaces also were "houses" owned by white society, who in turn were the "proper judge" of who should sit where. Until legislation could make segregation official, the force of social convention succeeded in making it the rule.[5]

The vulnerability of civil rights legislation did not make Douglass abandon it as a necessary strategy to social change, rather he felt that such laws had to be joined to black ownership of and acceptance into respectable properties. Even when the national Civil Rights Act was declared unconstitutional by the Supreme Court in 1883, Douglass argued that the legislation, while it could not be enforced, did have an effect: "That bill, like all advance legislation, was a banner on the outer wall of American liberty, a noble moral standard, uplifted for the education of the American people. There are tongues in trees, books, in the running brooks. . . . This law, though dead, did speak." While Douglass argued for the importance of legislation, he also suggested it was one-dimensional—a moral standard hung on the "outside" contradicted by popular sentiment and social convention on the "inside." Houses, on the other hand, were two-dimensional. During the antislavery campaign, Douglass and his colleagues sought to change the hearts and minds of Americans by revealing to them the horrors hidden inside the private world of the plantations. Douglass reapplied that strategy during Reconstruction: by prominently displaying to the public gaze his own family's domestic life, set in a handsome house on a hill for a pedestal, Douglass sought once again to change Americans, inside and out.[6]

At first glance, Douglass's house seems a rather conventional bourgeois home—an Andrew Jackson Downing spin-off in the country Gothic style (fig. 1). That and its elevated site might simply suggest Douglass's rise from rags to riches and his assimilation into white bourgeois society. The house was a conspicuous tribute to Douglass's own social ascent, certainly. But when considered against his conquests of

American Home

Fig. 1. Present-day Cedar Hill, now the Frederick Douglass National Historic Site, Washington, D.C. (National Park Service; Photo, Bill Clark.)

segregated spaces, as chronicled in his autobiographies (he wrote three), Douglass's home offers a direct challenge to those who would divide the national landscape along the lines of the plantation. The challenge that Douglass poses to the nation is underscored by the view from his front veranda. The city of Washington, with the Capitol building in the foreground, spreads itself out at Douglass's feet. His position as the nation's overseer materializes the somewhat equivocal stance Douglass took toward the federal government: he wanted both to be rewarded by it (he was given three minor posts) and to judge it from on high. That an ex-slave would enjoy this prospect is doubly ironic since perhaps the only other person to have possessed such a rare view of the capital city was another of its most staunch critics, Robert E. Lee. Lee's mansion, which was confiscated after he joined the Confederacy, still stands on the hill across the Potomac River from the Lincoln Memorial.

Douglass's estate was located in what was an intended white segregated suburb called, ironically, Uniontown. In fact, the house belonged to Uniontown's segregationist developer, who had gone bankrupt. Here Douglass chose to create the family home that slavery and racism had denied him. Douglass, with his sense of irony as well as his urge to transform segregated space, also must have been drawn to the house for its modest resemblance in situation and architecture to a plantation home. The white columns; the veranda, which extends the whole width of the house; and the commanding prospect recall essential features of Douglass's original plantation home, Colonel Lloyd's Wye House in nearby Eastern Maryland: "The great house itself was a large, white, wooden building, with wings on three sides of it. In front, a large portico, extending the entire length of the building, and supported by a long range of columns, gave to the whole establishment an air of solemn grandeur."[7] Douglass consciously pursued this parallel to Wye House by developing Cedar Hill into a small plantation. The original property included the house and ten acres of land. Douglass doubled the size of the house and added five acres of land to its property. He created extensive gardens and a woodland park—two features of Col. Lloyd's estate that Douglass particularly admired. He built at least seven outbuildings, including a carriage house, stables, servant quarters, and a strange structure that recalls the slave cabins in which he grew up. But Douglass then reverses this familiar, color-coded landscape: he turns the "big house" into the rightful home of his black, maternal ancestry—

rather than that of his white, paternal ancestry. (Douglass did not know who his father was, but believed he was white; at one point he speculated it was the overseer at Col. Lloyd's plantation.) Similarly, Douglass turns the "slave" cabin into a gentleman's private study. Through his estate, Douglass reclaimed his original plantation home, altering its landscape, however, to accommodate him as its master.

Douglass's treatment of his estate challenges conventional definitions of race in three ways. Through his name for the estate, Douglass redefines his black family's history from one of slavery to one of nobility. Through his treatment of the slave cabin, he challenges the possibility of meaningful distinctions based on race. Through his interior decor, Douglass redefines the American family based on a shared morality rather than genealogy.

Douglass suggests the distinguished pedigree of his maternal family in his autobiographies. He calls his mother "sedate and dignified" and likens her to an Egyptian pharaoh. Similarly, his grandmother was "held in high esteem" and privileged to live apart from the other slaves in a cabin, which the young Douglass considered a "palace." The name Cedar Hill substantiates Douglass's claim to nobility. He named the estate not only for the cedars that surrounded his house but also for his self-designated birthplace. In 1878, shortly after his purchase of Cedar Hill, Douglass revisited the site of his grandmother's cabin—where he had spent the first six years of his life—believing it to be the place where he was born. The cabin had been destroyed by time. But Douglass remembered, and found, a tall cedar that stood nearby. Here, he ceremoniously proclaimed (he had brought witnesses), was his birthplace. As Douglass quipped, "Genealogical trees did not flourish among slaves." Douglass makes up for this lack by inventing his own family tree—the cedar—a symbol for majesty. In the Bible, "cedars of Lebanon" attest to the majesty and omnipotence of God. In the nineteenth century, the term *cedar* was used to describe someone as a pillar of the community, as Douglass and his grandmother were.[8]

One literary reference makes Douglass's family the heroes of a romance: a genre of which Douglass was particularly fond. In Shakespeare's romance *Cymbeline*, a popular play in the nineteenth century that Douglass owned, the sons of Cymbeline, the king of Britain, have been stolen. In a prophetic dream Cymbeline is represented by "the majestic cedar" whose "lopped branches," which "being dead many

years, shall after revive, be joined to the old stock and freshly grown."
The image is interpreted to prophesy the return of Cymbeline's sons.
Douglass's literary father (from whom he took his name) was Sir James
of Douglas, a character in Sir Walter Scott's *Lady of the Lake.* Sir James
was also nobility and was wrongfully banished from his estate. Placed
within the literary context from which Douglass fashioned an identity
for himself, Cedar Hill becomes the estate from which Douglass's noble, enslaved family had been dispossessed and to which he trium-
phantly returns at the end of his life. Through literary references, Douglass presents what might seem strange as a natural event: his purchase
of a segregationist's home does not mark usurpation, an overthrow of
the master by the slave, but the restoration of a natural order, of the
cedar tree that slavery so barbarically lopped.[9]

Douglass gave material representation to this literary argument as
well. When he visited the site of his grandmother's cabin, he brought
back some of the soil from the base of the cedar tree to Cedar Hill.
This gesture confirms that the name Cedar Hill is not a kind of person-
ally coded oxymoron, ironically contrasting depths from which Douglass originated to the heights that he attained. Rather, through the
name, the situation, and the very soil of his estate, Douglass elevates
his maternal ancestry to its proper social position, joining the two seemingly irreconcilable ends of his life—the cedar and the hill—into a
structural whole. This interpretation presents Cedar Hill as an inherited
family estate, rather than the more conventional interpretation of it as
the new acquisition of a self-made man. The extremely long flight of
steps leading from the street to Douglass's front door reenacts, certainly,
his ascent from slavery to his position as one of the most famous men
in America. Perhaps the stairs also serve to heighten the ceremony with
which Douglass restores his maternal heritage to its proper place.

The strange cabin that Douglass had built behind the house expo-
ses the difficulty of making meaningful distinctions based on race (fig.
2). Like many slave cabins, the structure (a reproduction of which now
stands) is composed of one small room, roughly ten by twelve feet; it
has no windows and only one low doorway and a fireplace for light. In
this unlikely space, Douglass put a desk, chair, bookshelf, and lounge;
this cabin was his retreat when he wished to work in peace. Douglass's
placement of bourgeois furniture of leisure and of reading and writing
into a space that, when associated with slavery, afforded almost no lei-

Fig. 2. "The Growlery," Cedar Hill, ca. 1890. (National Park Service; Photo, Bill Clark.)

sure whatsoever for a typically illiterate people, can be attributed in part to his rhetorical use of radical inversions. At the same time, however, the cabin challenges the assumption that all slaves, and blacks generally, were illiterate. Douglass stressed the fact that his mother taught herself "against all odds" to read, and claimed that it is "not to [his] admitted Anglo-Saxon paternity, but to the native genius of [his] sable . . . uncultivated mother," that he owes his inherited love of letters. The cabin symbolizes this bequest.[10]

What is more, if we forget that Douglass was black and think of him simply as an American writer, then we can recognize the cabin as a more familiar literary retreat.[11] Made of stone and picturesquely covered with flowering vines, the cabin evokes that adored "rustic cottage" of the Romantics, while its spare roughness suggests Thoreau's cabin at Walden. Douglass's name for his retreat—"The Growlery"—suggests a lion's den, but the name actually comes from Dickens and refers to a gentleman's study; in *Bleak House,* a character shows his den to a guest: "This as you must know is my Growlery, when in bad humor I come here to growl." Douglass creates a structure that integrates these seemingly incongruous sources and that, hence, cannot be labeled definitively as "black" or "white," "African" or "European." [12]

As such, the Growlery frustrates what Douglass sees as a peculiarly American obsession to pigeonhole things in terms of race. When Americans hear of an unknown person, Douglass observes:

The first question that arises in the average American mind concerning him and which must be answered is, Of what color is he? and he rises or falls in estimation by the answer given. It is not whether he is a good man or a bad man. That does not seem of primary importance. Hence I have often been bluntly and sometimes very rudely asked . . . in what proportion does the blood of the various races mingle in my veins, especially how much white blood and how much black blood entered into my composition? . . . Whether I derived my intelligence from my father, or from my mother, from my white, or from my black blood?

The interior decor of Douglass's home answers the question Douglass thought people should ask about a man: it documents his goodness rather than his genetic makeup. Of course, he did not own any of the family heirlooms—the pictures of ancestors, the quilts or teacups by which our homes typically identify our racial and cultural makeup. Instead, Douglass displays pictures and heirlooms of abolitionists, both white and black; these crowd the walls and shelves of his home—constituting a moral, political family for him rather than a genealogical one. To these people, Douglass said, who were "ready to own me as a . . . brother against all the scorn . . . of a slavery-polluted atmosphere, I owe my success in life." Among the very long list of those represented in this moral, family portrait gallery are: Wendell Phillips, William Lloyd Garrison, Blanche K. Bruce (the first black U.S. senator), Rev. Henry Highland Garnet (the ex-slave and outspoken reformer/abolitionist), Elizabeth Cady Stanton, and Susan B. Anthony. Douglass, this decor emphatically states, descends from a line of good people, of freedom fighters. If his own mix of black and white blood seemed strange to some, it seems much more natural in the biracial pantheon of his home. [13]

As the exterior of Cedar Hill integrates the plantation, so its interior

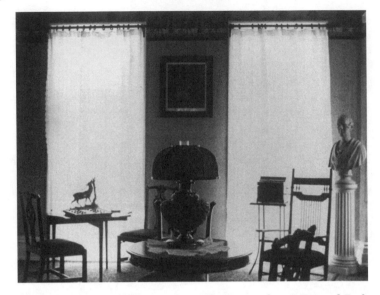

Fig. 3. East Parlor, front, Cedar Hill, present day. (National Park Service; Photo, Bill Clark.)

integrates the bourgeois American family home. Abolitionist souvenirs take their place beside more conventional bourgeois objects. Figure 3 shows one end of the East Parlor. (While some of the positions of objects in the house are placed by curators according to photographs from the period, others are placed simply by guesswork.) The table in the foreground belonged to civil rights advocate and U.S. Senator Charles Sumner; it was purchased by Douglass at an auction following Sumner's death. The bust to the right is of abolitionist Wendell Phillips, one of three representations of Phillips in the house. The bust exemplifies the decor's conflation of visionary politics with a genteel decor. Phillips is given a conventional classical treatment, despite his very radical views against capitalism and its "enslavement" of the laboring class. Here the uncompromising and extremist Phillips is presented as a founding father, perhaps recalling the idealism with which the nation began. Across from Phillips is a large portrait of Douglass. A portrait of Douglass's first wife, Anna Murray, hangs between the two windows. Giving these politically loaded furnishings a more conventional look

Fig. 4. East Parlor, rear, Cedar Hill, present day. (National Park Service; Photo, Bill Clark.)

are the wallpaper and border, the Brussels lace curtains, the statue of Venus, the small bust on the mantle, and various landscape paintings (fig. 4). The rocker is from Haiti, a gift to Douglass when he served there as the American Consul General. Its back and seat are of tooled leather; the wooden sides are carved with medallions depicting figures of black men. The somewhat incongruous lace antimacassar conventionalizes this conversation piece. In the mirror above the fireplace is a reflection of the portrait of Lincoln hanging directly across in the West Parlor.

The West Parlor continues the eclectic decor (fig. 5). Here is the piano, the essential feature of a middle-class home. On top of it is Hiram Powers's symbolically complex statue of a Greek slave, a reminder us that blacks were not the only race to have been enslaved. But the neoclassical statue also serves as an allegory of democracy: the chains of slavery, modestly placed across the woman's genitals, are also chains of

Fig. 5. West Parlor (and dining room through doorway), Cedar Hill, present day. (National Park Service; Photo, Bill Clark.)

chastity and symbolize the self-restraint necessary for self-government.[14] The statue is another one of Douglass's unexpected rhetorical inversions. Because of their history of enslavement, it was argued that African Americans were incapable of self-government and therefore should be denied the vote. But Powers's statue instead suggests that ex-slaves might be better prepared to meet the demands of an ideal democratic government, having learned to sacrifice their own immediate desires for a higher goal (such as freedom) and the common good. To the left of the statue, on the easel, is another portrait of Phillips; behind him on the wall hangs a portrait of General Dumas, father of writer Alexander Dumas (who was part black); and out of view directly beneath is a picture of President Hippolyte of Haiti. Figure 5 also gives a view into the dining room with its solid oak dining table, butler's table and sideboard, and the good china displayed there.

The eclectic decor redefines the American family along Douglass's vision of what he termed "a composite American nationality." It is a family of both races, joined not only by principles and ideals but love — joined, in other words, not simply in the public sphere but in the home. To the many who criticized Douglass's marriage to a white woman, these virtuous and refined surroundings defend his act as perfectly natural — a fulfillment of the belief in racial equality.[15]

The relatively open floor-plan of Douglass's house, which he augmented through the addition of several rooms, deserves mention. Douglass's vision of a free exchange between conventional opposites is initiated by his front hallway and main entry. Dell Upton has discussed how plantation owners underscored their "centrality" and importance by creating a highly "articulated processional landscape" of successive architectural barriers and formal entrances to their mansions.[16] In Douglass's house, however, a modest entry hall offers the visitor a generous overview of the house. (This admittedly is after one has ascended the long flight of steps — ceremonial yes, but also easily accessible, leading directly from the street to the front door.) To the left is the more formal East Parlor (where Douglass received his visitors) and beyond that, Douglass's library. To the right is the West Parlor, which was the family parlor or music room. The dining room is straight ahead, with the kitchen and laundry in view (if the door is open) beyond. The stairs to the second floor are easily accessible to the front hall; the door to the men's guest room is visible to the left at the top of the stairs.

On first consideration, the house appears to be divided into two halves: the more formal eastern side reserved for "male" activities of conference and study; the more private western half reserved for family or "female" activities of leisure and domestic work, such as serving food and its preparation. The second floor continues this pattern: Douglass's bedroom and the male guest bedroom are on the east side, while all the women's bedrooms are on the west. But the dynamic flow of space created by the intersection in the front hallway suggests a reciprocal relationship exists between the two halves. The east and west parlors are different but also very similar: both contain artwork, political portraits, good and less good furniture. They look directly into one another (although portieres could be drawn to separate them); this lay out sets up a mirror relationship between them, fulfilled by the mirror above the East Parlor mantel, which reflects the portrait of Lincoln that hangs above the West Parlor mantel. The natural lighting of the two parlors reiterates this idea of reciprocity and exchange. At any one time of day, one parlor is lighter or darker than the other, as the sun moves across from east to west. In the morning the East Parlor is light, the West Parlor dark. By the late afternoon, however, the roles have been reversed. The West Parlor thus gets lighter as the East Parlor gets darker. The front hallway presents you with a choice—between east and west, male and female, formal and causal, work and leisure, light and dark—but also suggests that the choice is false. As it happens, it was at this precise juncture that Douglass died, at seventy-seven, while getting ready to leave for an evening public appearance in 1895.

Douglass's autobiographies suggest that he saw access to prohibited spaces as crucial to the fight for racial equality. Segregated spaces offered physical "proof" of the differences between the races. When John Van Hook, the segregationist developer of Uniontown, built the house, it was a testimony to white supremacy: at the feet of his property spread his attempt to engrave racial differences on the social, political, and physical landscape of the neighborhood. Douglass acquired the property and used it to prove the opposite point. Throughout the property he argues that the distinctions black and white are not real, are not material, but are arbitrary. Not only do the estate's name, the Growlery, and the interior elude racial classification, but they also give material reality to Douglass's own definition of himself, beyond terms of race.

The political vision offered by Cedar Hill is idealistic, of course. The new class of freedmen encountered innumerable obstacles in their efforts to save money and acquire property during Reconstruction. Perhaps the most sensational tragedy was the collapse of the Freedman's Savings and Trust Company, where many African Americans had been lured into placing their savings. Reckless speculations by the bank's predominantly white trustees caused depositors to lose half or more of their life's savings. Douglass knew very well the difficulty of acquiring property; he himself speculated heavily in real estate and oversaw the dismantling of the Freedman's bank. He knew that property holders often refused to sell to African Americans or forced them to pay higher prices. Yet to some degree he continued to lure his audience away from traditional sources of self-esteem, such as religion and black separatism, to the capitalist system of conspicuous consumption: "The only way you can make yourself respected is to get something somebody else wants," Douglass preached. Certainly he cannot be criticized for encouraging the desire for decent, even bourgeois property. But Douglass may be faulted perhaps for being not only idealistic but misleading— for failing to appreciate the degree to which his own success was an exception. Most African Americans who achieved bourgeois lifestyles still found themselves excluded from the social and political life of the nation. And even Douglass probably chafed at never having been offered an important government post. Anyone who entered into the system of conspicuous consumption made themselves vulnerable to the volatile fluctuations of public opinion and the real estate market: African Americans made themselves doubly so.[17]

Douglass's own life even conflicted with the political vision he projected at Cedar Hill. In fact, Douglass had to some degree fallen out with almost all of his abolitionist friends by the time he honored them in his home. (For example, he rejected the political vision of his mentor and publisher, William Garrison, when Douglass started his own newspaper.) Further, Douglass's children deeply resented his second wife, both for her youth and her race. Cedar Hill has survived not as a genuine family home but as a polemic for racial equality and the abilities of African Americans. Douglass willed the estate to his wife Helen, rather than to his children; after his death, they sued her for possession of the estate. Helen had to purchase the house from Douglass's children to preserve it as a monument to her husband and, in her words, a "Mount Vernon for colored people"—not a family home but one of America's "First Homes," now owned by the National Park Service.[18]

I have attributed Douglass's reconstruction of his house to his rhetorical skill, marked by his signature ironic wit. I conclude with an image of the literary genius that animates the house: Douglass at work in his library (fig. 6). Like the house, the image is a conscious, posed autobiographical statement. (Notice, for instance, the contrived inclusion of Douglass's violin, which is exhibited to his right on the desk.) Douglass pretends not to see the photographer who has caught him "at work." He is busy with his writing, surrounded by books and intellectual clutter; the doors of the bookcase are open, signifying that the books are in use. Here is Douglass, the cultured man of letters. Like the house, he turns his back on racial definition. Rather than his face, and the color of his skin, we see only his white head of hair. Douglass does not hide behind his white hair, as he does not hide behind the white "face"

Fig. 6. Frederick Douglass in his study at Cedar Hill. (National Park
Service.)

of his big house; rather the image eludes the question of race altogether.
It defines Douglass by his books, his prosperity, his occupation, his hat,
his home.

---

[1] Frederick Douglass, *My Bondage and My Freedom* (1855; reprint, Chicago: University of Illinois Press, 1987), p. 245.

[2] Douglass, *My Bondage*, p. 245. Douglass frequently makes literary allusions; here there is an unmistakable echo to the famous scene in *Moby Dick* (1850) in which Queequeg and Ishmael share a bed. Douglass uses the word "colorphobia" in Frederick Douglass, *Life and Times of Frederick Douglass* (1892; reprint, New York: Macmillan, 1962), p. 457. "Dead letter" appears in his speech, "This Decision Has Humbled the Nation," Washington, D.C., October 22, 1883, in John W. Blassingame and John R. McKivigan, eds., *The Frederick Douglass Papers: Speeches, Debates, and Interviews*, ser. 1, 6 vols. (New Haven: Yale University Press, 1992), 5:121.

[3] Douglass quoted in William S. McFeely, *Frederick Douglass* (New York: W. W. Norton, 1991), p. 275.

[4] Thomas R. Johnson, "The City on the Hill: Race Relations in Washington, 1865–1885" (Ph.D. diss., University of Maryland, 1975), pp. 219–22.

[5] *Evening Star* (Washington, D.C.), June 7, 1869, quoted in Johnson, "City on the Hill," p. 183.

[6] "This Decision Has Humbled the Nation," in *Douglass Papers*, 5:121.

[7] Douglass, *My Bondage*, p. 47.

[8] Douglass, *Life and Times*, pp. 28–29.

[9] "Cymbeline," in *The Complete Pelican Shakespeare*, ed. Alfred Harbage (New York: Viking, 1969), act 5, sc. 5, line 456; act 5, sc. 4, lines 141–47.

[10] Douglass, *My Bondage*, p. 42.

[11] I am grateful to Dell Upton for this observation.

[12] *Oxford English Dictionary*, s.v. "Growlery."

[13] Douglass, *Life and Times*, pp. 512–13, 467.

[14] I owe my reading of Powers's statue to a conversation with Jay Fliegelman, January 1993.

[15] "Our Composite Nationality," Boston, Mass., December 7, 1869, in *Douglass Papers*, 4:240.

[16] Dell Upton, "White and Black Landscapes in Eighteenth-Century Virginia," in *Material Life in America, 1600–1860*, ed. Robert Blair St. George (Boston: Northeastern University Press, 1988), p. 364.

[17] Douglass, "Recollections of the Slavery Conflict," in *Douglass Papers*, 4:373. On the failure of the Freedman's bank, see Carl R. Osthaus, *Freedmen, Philanthropy, and Fraud* (Urbana: University of Illinois Press, 1976), chaps. 5 and 6. On the social acceptance of bourgeois blacks in Washington, see Johnson, "City on the Hill," p. 291. On Douglass's career disappointments, see McFeely, *Frederick Douglass*, pp. 305–6.

[18] Sharon Harley, "A Study of the Preservation and Administration of 'Cedar Hill' " (Washington, D.C.: U.S. Department of the Interior, National Park Service Publication, n.d.), p. 15.

Manufacturing and Marketing the American Bungalow

The Aladdin Company, 1906–20

Scott Erbes

By 1920 bungalows had saturated much of the United States' landscape and popular culture. Ensconced in the living room of their bungalow, middle-class family members could regale each other with tales from a Bungalow Boys adventure novel while enjoying a box of Russell Stover's bungalow candies. Propelled by bungalow rapture, one author even suggested that Marie Antoinette's palace, the Petit Trianon, was her version of a bungalow. A timely match between supply and demand encouraged America's bungalow mania. On the supply side, the bungalow offered profit-hungry builders and suppliers an easily standardized, aesthetically appealing house type. Writers for popular periodicals such as the *Ladies' Home Journal* contributed to demand by promising consumers a new, improved domestic life with the purchase of a bungalow.[1]

The Aladdin Company, a major manufacturer of mail-order

The author thanks Greg Olson, Rebecca Young, and Josie Gordon for their help. For her unstinting and patient assistance, he thanks Eleanor McD. Thompson. And special thanks go to Stephanie Erbes for her encouragement and support. This essay expands on themes introduced in the author's master's thesis, "The Redi-Cut Dream: The Mail Order House Catalogs of the Aladdin Company, 1906–1920" (University of Delaware, 1990).

houses, was one of bungalow mania's many profiteers. It, along with other house-by-mail enterprises, serviced and encouraged bungalow mania by combining industrial production with mass marketing. Production efforts exploited the bungalow's capacity for standardization, reducing it to a set of interchangeable, similarly sized spaces. To ensure demand, the company's catalogues enticed consumers with seductively phrased descriptions, glowing testimonials, and handsome illustrations. Aladdin's marketing of the bungalow, as derived from the abundant writings of Gustav Stickley, Henry Saylor, and other design reformers, centered on its properties as a recuperative retreat; in the bungalow, the catalogues insinuated, consumers could escape life's worries and commune with nature. This idealized image, along with the bungalow's distinctive aesthetic qualities, soon set it apart from other house types produced and marketed by Aladdin. The successful mating of promotion and production eventually made the bungalow a prominent part of America's architectural vocabulary at the turn of the century. But it proved to be more than just a fad. Not only did the bungalow influence houses during succeeding decades, but its legacy as a mass-produced mass-marketed commodity can still be seen in today's ever-growing suburbs. There, intensely marketed houses multiply in a limited range of repetitive designs.

Founded in 1906 in Bay City, Michigan, by brothers William and Otto Sovereign, the Aladdin Company was one of several firms that sold precut houses by mail on a large scale during the early twentieth century; the company was founded two years prior to Sears, Roebuck's entry into the house-by-mail industry. Inspired by an acquaintance who sold precut wooden boats by mail, the brothers started the enterprise with a small investment and no architectural experience (William was trained as a lawyer and Otto worked in advertising). Sales figures reflect their success: by 1917 they were selling more than three-thousand houses per year. Their customers, spread across the country's urban, suburban, and rural landscapes, included individual buyers as well as speculative builders. Industrial firms also purchased Aladdin houses, perhaps inspired by the company's Orwellian motto, "A housed labor supply is a controlled labor supply." Industrial customers included the DuPont Company and several coal mining companies as well as Austin Motors in Birmingham, England, which ordered 250 houses. Aladdin prospered during the first two decades of the century, expanding its offerings to include furniture, plumbing fixtures, heating equipment, and other products. The Great Depression, however, cut sales to a few hundred units per year. After regaining some momentum in the 1950s, sales fell during the 1960s and 1970s, eventually forcing Aladdin to close in the late 1980s.[2]

Shipped by train, an Aladdin house included all the precut framing, nails, paint, and other items necessary for a complete house, except masonry. The company followed standard building conventions of the period, using a framing system composed of two-inch-thick lumber of various widths (fig. 1). Best described as platform framing, a variation on balloon framing, Aladdin's system used wall studs cut to a length equal to the height of each story. The first floor thereby served as a platform for the second and so on. As with balloon framing, platform framing's reliance on standardized, dimensional lumber lent itself to the production of precut houses. Many of the other elements of an Aladdin house were also standardized. Materials ranging from millwork and windows to lock sets and paints, for example, were virtually identical to those found in houses ordered from other suppliers or even those built locally. Such components had been mass produced since the second half of the nineteenth century. Aladdin, like Sears and other mail-order house firms, also adopted new technologies such as plasterboard, a predecessor of today's drywall, and steel bridging, which was used to tie together floor joists. The company thus consolidated several decades of development in the industrialization of housing into a single, buyer-friendly package. At the same time, it expanded the process, turning the house frame itself into a factory product. This industrial approach to production made economic sense given the rising construction costs of the early twentieth century.[3]

Although its houses used familiar materials and framing techniques, Aladdin still had to overcome the relative novelty of selling houses by mail. To assuage public hesitation, its catalogues were liberally dosed with clever slogans such as "Sold by the Golden Rule" or "Built in a day" and gimmicks such as the "Dollar-a-Knot" guarantee (customers were offered $1 for every knot found in Aladdin's siding, flooring, or other finish materials). Despite such blatant salesmanship, the catalogues still reflect the popular zeitgeist that surrounded the bungalow. Promotional themes for the bungalow, for example, were borrowed from authors such as arts and crafts promoter Gustav Stickley and

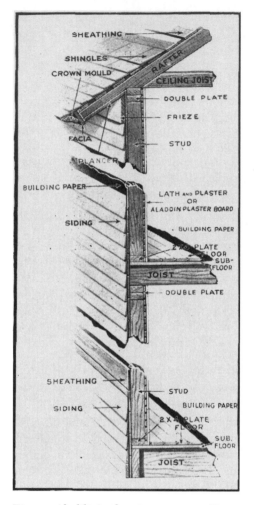

Fig. 1. Aladdin's framing system. From Aladdin Co., *Aladdin Homes* (Bay City, Mich.: By the company, 1918), p. 13. (Winterthur Library.)

periodicals such as *Ladies' Home Journal*. But unlike these prescriptive sources, Aladdin did not have an ideological ax to grind. Its catalogue writers therefore avoided prescriptive exhortations and instead tried to appeal to the mass, middle-class market.

Along with verbal appeals, Aladdin also tempted customers with handsome illustrations. As a result, the 1906 to 1920 catalogues alone provide illustrations and floor plans for more than 150 different houses. Sixty-five of these are bungalows of which the Winthrop is a typical example (fig. 2). Its low, horizontal massing; open floor plan; broad eaves; and exposed rafter ends and gable brackets were shared, in whole or in part, by the company's other bungalows. Size and price ranges for Aladdin bungalows respectively spanned 480 to 1,584 square feet and $313 to $1,578 in 1916. By comparison, Aladdin's flagship home, the two-story 2,700-square-foot Villa, cost $3,420.[4]

Theoretically, the bungalows produced by Aladdin and other companies traced their lineage to the *bangla*—a low, hutlike, often impermanent dwelling with a hipped roof indigenous to Bengal, India, and the surrounding region. Appropriated by European colonists beginning in the seventeenth century, the bangla grew in scale and pretension throughout the next two centuries. During the late nineteenth century, some knowledge of these structures spread to England and, no doubt, to the United States. But in the United States, the extent of knowledge was limited, leading to a free interpretation of the term and its meaning. For example, Aladdin's bungalows owed less to the bangla than to two intertwined architectural types: small cottages of the late nineteenth and early twentieth centuries and the early bungalows built in California. Like the bangla, these two building types were often simply constructed with a minimal amount of finish and frequently were intended only for temporary or seasonal occupation. Despite temporary or seasonal connotations, they supplied the visual and spatial models on which the year-round bungalow was based.[5]

Referred to as "bungalows" by at least 1905, early California bungalows, not surprisingly, provided the stylistic model for Aladdin's bungalows. The California bungalow was usually one story with a broadly pitched roof, exposed rafter ends, and a rather rustic, organic look; this aesthetic, in turn, had been influenced by a number of sources including the large, so-called shingle style and stick style vacation dwellings built in the East during the late nineteenth century. Unlike the year-

The Winthrop $1,095.35

Price, $1,153
Cash discount, 5%
Net price, $1,095.35

CAN you imagine this bungalow nestling among trees and shrubbery on your own lot? A few cobblestones are gathered from nearby fields and when blended with brown stained shingles, natural shrubbery and a setting of velvety green, the observer is fascinated.

A bungalow should always be set close to the ground. When local conditions seem to make this impossible, the same results can be secured by terracing close to the building.

The Winthrop is of the pure bungalow type—low, a touch of rough stones, bracketed eave supports, heavy timber work, shingles, and broken outlines.

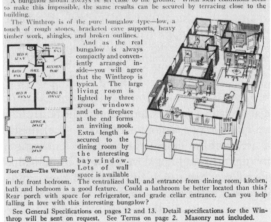

And as the real bungalow is always compactly and conveniently arranged inside—you will agree that the Winthrop is typical. The large living room is lighted by three group windows and the fireplace at the end forms an inviting nook. Extra length is secured to the dining room by the interesting bay window. Lots of wall space is available

Floor Plan—The Winthrop

in the front bedroom. The centralized hall, and entrance from dining room, kitchen, bath and bedroom is a good feature. Could a bathroom be better located than this? Rear porch with space for refrigerator, and grade cellar entrance. Can you help falling in love with this interesting bungalow?

See General Specifications on pages 12 and 13. Detail specifications for the Winthrop will be sent on request. See Terms on page 2. Masonry not included.

Fig. 2. The Winthrop. From Aladdin Co., *Aladdin Homes* (Bay City, Mich.: By the company, 1917), p. 67. (Winterthur Library.)

Fig. 3. The tent-house of southern California. From Henry H. Saylor, *Bungalows: Their Design, Construction, and Furnishing, with Suggestions also for Camps, Summer Homes, and Cottages of Similar Character* (2d ed., New York: McBride, Nast, 1913), p. 33. (Winterthur Library.)

round bungalows later sold by Aladdin and others, early California bungalows were much more rudimentary affairs, due, in some cases, to their use as seasonal dwellings. The so-called tent bungalow fell into this category (fig. 3). Tent bungalows typically combined a hipped roof and a simple balloon frame with "walls" made from canvas panels, giving them a profile remarkably similar to that of the southeast Asian bangla.[6]

The simple frame construction and unfinished interior of the early California bungalow also made it useful as a temporary dwelling. For example, the thousands of "shacks" built on posts to house refugees of the 1906 San Francisco earthquake followed the emerging bungalow aesthetic, incorporating exposed rafter ends and olive-colored paint. In response to the state's temperate climate and the need for housing in the face of explosive growth, the first "permanent" bungalows were also simply constructed; even the 1903 Arturo Bandini house, one of the early bungalows designed by Charles and Henry Greene, had exposed roof trusses and board-and-batten interior wall surfaces. Sometimes built with their sills laid directly on the ground or on a crude foundation, year-round bungalows in California were generally larger and better finished than their temporary counterparts. Nevertheless, one contemporary commentator still referred to them as "flimsy." Eventually, the year-round bungalows sold by Aladdin and others would replace the "flimsy" California models with structures suitable for less-forgiving environments. Even so, Aladdin's new bungalows maintained their visual ties to their California predecessors.[7]

Both the year-round bungalow and its aesthetic model, the California bungalow, were in turn indebted to the small, often nondescript cottages popularized during the late nineteenth and early twentieth centuries. These structures, commonly used as seasonal or impermanent dwellings, established the spatial models on which the bungalow was based. Derived in part from the camp tents found at religious camps and other retreats, the vacation cottages being built beginning in the 1860s had open plans, rectangular massing, and only a few rooms. These seasonal structures were very similar to the "settler's cottages" illustrated by plan-book publisher Palliser. Their single-story, gabled structures had two or three unplastered rooms, vertical siding (perhaps board and batten), and few stylistic flourishes. These dwellings cost $200 or less to build and were said to be suitable for "a small family of limited means." Supported by posts set into the ground, they were related to a centuries-old tradition of impermanent, earthfast building.[8]

Aladdin's summer cottages—among the company's first products—followed the nineteenth-century cottage tradition. Built on blocks rather than on foundations, these structures were sparse and utilitarian. The Erie, although a later, year-round version of one of Aladdin's first cottages, nonetheless retains the spatial and visual qualities of the earlier model (fig. 4). Inside, it had only three rooms (which would have been unplastered in the original cottage). Outside, the front-gabled dwelling is stylistically nondescript except for the capitals on the porch columns. (Unlike the Erie, the original cottage was clapboarded, not shingled.) Aladdin usually referred to vacation dwellings like the Erie's predecessor as cottages. It did, however, label the largest of these plain, vaguely Victorian structures a *bungalow*, reflecting the late nineteenth-century use of the term.[9]

Aladdin's later, year-round bungalows shared a direct spatial rela-

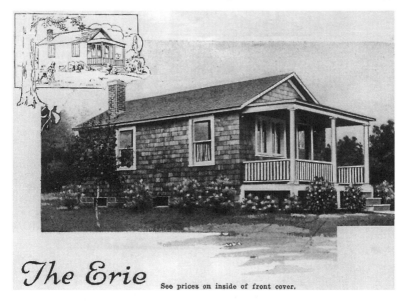

The Erie   See prices on inside of front cover.

Fig. 4. The Erie. From Aladdin Co., *Aladdin Homes* (Bay City, Mich.: By the company, 1918), p. 61. (Winterthur Library.)

tionship with their cottage forebears. The plan of Aladdin's three-room Style C cottage (the forerunner of the Erie), for example, can be detected in the Style F — the cottage noted previously that Aladdin labeled a *bungalow* (fig. 5). The basic spatial configuration of the Style F, in turn, influenced year-round bungalows such as the Winthrop. Similar relationships can be traced between other cottages and bungalows sold by the company. In each case, the simple, rectilinear, relatively informal plans of the cottages were expanded and modified to create houses suitable for year-round use. At a minimum, these houses contained a living room and dining room (the two usually joined by an open archway), a bathroom, a kitchen, and one bedroom. Hallways were also often incorporated to separate public and private spaces. Despite such changes, the basic core of the summer cottage remains recognizable.

The year-round bungalow produced by Aladdin and others thus emerged both visually and spatially from a series of house types that were essentially transitory. Whether used as seasonal dwellings or tem-

Fig. 5. Comparative floor plans of Aladdin's Style C and Style F cottages and Winthrop bungalow. After North American Construction Co., *Aladdin Knocked-Down Houses, Summer Cottages, Dwelling Houses, Auto Garages, Boat Houses* (Bay City, Mich.: By the company, [1908]), pp. 5, 7; and North American Construction Co., *Aladdin Houses* (Bay City, Mich.: By the company, 1913), p. 63. Key: (LR) living room; (DR) dining room; (K) kitchen; (BR) bedroom; (B) bath; (H) hall. (Drawing, Scott Erbes and Rebecca Young.)

porary shelters, structures such as inexpensive, late Victorian cottages and early California tent bungalows and "shacks" were built to keep costs and construction time to a minimum. As a result, they were small buildings with open floor plans; a sparse, rustic look; and a minimal level of finish. The year-round bungalow's roots in such structures represented a dramatic break from the relatively large, two-story, spatially segmented house idealized by many late nineteenth-century, middle-class Americans; a new archetype—smaller, simpler, less formal—was entering the country's architectural vocabulary.[10]

The bungalow's roots in temporary dwellings were recognized by many contemporary commentators. Those devoted to "reforming" the middle-class house praised the qualities that united the vacation cottage and the year-round bungalow: smaller size, aesthetic simplicity, informality, and a supposedly intimate connection with nature. Others were less enthusiastic about the use of bungalows as year-round dwellings. Frederick Coburn, for example, noted in 1906 that many city dwellers were beginning to occupy their summer bungalows on a year-round basis. He believed, however, that the move was due to financial hardship. He claimed that city families who toughed out the winter in their bungalows did so only because they could not afford to live in the city.[11]

Apart from Stickley's *Craftsman*, the *Ladies' Home Journal*, and like-minded periodicals, some magazines and architectural journals also questioned the bungalow's legitimacy. Reactions varied from mild disapproval to harsh rebuke. *House Beautiful*, for example, merely suggested that the bungalow was best used as a summer dwelling; it was especially suited to the task because it could be staffed by only one servant. Most other writers were more critical, seeing the small, one-story year-round bungalow as an ill-conceived architectural trend. Architect Wilson Eyre stated, "In general, I do not believe in the one-story house for an all-year dwelling. It is a fad which, like Mission furniture, is being much overdone." H. Van Buren Magonigle drew the same conclusion, believing that a one-floor house was to be feared because it could not adequately protect "timid women" from burglars and "tramps." Ultimately, many of the criticisms focused on the bungalow's nontraditional, essentially ahistorical roots. A writer for *Country Life in America* directly dismissed the bungalow on these grounds: "All lasting styles of architecture are the result of traditional evolution, which is entirely wanting in the true bungalow so far as we as a people are concerned." Eyre weighed in with a similar comment, claiming, "this bungalow style is not destined to produce any lasting effect on domestic architecture in America."[12]

To architects critical of the bungalow, such as Eyre and Magonigle, the bungalow fad was an affront to architectural purity and, by association, architects. As Magonigle, editor of *The Architect*, put it, "With the ready faculty Americans seem to possess (and the real estate operator in particular) for the corruption of meanings, it [the term, *bungalow*] has come to mean about anything the advertising agent cares to apply to it." As the self-appointed guardians of architectural standards and aesthetic purity, architects thus blamed nonarchitects for the perceived bastardization of the bungalow. Attacks on nonarchitects, such as builders and plan-book writers, however, actually began during the late nineteenth century—prior to the advent of the bungalow. But in

the case of the bungalow, one suspects architects were not only concerned with stylistic improprieties; some, no doubt, feared competition
from Aladdin and others who readily exploited the bungalow's suitability for standardized design and factory production.[13]

The floor plans of Aladdin's bungalows illustrate the company's
philosophy of standardized design. Bungalow plans (and those of some
of the company's other house types) were conceived as a set of squares
and rectangles available in a range of more or less standardized sizes.
The relationships illustrated in figure 5 reflect this approach: the Style
F is simply a Style C with two additional 8-by-10-foot units attached to
the back. The relationship between the Style F and the Winthrop is
more complex, yet the basic set of rooms in the Style F, although supplemented and expanded, can still be recognized in the Winthrop's
floor plan. From an industrial standpoint, this systematic, rational approach to architectural design was extremely practical. By using room
units of the same size or by expanding them in increments (often based
on standard lumber dimensions that increased by two- or four-foot
lengths), framing members could be cut in a standardized range of
lengths for use in a variety of models. Creating new bungalows was also
vastly simplified; one needed only to "assemble" the same rooms in
different configurations and, if desired, proportionally expand or contract the house's overall dimensions. Even small changes, such as shifting a rectangular living room from the short to the long side of a rectangular structure, created a completely different bungalow model.[14]

Other designers and suppliers also treated bungalows as a standardized type, particularly in regard to their floor plans. Francis Downing
and Ulric Flemming, for example, have shown how a shared set of
conventions was used to create the plans of several bungalows in Buffalo, New York. Architectural writers (at least those inclined to favor
the bungalow) also recognized the ease with which bungalow plans
could be developed and manipulated. William Draper Brincklé, discussing bungalow design and planning in 1911, demonstrated how a
four-room bungalow plan could be easily expanded by joining additional, similarly sized units to the four original ones. The standardization of bungalow design, spread through magazines, catalogues, plan
books, and other publications, is particularly apparent when comparing
Aladdin's bungalows to those offered by other mail-order manufacturers
and plan-book authors. For example, Aladdin's 1911 Oakland bungalow

and Henry Wilson's Plan 185 bungalow were virtually interchangeable. Similar relationships could be drawn among bungalow designs illustrated by Aladdin, Sears, and many other suppliers and promoters. In the context of architectural standardization in America, the bungalow represented an extension of late nineteenth-century efforts such as the suburban Chicago houses built by Samuel Gross; he built both small and large structures following standardized plans and a late Victorian aesthetic. But unlike Gross's localized marketing and production, the bungalow eventually became a standardized, national house type. Its ease of design and construction as well as its suitability for factory production were, in part, responsible for its nationwide popularity.[15]

On the supply side, then, the bungalow offered many benefits. For builders, plan-book writers, and mail-order companies, bungalows were easy to design, standardize, and produce or build in quantity. For housing reformers, bungalows represented a simple, informal antidote to late Victorian architectural excess. But if bungalows were to produce profits for suppliers and fulfill the reformers' dream of a new, middle-class architecture, consumers first had to buy them. Marketers and promoters had to convince buyers that they wanted smaller, informal houses grounded in the vacation cottage. The approach taken by Aladdin paralleled that used by other bungalow advocates. The company's promotion of the bungalow focused on its qualities as a retreat—an idea fostered in the late nineteenth century. Like the late Victorian house, the bungalow supposedly offered physical and psychic refreshment for its residents, but Aladdin updated elements of the late Victorian ideal to accommodate the bungalow's roots in vacation dwellings. In doing so, Aladdin insinuated that the bungalow offered best features of the vacation cottage on a year-round basis.[16]

One of the virtues associated with the cottage was its intimate relationship with nature. In Aladdin's words, "The summer cottage has a strong influence on the life of thousands of Americans. It affords the necessary contact with nature and outdoor life." According to Aladdin's catalogue illustrations and written copy, the ideal bungalow promised the same intimacy with nature thanks to its organic aesthetic and its integration with its surroundings. The Winthrop, for example, was pictured with cobblestone porch footings, extensive landscaping, and a backdrop of towering trees (see fig. 2). The Winthrop's text further emphasized its idyllic charms: "Can you imagine this bungalow nestling among trees and shrubbery on your own lot? A few cobblestones are gathered from nearby fields and when blended with brown stained shingles, natural shrubbery and a setting of velvety green, the observer is fascinated." Other bungalows were similarly promoted, transforming them into year-round nature retreats.[17]

The emulation of the vacation house's idyllic setting took on added gravity in light of the period's prescriptive literature. During the late nineteenth century, writers viewed the relationship between the house and its setting in moral terms. They argued, based on the principle that nature illustrated God's divine will, that house sites that provided contact with nature (those situated on suburban or rural lots) encouraged moral fortitude. Writers in the early twentieth century continued this theme, presenting nature as a sort of book written by God; studying this book provided important moral lessons. The ideal bungalow played into these philosophies by assuming the image of a cottage nestled in the woods, offering nature's tranquillity as well as its moral inspiration.[18]

Moral overtones colored the relationship between the vacation dwelling and the bungalow's image as a nature retreat. The recuperative properties associated with the cottage, later echoed in the bungalow, offer an illustration. In promoting its cottages, Aladdin stressed their restorative powers: "[The cottage] appeals to healthy impulses and affords an opportunity for fresh air and the upbuilding of the health of oneself and family." The health benefits offered by the cottage also could be found in the bungalow. The text promoting the Edison of 1920, for example, insisted, "Each sleeping room affords plenty of air and light and physicians ascribe many of the present day ills to lack of these two life-giving remedies of nature." Aladdin's association between fresh air and family health was based, in part, on popular medical literature of the day that vigorously promoted the fresh air cure. But by appropriating the cottage's image as recuperative spa, the bungalow also tapped into the connection made during the period between good health and moral rectitude (a theme prevalent since the late nineteenth century). A bungalow that provided the "life-giving remedies of nature" therefore promoted moral well-being while also fostering family health.[19]

Moral overtones were also linked to the Aladdin bungalow's supposed simplicity. In some models, for example, simplicity was associated with aesthetic purity. In others, aesthetic simplicity was promoted as a visual symbol of the owner's upright character. References to simplicity, purity, and personal character invested both the ideal bungalow and its occupants with images of moral rectitude and abstemious living. This evocation of simple living once again reached back to the vacation cottage, one of the original icons of the simple life. According to wilderness literature, the writings of early environmentalists such as John Burroughs, and the pages of popular periodicals, such retreats — free from the complex clutter of everyday life — offered a closer relationship with nature and, by association, with God. For Aladdin, Stickley, and other bungalow promoters, the bungalow's open floor plan, sparse ornament, and rustic aesthetic evoked the same aura of simple living; it replaced the complexity and formality attributed to the late Victorian house with a home free from the corrupting power of overcivilization and overconsumption. But did customers respond to the bungalow's idealized image? Some, no doubt, were inspired by this promise of simple living. Others, interested in following the latest tastes, may just have been drawn to the bungalow's fashionable novelty.[20]

As a physical and rhetorical construct, the ideal bungalow had ties to popular culture that went beyond the work of prescriptive writers and bungalow suppliers. Indeed, its image as a curative, uplifting nature retreat—as a tranquil world apart—mirrored that of the Chautauqua retreat, one of the period's more popular and influential institutions. Founded in 1874 in upstate New York, Chautauqua retreats were soon established in Michigan, Ohio, Maine, and elsewhere. Each offered "a rural enclave for self-improvement, a sylvan retreat away from the pressures of urban life, and a collective cultural enterprise for moral and intellectual rearmament." For those who could not afford a vacation house at a Chautauqua retreat, traveling tent Chautauquas offered escape and uplift in smaller doses through inspirational speeches, plays, and other events. Speakers and programs at both types of Chautauqua gatherings often dealt with progressive issues such as women's suffrage and the urban poor, helping to give these issues a wider hearing; in this sense, Chautauqua and the ideal bungalow drew from the same reformist philosophies. Chautauqua gained widespread support primarily among the Protestant middle class (although there were also Catholic Chautauquas): in 1904 there were eighty-six independent Chautauqua retreats, and by 1921 traveling Chautauqua meetings were reaching some nine thousand communities.[21]

As with the ideal bungalow, a sense of retreat was an essential component of the Chautauqua enclave. With its curving avenues set in the woods (often alongside a lake), the Chautauqua "camp" provided an inspiring, idyllic landscape; this intimacy with nature encouraged "high thinking and natural living." More important, the Chautauqua setting offered the chance to learn nature's divine lessons (in addition to religious services and other spiritual programs). The moral qualities invested in nature and its study were made explicit at the New York Chautauqua, where Palestine Park featured re-creations of biblical landscapes. Even away from such blatantly didactic landscapes, visitors could still benefit from the contemplation of the divine world. According to Thomas Schlereth's analysis, the Chautauqua camp represented a middle landscape between the primitive and the civilized that offered moral and physical regeneration.[22] As we have seen, the bungalow's idealized image embodied the same principles; presented as a tranquil nature retreat, it offered an escape from everyday chaos and a chance for moral rejuvenation. The relationship between Chautauqua and the ideal bungalow, like its associations with the vacation house and the period's prescriptive literature, again grounded it squarely in the period's popular culture. Such connections could only increase the bungalow's appeal.

In Aladdin's hands, the image of the bungalow proved remarkably elastic. By 1918 the ideal of the bungalow nestled in the arms of nature was being supplemented by other promotions. One example exploited the bungalow's California roots, implying that the purchase of a bungalow brought with it a bit of California living. The bungalow's roots in California were well recognized by Aladdin and others.[23] Aladdin had acknowledged the connection as early as 1909 when it named its first stylistically recognizable bungalow the California.

The associations made between the bungalow and California, however, were not simply based on their geographic relationship; they also exploited the bungalow's symbolic ties to the California dream. At the turn of the century, California was seen as a romantic frontier of perfect weather, warm seas, and limitless opportunity. The bungalow, so often associated with California and its growth, became a metaphor for these idyllic qualities. Its relative novelty and revolutionary simplicity symbolized California's perceived freedom from established cultural strictures, while its organic aesthetic and intimacy with nature embraced the state's tranquil environment. This quality—the bungalow's capacity to symbolize California's romantic appeal—was used in Aladdin's promotional materials. The aptly named Pomona, for one, offered to carry this romance back across the Rockies to the Midwest and East. The 1918 text accompanying the Pomona tells the story of a California woman who married and moved to New York. Although happy, she desperately wanted to recapture in her house the atmosphere of her beloved California. Thus was born the Pomona, described as "a worthy representative of the delightful little California town of that name, from which the 'girl of the golden west' came." For those unable or unwilling to go west, bungalows like the Pomona offered a chance to possess a piece of the state's romance; even if one could not directly experience the new frontier, one could at least own the house that settled the new frontier.[24]

The idealization of the bungalow's California roots furthered its image as a haven from everyday cares (albeit with a slightly different spin). If potential customers still were not swayed by this image of carefree living, perhaps they would be enticed by the bungalow's patriotic pedigree, a virtue frequently noted by Aladdin and other bungalow promoters and suppliers (despite the form's roots in southeast Asia). Such nationalistic overtones were attached to Aladdin's Plaza bungalow: not only was it a good example of California architecture, but it was also "rock-ribbed American." Promoting the bungalow in nationalistic terms responded, in part, to the arts and crafts and colonial revival movements. Both movements hoped to establish a uniquely "American" design aesthetic, whether inspired by indigenous landscapes (as with the Prairie School) or by the architecture of colonial forefathers. The disillusionment with European cultural models created by World War I also may have helped to promote the patriotic bungalow.[25]

Whatever the sources, the image of the bungalow as a distinctly American house type helped lend it cultural credibility. Associations made between the bungalow and the log cabin served the same ends. Warfield Webb was one of several bungalow promoters who made this connection. He stated, "Even our cabins, as built several hundred years ago, might be termed bungalows, insofar as the type is concerned, for they are in several important details identical with the more recently adopted style of this house." Echoing Webb, another writer commented, "The log cabin is the primitive bungalow, or shall we say that the bungalow is the 'up-to-date' log cabin." To some extent, the connection between the bungalow and the log cabin derived from the bungalow's associations with vacation houses. Bungalow advocate Henry Saylor, for example, showed how to turn a vacation dwelling into a log bungalow simply by nailing split log slabs to the stud frame. Similarly, other log bungalows looked like miniature versions of grand, late nineteenth-century Adirondack log retreats. The relationship between the bungalow and the log cabin, however, also tapped into a more pervasive sentimentalization of the log cabin. With the closing of the frontier, the log cabin became a symbol of America's victorious westward expansion. And in an era of urbanization and industrialization, it also came to symbolize a more simple, Edenic way of life.[26] As we have seen, the bungalow offered to recapture these same qualities (with the added benefits of a kitchen and indoor plumbing).

The bungalow's elaborate image—part nature lodge, part California dream house, part log cabin—no doubt helped it to become an acceptable form of year-round housing. For Aladdin, the bungalow's distinctive image also helped differentiate it from other house types, which, at the time, ranged from large colonial revival structures to small, plain dwellings. Aladdin, in effect, created a product line of different house types, with each type catering to different consumer tastes, preferences, and incomes. Distinctions were drawn between the bungalow and Aladdin's more aesthetically simple models in the text of the company's catalogues. Ranging from one to two stories in height, these clapboard houses generally had little ornamentation and simple roof lines; some of the larger one-story houses in this group used the same floor plans as Aladdin's bungalows. Ironically, this group also included year-round versions of the vacation cottages that had influenced Aladdin's bungalows (see fig. 4).

The marketing of the Michigan (fig. 6), a plain, two-story model priced slightly less than many of Aladdin's bungalows, shows how the firm implicitly pitted less expensive, more conservative models against the bungalow: "[The Michigan] is a conservative design of a type that has always found a number of admirers among home builders. Among the great number of people building new homes each year, a large percentage are not attracted to types decorated with embellishments and novelties that, to use their words, 'come and go every year.' Their preference runs to simplicity, service and durability."[27] For middle-class

See prices on inside of front cover.

Fig. 6. The Michigan. From Aladdin Co., *Aladdin Homes* (Bay City, Mich.: By the company, 1918), p. 34. (Winterthur Library.)

consumers who saw the bungalow as little more than a passing novelty (and for those looking for a less expensive house), the Michigan offered a plain, pragmatic alternative. The conservatism offered in the Michigan also could be found in other, similar models. In 1916 the Jersey and the Portland, both relatively plain, gabled houses, were respectively renamed the Princeton and the Yale. The new Ivy League names carried connotations of tradition and a certain exclusivity (the latter useful for selling less-expensive models), recalling ivy-covered academic structures rather than the idealized rusticity associated with the bungalow.

The promotion of the Michigan and related houses, when compared to the marketing of the bungalow, shows how Aladdin tried to develop distinct personalities for its different house types, despite the fact that all types shared the same structural system and many shared the same floor plans. Such differentiation was crucial to a company catering to a wide range of consumer tastes. As the promotion of the Michigan showed, tangible stylistic differences provided one method of differentiation, but abstract, nonvisual distinctions also were created through the text and images attached to each house type. Like the period's fledgling automobile manufacturers (General Motors was incorporated in 1908), Aladdin created unique personas for products that were in many ways similar except for their outer skins.

For consumers, a line of distinctive house types provided the opportunity to purchase both a house and the associations that accompanied it. A bungalow, for example, might symbolize its owner's "progressive" pretensions or his or her preference for the latest stylistic fashions. A more plain house, on the other hand, might suggest more traditional tastes and values. Through Aladdin's catalogues, the associations attached to a given house type enjoyed wide distribution, and the designs and rhetoric produced by Aladdin mirrored the work found in other catalogues, plan books, and prescriptive literature. Aladdin's product line was therefore part of a larger, standardized language of architecture and architectural symbols that permeated American mass culture during the early twentieth century. In purchasing a house, be it a bungalow or another house type, the consumer established an architectural identity not only within the local community but also within the larger popular culture; like other mass-produced mass-marketed goods, houses could create relationships and disparities among mass-market consumers.[28]

During the early twentieth century, many middle-class, suburban consumers came to occupy a new bungalow. Aladdin, through its products and catalogues, played an important role in both supplying and stoking this popular fervor for the bungalow. The company's 1906 to 1920 catalogues, although only a fragment of the bungalow story, provide unique insights into the bungalow and the mechanics of its supply and demand. In the hands of Aladdin and other similar firms, the bungalow became a standardized commodity churned out and packaged like other mass-produced goods of the period. To encourage purchases, Aladdin matched its production capacity with persuasive verbal and visual marketing. Accordingly, the bungalow came to life as an idealized retreat, promising everything from good health to a piece of the California dream. This mating of mass production and mass marketing firmly anchored the bungalow in America's popular consciousness and on its suburban and rural landscapes. And yet, even after bungalow mania began to fade, the form itself remained. In the small Tudor house of the later 1920s, the Cape Cod of the 1930s, and the ranch of the 1940s and 1950s, one still sees the bungalow's informal plan and simple aesthetic as well as its legacy of standardized design. These accomplishments aside, however, it never could quite measure up to Marie Antoinette's Petit Trianon.

---

[1] H. P. Keith, "What to Put in the Bungalow," *Keith's Magazine on Home Building* 33, no. 4 (April 1915): 237. The influence of popular periodicals on interior design and architecture is discussed in H. Allen Brooks, *The Prairie School: Frank Lloyd Wright and His Midwest Contemporaries* (Toronto: University of Toronto Press, 1972), pp. 23–24; David E. Shi, *The Simple Life: Plain Living and High Thinking in American Culture* (New York: Oxford University Press, 1985), pp. 181–89; and Jean Gordon and Jan McArthur, "Popular Culture, Magazines, and American Domestic Interiors, 1898–1940," *Journal of Popular Culture* 22, no. 4 (Spring 1989): 35–60.

[2] The firm was known as the North American Construction Company until 1917. On William and Otto Sovereign and the founding of Aladdin, see Otto E. Sovereign, *Fifty Million Dollars on a Shoestring: A Tale of Fifty Years of Business (and Fifty Years of Fun)* ([Bay City, Mich.]: By the author, 1951); and Robert Schweitzer and Michael Davis, "Aladdin's Magic Catalog," *Michigan History* 68, no. 1 (January 1984): 24–33. On the company's history of success, see Robert Schweitzer and Michael W. R. Davis, *America's Favorite Homes: Mail-Order Catalogues as a Guide to Popular Early Twentieth-Century Houses* (Detroit: Wayne State University Press, 1990), p. 84. Aladdin Co., *Industrial Housing* (Bay City, Mich.: By the company, 1920), p. 86. This catalogue also illustrates several model Aladdin towns. For the Birmingham project, see Sovereign, *Fifty Million Dollars*, p. 25. Aladdin's first merchandise catalogue, *Aladdin Homecraft Marketplace* (Bay City, Mich.: North American Construction Co.), was published in 1915. The origins of mail-order housing in America can be traced in mid to late nineteenth-century planbooks such as Samuel Sloan, *The Model Architect: A Series of Designs for Cottages, Villas, and Suburban Residences,* 2 vols. (Philadelphia: E. S. Jones, 1852); periodicals such as *Godey's Lady's Book*; and the work of firms such as Palliser, Palliser, and Co. of Bridgeport, Conn. On mail-order plans and houses during the nineteenth and early twentieth centuries, see Patricia Poore, "Pattern Book Architecture: Is Yours a Mail-Order House?" *Old House Journal* 8, no. 12 (December 1980): 183–93; James L. Garvin, "Mail-Order House Plans and American Victorian Architecture," *Winterthur Portfolio* 16, no. 4 (Winter 1981): 309–34; Thomas Harvey, "Mail-Order Architecture in the Twenties," *Landscape* 25, no. 3 (1981): 1–9; David M. Schwartz, "When Home Sweet Home Was Just a Mailbox Away," *Smithsonian* 16, no. 8 (November 1985): 90–100; Alan Gowans, *The Comfortable House: North American Suburban Architecture, 1890–1930* (Cambridge: MIT Press, 1986), pp. 41–63; Katherine Cole Stevenson and H. Ward Jandl, *Houses by Mail: A Guide to Houses from Sears, Roebuck, and Company* (Washington, D.C.: Preservation Press, 1986); and Schweitzer and Davis, *America's Favorite Homes*. On prefabricated construction, see Alfred Bruce and Harold Sandbank, *A History of Prefabrication* (1944; reprint, New York: Arno Press, 1972); Gilbert Herbert, *Pioneers of Prefabrication: The British Contribution in the Nineteenth Century* (Baltimore: Johns Hopkins University Press, 1978); and Anthony King, *The Bungalow: The Production of a Global Culture* (2d ed., New York: Oxford University Press, 1995), chap. 3.

[3] Aladdin's framing system and the relationship between balloon framing and stan-

dardization are briefly discussed in Fred W. Peterson, *Homes in the Heartland: Balloon Frame Farmhouses of the Upper Midwest, 1850–1920* (Lawrence: University of Kansas Press, 1992), pp. 196–200. On the development of standardized architectural components, see Gwendolyn Wright, *Moralism and the Model Home: Domestic Architecture and Cultural Conflict in Chicago, 1873–1913* (Chicago: University of Chicago Press, 1980), pp. 81–97. For Sears's use of new technologies, see Stevenson and Jandl, *Houses by Mail*, p. 30. Construction costs are discussed in Michael J. Doucet and John C. Weaver, "Material Culture and the North American House: The Era of the Common Man, 1870–1920," *Journal of American History* 72, no. 3 (December 1985): 560–87.

⁴ The physical properties that defined bungalows are analyzed in detail in Richard Mattson, "The Bungalow Spirit," *Journal of Cultural Geography* 1, no. 2 (1981): 75–92. North American Construction Co., *Aladdin Homes* (Bay City, Mich.: By the company, 1916).

⁵ The bungalow's southeast Asian roots are discussed in J. Lockwood Kipling, "The Origin of the Bungalow," *Country Life in America* 19, no. 8 (February 15, 1911): 308–10; Clay Lancaster, *The American Bungalow, 1880–1930* (New York: Abbeville Press, 1985), pp. 19–21; and King, *Bungalow*, chap. 1. King discusses the bungalow's early influence in England in chaps. 2–3. The loose interpretation of the bungalow in America is discussed in Brooks, *Prairie School*, pp. 20–21.

⁶ According to King, *Bungalow*, p. 142, the term *bungalow* was in use in California by at least 1905. Robert Winter, *The California Bungalow*, California Architecture and Architects no. 1 (Los Angeles: Hennessey and Ingalls, 1980). For the bungalow's roots in late nineteenth-century vacation houses, see Lancaster, *American Bungalow*, pp. 71–73, 77–94. On tent bungalows, see Henry H. Saylor, *Bungalows: Their Design, Construction, and Furnishing, with Suggestions also for Camps, Summer Homes, and Cottages of Similar Character* (2d ed., New York: McBride, Nast, 1913), pp. 33–35. The relationship between tents and bungalows is also discussed in Kipling, "Origin of the Bungalow," p. 308; and Lancaster, *American Bungalow*, pp. 181–88.

⁷ "The California Bungalow," *Architectural Record* 19, no. 5 (May 1906): 394. See Lester Walker, *Tiny, Tiny Houses* (Woodstock, N.Y.: Overlook Press, 1987), pp. 68–73, for an illustrated discussion of earthquake shacks. For the Arturo Bandini house (Pasadena), see Randell L. Makinson, *Greene and Greene*, 2 vols. (Salt Lake City, Utah: Peregrine Smith, 1977), 1:70–72. Southern California's growth during the late nineteenth and early twentieth centuries is discussed in Robert M. Fogelson, *The Fragmented Metropolis: Los Angeles, 1850–1930* (Cambridge: Harvard University Press, 1967), p. 79.

⁸ For the relationship between bungalows and nineteenth-century cottages, see Clifford Edward Clark, Jr., *The American Family Home, 1800–1960* (Chapel Hill: University of North Carolina Press, 1986), p. 185. On American religious camp architecture, see Pauline Fancher, *Chautauqua: Its Architecture and Its People* (Miami: Banyon Books, 1978); Walker, *Tiny, Tiny Houses*, pp. 46–59; Ellen Weiss, *City in the Woods: The Life and Design of an American Camp Meeting on Martha's Vineyard* (New York: Oxford University Press, 1987); and Ellen Weiss, "Bay View, Michigan: Camp Meeting and Chautauqua," in John S. Garner, ed., *The Midwest in American Architecture* (Urbana: University of Illinois Press, 1991), pp. 145–58. Palliser, Palliser, and Co., *Palliser's New Cottage Homes and Details* (1887; reprint, Watkins Glen, N.Y.: American Life Fndn., 1976), pl. 7. On earthfast construction in colonial America, see Cary Carson et al., "Impermanent Architecture in the Southern American Colonies," *Winterthur Portfolio* 16, nos. 2/3 (Summer/Autumn 1981): 135–96. For the links among Palliser's cottages, impermanent architecture, and the bungalow, see Gowans, *Comfortable House*, pp. 78–82.

⁹ King, *Bungalow*, p. 142. North American Construction Co., *"Aladdin" Summer Cottages* (Bay City, Mich.: By the company, [1906]).

[10] For a comparison of the late nineteenth-century house and the bungalow, see Margaret Marsh, "From Separation to Togetherness: The Social Construction of Domestic Space in American Suburbs, 1840–1915," *The Journal of American History* 76, no. 2 (September 1989): 515–20. See also Wright, *Moralism*, pp. 244–47.

[11] On the bungalow and architectural reform, see Wright, *Moralism*, pp. 234–36, 240–44, 251; Clark, *American Family Home*, pp. 132, 162–63; King, *Bungalow*, pp. 134–37. Frederick W. Coburn, "The Five Hundred Mile City," *World Today* 11, no. 6 (December 1906): 1251–60.

[12] Mary W. Mount, "Bungalow Furnishings," *House Beautiful* 32, no. 3 (August 1912): 75–76. Wilson Eyre, "The Purpose of the Bungalow," *Country Life in America* 19, no. 8 (February 15, 1911): 305. Magonigle quoted in Phil M. Riley, "What Is a Bungalow?" *Country Life in America* 22, no. 6 (July 15, 1912): 12. Riley, "What Is a Bungalow?" p. 11. Eyre, "Purpose of the Bungalow," p. 305. Even inveterate bungalow supporter Henry Saylor admitted that bungalows were best suited as temporary or seasonal dwellings; see Saylor, *Bungalows*, p. 20.

[13] Magonigle quoted in Riley, "What Is a Bungalow?" p. 12. On the earlier battles between architects and builders, see Wright, *Moralism*, pp. 21 26, 46–78. On the tension between architects and mail-order suppliers during the early twentieth century, see Gowans, *Comfortable House*, pp. 63–67.

[14] According to Schweitzer and Davis, *America's Favorite Homes*, p. 99, Aladdin intentionally designed its houses based on standard lengths of milled lumber. The variation of a standardized set of rooms in a more or less standardized range of dimensions is similar to the design approach associated with some vernacular structures; see, for example, Henry Glassie, "The Variation of Concepts within Tradition: Barn Building in Otsego County, New York," in H. J. Walker and W. G. Haag, eds., *Man and Cultural Heritage: Papers in Honor of Fred B. Kniffen*, Geoscience and Man, vol. 5 (Baton Rouge: Louisiana State University Press, 1974), pp. 177–235.

[15] Frances Downing and Ulric Flemming, "The Bungalows of Buffalo," *Environment and Planning B* 8, no. 3 (1981): 269–93. William Draper Brincklé, "Planning the Bungalow," *Country Life in America* 19, no. 8 (February 15, 1911): 319–21. The bungalow's adaptability is also noted in Charles Vaughn, *The Little Book of Bungalows and Cottages* (New York: Woman's Home Companion, 1921), p. 3; and Clark, *American Family Home*, p. 183. Henry L. Wilson, the self-proclaimed "Bungalow Man," was a major publisher of bungalow plans and specifications that could be ordered by mail; see Henry L. Wilson, *The Wilson Bungalow* (5th ed., Chicago: By the author, 1910). On Wilson's work, see Jan Cohn, *The Palace or the Poorhouse: The American House as a Cultural Symbol* (East Lansing: Michigan State University Press, 1979), p. 100. On the standardization of houses in Chicago's late nineteenth-century suburbs, see Wright, *Moralism*, pp. 40–42.

[16] On the late Victorian house as a retreat, see Wright, *Moralism*, pp. 97–102; and Clark, *American Family Home*, pp. 24–34. The continued use of this idea in the early twentieth century is discussed in Wright, *Moralism*, pp. 132–49; Clark, *American Family Home*, pp. 153–55; and Cheryl Robertson, "Male and Female Agendas for Domestic Reform: The Middle-Class Bungalow in Gendered Perspective," *Winterthur Portfolio* 26, nos. 2/3 (Summer/Autumn 1991): 124. The connection made between the vacation home and the ideal bungalow has also been noted in Clark, *American Family Home*, pp. 180–81; Gowans, *Comfortable House*, pp. 77–78; Richard Guy Wilson, "American Arts and Crafts Architecture: Radical though Dedicated to the Cause Conservative," in Wendy Kaplan, ed., *"The Art That Is Life": The Arts and Crafts Movement in America, 1875–1920* (Boston: Little, Brown, 1987), p. 117; and King, *Bungalow*, p. 142.

[17] North American Construction Co., *Aladdin Summer Cottages, Garages, Pergolas,*

Sleeping Porches, Sun Rooms, Arbors, Trellises (Bay City, Mich.: By the company, 1913), p. i. Aladdin Co., *Aladdin Homes* (Bay City, Mich.: By the company, 1917), p. 67.

[18] On the moral dimensions of the late nineteenth-century suburban house, see Wright, *Moralism*, pp. 26–28; on the connection between nature and morality, see Margaret W. Morley, "Nature Study and Its Influence," *The Outlook* 68, no. 13 (July 27, 1901): 737–39; and C. F. Hodge, "Nature Study and Citizenship," *The Chautauquan* 37, no. 5 (August 1903): 438–39. For a more general perspective, see Peter J. Schmitt, *Back to Nature: The Arcadian Myth in Urban America* (New York: Oxford University Press), pp. 141–45; James Oliver Robertson, *American Myth, American Reality* (New York: Hill and Wang, 1980), pp. 115–16; Robert M. Crunden, *Ministers of Reform: The Progressives' Achievement in American Civilization, 1889–1920* (New York: Basic Books, 1982), pp. 117, 145–46; and Shi, *Simple Life*, pp. 195–201.

[19] North American Construction Co., *Aladdin Summer Cottages*, p. i. Aladdin Co., *Aladdin Homes* (Bay City, Mich.: By the company, 1920), p. 90. On ventilation and health, see Richard Cole Newton, "The New Method to Keep Us Well," *Ladies' Home Journal* 25, no. 5 (April 1908): 26; Wright, *Moralism*, pp. 29–31; Shi, *Simple Life*, pp. 201–4; Harvey Green, *Fit for America: Health, Fitness, Sport, and American Society* (New York: Pantheon Books, 1986), p. 77; and Witold Rybczynski, *Home: A Short History of an Idea* (New York: Viking, 1986), pp. 132–37. On health and morality, see Clark, *American Family Home*, pp. 101–2.

[20] North American Construction Co., *Aladdin Homes*, p. 22. Aladdin Co., *Aladdin Homes* (1917), p. 54. On the simple life, see Schmitt, *Back to Nature*, pp. 125–40, 167–76; Shi, *Simple Life*, pp. 181–89, 195–201; and King, *Bungalow*, pp. 132–34. On the architecture of simple living, see Gustav Stickley, *Craftsman Homes: Architecture and Furnishings of the American Arts and Crafts Movement* (1909 reprint, New York: Dover, 1979), p. 194; Charles Keeler, *The Simple Home* (1904; reprint, Santa Barbara: Peregrine Smith, 1979), pp. 36–37; Brooks, *Prairie School*, pp. 20–21; Wright, *Moralism*, pp. 240–44; and Clark, *American Family Home*, pp. 146–49. On the concept of simplicity as a form of fashion and status, see Thorstein Veblen, *The Theory of the Leisure Class* (New York: Macmillan Co., 1912), pp. 155–66; the theme has been further developed by Winter, *California Bungalow*, p. 48; Cheryl Robertson, "House and Home in the Arts and Crafts Era: Reforms for Simpler Living," in Kaplan, *"The Art That Is Life,"* pp. 336–40; and King, *Bungalow*, p. 155.

[21] Thomas J. Schlereth, "Chautauqua: A Middle Landscape of the Middle Class," *Henry Ford Museum and Greenfield Village Herald* 13, no. 2 (1984): 25. Eldon E. Snyder, "The Chautauqua Movement in Popular Culture: A Sociological Analysis," *Journal of American Culture* 8, no. 3 (Fall 1985): 80–85; and Alan Trachtenberg, " 'We Study the Word and Works of God': Chautauqua and the Sacralization of Culture in America," *Henry Ford Museum and Greenfield Village Herald* 13, no. 2 (1984): 3–4. Snyder, "Chautauqua Movement," pp. 85–89. See also Theodore Morrison, *Chautauqua* (Chicago: University of Chicago Press, 1974); Roland Mueller, "Tents and Tabernacles: The Chautauqua Movement in Kansas" (Ph.D. diss., University of Kansas, 1978); and Weiss, "Bay View, Michigan."

[22] Schlereth, "Chautauqua," pp. 23–24; Trachtenberg, " 'We Study the Word and Works of God,' " p. 6.

[23] See, for example, "California Bungalow"; King, *Bungalow*, pp. 142–45.

[24] Aladdin Co., *Aladdin Homes* (Bay City, Mich.: By the company, 1918), p. 32; Kevin Starr, *Americans and the California Dream, 1850–1915* (New York: Oxford University Press, 1973). For the bungalow's connection to the California dream, see Clark, *American Family Home*, pp. 179–80; and Winter, *California Bungalow*, p. 23.

[25] Aladdin Co., *Aladdin Homes* (1918), p. 31. On the bungalow's "Americaness," see

Clark, *American Family Home*, p. 185; and Gowans, *Comfortable House*, pp. 75–76. On World War I and the bungalow, see Rodney Douglas Parker, "The California Bungalow and the Tyrolean Chalet: The Ill-Fated Life of an American Vernacular," *Journal of American Culture* 15, no. 4 (Winter 1992): 13–15.

²⁶ Warfield Webb, "Why Bungalows Are So Popular," *Keith's Magazine on Home Building* 33, no. 4 (April 1915): 245. "Some California Bungalows," *Architectural Record* 18, no. 3 (September 1905): 223. Saylor, *Bungalows*, p. 103. For a quasi-Adirondack log bungalow, see "Some California Bungalows," p. 222; for Gustav Stickley's log club house at his Craftsman Farms complex in Parsippany, N.J., see Mark Alan Hewitt, "Words, Deeds, and Artifice: Gustav Stickley's Club House at Craftsman Farms," *Winterthur Portfolio* 31, no. 1 (Spring 1996): 23–51. On the sentimentalization of the log cabin, see Cohn, *Palace or the Poorhouse*, pp. 175–92.

²⁷ Aladdin Co., *Aladdin Homes* (1918), p. 34. The Michigan cost $876 in 1916.

²⁸ The connections made among houses, consumption, and the creation of identity draw on theories developed in Michael Schudson, *Advertising, the Uneasy Persuasion: Its Dubious Impact on American Society* (New York: Basic Books, 1984), pp. 151–68. His work incorporates theories first expressed in Mary Douglas and Baron Isherwood, *The World of Goods: Towards an Anthropology of Consumption* (New York: W. W. Norton, 1979). Judith Williamson, *Decoding Advertisements: Ideology and Meaning in Advertising* (London: Marion Boyars, 1978); and Torben Vestergaard and Kim Schroeder, *The Language of Advertising* (Oxford: Basil Blackwell, 1985) also offer a cultural analysis of advertising.

Household Encounters
Servants, Slaves, and Mistresses in Early Washington

Barbara G. Carson, Ellen Kirven Donald, and Kym S. Rice

In the woods near Samuel Harrison Smith's house outside Washington stood a ramshackle hut occupied by a poor woman who supported herself with piecework. When Margaret Smith offered to find the woman a position as a domestic servant "where her useful experience . . . would have procured her a comfortable existence," she refused and observed that "independence, however humble, was far preferable" to servitude. As this story illustrates, the nature of domestic service was shifting in early America. Ideas about equality were evolving. Likewise, attitudes about the value of women's traditional activities were changing. Fewer individuals wanted to be servants. Eventually market relations replaced household paternalism. Elite women struggled to run their households under new circumstances. In the early nineteenth century, many writers, especially foreign travelers, associated these specific conditions of American life with a severe "servant problem."[1]

This study of relationships between servants and their mistresses in the nation's capital draws largely on the correspondence and diaries of elite women, including Anna Maria Thornton, who came to the city in 1794 with her husband Dr. William Thornton, the first architect of the U.S. Capitol; Margaret Bayard Smith, who arrived in 1800 as the bride of newspaper editor Samuel Harrison Smith; Louisa Catherine

Adams, wife of John Quincy Adams, who was first secretary of state and then president; and Elizabeth Wirt, whose husband, William, became President Monroe's attorney general. These women left extensive writings about their household management and word pictures of domestic encounters. Other sources help to establish a context against which to view the details of the conflicts among mistresses, servants, and slaves found in the writings of these women.[2]

This essay looks specifically at domestic servants and service in Washington in the early national period. A rich body of material, of which this essay draws on only in small part, allows for the examination of several important issues. Focusing on features of domestic servitude, including women's roles as domestic supervisors and moral managers, and on features specific to Washington, including race relations in the home and in the community, this essay suggests the ways in which issues of political, economic, and social equality are reflected within the world of domestic Washington.

SETTING THE SCENE

When the federal government arrived in 1800, only the most rudimentary parts of Washington City were constructed. The scattered public buildings, including the Capitol and the President's House, stood unfinished, and the city still consisted mostly of woods and farmland (fig. 1). Only a few rutted streets were cleared. As late as 1827, an English visitor grumbled to her sister, "One is tempted to ask even in the heart of the city, 'Where is Washington?' "[3]

The new District of Columbia also incorporated the tobacco port of Georgetown, Maryland, and, until 1846, the city of Alexandria, Virginia. Not just physical proximity allied the District of Columbia to the larger region of the South. Local government adopted and upheld the laws of Maryland and Virginia; as a result, the city was, in the words of one critic, "an emporium of slavery." Slavery in the nation's capital, Basil Hall observed in 1828, was "felt in its remote ramifications in every class of the society."[4] Certainly there was no place where the contradictory nature of American freedom and democracy was more evident.

The "City of Washington" was first settled in neighborhoods near the public buildings (fig. 2). The composition of city neighborhoods

Fig. 1. Anthony St. John Baker, *The White House and Grounds,* ca. 1826. Watercolor; H. 7¾", W. 11⅝" (Huntington Library, San Marino, Calif.)

was still fluid, and people lived near where they worked. Sometimes within the same dwelling or as next-door neighbors could be found both rich and poor, professional tradesmen and artisans, and skilled and unskilled laborers. Blacks and whites lived in close proximity. In 1820 one of wealthy John Tayloe's nearest neighbors was Anna Black, an enslaved head of household.[5]

During the winter season, when elected officials were in residence, elite families regularly socialized with one another and with visitors to the city. Diaries and letters record the frenetic daily round of calls, teas, dinners, suppers, balls, and other social events. Such elite entertaining practices depended on the daily service of men, women, and children. During the season, servants were needed by locals and visitors alike to take care of household activities and to perform at social functions. Margaret Bayard Smith claimed that "few persons [in Washington] realize how dependant they are on servants, not only for their comfort, but for their estimation in society."[6]

Fig. 2. Thomas Doughty, *The Capitol. Washington, D.C./West Front from City Hall*, 1832. Lithograph; H. 5⅛", W. 8" (Kiplinger Washington Collection.)

CHARACTERISTICS OF DOMESTIC SERVITUDE IN WASHINGTON

The Washington servant pool was largely drawn from the city's growing African American population, which in this period was increasingly free. Urban economic opportunity for blacks remained confined to employment in personal service to whites or within a narrow range of artisan activity. Elite whites employed black men, women, and young children as their maids, nurses, manservants, waiters, cooks, laundresses, gardeners, stable hands, and coachmen on both a permanent and a temporary basis. In 1820 more than half of all white households in the city's better neighborhoods employed free or enslaved blacks as help. In general, slaveholding in the city was widespread, but the numbers in individual households were small—between one and three slaves. Elite households with eight to fourteen servants were rare.[7]

Many white Washingtonians (including northerners like Margaret

Smith) secured their domestic servants through a common southern practice that hired out slaves on yearly contracts. Sometimes encouraging more independent working and living arrangements for enslaved individuals, "hiring out" provided African Americans with an important measure of autonomy. The system evolved such that enslaved African Americans negotiated their own hiring agreements, living arrangements, and wages independent of their owners' requirements. In August 1829, Anna Maria Thornton was surprised to meet Barney, a former slave in her neighborhood, who had earned enough from self-hire to buy his freedom.[8]

Washington's economy was underpinned by the sale of food, lodgings, goods, and the other conveniences provided by locals to government officials during the six months that Congress was in session. The resident population, especially merchants, boardinghouse keepers, and the like, depended on this annual influx for their livelihood. "Winter is harvest time in Washington," quipped a character in Margaret Bayard Smith's unpublished novel, "Lucy," set in Washington following the War of 1812.[9]

Many residents, black and white, found temporary work—with long hours and burdensome duties—in hotels, taverns, and private residences. Few establishments or families maintained the kind of large permanent staff that the population influx and city social life necessitated. In "Lucy," a free African American character informs the heroine, "Congress will soon meet. . . . I can get a place as a Coachman or waiter any day I please, either among the quality or at Taverns. By the month or by the day—I can make my [two is crossed out] three dollars a day at any of the secretaries, on their dinner days, for you know they count me as an excellent waiter, & as much as the houses of quality just for tending at an evening party." Later, at home with his family, the man muses, "Its only a pity they [the Congress] would not stay the whole year round, we should soon have a city, worth calling a city then, for they would find abundance of work for all sorts of folk. . . . Its always feast or famine."[10] As Margaret Smith recognized, one feature of working-class life in early Washington was seasonal high unemployment.

HOUSEHOLD ORGANIZATION

This ebb and flow in social activity and the subsequent need to hire additional help can only have complicated the daily demands of household organization. Louisa Catherine Adams, wife of President John Quincy Adams, provides a clear picture of the complexity of running a large elite household. Her organizational scheme and list of duties provide insights into the character and behavior she considered acceptable for servants, the hierarchy among servants, and relationships between master, mistress, and male and female servants. Within the house Louisa Catherine Adams gave orders to both male and female members of the staff. The family employed four upper servants, a female housekeeper, and three men—the steward, the butler, and the cook. Probably she consulted most closely with the steward, who had "charge of all the expenses of the family."[11]

The butler took charge of John Adams's clothes. Together these two men supervised the porter at the door and the two boys who carried wood and coal, laid fires, accompanied the carriage, and waited table. At mealtime the butler took charge of the food, the steward of the wine. Along with the coachman and the ostler, these seven men comprised the visible portion of the staff. The cook and possibly his kitchen helper or scullion, whose gender was not specified, were the only males who did not work in the public arena.

The Adams's housekeeper oversaw "all the female part of the Household." Six female servants cleaned house, laundered and repaired the linen, cared for the sick, and milked the cows. At least in the Adams's household, the male cook worked closely with the female housekeeper. She gave out all provisions, and if the scullion was "impudent or disrespectful," the cook applied to the housekeeper to send the offender off and engage another. Louisa Catherine Adams's instructions imply that she at least confirmed firing and hiring decisions for all lower staff except the scullion.[12]

Adams aimed for a clean, well-ordered establishment where the rituals of greeting and serving guests would be conducted "properly," a word she used repeatedly. She anticipated personnel problems. If a staff member broke her rule against quarreling, "dismissal without further enquiry" was the penalty. Adams specifically cautioned the "coloured females" not to exhibit impudence or disrespect "to any of the white people in the family."[13]

Louisa Catherine Adams's instructions reveal her expectations that servants should adhere to certain types of behavior—perhaps along the lines of those outlined in 1827 by a Washington magazine that detailed

Fig. 3. John Lewis Krimmel, woman ironing, 1819. Watercolor; H. 4⅞", W 7". (Joseph Downs Collection of Manuscripts and Printed Ephemera, Winterthur Library.)

the ideal characteristics of good servants. They were to be clean, neat and tidy in appearance, sober, truthful, industrious, conscientious, and honest. They were to avoid coarse and vulgar language and never to repeat family tales. Envy of masters and mistresses was to be avoided. "Mildness, meekness and amiability" were traits to cultivate. Deferential behavior was desirable in a world where it was right "that one portion of the community should aid, assist or, if you please, labor for the other."[14]

ELITE DOMESTIC MANAGERS

In elite Washington households, as in those elsewhere, housework was still housework (fig. 3). Its tedious routine exasperated Margaret Smith. "The business of a family is everyday alike, every day the house is to be put in order, the food prepared & the clothing made or mended— Does it then require the whole of life to support life? Few are exempt from this necessity—at times how insignificant and how wearisome do these domestic employments seem."[15]

Elite women were neither partners in drudgery nor creatures of leisure. They were active domestic managers. In 1801 new mother Margaret Smith reported to her sister that she was on the mend and eager to return to her duties: "I am determined to see after every thing myself & in all respects to be industrious & economical."[16] Like Smith, the women studied here made comments about supervision of the routine of house cleaning and laundry and noted servants running errands and making preparations for meals. Some tasks they took special pride in performing themselves. On one occasion Smith showed off her dairy and the butter she made to guests who came to her country house. More typically, sewing and child care were among the duties the mistresses took on themselves.

Louisa Catherine Adams, for instance, oversaw the large staff of servants necessary for the household of the secretary of state to function smoothly. Household accounts record wages paid to numerous individuals for domestic service, some employed full time and others hired as needed. The Adamses entertained frequently and on a large scale. In January 1820, Louisa Catherine Adams recorded, "Very busy all day preparing for my Ball tomorrow, taking down bed, and furniture of every description, . . . I cannot therefore pretend that the day was passed quietly. However we were all pleased at having accomplished this great labor. . . ." The next day she continued, "We were so busy all the morning, as to be almost exhausted by this time our company arrived. . . . We had about three hundred, perhaps more, and the evening was more than commonly animated. . . . we retired to bed much fatigued, and I not much pleased at the prospect before me of the cleaning and scrubbing."[17]

Both before and after her husband's death, Anna Maria Thornton directed the daily activities of the men and women who worked in her home (fig. 4). Her diaries and ledgers, which record routine chores as well as the occasional hiring of outside help, demonstrate Thornton's constant use of her management skills. In 1833 she noted, "I intended to go out—but thought it better to keep the Servants at work." Troubled by problems with an alcoholic female slave, she confessed in her diary, "It is very contrary to my wishes & feelings to sell any of them—but if they will not behave—what can I do—I cannot afford to give them

Fig. 4. Gilbert Stuart, *Anna Maria Brodeau Thornton*, 1804.
Oil on canvas; H. 28¾", W. 24". (National Gallery of Art,
Washington, D.C.)

free[dom]." After the drinking problem accelerated, Thornton sold the
slave (and her child) without remorse.[18]

A mistress's sense of duty usually extended into responsibility for
the moral and religious life of servants in their house and into charitable
acts for others outside their own four walls. In Margaret Smith's novels,
elite women often provide a range of educational opportunities for indigent children and perform other charitable acts for the "worthy poor."
Smith herself taught Bible classes to the white and black children in

her household, including a hired slave named Philip. "This evening
I have given the children a long & satisfactory lesson—It is now
ten o'clock, but he is so delighted with his book, he is still pouring
over it."[19]

Teaching Philip reading was easier than instilling virtue in another
servant. Although Smith had "suffered scarcely a week . . . without
giving her the most affectionate advice & enforcing that advice with
an exhibition of all the misery . . . sin would bring," the unmarried
Polly still became pregnant. Because she expressed no embarrassment
or remorse in her situation, Margaret Smith reluctantly concluded the
maid was beyond reformation and found her another place.[20]

WORKING AND LIVING CONDITIONS

Accommodations in Washington for resident servants undoubtedly
ranged widely, but more were probably deplorable than comfortable.
Race undoubtedly was a key factor in determining sleeping arrangements. Writing of the region in the 1820s, Frances Trollope observed
that "domestic slaves are, generally speaking, tolerably well fed, and
decently clothed; and the mode in which they are lodged seen as a
matter of great indifference to them." Possibly, but more likely the indifference was on the part of the owner. The best evidence for servants'
sleeping arrangements for Washington applies to commercial establishments. In the winter of 1811–12, Harriet Otis, the stepsister of Congress-
man Harrison Gray Otis, resided at a boardinghouse with other family
members. One evening she visited a sick slave who was "stretched on
a bed of rags covered with old carpeting in the corner of a noisy
kitchen." In 1816 the British traveler David Baille Warden anticipated
Trollope's later observation stating, "Most of the slaves of Washington
are well clad and nourished. . . . In some of the taverns, they sleep on
the floor of the dining-room, which the master, for obvious reasons,
ought to forbid." More than thirty years later Charles Lyell contrasted
his experiences in Washington. "The principal hotels . . . have improved, and we were not annoyed . . . by the odors left in the room by
the colored domestics, who had no beds but slept anywhere about the
stairs or passages without changing their clothes."[21]

Washington probate inventories and scattered insurance records for Alexandria provide scant evidence of accommodations of servants in private homes. Analysis of 418 Washington inventories dating between 1806 and 1826 reveal the presence of slaves, either owned or hired, in nearly half the households. (In additional cases free labor may have accounted for some domestic work.) Only sixteen of these documents (3.8 percent) list objects specifically associated with servants or slaves. In all but one instance the items were bedding, and their placement suggests a location in or near the kitchen. In Washington during those years, most kitchens of elite and even more ordinary residences were either in cellars or in detached or semidetached outbuildings. Mutual Assurance policies for Alexandria describing both contiguous and separate structures as "Dwelling & Kitchen" bolster the likelihood that domestic help slept in or near kitchens on the floor on portable pallets or mattresses.[22]

Clear distinctions between accommodations for slaves and white upper servants are revealed in correspondence between Elizabeth and William Wirt (fig. 5). Writing from Richmond prior to the family's move to Washington in December of 1817, Elizabeth Wirt reveals that the problem of living quarters for her slaves was one that troubled her. Lack of adequate space caused a female slave going into labor to share a room with a male slave immobilized with a broken leg, a situation that Wirt felt "ought not to be." Her sense of propriety was offended. In another letter, she complained, in reference to a home that the Wirts were considering purchasing, that the housing for servants was not in the outbuildings as she had anticipated. Her solution to this dilemma was to suggest that the current stable be converted to "servants rooms."[23] While she may have given some thought to the basic needs of her slaves, her primary concern was to establish what she considered a proper distance between her family and the slaves who lived on the Wirt's property.

Following the family's move to the nation's capital, these sorts of difficulties seemed no longer to trouble Wirt. Perhaps her desire to physically separate slave housing from family quarters was adequately met by the new house, which, in addition to its ten rooms, had "all necessary out houses" spread out over "beautiful & spacious grounds." Instead, her problems revolved around the housing of her white servants. When William Wirt wrote to hire a housekeeper, Mrs. Lane, in 1818, he promised to receive her "as an equal & a friend" who would

Fig. 5. Cephas Thompson, *Elizabeth Gamble Wirt*, ca. 1818. Oil on canvas; H. 30″, W. 25″. (National Portrait Gallery, Smithsonian Institution.)

"eat at our board and live in our company" with her own "neatly furnished" chamber. Six months later Wirt complained that Mrs. Lane was not worth either her one hundred dollar salary or the "one constant fire" kept in her room. Another white servant, Stephen, whose duties are not clear, complained to Wirt that his room was "not comfortable enough" and that he had "not a servant . . . to clean . . . for him every day." Although Wirt complied and had "his room cleaned out and a new bed arrangement made," she was clearly annoyed and predicted

Fig. 6. Anne-Marguerite Rouille de Marigny, Baroness Hyde de Neuville, *Cook in Ordinary Costume*, before 1822. Watercolor; H. 7½", W. 6½". (New-York Historical Society.)

that "Stephen won't answer long."[24] Apparently, the problem with white servants was not propriety or proximity but one of attitude and expectations.

Servants' dress on-the-job reflected their status and varied with their visibility before the public and guests (fig. 6). Upper servants, such as tutors and housekeepers, both male and female, usually wore their own clothes, which resembled those of their employers as much as possible. Lower female servants wore ordinary clothes.[25] More frequently in public, male servants, coachmen, footmen, doormen, and waiters often wore a uniform known as *livery*. Like a military uniform, this costume not only marked their specific position in household hierarchy but also signaled to all the ability of their masters and mistresses to command their labor.

As a group, urban domestic servants were said to have been among the first to step out of the clothes of their station. When bed and board were provided, servants could spend some of their wages on new or secondhand personal adornment. Eliza Dodd, a Georgetown milliner who had many fashionable customers, also sold ribbons, laces, and hats to a few white and African American servants.[26] Servants who worked for elite families could observe firsthand how to dress fashionably. Clothes received as gifts from employers, though probably outmoded in cut and likely to be worn, faded, mended, or obviously remodeled, were still a step up from those available to many Washington residents.

Servants responded to situations requiring special care in dressing. In Smith's "Lucy," a maid busily works on a dress for one of the many parties to which she has been invited. She plans to wear her own clothes to some and for others to borrow covertly from her mistress's wardrobe. "It won't be near such a sin, as not paying a body their wages. It's only takin whats ones own, as a body may say." On the days when his family expected callers, one fictional male servant wore his Sunday clothes. On the other hand, an experienced tavern waiter was demoted to second fiddle because his shirt was not freshly laundered.[27]

Masters, conversely, bought livery. In the United States generally few domestic servants wished to announce their subservient status, and by the nineteenth century, liveried servants chiefly were found in the slaveholding South. Writing to family in England, Margaret Hall explained that in months of travel in the northern United States and Canada she had not seen any liveried servants except in two Philadelphia houses. The farther south she traveled, the more liveried servants she noticed. When Hall called on the elegant and old-fashioned Charles Carroll at his Maryland estate, she observed with approval "no less than three servants in livery."[28]

In Washington many servants in elite households wore livery. But no matter how grandly a few were dressed by their American masters, foreign ministers, representing their European governments, outdistanced the elite citizenry with the splendor of their servants' costumes. On New Year's Day at the White House in 1814, the "gorgeous footmen with chapeaux bras, gilt braided skirts and splendid swords" dazzled one visitor. On another occasion, a guest at a dinner party given by the British Minister Charles Vaughn made special note of the livery worn by his servants. Three servants were required to open the door, conduct guests upstairs, and announce their names to the minister's secretary. All were "in a dress that would have become a field marshall—a white coat trimmed with red and yellow buttons—a red waistcoat and red satin breeches with white stockings and shoes with buckels—all as clean and neat as possible." Some American guests may have marveled at the white and red uniforms, but others regarded liveried servants with less respect. "Our people are frequently laughed at for wearing livery," noted one of Vaughn's predecessors.[29]

How many Washington masters dressed their male servants in livery? Few of the documents examined for this essay reveal whether servants in elite city households were required to wear livery. John Tayloe III, at his house in Washington, provided his male servants—porters, waiters, and grooms—with "Blue Quaker Cut Coats Turned up with Red—Red Vests—Collers & Pockets Gold laces—Breeches, Whitest long stockings, Shoes & Buckles—The full Costume Shoulder straps or Small Epaulettes." President Thomas Jefferson paid a tailor more than £18 for the materials, blue fabric, red lining, silver lace trimming, and labor to make four livery coats. Fictional writers and would-be poets emphasized the red color and lace worn by White House servants, many of whom were African Americans. They thought it incongruous that men who could wield strong axes were "set up with lace upon their backs: And those so fit for toting rails, Were patched with red down to their tails." The general American attitudes toward equality in dress was expressed bluntly in Smith's "Lucy," in which an invitation to "our Sam" to attend a servants' party specified, "Gentlemen with livery not admitted."[30]

THE SERVANT PROBLEM

In America between 1800 and 1835, most individuals who wrote about domestic management, whether for publication or in private, acknowledged some sort of servant problem. Masters, mistresses, and visitors all complained about the quality of the service or about the attitudes with which it was rendered. Scottish writer Basil Hall was not even sure *servant* was the accurate term. He had difficulty summoning "the helps, or hirelings, or whatever name they think it degrading to go by." Attending to another person's personal comfort and convenience somehow offended Americans' complicated notions about equality. As Tocqueville expressed it, "In democracies servants are not only equal among themselves, but it may be said that they are, in some sort, the equals of their masters."[31] On the part of both black and white, distaste for deferential behavior and the dislike of household chores were widespread.

Race shaped the nature of domestic servitude in early Washington. The majority of the city's servants, whether free or enslaved, were African Americans. In Washington the servant problem had several related components—quality of performance, servant's attitudes, and different expectations of deference associated with race. Elite housewives criticized their servants for having too little skill, requiring too much close supervision, failing to stay on the job, displaying ill-temper, drinking, stealing, or behaving promiscuously. They sometimes complimented good work and often gave mixed reviews. Unlike European travelers who so frequently made sweeping statements about the "total want of good servants in America," they faced their servant problems individually and daily.[32]

Increasingly, probably in response to the servant shortage, poor children were apprenticed as household servants. Nancy Hopewell's indenture to Samuel Collingwood of Georgetown specified, for example, that the eleven-year-old would be "taught sewing, washing, cooking and other requisites common for persons in her situation to learn in order to become a useful Servant and be able thereby to Earn a livelyhood." Like Hopewell, most Washington domestic servants were free black, female, and young.[33]

While asylums were expressly founded, in both Boston and New York, to train female orphans as domestic servants, the purposes of the Washington City Female Orphan Asylum were less clear-cut. Founded after the War of 1812 by a group of "lady manageresses" (including Margaret Smith) for indigent white girls, the institution opened its doors in 1815. Following a program of "religious instruction [and] moral example," residents of all ages rose at first light, washed up, cleaned their rooms, performed chores around the house or outside in the garden, and offered a prayer together before breakfast. Following morning and afternoon instruction in reading, writing, sewing, and knitting, the older girls shared cooking, cleaning, and laundry duties. The manageresses designed the closely supervised daily routine to leave inmates with the "habits of industry inculcated on their minds."[34]

Early records suggest that discipline was sometimes a problem. Accounts of good and bad behavior were kept. Difficult girls apparently were "placed out" or "put out" at ages as young as five, as domestic servants. From the few households identifiable from orphanage records, the individuals who employed the eight young women placed out between 1818 and 1822 included several tradesmen, a teacher, and a boardinghouse keeper.

Ideally, at fourteen or fifteen years of age, when successful graduates of the asylum were "capable of earning their living they . . . [were] bound out to some reputable persons or families." Perhaps the "bound out" girls found steady work of the type the manageresses envisioned for them: employment in elite households as upper servants, such as housekeepers or governesses, with some financial security and stability.[35]

A life in household service, however, did not appeal to many native whites, even poor ones. When Mrs. Seymour, the heroine of Margaret Smith's *Winter in Washington*, suggested to an indigent woman that her hungry children be put "out to service," the woman replied angrily, "Put them out to service indeed! Do you suppose they are slaves?" The children were mulattos; their mother a white woman, their father a free black. During Richard Cobden's visit to the Buchanan White House in 1859, he noticed that all of the staff were foreigners. "Native American Citizens will not (at least the better part of them) undertake the duties of a menial servant even for their president. They will attend upon horses, or even pigs, but will not wait on the person of their fellow man." White servants who were difficult to obtain in Washington also proved expensive and unreliable. Other sources confirm David Warden's observation that "from interests, caprice, or the love of change, they seldom remain long with the same master."[36] In Washington, domestic service may have been downgraded because of the racial composition of the labor force. For whites, other occupations were preferable.

Nevertheless, many whites and blacks worked together in Washington households, although relationships were far from harmonious. One local newspaper advertisement in 1820 promised a position for a white servant that involved no contact with blacks. Warden reported that some white servants were "unwilling to associate with blacks."[37] African Americans probably resented whites who did similar jobs but received higher wages and, in most cases, had better living and working conditions.

The black servants of families like the Wirts, the Thorntons, the Adamses, and the Smiths may well have been among the crowds of African Americans who filled the visitors' galleries when Missouri statehood was debated in Congress in 1820. Troubled by the keen interest of enslaved Washingtonians in the question, newspaper editor William Seaton commented to his wife, "They know it to be a question of servitude or freedom, and imagine that the result will immediately affect their condition. . . ." As black Washingtonians explored notions of freedom, racial attitudes among whites were hardening. The growing numbers of free blacks in Washington caused some concern. A grand jury echoed popular sentiment in 1821 when it said, "We . . . present the rapid increase of Free People of Colour, within said country, as an evil." That year a new charter took effect that extended the city's earlier "black codes" to seriously restrict the lives of free African Americans, thereby endangering their status. The ten o'clock curfew imposed on city blacks must have hindered short-term evening employment and living out.[38]

Every suspicious fire, poisoning, and unsolved murder was attributed to a conniving slave or thought to have had the assistance of a free black. White women were particularly fearful. Forced to sit with her ill mother in 1830, Anna Maria Thornton, distrustful of her several black household servants, confided to her diary, "I have staid at home so much with her . . . [because I] have nobody to leave with her" — meaning no white person. Residents had only to look to neighboring Virginia, site of the rebellions of Gabriel in 1800 and Nat Turner in 1831. For white southerners, Turner's uprising, in which several dozen whites died, confirmed their worst fears about African Americans.[39]

Two revealing episodes illustrate how desires for freedom and equality — and the means to obtain them — were uppermost in the minds of some enslaved African Americans. Captured as a runaway in Baltimore, Frederick, who belonged to William Wirt, was unrepentant about his attempt at liberation. Elizabeth Wirt was affronted (and made uneasy) by "the freedom, boldness, and almost fierce defiance with which he spoke and defended himself—declaring that freedom was what he aimed at & that he had done no one harm in his attempt." Evidently a valuable servant, Frederick was not sold or severely punished for running away but absorbed back into the household. About a year later Frederick successfully "stole himself." Assisted by other Wirt slaves and armed with cash he obtained by selling off goods from the family's storeroom, Frederick was last seen "walking briskly up the road" some miles outside Washington. A furious Elizabeth Wirt admitted that "it was difficult to overtake him. . . . I shall be not a little vexed if he should get off clear, it will be so bad an example to those who now remain behind."[40]

A series of confrontations occurred between Anna Maria Thornton and a young slave, Arthur Bowen, the son of her long-time domestic servant, Maria. Left debt-ridden and widowed in 1828, Thornton hired out many of her slaves, including Bowen, for much-needed income. The young man engaged in classic tactics of slave resistance by refusing to work, pretending to be sick, and taking time off without permission. On August 5, 1835—"a dreadful night"—Thornton wrote in her diary that Arthur's rebellion took a nasty turn. As Thornton's elderly mother no longer could climb stairs, the women slept together with Arthur's mother in the downstairs parlor. "Arthur entered our room at 1/2 after one o'clock with an axe—with the intension we suppose to murder us." Fortunately, his mother "seized him and got him out." Although rattled by Arthur's enmity, Thornton interpreted his actions as drunken antics.[41]

Word of the incident apread quickly and inflamed antiblack sentiment then growing in Washington. When an angry mob of white "mechanics" appeared outside her house, Thornton had Arthur locked up for his own protection. Against her wishes, the authorities formally charged him with burglary and attempted murder. Spurred by the jailing—coupled with antiabolitionist sentiment rising among disaffected poor whites—the mob reassembled on the night of August 12, 1835, stormed Capitol Hill, and destroyed a black school, several houses, a brothel, and a popular black-owned restaurant named Snow's. The so-called Snow Riots, however, sparked Washington's enactment in 1836 of the most restrictive legislation yet imposed against free blacks in the pre–Civil War South. Eventually Thornton arranged for Arthur's sale and transport to Florida, far away from home and family.⁴²

A "WISE AND BENEVOLENT ARRANGEMENT OF SOCIETY"

The Declaration of Independence may have asserted that all men are created equal, but in the early nineteenth century, inequality was believed to be sanctioned by God and the Bible. It was deeply embedded in social practice. In 1827 a Washington newspaper article assured readers that "there is nothing mean or degrading in the fact, that Providence, in his wise and benevolent arrangement of society, has ordained that one portion of the community . . . should labor for the other."⁴³

This world view was challenged in an extraordinary conversation recorded by Margaret Smith. Accused by Smith of theft, Sukey, a hired slave, insisted on her innocence: "God who made you . . . made me likewise. . . . Here we are very different, you are a fine lady, that dress in silks & muslims & know how to read & write. [I am] a poor slave, covered with rags & know not one letter but when we die . . . the only difference will be that your coffin will be a little gayer than mine."⁴⁴

---

¹ Poor woman quoted in David Baille Warden, A *Chorographical and Statistical Description of the District of Columbia* (Paris: Smith, 1816), p. 164. On the "servant problem," see Jeanne Boydston, *Home and Work: Housework, Wages, and the Ideology of Labor in the Early Republic* (New York: Oxford University Press, 1990); Carol S. Lasser, "The Domestic Balance of Power: Relations between Mistress and Maid in Nineteenth-Century New England," *Labor History* 28 (Winter 1987): 5–22; Daniel E. Sutherland, *Americans and Their Servants* (Baton Rouge: Louisiana State University Press, 1981), pp. 1–22; David M. Katzman, *Seven Days a Week: Women and Domestic Service in Industrializing America* (New York: Oxford University Press, 1978).

² Anna Maria Thornton diaries, 1793–1863, Anna Maria Thornton Papers, Manuscript Division, Library of Congress, Washington, D.C. (hereafter MDLC); Elizabeth Wirt correspondence is in the William Wirt Papers, Maryland Historical Society, Baltimore; Margaret Bayard Smith Papers, MDLC, contain both correspondence and journals; excerpts from her papers are published in Gaillard Hunt, ed., *The First Forty Years of Washington Society* (New York: Charles Scribner's Sons, 1906); Louisa Catherine Adams's diaries, household accounts, and correspondence are part of the Adams Family Papers, Massachusetts Historical Society, Boston. Microfilm copies of the Wirt correspondence and the Adams Family Papers are at the Library of Congress.

³ Margaret Hall, *The Aristocratic Journey: Being the Outspoken Letters of Mrs. Basil Hall Written during a Fourteen-Months Sojourn in America, 1827–1828*, ed. Una Pope-Hennessey (New York: G. P. Putnam, 1931), December 29, 1827, entry.

[4] Jesse Torrey, *A Portraiture of Domestic Slavery* (Philadelphia, 1817), p. 41; Basil Hall, *Travels in North America in the Years 1827 and 1828*, 3 vols. (Philadelphia: Carey, Lea and Carey, 1829), 3:48.

[5] In 1820, Ward 1—Washington City's elite neighborhood, located between George-town and the President's House—included 337 white households, 59 free black house-holds, and 17 households headed by slaves; see 3d U.S. Census for the District of Colum-bia, National Archives, Washington, D.C. (microfilm).

[6] Washington's social scene is described in Barbara G. Carson, *Ambitious Appetites: Dining, Behavior, and Patterns of Consumption in Federal Washington* (Washington, D.C.: American Institute of Architects Press, 1990). The quote is in Margaret Bayard Smith's unpublished novel, "Lucy," fol. 3392, Smith papers, MDLC. We are grateful to Fredrika J. Teute for identifying "Lucy" and Smith's other unpublished novel, "Julia," in the William Thornton Papers, reel 5, MDLC.

[7] In 1820 just a little more than one third (35 percent) of the white households appear to be slaveholding; among those, some 37 percent owned or employed only 1 slave. Wealthy residents or business persons formed the 7 percent of the ward that owned 10 or more individuals.

[8] For a summary of "hiring out," see David Goldfield, "Black Life in Old South Cities," in Edward D. C. Campbell, Jr., and Kym S. Rice, eds., *Before Freedom Came: African-American Life in the Antebellum South* (Charlottesville: University Press of Vir-ginia, 1991), pp. 130-33. Thorton diary, August 18, 1829, entry, MDLC.

[9] Smith, "Lucy," fol. 3338, Smith papers, MDLC.

[10] Smith, "Lucy," fol. 3357, fol. verso 3357, Smith papers, MDLC.

[11] Louisa Catherine Adams, "Instructions for Servants," undated, Adams Family Pa-pers (microfilm, MDLC). The document probably was written when John Quincy Adams was either secretary of state (1817–25) or president (1825–29). Presumably, because the coachman and the ostler lay outside the domestic realm, the former took his orders di-rectly from John Quincy Adams and in turn directed the latter.

[12] Adams, "Instructions for Servants."

[13] Adams, "Instructions for Servants."

[14] *Mrs. Colvin's Weekly Messenger, Containing a Variety of Original and Selected Articles on Subjects Interesting to Society from 22d July, 1826 to 18th August 1827*, 2d ser., vol. 1 (Washington, D.C.: Mrs. A. S. Colvin, 1827), p. 85.

[15] Smith papers, journal, September 17, 1806, MDLC.

[16] Smith to her sister, November 15, 1801, MDLC.

[17] See, for example, wages paid to "extra waiters at table and cook," February 23, 1819, household account book 1799–1822, Adams Family Papers (microfilm, MDLC). Adams diary, January 17, January 18, 1820, Adams Family Papers (microfilm, MDLC).

[18] Thorton diary, October 3, 1828, MDLC.

[19] Smith diary, April 7, 1807, MDLC.

[20] Smith diary, November 15, 1801, MDLC.

[21] Mrs. [Frances] Trollope, *Domestic Manners of the Americans* (1832; reprint, Barre, Mass.: Imprint Society, 1969), p. 192; January 24, 1812, Harriet Otis diary, Harrison Gray Otis Papers, Massachusetts Historical Society (microfilm, MDLC); Warden, *Description of District of Columbia*, p. 47; Charles Lyell, *A Second Visit to the United States of North America, Volume I* (New York, 1849).

[22] Mutual Assurance records survive for Alexandria, Va., for 1796, 1805, 1815, and 1823. One policy of 1796 labeled a "servants' hall," which was 15 by 20 feet and shared a party wall with the kitchen, which in turn was connected to the main house. An 1805 policy insured 3 connected brick structures. Two were dwellings and the third at the rear "a brick Kitchen & servants hall 1-1/2 stories high 24 x 24 feet. . . ." By 1815 this structure

had been altered and was now described as "a Dwelling & Kitchen." This combination appears in about one-fifth of surviving policies for 1815 and 1823. Only one "servants' room" is specified, which is on the second story of a wooden stable, which measured 12 by 21 feet (Mutual Assurance policies, Library of Virginia, Richmond [microfilm, Lloyd House, Alexandria, Va.]).

[23] Elizabeth Wirt to William Wirt, Richmond, January [?], 1816, and January 13, 1816, both William Wirt Papers, Maryland Historical Society (microfilm, MDLC).

[24] William Wirt to Harriet Lane, May 29, 1818; Elizabeth Wirt, Washington, to William Wirt, November 29, 1818; Elizabeth Wirt to William Wirt, September 22, 1818, all in Wirt Papers (microfilm, MDLC).

[25] Uniforms were imposed on housemaids only in the middle of the nineteenth century.

[26] On fashionable dress of urban English servants, see Neil McKendrick, John Brewer, and J. H. Plumb, *The Birth of a Consumer Society* (Bloomington: Indiana University Press, 1982). Eliza Dodd account book, 1821–33, Historical Society of Washington, D.C.

[27] Smith,"Lucy," fol. verso 3391, Smith papers, MDLC; Margaret Bayard Smith, *What Is Gentility?* (Washington, 1828), p. 124; Harrison Gray Otis to Sally Foster Otis, February 21, 1819, Otis Papers, Massachusetts Historical Society (microfilm, MDLC).

[28] Robert Roberts, for example, does not mentioned livery in his "Hints to House Servants on Their Dress," in *The House Servant's Directory* (Boston, 1827), pp. 76–78. Hall, *Aristocratic Journey*, pp. 158, 217–18. When the Halls returned to England, Margaret took special pleasure in the sight of liveried footman (Hall, *Aristocratic Journey*, p. 302).

[29] [Josphine Seaton], *William Winston Seaton of the "National Intelligencer"* (Boston: James R. Osgood, 1871), pp. 113–14; John Davis to Eliza Davis, January 13, 1826, Davis Papers, American Antiquarian Society; British Minister Francis James Jackson, October 7, 1809, quoted in Beckles Wilson, *Friendly Relations: A Narrative of Britain's Ministers and Ambassadors to America, 1791–1930* (1939; reprint, Freeport, N.Y.: Books for Libraries Press, 1969), p. 67.

[30] Carson, *Ambitious Appetites*, pp. 94–95. Harry Nimrod, *The Fudge Family in Washington* (Baltimore: Joseph Robinson, 1820), p. 39. Smith, "Lucy," fol. 3394, Smith papers, MDLC.

[31] Christine Stansell suggests that having a servant problem was part of the way elite people defined themselves; see Christine Stansell, *City of Women: Sex and Class in New York, 1789–1860* (Urbana: University of Illinois Press, 1982), p. 161. Alexis de Tocqueville, *Democracy in America*, trans., George Lawrence (New York: Anchor Books, 1964), p. 576. Some years later, Caroline Kirkland expressed insight into the matter: "This state of things [servants who refused to acknowledge their so-called inferiority with deferential behavior] appalled me at first; but I have learned a better philosophy since. I find no difficulty now in getting such aid as I require, and little in retaining it as long as I wish, though there is always a desire of making an occasional display of independence. Since living with one for wage is considered by common consent a favor, I take it as a favor; and,this point once conceded, all goes well" (Mary Clavers [pseud. for Caroline Mathilda Kirkland], *A New Home—Who'll Follow? or, Glimpses of Western Life* [1839: reprint, 1965], p. 63).

[32] For the life of a twentieth-century Washington domestic, see Elizabeth Clark-Lewis, " 'Duty and Fast Living': The Diary of Mary Johnson Spow, Domestic Worker," *Washington History* 5, no. 1 (Spring–Summer 1993): 46–65. Hall, *Travels in North America*, 2:156.

[33] Indenture dated August, 8, 1811, Record of Apprentices' Indentures Commencing the 21st of May 1801 and ending 17 December 1811, entry 127, J. H.1, Record Group 21, National Archives, Washington, D.C. See also Stephanie Coles, "Servants and Slaves:

Domestic Service in the Border Cities, 1800–1850" (Ph.D. diss., University of Florida, 1994). Coles argues that in southern border cities like Washington, the legal apprenticeship of young children increasingly became a source for servants in the antebellum period.

[34] Constitution, Washington City Female Orphan's Asylum Society, 1815–51, vol. 1, box 34, Hillcrest Children's Center Records, MDLC.

[35] Proceedings, Washington City Female Orphan's Asylum Society, 1815–51, vol. 1, box 34, Hillcrest Children's Center Records, MDLC.

[36] Margaret Bayard Smith, *A Winter in Washington*, 2 vols. (Washington, D.C.: Pishey Thompson, 1824), p. 134; *The American Diaries of Richard Cobden*, ed. with and intro. and notes, Elizabeth Hoon Cawley (New York: Greenwood Press, 1969), p. 180; Warden, *Description of the District of Columbia*, p. 45.

[37] *Daily National Intelligencer*, December 5, 1820, p. 3, col. 5; Warden, *Description of the District of Columbia*, p. 45.

[38] [Seaton], *William Winston Seaton*, p. 132; the grand jury citation is quoted in Leonard P. Curry, *The Free Black in Urban America, 1800–1850* (Chicago: University of Chicago Press, 1981), p. 82. For more information, see Mary Beth Corrigan, "The Ties That Bind: The Pursuit of Community and Freedom among Slaves and Free Blacks in the District of Columbia, 1800–1850," in Howard Gillete, Jr., ed., *Southern City, National Ambition* (Washington, D.C.: Octagon Museum and the Center for Washington Area Studies, 1995), pp. 69–90.

[39] Thorton diary, May 28, 1830, MDLC.

[40] Elizabeth Wirt to William Wirt, November 4, 1819; Elizabeth Wirt to Laura Wirt, October 5, 1820, both, Wirt Papers (microfilm, MDLC).

[41] See, for example, Thorton diary, May 28, 1830, MDLC.

[42] Actual incidents of large-scale racial unrest were relatively rare in Washington, D.C., although white citizens apparently worried about attacks by blacks. In 1814, when the city was burned by the British during the War of 1812, whites formed patrols with the intent of putting down an anticipated black revolt; see *The Diary of Elbridge Gerry, Jr.*, preface and footnotes by Claude G. Bowers, foreword by Annette Townsend (New York: Brentano's, 1927), pp. 198–99. Arthur's story unfolds in Thornton's diary, beginning on August 5, 1835, and continues until his sale in July 1836. The characterization of the new legislation appears in Curry, *Free Black in Urban America*, p. 99.

[43] *Mrs. Colvin's Weekly Messenger*, p. 85.

[44] Smith diary, undated after entry for July 4, 1806, MDLC.

Everyday Life on a Berkshire County Hill Farm

Documentation from the 1794–1835 Diary of Sarah Snell Bryant of Cummington, Massachusetts

Jane C. Nylander

Almost every day of her adult life, Sarah Snell Bryant (1768–1847) uncorked her ink bottle, picked up her pen, and made an entry in her diary (fig. 1).[1] After noting the state of the weather, she wrote about her daily work, the progress of the agricultural season, the health and activities of other members of the household, people who came to call or to whom she paid visits, and other details of her life as a doctor's wife in Cummington, Massachusetts. The diary reveals the influence of changing circumstance—the arrival of children, the supervision of hired help and restless adolescents, and the emotional pain and diminished circumstances of widowhood. Above all, it defines the never-ending nature of the daily round of housework, food preparation and preservation, dairying, textile production, sewing, and laundry. While most women's diaries of this era are more introspective and/or spiritual in nature, Sarah Bryant's diary is unusual for its length and level of detail.

During the first years after Sarah Snell married Dr. Peter Bryant in 1792, the couple rented rooms or small houses either in Cummington or nearby Plainfield. In 1799 they moved in with Sarah's parents,

Fig. 1. ["Mr. Clark"], *Sarah Snell Bryant* (1768–1847). Oil on canvas; H. 29½″, W. 24½″. (Trustees of Reservations, Bryant Homestead, Cummington, Mass.) On October 29, 1829, Sarah's diary entry states, "Mr. Clark from New York came to take my portrait."

Ebenezer and Sarah Snell. In 1801 Peter built a four-room addition to his father-in-law's seven-year-old gambrel-roofed farmhouse, thereby providing both a medical office for himself and some privacy for his growing family (fig. 2). The furnishings and living spaces of the two families were co-mingled from this time. Upon her father's death in 1813, Sarah and her eldest son, Austin, each inherited half of his portion

Fig. 2. Peter Bryant's "new house" and office, 1801. (Society for the Preservation of New England Antiquities, Boston.) Bryant built a perpendicular addition onto the facade of the house of Sarah's parents, Ebenezer and Sarah Snell. In 1842 this portion of the building was moved to a new location and used thereafter as an independent house.

of the house along with the sixty-seven acre farm.[2] Already established on a nearby farm, Sarah's brother, Ebenezer Snell, Jr., inherited his father's desk-and-bookcase, a "great Bible," and half of his father's library of books. Sarah inherited a tall-case clock and divided the remaining household furniture with her sister, Abigail Fish.

By the time of Peter's death in 1820, one room of the home was embellished with a carpet, and the furniture included a sideboard and a sofa in addition to nine beds with seven bedsteads, bedding, a dozen dining chairs, and the tall-case clock, as well as the usual assortment of tables and chairs, chests of drawers, wash- and candlestands, looking glasses, and another desk-and-bookcase. There was a small amount of silver and an unspecified assortment of pewter, glass, crockery, and other tableware along with cooking, dairying, and weaving equipment, candlesticks, and a stove.[3]

Because the appraisers of Peter's estate did not list the contents of the household in a room-by-room format, it is difficult to know how the furnishings were arranged and what functions took place in specific rooms. Sarah's diary gives few clues. When she mentioned a room other than a kitchen, it was usually identified by the occupant ("mam's room," "boys' room") or its compass point ("northwest room," "southwest room"). The center of Sarah's workday world was undoubtedly the kitchen, and she referred to her work spaces variously as "middle kitchen," "long kitchen," "back kitchen," and "new kitchen," in addition to a buttery. The middle kitchen and long kitchen may have been the same, using the center chimney of the older house.

Like many married women of her time, Sarah was either pregnant or nursing a baby almost continuously for fourteen years, for she had seven children, five boys and two girls, born at roughly two-year intervals between 1793 and 1807.[4] None of the children died in infancy. She maintained a regular schedule of work right up until the very last days before each child was born, sometimes cutting down on strenuous physical labor such as weaving and increasing the amount of time spent cutting out clothing or working on other projects that were less taxing.

Diary entries were usually suspended for a few days when a child was born, but the record was soon filled in. The entry "Unwell. Seven at night a son born. Mamma and Mrs. Shaw were here" indicated William Cullen's birth on November 3, 1794; the following July "unwell at night . . . a son born a little before sunset" announced the arrival of Cyrus. Two women had come to assist during Cyrus Bryant's birth, but his mother did not linger long in bed. Two days after delivery she "got up" and soon resumed care of her family. When her first daughter, Sarah, was born on July 24, 1802, the new mother "sat up" the next day, "walked in the kitchen" on the twenty-sixth, "went outdoors" on the twenty-seventh, and soon resumed her sewing. Often her first task after childbirth was sewing infant's clouts [diapers]. In a busy farm household there was no time for a long confinement or the urban ritual of a "sitting up week."

Sarah's responsibility extended beyond the care of her husband, parents, and children. Most of the time the family also included at least

Fig. 3. Bryant Homestead, 1865. (Society for the Preservation of New England Antiquities, Boston.)

one hired man and one hired girl. At the height of his career, Dr. Peter Bryant gave medical instruction to as many as ten young men at once; many of them boarded with the Bryant family. Despite the complications of shared dwelling spaces, authority and responsibility were centered in the head of household and his wife. After Peter died, authority shifted to his son Austin, even though the widowed Sarah continued to live and work in the same house where she had been first daughter and then mistress for decades (fig. 3); in fact Sarah lived with at least some of her children for twenty-nine years. Throughout her life, the coming and going of friends, family, help, travelers, young people, daytime workers, and some seasonal laborers made change a household constant. Complex personalities and people with diverse political and religious opinions gathered around the family table, brought news, and sparked the conversation. Members of the nuclear family came and went to watch with the sick and the dead, to assist births, to help with seasonal work, to visit relatives, to secure education, to embark on business ventures, or to seek information and advice.

Sarah expressed considerable satisfaction when she was able to employ steady and reliable household help, for there was a tremendous amount of work to be done. Difficult personal circumstances, such as childbirth or illness, sometimes put her in the position of keeping a lazy or unreliable servant. The winter of 1806–7 was a particularly bad time for her. Nancy Thayer had lived with the family only since July 17 and had gone home for six weeks between August 1 and September 17 when suddenly on September 24 she "went home bag and baggage." Left with her own six young children to care for in addition to her husband, her parents, and a number of boarding students, Sarah was without settled help throughout the difficult harvest season, cold winter, and busy spring. During this time she employed five different women, including the temperamental Nancy Thayer, on a sporadic basis, for weaving, candle dipping, spinning, and general housework until Nancy's sister Sukey came to live for six weeks on May 29, 1807. Sukey's employment may well have been related to Sarah's impending delivery of John Bryant, who was born on July 22. Sukey Thayer went home on August 3, and thereafter Temperance Barber came weekly to do the washing until Polly Hamilton came to live in on September 7. Although Polly remained with the Bryant family for a year, it was not until John, the youngest child, was seven years old and a hired girl named Martha arrived in 1814 that the situation stabilized. Martha remained in the Bryant household for nearly five years—perhaps her situation was more interesting because of the companionship of the Bryants' daughter Sally, who was twelve years old when Martha arrived. Sally and Martha often did chores together, visited mutual friends, and attended apple paring bees and other work parties during the time Martha was part of the household. As the Bryant daughters grew older and were able to share more of the burden of household work, especially spinning, Sarah employed day laborers for laundry, seasonal cleaning, and other particularly burdensome tasks.

Sarah Bryant was a hands-on manager. Even though she enjoyed an elevated social status and some economic advantages, she organized the complicated work of her household and actively participated in most of it. Routine chores assigned to hired girls included most of the heavy indoor work, such as washing, ironing, dishwashing, cleaning; scouring pots, kettles, floors, and pewter; spinning wicking and making candles; picking geese; making starch; and hatcheling, spinning, and bleaching linen. She usually warped and set the looms herself, but the hired girls did all the spinning and much of the routine weaving while the children were young. Apparently Sarah, and her mother while she was alive, did much of the cooking, leaving more onerous tasks of food preparation to the hired girls. After butchering was done on December 6, 1800, for example, Chloe "cleaned the creature's feet."

In her diary Sarah never mentioned dusting furniture, making beds, setting tables, sweeping or mopping floors, yet these tasks were certainly performed on a routine basis. With doors opening directly from the unpaved dooryard and with windows wide open in the summertime, dust swirled into the house on every current of air, and mud was tracked in whenever it was wet outside. Downdrafts blew clouds of ashes out of the fireplaces, and all sorts of chaff fell out of the firewood as it was carried into the house. Stray fibers and bits of dirt flew from the spinning wheel and the loom. Of course the floors and rooms needed to be swept and dusted regularly. These tasks were a regular part of everyday life, unworthy of documentation.

Perhaps routine tasks were only recorded in the diary when part of a reciprocal work arrangement for which there was some value, when done by an employee, or when particularly difficult. For example, Sarah "scoured the floor" on September 15, 1796, "washed the buttery" on September 29, and then, within the next week, whitewashed the bedrooms, kitchen, and west room. This was hard work and had to be done promptly, for once temperatures dipped below freezing inside the house, these chores would have been impossible. The next entry that recorded that she had "washed the floor" was on June 11, 1798; at that time she was eight months pregnant, and it could not have been an easy thing to do. The task is not mentioned again until June 13, 1799, and it seems unlikely that the floor had not been washed for a whole year.

In addition to writing about tasks that were accomplished under difficult circumstances, Sarah also recorded massive tasks that were done only once or twice a year: scouring pewter, "cleaning up" or "cleaning out" rooms, picking geese, scouring the buttery, whitewashing, making soap and candles, and the tasks associated with butchering. Still, from the patterns of her diary entries, much can be learned about weekly and seasonal routines, particularly food production and preservation, clothing production and care, and textile production.

The Bryant family relied on their own farm produce for their primary food supply. They purchased tea, coffee, sugar, molasses, salt, spices, and an occasional barrel of flour from local storekeepers, using butter and cheese for the majority of their store credits.

Sarah kept a kitchen garden and expected her sons to help with soil preparation, sowing, and weeding when they were young boys. At various times, the diary mentions harvesting or cooking green peas, corn, string beans, onions, green squash, cabbages, and potatoes. Most of these were grown in quantities large enough for winter storage as well as summer consumption. During the unusually cold year of 1816, which is still referred to in New England as the year without a summer, the cucumbers were very late. On Wednesday, August 21, the Bryants "had a mess of cucumbers last Monday the first we have had this summer" and the same day suffered from "frost at night which killed vines in low lands and some corn."

Reflecting the tremendous importance farm families placed on the production and preservation of an adequate supply of food, Sarah's diary gives far more attention to food processing and preservation than to the daily work of cooking or the details of menu composition. Clearly her long-term concern was to ensure her family an adequate supply and to avoid wasting anything. At the end of each December she often commented on the successes and failures of the agricultural season and the health of the community in general. The entry for December 31, 1808, is typical: "The season has been fruitful very good for Dairy hay quite plenty, fruit aplenty as common in these parts but scarce in the lower towns."

Sarah often combined her weekly baking with either washing or ironing, all of which required keeping a fire and remaining in or near the kitchen. Her timesaving practice was exactly the opposite of that suggested a decade or two later by the authors of household advice books, who urged women to separate these arduous jobs. Baking was most often done on Saturday, and it could extend early or late in the day; on January 7, 1808, she "baked before sunrise," while on October 17, 1814, she "baked pies in the evening."

Usually, Sarah's diary entry was simply the word "baked"; many more specific entries indicated that the bulk of the baking was composed of bread and pies, the latter sometimes further described as egg, minced, chicken, apple, pumpkin, or squash. It is unclear whether the "grate apple pie" baked on December 11, 1817, was made of grated apples or was unusually large. Gingerbread, sweet cake, pound cake, "bisquit," plain and apple custard, and squash pudding were also baked from time to time. As early as 1808, there is an occasional reference to "white bread," indicating that at least some of the wheat grown on the Bryant farm was ground into flour for the family's own use. Usually meats were roasted in front of an open flame, but on August 20, 1808, the same day that white bread was mentioned for the first time in the diary, the meat was "baked."

Although any of these goods could be baked on the hearth in a Dutch oven, at least one kitchen of the Bryant house had a large oven constructed as an integral part of the fireplace. Normally Sarah only heated the oven once for each baking day, but as the family expanded in the 1820s, this routine changed. On October 30, 1826, she had to "heat the oven twice" in order to bake a sufficient quantity of "bread and pies," and during the winter of 1827–28, she often had to "heat the oven three times."[5] Her usual diary entries on the day or two before Thanksgiving simply indicate that she "baked pies"; the diary gives no indication of baking unusual kinds or large quantities in conjunction with the holiday.

Butter- and cheesemaking in the Bryant family were both for family use and for store credit. Before he died in 1820, Peter Bryant had such confidence in his wife's skill at handling this particular aspect of the household economy that he bequeathed the dairy operation solely "to the discretion and good management of my beloved wife, Sarah." The diary contains little documentation of the work involved in managing dairy—weaning calves, selling veal, hiring girls to do the milking, supervising their work to be sure the cows were well stripped of milk, straining milk, scrubbing and scalding milk pails, washing the milk pans and straining cloths, setting milk for butter or cheese, skimming cream, churning, working butter, exchanging milk, making cheese, and cleaning out the buttery at the beginning and end of each season—yet all these tasks were essential.

Sarah seldom noted the quantities of butter that she churned; when she did they were relatively small, such as the two pounds she made on April 10, 1817. During hot weather, when milk production was at its greatest and butter could not be made and preserved safely, the excess milk was turned into cheeses of various sorts. This profitable work was clearly of much greater interest to Sarah.

Cheesemaking usually began in a small way in June, when "new milk cheese" was made in addition to butter. Sometime during the latter part of June, Sarah began to "exchange" milk with her neighbor,

Mrs. Briggs, a process that continued until near the end of September, when the weather was again cool enough for buttermaking. A common practice, the exchange of milk meant that families with only a small number of cows pooled their resources to ensure that each would have enough milk to make good-size cheeses on certain prearranged days of the week.[6]

Sarah sometimes used sage to flavor a new milk cheese. She frequently made "four meal" cheese of 75 percent skimmed milk; such a cheese was half the richness of a "two meal cheese" made with "one milking of new milk and one of skimmed to the cheese," while the cream of the second milking was set aside for butter.[7]

Since butter- and cheesemaking had to be done in a cool room, the buttery was located on the north side of the house, convenient to an ample supply of running water and not too far from the cow barn. The buttery was equipped with plenty of shelves for the shallow milk pans in which the cream rose after the morning and evening milking. More shallow shelves were used for the growing supply of cheeses, which had to be wiped and turned each day during the cheesemaking season. Sarah Bryant carefully scrubbed her buttery each autumn, after the weather turned cold, milk began to freeze on the open shelves, and the family supply of cheeses had to be carried to the cellar for winter storage.

During the early years of her widowhood, Sarah produced large quantities of cheese for sale. On October 1, 1822, she "sold 302 lbs. of cheese to a Mr. Loud of Abington." Three years later on September 29, "Mr. Globe carried away six hundred pounds of cheese at six cents per lb." Having been paid only thirty-six dollars for making 602 pounds of cheese, Sarah's only comment in her diary was "washed out the buttery."[8]

The Bryants, like many other families, usually did their butchering in late November or early December, after Thanksgiving and when cold weather could be relied on to help preserve the meat. The women's work included cleaning tripe; trying out tallow, or hog's lard; using the animal's head and feet for making head cheese or baking foot pies; and cleaning "the guts."[9]

In late winter, Sarah described the tapping of maple trees, making sugar troughs, cutting firewood, sledding kettles and other equipment to the woods; and she noted the extent of the sap run and the quantities of sugar produced. When Austin Bryant began his efforts to improve profitability of the family farm in the late 1820s, he made additional sap troughs, borrowed extra kettles, boiled large quantities of sap, and set out new maple trees. Most of the work was done in the woods, although occasionally they "sugared off in the house." After all the hard work was done, sharing the fresh sweet sugar was a welcome treat; sometimes neighbors joined the family for a sugaring party in the woods.

As each season advanced, Sarah's diary records the fruitfulness of animals as well as changes in the growth of plants. On February 21, 1833, she noted, "hens begin to lay," and in late May or June of many years she observed the swarming of bees. She often noted the date of the first blooming of plums, apples, peaches, and cherries in the orchard, and she worried over the threat of late frost during the blooming season. Her diary records the first sowing of grains and garden vegetables, and she took satisfaction in recording the date when the first peas and cucumbers were gathered in the garden. Spring 1805 must have been exceptionally cold, for on June 11 they experienced "frost at night which killed the cucumber vines." Even so, nothing could compare with 1816.

Sarah describes in her diary eating or picking strawberries, raspberries, blackberries, and thimbleberries, none of which appears to have been cultivated on the Bryant farm. The family did grow currants, which were used in 1818 for currant wine, and they obtained quinces from an unidentified source for quince sauce. The ripening of peaches and watermelons provided an excuse for hospitality or visiting.

Apples were stored whole and used for cider, applesauce, and pies. Anticipating good crops of apples, the Bryants often hired a cooper to repair and hoop barrels sometime in September or early October. On the Bryant farm, apple picking usually occupied the men for a week in mid October, after which some barrels of whole apples were stored in the cellar, and others were carried to the cider mill. Making barrels of applesauce for winter storage was a time-consuming kitchen project in November, beginning with several days and evenings devoted to paring and cutting apples and boiling cider for "cider molasses," the sticky sweet syrup that was the basis for applesauce. After boiling both the cider and the sauce, securing a good quantity and restoring order in the kitchen, Sarah often recorded her satisfaction: "Finished making the sauce—washed up the kitchen," she wrote on October 29, 1814, and she "made three kettles of applesauce & *finished*" on November 16, 1820.

Sarah did her laundry on an irregular schedule in the early years of her marriage, but as soon as she had a settled dwelling place, she "washed" almost every Monday or Tuesday and did some ironing almost every Saturday for the rest of her years in Massachusetts. Her brief diary entries about laundry chores underscore the ordinary quality of the work routine.

In the best of weather, doing laundry meant a day outdoors carrying large quantities of water in heavy and awkward wooden containers, maintaining fires, and tiresome lifting, rubbing, and scrubbing. The Bryants had a piped water system that conveyed water from a spring to the house and barn, but it sometimes froze solid in very cold weather. In wintertime, when laundry was done inside, warm steam from the boiling water filled the room, but spilled water might still freeze on the floor, and drying was never accomplished easily. In the coldest weather, clothes put outdoors to dry would freeze stiff, but a brisk wind caused most of the water to evaporate before they were brought in. On stormy days in the winter, the Bryant kitchen must have featured a clothesline stretched in front of the fireplace and hung with garlands of drying diapers and wet stockings, a pile of stiffly frozen shirts and bedsheets, and the smell of wet warm wool. The picture did not always change in summer; Sarah's laundry took an entire week to dry during the rainy weeks of June 17 and August 27, 1831. Still, laundry was done on rainy days and in glorious spring sunshine, in hot weather and cold. When it was all over, her most frequent diary entry was simply "washing done."

Laundry was the task most frequently delegated to hired help or to daughters, and some women performed this task as day laborers. After twenty years of finishing her entire washing in a single day, Sarah seems to have adopted an even more time-consuming procedure. Beginning on June 7, 1819, during the summer months, the clothes were "steamed" on Monday and the washing "finished" on Tuesday. Although the diary carefully records these weekly activities for another sixteen years, there is never a clue as to how the process had changed. Most likely Sarah adopted the habit of bringing the most soiled clothes to a boil and soaking them overnight in soapsuds before boiling them again and rinsing. This step may have avoided the process of beating heavily soiled clothes with a stick to loosen the dirt before boiling them.

Although Sarah's diary indicates faithful weekly washing throughout the year, ironing was not done every single week. Ironing was done less frequently in winter than in summertime, probably because the woolen clothing worn in winter was less frequently laundered than the linen and cotton worn during the summer. This task was often postponed until Saturday when other kitchen chores requiring steady fires, especially baking, were undertaken. Sometimes, as on March 10, 1798, candle dipping also was done on ironing day. Sarah dipped candles once a year, making between twenty-two and thirty pounds at a time, depending on the available supply of tallow.

Diary entries for Saturdays almost always indicate that Sarah mended as well as ironed on that day. After the hard work of ironing, which she usually combined with baking, it must have been a satisfying pleasure to sit comfortably in a chair and work through a basket of mending, having all in order at the close of the week.

The individual pieces of clothing and bed and table linen that passed through the laundry tubs and under the flatirons were no strangers, of course. Documented in the diary are the variety and quantity of the work involved in preparation and production of a family wardrobe and also how this work fit within the rhythm of her daily life. Six days a week, almost without fail, Sarah sat down and picked up her needle to work on a garment for someone in the family—husband, parent, child, hired girl, farmworker, daughter-in-law, or grandchild. As part of her instruction in domestic economy, she cut out gloves and gowns for her hired girls, but she also expected them to sew themselves.[10] Sarah herself mended and sewed for her help, making shirts, frocks, gowns, caps, pelisses, tuckers, and bonnets for the girls and leather mittens, waistcoats, vests, spencers, coats, pantaloons, and trousers for the hired men.

Once in a great while, Sarah sewed for someone outside the family, usually as part of a reciprocal work arrangement or for someone in special need. Over the course of a lifetime, she made literally hundreds of garments. Some of these were projects small enough to be carried along when going visiting in the afternoon. Sewing offered an opportunity to sit down while continuing to be productive, but it required good light as well as close attention; knitting was a better job for the evening hours. On September 10, 1801, Sarah made two handkerchiefs while visiting her neighbor Mrs. Austin. She could just as easily have carried sleeves for a gown, breadths of a skirt to be assembled, or a partially completed stocking. Sometimes, the visit itself was focused on critiquing a new style, cutting and fitting a particularly difficult pattern, or sharing a clever technique of turning a heel. On June 15, 1810, she "made bonnets with Mrs. Snell & Briggs"; the following day she went to Mrs. Snell's "to finish" her bonnet.[11]

Sarah's diary contains a remarkably detailed list of her sewing projects, but it is not possible to develop an accurate inventory of the number of garments owned by each adult or child in the family. Additional sewing was done by Sarah's mother, the hired girls, daughters, and daughters-in-law. Without question Sarah Bryant coordinated the fabric selection, pattern making, and sewing efforts of all these people; she also did much of the cutting out of clothing as well as a great deal of the actual sewing. Still, this diary record of her own work gives us an unusually detailed picture of wardrobe composition for each member of the family.

Perhaps most interesting to the modern reader is the relatively small number of garments made in each year for each individual. Clothing was clearly intended to be kept in good repair and worn for a long time. Even during pregnancy or lactation, no special garments were needed. Sarah could adjust the waistline of her gown, let out the drawstrings of her petticoats, drape a handkerchief over her bosom, and pin it all together with long, strong common pins. Most of the children's garments were worn for several years; they were made with broad bodies gathered on drawstrings and generous tucks and hems that could be let down and out as they grew. As babies, the Bryant children were dressed alike in shirts, slips, coolers, covers, frocks, gowns, and petticoats.[12] Austin had his first coat and trousers at twenty-eight months of age, Cullen at thirty-one months of age, and Cyrus at twenty-nine months—presumably at the conclusion of successful toilet training. Throughout their childhood, their mother made most of their clothing, including stockings, mittens, and some shoes. She usually made one or two shirts and pairs of trousers for each boy and two or three gowns, petticoats, and tyers (long bibbed aprons), and one bonnet for each of the girls. With a family of seven growing children, clothing was passed along, mended, and altered to fit whoever needed it.

Even in years of relative prosperity, Sarah's own wardrobe was small by modern standards. In 1801 the young mother of three children acquired three new shirts, one half robe, two silk gowns (one of them made of Italian striped silk), two short gowns (one of them calico), and one worsted skirt, or petticoat, to wear with the short gowns. She also acquired a satin cloak, a muslin shawl, a spencer, and a tippet as well as a sable muff, a black silk handkerchief, a pair of gloves, a fur cap, another cap, and a white bonnet, two pairs of shoes, and four pairs of stockings, one of them cotton. This lavishness can be compared to 1820, the year her husband died, when her total clothing acquisitions were confined to a homespun plaid wool gown, a calico gown, a pelisse, a mourning bonnet, one pair of stockings, and the repair of her shoes.

Sarah was careful to maximize the investment in time and materials that her family's clothing represented. Her own scarlet cloak or riding hood, which she first cut out in 1797, is a good example of her prudence and thriftiness. Although she added a satin cloak to her wardrobe the next year and acquired great coats in both 1799 and 1808 and a woolen habit in the cold year of 1816, she made alterations to her old scarlet cloak in 1819 and repairs to it the following year. Apparently she gave up trying to make it presentable in 1825, for in that year she noted that she had made a gown out of her red riding hood, and she had no other since the first one she had made nearly thirty years before.

When Peter Bryant died in 1820, his will directed that his new "Drab Great Coat" be given to his eldest son, Austin, his blue cloak to his second son, William Cullen, his best hat to Peter Rush, and his second best hat to Cyrus. The appraisers of his estate listed the value of his clothing, singling out a cloak valued at $18, a coat valued at $12, a great coat valued at $14, and a watch valued at $18; the remainder, including the two hats, was simply listed as "sundry other articles of clothing" worth $75.[13] According to his wife's diary, his new coat had been made in 1816. Prior to that, he had not had a new great coat since 1799, although it had been altered in 1804, and it is hard to believe that it could still be worth $14 in 1820. Still, this example of "one handsome coat" being handed down from father to son is testimony to the durability of the fabric and the timelessness of the design.

Sarah Bryant's diary gives much more information about the composition of Peter's wardrobe than does his probate file. Sarah made him an average of five new shirts each year along with two to four pairs of trousers or pantaloons, a coat, and a jacket or two. She also made him a pair of mittens and one or two pairs of new stockings annually. Although he wore small clothes, or knee breeches, until at least 1806, he never had a new pair after that time. The diary reveals that Peter wore both drawers and under waistcoats, the latter made of flannel, especially as his consumption worsened in 1818 and 1819. Five years after Peter's death in 1820, his widow made over his blue wool coat for their eighteen-year-old son, John. This may have been anticipated, for Peter's will specified that all the residue of his wearing apparel be given to Sarah "to be distributed among his 3 youngest sons."[14]

In her diary Sarah usually specified the name of the person for whom each garment was made. Some fabrics were purchased from local storekeepers, and cloth for coats, pantaloons, shirts, aprons, tyers, and winter gowns was woven within the family. Whenever Sarah traveled outside Cummington, especially when she went to Northampton or Boston, she brought back fabrics, trimmings, or small articles of clothing. Peter sometimes brought fabrics when he returned from an urban area, and William Cullen sometimes sent his mother gifts of fabric from New York after he moved there in 1825. When Sarah traveled to visit her brother, the Reverend Ebenezer Snell, and his family in Brookfield, Massachusetts, she usually "went a shopping," taking advantage of the momentary lull in her household work to select fabrics and sewing supplies at the local Brookfield store or at the larger number of shops in Northampton.

Sarah's first extant diary [1794] is written in *The New Ladies Memorandum Book, for the Year 1796,* a London publication containing space for diary writing as well as a variety of useful information and illustrations of "The Most Fashionable Dresses of the Year 1793." No other ladies magazines or fashion prints known to have been owned by Sarah Bryant have been identified. Still, she must have been interested in fashion. Whenever she traveled, she had opportunities to observe new styles and to confer with female friends and relatives about patterns and methods of clothing construction. When Peter's sister Charity visited Cummington, she often brought a new style of gown or bonnet trimming, which Sarah was quick to copy. While visiting in Cummington in September 1808, Charity cut out "a gown and spencer of black lutestring" for her sister-in-law. Charity may have had particular skill in designing and fitting gowns or she may have had knowledge of a new style or pattern that she could best convey with her scissors. In Sarah's busy world, the help itself was welcome, but the opportunity for innovation was not to be missed. Similar information could have been purchased from dressmakers or tailors, but she seldom patronized these professionals.

As her children grew, so did their interest in taste and fashion.

William Cullen Bryant wrote to his father in 1815, "It would be convenient for me to have an additional pair of thin pantaloons this summer—If my mother should think proper to send down a pair by you
next June I should like to have them middling large—and made upon
the tight knee and bell-muzzle plan." His brother Rush was even more
concerned that his mother in rural Cummington might not know what
a young man had in mind, and he convinced Cullen to write to their
mother, "Peter [Rush] seems to think that he must have a cloak but
wishes that the plaid may not be bought till he comes home, as he
would like a voice in the choosing of it. It took nine yards for my cloak
but it is made very full.—He likewise wishes me to say that he will need
another pair of pantaloons this winter."[15]

When Peter Bryant died in 1820, the appraisers of his estate found
three large and small spinning wheels as well as a "Loom and Slaies"
among the agricultural equipment. His wife's detailed diary provides a
clear picture of the way in which these tools were used, as well as the
quantity of textile production each year. Analysis of her daily entries
reveals seasonal patterns as well as changes in her work habits and production over a lifetime. From other sources, it seems that her story was
typical of many women in prosperous households in the years between
the American Revolution and the initial impact of the industrial revolution. The diary also demonstrates vividly how the apex of domestic production coincided with the firm establishment of industrialization.

On the Bryant farm, linen and tow were processed in the spring,
and wool was processed in the fall and early winter. Each season's production of wool and flax was turned into finished yard goods within
one year. On November 14, 1820, Sarah noted that she had "warpt a
piece for flannel—it's the last woolen piece we have to weave." Martha,
a hired girl, drew in the piece the next day, and just four days later, on
Monday, "Martha finished weaving the wool." Weaving was sometimes
hampered by extraordinarily cold weather, as noted on December 24,
1831: "wove on the plaid—have not wove any for two weeks . . . very
cold so that I could not weave." Toward the end of December or early
January, the year's weaving was usually finished. "Got out my piece of
blue, the last for this season," Sarah wrote on December 25, 1827, but
soon, no later than February or early March, flax preparation and linen
spinning began again, and in the first warm days of May it would be
time to wash and shear the sheep.

As a married woman with two young children, Sarah spun linen and tow six days a week from January 1 to April 27, 1797, toward the end of this time producing four skeins or thirty knots per day for sixty days—with the exception of one five-day period and Sundays, of course. The pace did not even slacken on February 4 when Sarah was "almost sick with a cold." This work completed, she then began to spool, warp, and weave pieces averaging thirty-four yards in length until June 26. After taking a break to teach school from June 26 to mid September, on the fifteenth, she began again by drawing in a piece and weaving it off. Before 1800 the diary seldom mentions the composition or intended use of each woven "piece," specifying only shirting, handkerchiefs, a diaper, twenty yards of tape, and a horse blanket.

After 1800, when her husband's medical practice began to be more successful, Sarah started relying on hired girls to do more of the work of textile production, although she always spooled and warped the pieces to be woven and continued to do some spinning. She owned her own spooling and warping equipment and often assisted neighbors in their use of it. Sometimes, however, she spooled her own warps at other houses, perhaps because of extraordinary complexity or size, or because her own equipment was being used by others. Wool was carded by machine at a mill in Chesterfield after 1800 and, locally, at Mr. Darias Ford's mill from 1816 until it was destroyed by fire on October 23, 1823. Sarah acquired a new loom in 1805, and she occasionally wove for others, including her mother, her sister-in-law, the minister's wife, and a few neighbors. Rarely, a neighbor used the Bryant loom for her own work. Sarah's own daughters began to help with the spinning when they reached the age of eleven, but the bulk of the spinning was done by hired girls until 1820.

Fabrics woven on the Bryant farm included cotton, linen, and flannel sheeting; dimity, cheesecloth, table linen, checked linen, shirting (both linen and flannel); a carpet; and a rag coverlet. They also wove kersey for a loose coat and unspecified amounts of woolen and worsted, which were finished at a clothiers. Fabrics were woven for short gowns; boys' trousers; common pantaloons; aprons; woolen and linen tyers; pocket, common, and bundle handkerchiefs; pillowcases; and bags, but the diary does not identify either the fibers or colors of any of these.

Fabric for tyers was once made with madder and white stripes; woolen quilt linings were usually dyed yellow. Dyestuffs used in the Bryant family included locally gathered peach leaves, goldenrod, butternut bark, smartweed, and hemlock, while annetto, indigo, copperas, and madder were purchased. Dyes were used for linings and knitting yarn as well as for recoloring old clothing.

During the 1820s, one of Austin Bryant's efforts to increase the productivity of the family farm was to increase flax production. Although in 1821 they had only 36¾ pounds of flax to process, by 1834 they had more than a hundred pounds. On most New England farms at this time, flax was being abandoned in the face of the increasing production of inexpensive cotton in the water-powered mills. Still, Austin and Sarah persisted in trying to improve the world they knew.

With her eldest son in charge of the farm and no husband or young children to care for, Sarah spent much more time weaving during the 1820s than she had earlier in her life. On July 14, 1820, they moved the loom into Peter's old medical office, and within the week Sarah drew in "a piece for Adeline striped blue and white for trousers." During the summer of 1820, Sarah and a hired girl wove bedticks, shirting, dimity, flannel and "fine flannel" bags, cheesecloth, and fabric for trousers, before the loom was "taken down and carried to the chamber" on September 6. During November and December, Sarah wove a piece of blue cloth for a coat for herself. Interrupted frequently by other tasks, she finally finished it on December 13, commenting in her diary that it "has been in for a long time." In the fall of 1823, a flurry of dyeing "mixed yarn with golden rod," "green," "red with madder," and "coloring with peach leaves" preceded something new: "colored yellow for a plaid gown." The gown was woven in November, and after the first yard was completed, Sarah noted with some satisfaction on the seventh, "I like my plaid much." She finished the weaving on December 4 and cut out the gown on January 8; her daughter Louisa stitched it for her in three days. The notation "homespun plaid is my gown" suggests that both homespun and plaid were unusual in 1823, but during the next few years both Sarah and her daughters had a number of homespun gowns, probably reflecting straitened economic circumstances after Peter Bryant's death as well as their pleasure in experimenting with color and design. Plaids were undoubtedly more interesting and satisfying to weave than plain white sheeting or shirting. The challenge of producing compatible colors with natural dyestuffs, developing a pleasing pattern, and the steady pleasure of watching the colorful pattern emerge on the loom clearly appealed to Sarah.

The new emphasis on weaving in her life during the 1820s is re-

flected in the seasonal relocation of the loom to the office in summer
and to her chamber in winter and by an increasing number of diary
entries that indicate that Sarah was actually doing the weaving herself.
During this period the diary also records more complex projects and
more technical detail such as using "a thirty four reed" or "a thirty two
for shirts."[16] In 1828 Sarah Bryant proudly noted that she began weaving
table linen in "double diamonds," with eight wings, or harnesses, on
the loom. Late in the summer she wove table linen in a damask pattern.
In 1833 her ambition got ahead of her, and she tried a "12 wing damask"
in a number sixty reed, but she could not get it to work and eventually
cut it out of the loom and reverted to her practiced eight-wing pattern.

Unfortunately for Sarah, just as she was beginning to experiment
with complex color and design, her family fortunes diminished, and
she was forced to weave coarser goods for the sake of the income they
could generate. She began to do weaving for her neighbors, especially
warp-striped carpets. She also made and sold both bags and flannel in
pieces up to forty-five yards. On November 1, 1830, she recorded that she
"went to Greenfield a shopping—carried some flannel—bought some
shawls, Adeline silk levantine for a gown & numerous other articles."
On December 17, Austin sold their forty-five-yard piece of fine flannel
to Mr. Hubbard, and in November 1832 she struggled over a seventeen-
yard piece of flannel, which she described as "very tender" and not easy
to weave; on the twenty-third she got it out of the loom, and Adeline
immediately carried it to Mr. Mitchell's store and used it as a credit
for the purchase of some dark calico to make gowns for herself and
Louisa. Although Austin "sold His wool"—190 pounds in June 1834,
Sarah continued weaving, both for the family and for sale, right up until
March 20, 1835. On the twenty-first they "took down the loom;" four
days later Sarah departed for a last visit to her brother and his family
in Brookfield, and in May the entire family moved to Illinois. Her last
weaving projects in Massachusetts were the kind that would be easily
portable—towels, bags, and suspenders.

Sarah's textile work in the 1820s and early 1830s may be seen as
typical of that done on many prosperous New England farms during
that decade. The lists of awards that were made at the agricultural fairs
at the county and state level document the range of that work, including
woolen and linen yard goods, blankets, coverlets, pattern woven table
linens, and a variety of other handwoven textiles. Those who exhibited

at the fairs were usually the same people who raised merino sheep for their improved fleece, planted mulberry trees, and experimented with silk culture. Even Austin Bryant planted mulberry trees in 1833, the year before he sold the farm. After reeling nine skeins of silk from seventy-four cocoons that year, he and his mother visited the local expert, Deacon Cobb, to observe silk reeling. Never willing to leave a project unfinished, Sarah spent part of April 21 and 22, 1835, "reeling my silk" so that it could be taken with her to Illinois.

It is perhaps ironic that the success of these efforts at household textile production came just at the time when the inexpensive products of new textile factories would make domestic production uneconomical. Many people, like the Bryants, gave up the struggle and left their hill farms for promising agricultural opportunities in Ohio, Indiana, or Illinois. Later they and subsequent generations looked back to their New England experience with nostalgia.

On August 21, a busy Saturday in 1824, Sarah "scoured more than a hundred skeins of yarn—colored with smart weed some mixed yarn for filling to a piece—made five gallons of currant wine—churned." Relieved of some of the direct responsibility for household management by living with her son and daughter-in-law—and apparently almost untouched by the industrialization of the textile industry, which was accelerating at that very moment—the fifty-six-year-old widow continued to use her own skills and the products of the family farm. It really did not matter to Sarah what would become of the butter, who would drink the currant wine, or how the finished cloth would be used. In the thrifty world she knew, it was essential that not a thing or a moment be wasted. She, and others like her both then and now, believed that every thing and every minute could be turned to some kind of advantage by frugal and industrious people. Sarah's labor enhanced her life by earning cash or store credits, by creating products for direct exchange with neighbors, or by making it possible for her to step into a warm and colorful new winter gown, sip a flavorful homemade wine, or spread her butter thickly on a piece of freshly baked bread. She was gratified by the knowledge that her labor contributed to the support of her family, whether directly or indirectly, and that it also could permit her to be both hospitable and charitable with her neighbors.

The work accomplished by the individual members of the Bryant household contributed to the well-being of all of them. Much of it was

directly related to providing food, clothing, heat, and light, yet the Bryants were not self-sufficient, nor were any of their neighbors. Even families that were considered successful did not totally provide for themselves. Few owned enough land, tools, or raw materials or controlled
enough labor to be completely self-sufficient. The most prosperous people in any New England town were the most highly specialized in terms
of production and the most heavily involved in the extensive and complex interchange of goods and services that made possible the relative
self-sufficiency of the New England village.[17]

In these relationships as well as within each individual household,
the worlds of men and women overlapped in both house and barn,
dooryard and woodlot, kitchen garden and broad field. Sarah Bryant was
involved in this kind of complex economic and interpersonal exchange
throughout her life.

----

[1] Sarah Bryant continued to keep her diary until shortly before her death in 1847.
The 1794 volume is owned by the Trustees of Reservations at the Bryant Homestead at
Cummington, Mass.; the remainder of the diary is in the Houghton Library at Harvard
(hereafter HL).

[2] The farm was sold in 1835 when the family moved to Illinois. In 1842 the 4-room
section that Peter Bryant had added in 1801 was moved and used as a residence. In 1865
Sarah and Peter's son William Cullen Bryant repurchased the "old homestead" and made
drastic changes, raising the original building and constructing a new first floor underneath
it. He also built a small office on the site of the 1801 addition, replicating the gambrel
roof and other details. William Cullen Bryant's daughter Julia inherited the property and
made additional changes in 1894. Honored by many who believe that William Cullen
Bryant composed "Thanatopsis" inside it, the little house has served as a retreat for several
poets in the twentieth century. Today the house and grounds are open to the public as
a property of the Trustees of Reservations; Helen H. Foster and William W. Streeter,
Only One Cummington (Cummington, Mass., 1974), pp. 245, 352–55; Bryant diaries, 1801,
1835, HL.

[3] Inventory of Peter Bryant, May 23, 1820, Probate Office, Hampshire County, Mass.
The inventory was taken by Bryant's medical student Dr. Samuel Shaw, who later married
Peter and Sarah's daughter Sally, and by two close neighbors, William Packard and Dea-
con James W. Briggs.

[4] The Bryant children were Austin, born in April 1793; William Cullen, known to
his mother as Cullen, born November 3, 1794; Cyrus, born July 12, 1798; Sarah, born
July 24, 1802; Peter Rush, known to his mother as Rush and later called Arthur, born
November 28, 1803; Charity Louise, named for Peter Bryant's sister Charity and known
as Louisa, born December 20, 1805; and John, born July 7, 1807.

[5] Bryant diary, October 30, 1826, December 8, 1827, and subsequent references, HL.

[6] Bryant diary, June 1, 1814, June 15, 1826, HL. According to Stephen Walkley, whose
family in Southington, Conn., kept 5 cows and shared milk with another family who

kept 4, "the milk from nine cows would make a cheese about 8 inches in diameter and 4 inches high" ("Furnishing a Small New England Farmhouse," *Old-Time New England* 48, no. 3 [Winter 1958]: 83).

[7] Sarah Anna Emery, *Reminiscences of a Nonagenarian* (Newburyport, Mass.: William Huse, 1879), p. 8.

[8] Bryant diary, October 1, 1822, September 29, 1825, HL.

[9] Bryant diary, November 24, 1803, HL.

[10] Bryant diary, June 27, September 1, 1807, HL.

[11] Bryant diary, June 15, 1810, HL. Mrs. Snell and Mrs. Briggs were Sarah Bryant's nearest neighbors; Mrs. Snell was her sister-in-law, Ebenezer's wife.

[12] All were simple loose dresses fitted by gathering the fabric on a drawstring around the neck; coolers were made with either long and short sleeves; there was no waistband.

[13] Peter Bryant will, 1820, Hampshire County Courthouse, Hampshire County, Mass.

[14] Peter Bryant will, 1820, Hampshire County.

[15] William Cullen Bryant to Peter Bryant, Bridgewater, Mass., April 27, 1815, in William Cullen Bryant II and Thomas G. Voss, *The Letters of William Cullen Bryant. Vol. I 1809–1836* (New York, 1975), p. 55. William Cullen Bryant to Sarah Snell Bryant, Great Barrington, Mass., September 15, 1823, in Bryant and Voss, *Letters of William Cullen Bryant*, p. 145.

[16] Bryant diary, February 14 and May 11, 1820, HL.

[17] These ideas are well defined in Carol Shammas, "How Self-Sufficient Was Early America?" *Journal of Interdisciplinary History* 13, no. 2 (Autumn 1982): 247–72. Since 1982 many others have completed regional studies further refining this important point.

The Madisons at Montpelier

A Presidential Duplex in the Virginia Piedmont

Conover Hunt

"I wish you had just such a country home as this," Dolley Madison (1768–1849) wrote to a sister in 1820. "It is the simplest and most independent life."[1] The home was Montpelier, the family estate of her husband, President James Madison (1751–1836), located in Orange County, Virginia. Twice enlarged and extensively remodeled during Madison's long public career, the Montpelier of 1820 had grown from the original brick Georgian house constructed by Madison's father, Colonel James

This article was prepared for oral presentation in 1992 and has been updated to reflect newer discoveries at Montpelier by the staff of the National Trust for Historic Preservation. The author is indebted to the following individuals and institutions for assistance in the preparation of this article: Ann Miller, research historian, Orange County Historical Society; Larry Dermody, former conservation director, Kathleen Mullins, director, Marcy Modeland, director of interpretation, and Lynn Lewis, staff archaeologist, all at Montpelier; and Susan Schreiber, director of interpretation for the National Trust, all of whom were kind enough to review the material in 1997 for accuracy. Nancy E. Davis, former director of the Octagon House, and the American Architectural Foundation, Washington, D.C., was generous in supplying visuals. The architectural information contained herein represents an update of material originally published in Conover Hunt-Jones, *Dolley and the 'Great Little Madison'* (Washington, D.C.: American Institute of Architects Fndn., 1977).

119

Fig. 1. Montpelier as it appeared shortly before James Madison's death in 1836. J. F. E. Prud'homme after John G. Chapman (1808–89), *Montpelier, Va., The Seat of the Late James Madison*. Engraving. From James B. Longacre and James Herring, *The National Portrait Gallery of Distinguished Americans* III (Philadelphia, 1836), title page. (American Architectural Foundation; Photo, Virginia State Library.)

Madison, Sr. (1723–1801) around 1760 into an imposing Palladian residence befitting the fourth president of the United States (fig. 1).

Madison retired to Montpelier in 1817 to his "books & farm, to tranquility & independence." At that time his home included a separate apartment for his mother, Nelly Conway Madison (1732–1829), who lived there for sixty-nine years until her death at the age of ninety-seven. The estate was sold by a widowed Dolley Madison in 1844 and then passed through a variety of owners who added, subtracted, multiplied, and divided the mansion to create the twentieth-century architectural puzzle that became a property of the National Trust for Historic Preser-

Fig. 2. Montpelier, Orange County, Va., as it appeared when acquired by the National Trust for Historic Preservation in 1984. (American Architectural Foundation; Photo, William Barrett.) The central block dates to the Madison era and retains architectural elements from separate construction projects dating to 1760–65, 1797–1800, and 1809–13.

vation through the provisions of the will of Marion duPont Scott, the last private resident of Montpelier (fig. 2).[2]

The Montpelier estate of the present day contains 2,700 acres with ten miles of paved roads, a virgin wilderness forest, archaeological sites dating back ten thousand years, two 1929 horse-racing courses, a skeet-shooting range, and 136 structures—among them a pony barn, a Victorian bowling alley, railroad station, general store, several prefabricated Sears and Roebuck horse barns, and the main house, a 36,000-square-foot structure with seventy-seven rooms. Marion Scott's father, industrialist William duPont, made extensive architectural additions between 1900 and 1902, adding a second story to the wings of the Madison mansion and effectively doubling the size of the structure.[3] Several Madison-era rooms no longer exist in the modern floor plan, and quite a few

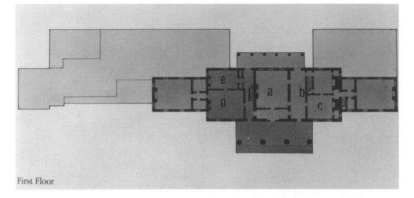

First Floor

Fig. 3. First-floor plan and present-day arrangement of rooms, Montpelier, Orange County, Va. (Montpelier, National Trust for Historic Preservation.) The footprint of the original house is the medium grey area
encompassing the center and right half of the mansion's central block.
The darkest grey areas (e, d, front portico) show the wing and portico
added by James Madison in 1797–1800. In medium grey (a, b, c, back
portico, and parallel side wings) is the footprint of Madison's 1809–13
remodeling and expansion. The palest grey areas (the outermost additions to the left and right back) date to 1900–1902 and reflect William
duPont's additions.

Madisonian architectural elements have been discovered in other, modern, parts of the house (figs. 3, 4).

The National Trust's program of architectural and archaeological
research at Montpelier began in 1986 and is continuing under the apt
title "The Search for James Madison." It is a search that will take years
to complete. One aspect of the challenge to architectural specialists
involves unraveling the chronology of alterations that were made by
James Madison, Sr., and his presidential son between about 1760 and
1813. Currently, planning is under way to create an exhibit that will
interpret James Madison's Montpelier and explore how the house
evolved during the past 250 years.

The invasive architectural research at Montpelier supports earlier
known written accounts of the evolution of the house during the Madison era and tends to confirm the thesis that Montpelier grew in phases
according to a long-range building program that then-Congressman

Fig. 4. Elevation of Montpelier showing additions, 1760–1902. (Montpelier, National Trust for Historic Preservation.) The original colonial mansion is seen as the right section of the central block. The left section and portico, shown in dark grey, date to James Madison's first addition in 1797–1800. The first-floor wings were added by Madison in 1809–1811, at which time he altered the interior of the central block. The palest grey and outermost additions are William duPont's, circa 1900–1902.

James Madison devised after his marriage to Quaker widow Dolley Payne Todd in 1794. Madison's plan was shaped by the domestic arrangements at the estate; its implementation was carried out over a period of fifteen years as funds became available.

The land upon which Montpelier was built was initially settled by Madison's grandfather, Ambrose Madison, in 1723. Archaeologists located the site for the home that Ambrose erected elsewhere on the grounds. Ambrose's son, James Madison, Sr., known as the Colonel, was a successful businessman and planter who became the county's richest citizen. He built the nucleus of the present mansion circa 1760 (fig. 5) to accommodate his wife Nelly Conway and their family, which grew to twelve children, seven of whom lived to maturity. James, Jr., was the eldest, and he remembered helping move light furniture into the house when he was a boy. Figure 5 suggests how the exterior might

Fig. 5. Conjectural elevation, Montpelier, 1760–65. (Montpelier, National Trust for Historic Preservation.)

have looked during the youth and early career of the future president.[4] The house remained essentially unchanged until 1797, when the younger Madison enlarged it.

The use of brick was unusual during the 1760s in the Virginia Piedmont, and the large rooms made an impressive statement amid the traditional story-and-a-half, hall-parlor frame residences that were then common in the area. Madison grew up in this colonial home, which was furnished with English and urban American imports interspersed with simpler articles manufactured in Virginia. Montpelier was his base during research to draft a constitutional plan for the United States, and it was home when he penned his part of the Federalist essays in an effort to assure its ratification. Madison knew that he would eventually inherit Montpelier from his father, a continuance of the old British custom of primogeniture, in which property passes to the oldest son. He was also heir to the cultural traditions of the Virginia gentry and had grown up using his father's library at Montpelier, a collection that the younger Madison later expanded into one of the finest in the nation.[5]

James Madison retired from Congress in 1797 and returned from Philadelphia to Orange County with his bride, her infant son John

Payne Todd, and Dolley's younger sister, Anna Payne. Both of his parents were still alive and in residence, so Madison, Jr., decided to create separate living quarters for his young family by adding a thirty-foot, federal-style wing onto the northwest (left) end of the Georgian house. Although Madison never traveled abroad, he was among the most well-read of the founding fathers, owned books on the architecture of Palladio and Vitruvius, and was familiar with the monuments of Europe.[6]

When he returned to Orange County, Madison may have believed that he had left politics behind him; although his life as a gentleman-farmer was short-lived (President Thomas Jefferson called him to Washington as secretary of state in 1801), Madison threw himself into Montpelier affairs. He served as the architect for the first Montpelier expansion project, relying on his good friend and neighbor Jefferson to supply workmen and nails from Monticello, to advise him on the correct terminology for brass door hardware, and to provide moral support while he suffered through his first and only documented attempt as architect-builder.[7]

Neighbor James Monroe, also engaged in construction during this period, borrowed some of Madison's workmen to assist him at Ash Lawn in Albemarle County. When British Minister Sir Augustus John Foster visited Montpelier in 1807, he made note that Madison "himself [had] superintended the building [and] prescribed the proportions to be observed . . . without the assistance of an architect."[8] The addition created two new rooms on the first floor of the house and several rooms above (see figs. 3, 4). The family moved into the unfinished addition before Christmas 1798.

Madison designed the formal portico on the front of the enlarged mansion but took his time plastering it. In April 1800, he wrote to Jefferson to ask "whether there be known in Philadelphia any composition for encrusting Brick that will effectively stand the weather." When Augustus Foster saw the portico in 1807, it remained unplastered, and the foreign minister expressed some concern that Madison had constructed his portico using "the hands of common workmen [with] very ordinary materials."[9]

This first Madison addition, executed between 1797 and 1800, created the duplex plan at Montpelier. It is tempting to explain the arrangement in terms of our modern attitudes toward resident mothers-in-law, but Dolley and Mother Madison lived under the same roof for twenty-two years and seem to have gotten along just fine. The Colonel died in 1801, shortly after Madison completed his addition, and left the property to his son James with a life estate for Mother Madison, who was subsequently known with affection as "the Old Lady." She remained at Montpelier until her own death in 1829, just seven years before that of James Madison.

The arrangement was by all accounts cordial but separate and equal. Mother Madison kept her own servants, her own hours for meals, her own colonial furniture, her own kitchen, and her own kitchen garden. Visitors who came to see the younger Madisons were graciously received by the Old Lady, but at a time before their dinner at 4:00 P.M. and after hers at 2:00 P.M. The apartments that she retained encompassed most of the southern (right), 1760, portion of the main house, at least on the first floor. During the final years of her life, she probably gave over many of the upper rooms, since her son had so much company. On one occasion, a visitor was astonished to learn from the ebullient Dolley Madison that there were twenty-three guests in residence, with "house room in plenty for more."[10]

The survival of many architectural elements of the 1760 era in Nelly Madison's section of the house suggests that the respectful son chose to delay modernizing the original interiors until the death of his mother. By the time she died, however, Madison was himself an old man crippled by arthritis. Whatever his intention, Madison was pragmatic, and there is now documentary evidence to support the idea that his first Montpelier addition was phase one of a larger plan to beautify the house and grounds into a physical metaphor of his stature as an enlightened thinker, Father of the Constitution, and author of the Bill of Rights. In all likelihood the timing for alterations to the house and grounds under his stewardship was a simple function of economics; when he had money, he spent it on his house.

For many years scholars searched for a watercolor sketch of Montpelier that was drawn by Dr. William Thornton in 1802–3, then framed and presented as a gift to the Madisons in the latter year. It was included on an 1836 inventory of pictures in the Madisons' dining room and is believed to be the only visual to show the mansion after the first expansion.[11]

This long-missing drawing was located in a private collection by former Montpelier Director of Research Ann Miller (fig. 6). It clearly

Fig. 6. William Thornton, *Montpelier*, 1802–3. Watercolor on paper. (Private collection.) This rare image of Montpelier, showing its appearance after the 1797–1800 expansion, shows James Madison's one documented exercise in architecture. The addition determined the basic shape of the central block that survives today.

shows the house with its first addition and the portico. Madison designed the portico in the Tuscan order and included all the requisite classical elements. Compare the watercolor with a photograph of the portico as it appears today (see fig. 2). Note that the columns now extend all the way to the ground in a most nonclassical manner, and the original porch has been rebuilt behind them. This major alteration took place during the 1860s.[12]

The 1802 Thornton sketch shows a garden temple on the front lawn; surviving building accounts show conclusively that the temple was not constructed on this location until 1810–11, during Madison's second building phase. Miller and former Montpelier Architectural Conservator Larry Dermody have suggested, and I concur, that the Thornton sketch represents a conceptual drawing of Madison's long-range plan for the house and grounds. Note that the Thornton sketch also depicts a classical urn on the roof; if this element was ever constructed, it does not survive.

Thornton was architect of the United States Capitol and Colonel

William Tayloe's Octagon House, both in Washington. Thornton and his wife, Anna, enjoyed a warm and lengthy friendship with the Madisons. By long-standing oral tradition in Orange County, both Thornton and Benjamin Henry Latrobe have been credited with designs for Montpelier, attributions that began to appear in print during the 1890s. To date there is no written documentation to confirm that either Thornton or Latrobe played any active design role at Montpelier. Anna Thornton recorded in her diary that the plans were discussed at length when the Thorntons visited Montpelier early in September 1802, but gave credit to Madison for the creative concepts.[13]

The last major expansion at the house during the Madison period of occupancy began shortly before James Madison assumed the presidency in 1809, having completed two terms as secretary of state. This phase went on for four years and actually reinforced the duplex footprint on the first floor of the mansion house. The timing coincided with a substantial raise in Madison's salary. The large scale of these additions attests to Madison's awareness that the presidency would attract a multitude of visitors to his Orange County home.

For this phase of construction Madison turned over the work to housewrights James Dinsmore and John Neilson, along with brickmason Hugh Chisholm—three workmen who had been involved in Jefferson's long-term building program at nearby Monticello. In September 1808, Jefferson wrote to Madison, "Mr. Dinsmore informs me you wish to employ Hugh Chisholm, a bricklayer now working for me in Bedford [Poplar Forest, Jefferson's country home near Lynchburg]." Dinsmore was the chief designer for the work, which was carried out under Madison's supervision.[14]

The expansion included the addition of the garden temple, a part of Madison's plan to create a park, which Anna Thornton described in 1802 as similar "to some of the elegant seats in England" (see figs. 1, 6). The temple survives today in a remarkable state of preservation. Its classical monopteron design is close to that of several other contemporary garden temples. A similar design for a circular temple appeared in Claude Perrault's *Livres d'Architecture de Vitruve* (Paris, 1684). Jefferson borrowed a work on Vitruvius from Madison in 1820, but it remains uncertain that this was the particular edition in the Montpelier library. The temple was placed over the ice house and ranks among the finest classical examples of landscape architecture in the United States.[15]

At the mansion house the workmen also added matching one-story wings, each with a basement kitchen, and erected a colonnade over-looking the rear lawn (see figs. 3, 4). The rear colonnade survives, now encased in duPont additions. Madison had the workmen add minor architectural trim to several of the interior apartments in the house, an obvious attempt to lend classical coherence to the different rooms.[16]

Madison also agreed to a remodeling of two major rooms on the first floor. The elegant central drawing room at Montpelier took its final form at this time, complete with elaborate doors with Venetian glass and side lights and triple-hung windows facing the rear lawn (fig. 3, room a). Dinsmore and Neilson also decorated Madison's largest 1797 room (fig. 3, room d), transforming it into the dining room. The rear colonnade was constructed in the Tuscan order, and Madison had the workmen lay a floor on its roof to serve as a terrace. This addition was handsomely fenced with Chinese railing. Oriental railings were also used on the roofs of the new one-story wings.[17]

As of this writing, Hugh Chisholm's brickmason bills have not been located, so it is uncertain just how much money Madison spent on his last Montpelier building phase. The carpentry bills from Dins-more and Neilson exceeded $4,200, a princely sum. Their accounts did not include the cost of erecting the foundations and walls of the one-story wings, underpinning old walls, or fabricating the columns for the temple and the rear colonnade. Chisholm was at work at Montpelier for a period of five years, submitting his final bill in 1814.[18]

Major construction at Montpelier was complete early in 1813, dur-ing the height of the War of 1812. After the British burned the White House in August 1814, the Madisons had to move many personal effects to Washington to decorate their temporary quarters.[19] The interiors at the main house in Orange County probably never looked complete until Madison retired from the presidency in 1817. Then, the house became the final storehouse for his and Dolley's possessions and a true mirror of their varied interests and tastes.

In its final form Montpelier was about 158 feet long and contained twenty-two rooms. Suitably monumentalized with classical portico, col-onnade, interior architectural details, and the classical garden temple, it became a fitting residence for a great republican. Madison conceived of the house as a focal point for the display of an extensive collection of fine and decorative art that he and Dolley had amassed during his long public career.

In 1828 Margaret Bayard Smith was moved to note during a visit to Montpelier that the drawing room "had more the appearance of a museum of the arts," giving "activity to the mind, by the historic and classic ideas that it awakened" (fig. 3, room a).[20] Here, Madison created his visual history of the United States from discovery through the republican era. He arranged his collection of portraits of the early discoverers of America in counterpoint to oil paintings of the first five presidents of the United States. These portrait groupings were divided by an Asher Durand print of the signing of the Declaration of Independence, which hung over the drawing room mantel.

A separate gallery on the first floor of the old part of the house (fig. 3, room b) was devoted to Madison's collection of Old Master paintings depicting both sacred and profane subjects. Madison never traveled abroad, but the collection was a clear reference to his status as an educated and civilized man. Many of the oils were purchased for Montpelier in Ghent in 1815 by Dolley's son, John Payne Todd. The Clock Room (probably room c) was the mansion's sanctuary, dominated by the ticking of the family tall-case clock.[21] It contained the sculpture collection, including portraits of notable political leaders from America and abroad and plaster casts from ancient statuary.

The dining room (fig. 3, room d) was the social center of the Madison's domain, with fine French cuisine and wines served amid prints and mementos, most of them pertinent to Madison's own career. The walls had engravings of battle scenes from the American Revolution, portraits of Madison's mentors and contemporaries, and the occasional political gift sent from a foreign head of state. The Thornton watercolor sketch of Montpelier, drawn in 1802, hung in this room.

The chamber (fig. 3, room e) had several uses during the Madisons' occupancy. After 1830, it served as James Madison's bedroom, its walls hung with souvenirs. Crippled with arthritis, the former president held interviews there and sat in a chair near the door during meals so that he could converse with guests at dinner. The dominant feature of this chamber was the iron French bedstead with crimson hangings sent by James Monroe from Paris during the 1790s. This mixture of elegant French furniture with personal mementos was somewhat typical of Madison's interests and created in one observer's eyes "an elegant little chamber" with a beautiful view of the rear lawn.[22]

Montpelier's furnishings created their own lesson in the dramatic changes in American history that Madison had helped to effect. Guests must have been struck by the contrast between Mother Madison's apartments and those of the former president. If one was a museum of British-colonial America, the other sported the finest trappings of the republican court, complete with French chairs from the palaces of Louis XVI and Napoleon, along with federal and empire examples made by cabinetmakers in New York, Washington, and Philadelphia.

Madison shared his great friend Jefferson's belief that art served best "to improve the taste of my countrymen, to increase their reputation, to reconcile to them the respect of the world & procure them its praise."[23] The intellectual content of the art at Montpelier and its didactic arrangement were reflections of the mind of Madison, who is remembered as one of the most intellectual American presidents.

Madison created the architectural statement in monumental classicism at Montpelier and arranged the interiors of his residence into a lesson in American history, but it was Dolley who ran the household and gave Montpelier its special reputation for warmth. Her own tastes were manifest in a love of color and light. "Hospitality is the genius of this house," wrote one guest in 1809, "and Mrs. M[adison] is kindness personified." Dolley Madison was among America's most gregarious first ladies; she never forgot a name and had a knack for putting even her most serious detractors at ease.[24] It was Dolley who became a mother to Nelly Madison as their years together at Montpelier grew into decades, and when James Madison became old and infirm, Dolley refused to leave his side.

James Madison died peacefully on June 28, 1836, in his little bedroom at Montpelier. The house is the last great early presidential home to enter the public domain. Many discoveries remain to be made at Montpelier, but the National Trust has opened the main house, several outbuildings, and the grounds so that modern Americans can join in the "Search for James Madison" and journey to Montpelier to meet the founding father at home. The Madisons are gone now, but Montpelier's land and architecture still contain the elements that provided emotional sanctuary and intellectual stimulation to James Madison for most of his eighty-five years. As its name implies, it is a most salubrious place, full of history and alive with activity. Visitors today share the feelings that the Madisons' guests did so many years ago. "They always made you glad to have come," recalled one contented visitor, "and sorry that you must go."[25]

[1] Dolley Madison to a sister [copy], Montpelier, July 5, 1820, Cutts Collection of the Papers of Dolley Payne Madison, Library of Congress, Washington, D.C. (hereafter, CC, DPM-LC).

[2] Thomas Jefferson to James Madison, April 15, 1817, Papers of James Madison, Library of Congress (hereafter, Madison papers). For a summary of the ownership changes that took place at Montpelier, see Ann L. Miller, "Historic Structure Report: Montpelier, Orange County, Virginia/Phase II: Documentary Evidence Regarding the Montpelier House, 1723–1983" (National Trust for Historic Preservation, Orange, Va., July 1990, typescript) (hereafter, Miller, "Historic Structure Report"). Architectural evaluations contained in Conover Hunt-Jones and Robert Rutland, *Dolley and the 'Great Little Madison'* (Washington, D.C.: American Institute of Architects Fndn., 1977), pp. 59–74, have been largely superseded by Miller's important work.

[3] Miller, "Historic Structure Report," pp. 4, 113–41.

[4] Miller, "Historic Structure Report," pp. 2–4, 7–12, 15–33. Hunt-Jones, *Dolley and the 'Great Little Madison,'* pp. 60–61.

[5] Miller, "Historic Structure Report," pp. 33–35. Inventory of the Estate of James Madison [Sr.], July 26, 1802, Madison papers. See also Hunt-Jones, *Dolley and the 'Great Little Madison,'* pp. 94–96. For a discussion of Madison's library and intellectual pursuits, see Hunt-Jones and Rutland, *Dolley and the 'Great Little Madison,'* pp. 97–109, Irving Brant, *The Books of James Madison* (Charlottesville, Va.: University of Virginia, 1965). For information about the life and career of James Madison, see Irving Brant, *James Madison*, 6 vols. (Indianapolis: Bobs-Merril Co., 1941–61).

[6] On Palladio, see Jefferson to Madison, Monticello, November 15, 1817, and Madison to Jefferson, Montpelier, November 29, 1817, both Madison papers. On Vitruvius, see Jefferson to Madison, Monticello, February 16, 1820, Madison papers. Thomas Jefferson borrowed copies of these books from Madison. For a discussion of the first addition to the house, see Miller, "Historic Structure Report," pp. 36–40.

[7] See Madison to Jefferson, December 25, 1797; Jefferson to Madison, January 3, 1798; Madison to Jefferson, February 12, 1798; Jefferson to Madison, February 22, 1798; Madison to Jefferson, March 4, 1798; Madison to Jefferson, April 29, 1798; Jefferson to Madison, May 10, 1798; Madison to Jefferson, May 20, 1798; Madison to Jefferson, October 31, 1798; Jefferson to Madison, November 3, 1798; Jefferson to Madison, November 17, 1798, all Madison papers.

[8] Madison to James Monroe, November 10, 1798, Gratz Collection, Historical Society of Pennsylvania, Philadelphia; Madison to Monroe, December 11, 1798, and July 20, 1799, both Madison papers. Foster quoted in Brant, *James Madison*, 3:459.

[9] Madison to Jefferson, April 4, 1800, Madison papers. Brant, *James Madison* 3:459.

[10] Many visitors commented on the Madisons' living arrangements. For the most complete description, see [Mary E. E. Cutts] manuscript draft for a biography of her aunt Dolley Madison, [1850–55], inconsistently paginated, CC, DPM-LC. Margaret Bayard Smith, *The First Forty Years of Washington Society*, ed. Gaillard Hunt (New York: Charles Scribner's Sons, 1906), pp. 81–83.

[11] Diary of Mrs. William Thornton, 7 vols., 1783–1861, vol. 1, September 5, 1802, and February 28, 1803, Library of Congress (hereafter, Thornton diary). [Dolley Madison], "Engravings in the Dining Room," n.d., DPM-LC; Miller, "Historic Structure Report," pp. 41–42.

[12] Miller, "Historic Structure Report," pp. 117–24.

[13] For a detailed discussion of the numerous design attributions associated with Montpelier, see Miller, "Historic Structure Report," pp. 61–63. Thornton diary, vol. 1, September 5, 1802.

[14] Jefferson to Madison, Monticello, September 5, 1808; Jefferson to Hugh Chisholm, Monticello, September 8, 1808; James Dinsmore to Thomas Jefferson, Monticello, February 24, 1809, all Thomas Jefferson Papers, Massachusetts Historical Society, Boston. Jefferson to Madison, Monticello, April 19, 1809; Jefferson to Madison, September 23, 1808; Dinsmore to Madison, Montpelier, April 20, 1809, all Madison papers. See also Miller, "Historic Structure Report," pp. 43–59.

[15] Thornton diary, vol. 1, September 5, 1802. Jefferson to Madison, Monticello, February 16, 1820, Madison papers. See also William B. O'Neale, *A Fine Arts Library: Jefferson's Selections for the University of Virginia together with His Architectural Books at Monticello* (Charlottesville: University of Virginia, 1976), pp. 368–70. James Madison in Account with Dinsmore and Neilson, carpentry accounts, 1809–14, Alderman Library, University of Virginia, Charlottesville (hereafter, Carpentry Accounts, UVA).

[16] Carpentry Accounts, UVA.

[17] Carpentry Accounts, UVA. Also, Dinsmore to Madison, Montpelier, April 20, 1809, May 4, 1809, May 16, 1809, May 26, 1809, October 29, 1809, all Madison papers.

[18] Hugh Chisholm to Madison, Charlottesville, Va., December 14, 1814, Madison papers.

[19] Hunt-Jones, *Dolley and the 'Great Little Madison,'* pp. 45–58. See also James Madison, Orange County Personal Property Tax Records, 1815, Virginia State Library, Richmond.

[20] Smith, *First Forty Years*, pp. 81–83. For a detailed discussion of the Madison interiors, see Hunt-Jones, *Dolley and the 'Great Little Madison,'* pp. 75–96. See also George Shattuck to Dr. G. C. Shattuck, January 24, 1835, Massachusetts Historical Society, Boston; J. G. Moffatt and J. M. Carriere, eds., "A Frenchman Visits Norfolk, Fredericksburg, and Orange County, 1816," *Virginia Magazine of History and Biography* 53, no. 2. (June 1945): 202–4; Ralph D. Gray, ed., "A Tour of Virginia in 1827: Letters of Henry D. Gilpin to His Father," *Virginia Magazine of History and Biography* 76, no. 3 (October 1968): 469; and John E. Semmes, *John H. B. Latrobe and His Times* (Baltimore: Norman, Remington Co., 1917), pp. 239–45. Miller offers an excellent summary of visitor accounts in "Historic Structure Report," pp. 66–89. There is also a lengthy description of the collection and its arrangement in Mary Cutts Memoir, CC, DPM-LC.

[21] The exact location of this room has always been conjectural; however, the invasive architectural research has clarified the location of Madison-era doorways, with the result that Ann Miller and this writer agree that the painting gallery occupied the original transverse room in the 1760 house. At one time I believed that the Clock Room was located in the rear of the house in the 1760 section. The discovery of an original doorway between the parlor and the old section has led Miller to offer the front room as a more logical site for the Clock Room.

[22] The chamber no longer exists in the modern Montpelier floor plan. On the bedstead, see Mary Cutts Memoir, CC, DPM-LC. Smith, *Forty Years*, p. 234.

[23] Harold Dickman, "Thomas Jefferson, Art Collector," in William Howard Adams, ed., *Jefferson and the Arts: An Extended View* (Washington, D.C.: National Gallery of Art, 1976), p. 128.

[24] Smith, *First Forty Years*, pp. 81–83. One comprehensive biography of Dolley Madison is Ethel Stephens Arnett, *Mrs. James Madison: The Incomparable Dolley* (Greensboro, N.C.: Piedmont Press, 1972).

[25] Smith, *First Forty Years*, p. 237; Arnett, *Mrs. James Madison*, p. 310.

Own Your Own Home
S. E. Gross, the Great Domestic Promoter

Emily Clark

Samuel Eberly Gross, a Chicago real-estate dealer in the late nineteenth and early twentieth centuries, built more than twenty-one subdivisions and ten thousand homes, mostly for working- and middle-class citizens. In doing so, he contributed to the stability of these Chicagoans by helping them become more self-sufficient. By studying his flamboyant advertising materials one can gain insights into the real-estate business in Chicago at the turn of the century. Two of the more interesting aspects of his career are his campaign to provide homes for the working-man and his marketing genius.

After serving in the Civil War and graduating from law school, Gross embarked on his real-estate career in Chicago in the late 1860s. His arrival in Chicago coincided with the post Civil War building boom. *Industrial Chicago* described the atmosphere in the city: "No sooner was the fall of the Confederacy heralded through the streets . . . than men, hitherto cautious, rushed into the arms of enterprise." Gross

Portions of this paper are based on research done for a Chicago Historical Society exhibition, "The Merchant Prince of Cornville: S. E. Gross and his subdivisions," and an article with the same title, appearing in *Chicago History* 21, no. 3 (December 1992). The author acknowledges the contributions to that research of co-curator and co-author Patrick Ashley. She also thanks her colleagues Amanda Kaiser and Tim Hagan for their assistance in locating Gross's ads in foreign-language newspapers. Gwendolyn Wright's excellent book, *Moralism and the Model Home: Domestic Architecture and Cultural Conflict in Chicago, 1873–1913* (Chicago: University of Chicago Press, 1980) provided a great deal of material that was helpful in placing Gross within a context of home building and home ownership in Chicago in the late nineteenth and early twentieth centuries.

eagerly joined the rush and purchased property on which he began to build houses in 1867. Even at this early stage of his career, he was confident in his business acumen and the investment opportunities provided by the rapidly growing city, for in 1868 he wrote to this mother, "What I invest in real estate is pretty sure of not being lost unless the city sinks."[1]

Chicago did not sink, but it was devastated by the Chicago Fire of 1871. To save his business, Gross gathered together his papers and rowed them to a tugboat in the Chicago River. He was thus able to resume his business shortly after the disaster. The rebuilding of the city after the fire attracted architects and builders from across the nation, who flocked to Chicago to take advantage of the building opportunities. The frantic pace of the city's rebuilding was checked by the nationwide depression of the mid to late 1870s. Building and development slowed down, and Gross, like other developers, suffered. He kept himself occupied by practicing law, studying literature, art, and the sciences, designing mathematical instruments, and patenting street paving systems and map improvements.

As building construction began to revive after the 1870s, Gross's career flourished. In the 1880s, he began developing working-class subdivisions throughout the Chicago area. For instance, his New City development drew prospective residents from the workers in the meatpacking plants and related industries of the Union Stockyards, and his Gross Park area catered to German laborers and businessmen from the nearby brickyards and Deering harvesting machinery manufacturing plant.

Gross's success in providing homes for the working classes can be tied to three factors—the location of his developments on the outskirts of the city, the close proximity of his subdivisions to the growing public transportation system, and advancements in building technology. According to the *Chicago Globe*, "He undertook to devise a plan by which [the industrial classes and wage workers], who more than any other, needed a home of their own with the independence, self-respect, better citizenship and stronger manhood its acquisition would give, could secure and pay for a cottage and lot and put their savings into something permanent instead of losing sight of them forever in rent paying." Gross's strategy worked. The working classes appreciated the affordable homes that he provided, particularly as he allowed them to make only a small down payment and continue with low monthly payments. For instance, his workingman's cottages sold from $800 to $2,000. (In the 1880s, the average laborer made $500 in one year.)[2] His simplest workingman's cottage consisted of a kitchen, parlor, and two bedrooms on one floor—without an indoor bathroom. In contrast, his later middle-class homes in Grossdale included such layouts as four bedrooms, a bathroom, a parlor, a sitting room, a dining room, a kitchen, a pantry, numerous closets, and a veranda, on two floors.

Building in the outlying areas of the city was critical since following the Great Chicago Fire the city government had passed building ordinances that limited the construction of frame buildings within city limits.[3] The ordinances, seemingly a natural reaction to the widespread destruction caused by the fire, were hotly debated by the city's populace. The working classes felt they were being unfairly thwarted in their attempts to provide themselves with individually owned homes. They could not afford the brick houses that could be built within the central city and yet were limited by their need to remain close to their places of employment—largely within city limits. The upper classes insisted that brick structures were safer and cheaper to maintain but failed to take into account the much higher cost of providing foundations for brick houses.

In January 1872, the working classes protested the fire ordinances by marching on City Hall and disrupting a meeting of the city council. One of their leaders was A. C. Hesing, editor of the *Illinois Staats Zeitung*, a local German-language paper. Hesing argued that because brick houses would cost three times as much to build as frame cottages and because the working classes would not be able to borrow the money to build the more expensive houses, their property (purchased before the fire) would depreciate and "the earnings of thousands of thrifty and industrious citizens would melt away. Instead of enjoying the blessing of independent homes," he continued, "our laboring people would be crowded into those terrible tenement houses, which are the curse of eastern cities. The effect of the great conflagration would then have been to make the rich richer and the poor poorer."[4]

Hesing exhorted his followers to meet at the corner of Illinois and Market on the evening of January 15, 1872, and march on City Hall "by the memory of the great fire, by their love of their homes and their little ones." The marchers, accompanied by a brass band, carried the

Prussian flag and transparencies with mottoes such as "Leave a home for the laborer," "No tenement houses," and "Don't vote any more for the poor man's oppression." The crowd grew as it neared City Hall and eventually got out of hand, running rampant within the city council chambers. Local newspapers described the marchers as "dirty ill-dressed ruffians" and "mongrel fire-bugs," among other insults. The *Tribune* claimed that the "majority of the 'procession' was composed of men who never owned a foot of ground, and never will if they do not spend less money for beer and whiskey." The *Times* interviewed Hesing the day after the march, and he claimed that he did not support the riotous nature of the crowd and was disturbed by its violence. However, when asked if he would advise resistance to the ordinances if they passed, he answered, "I am in favor of protecting the rights of laboring men. . . . The poor people are bound to rebuild their little homes, and I am with them." It seems clear from these accounts of the working-class riot against the fire ordinances that the people felt strongly that their right to an individually owned home was one of the most crucial to their future well-being. Gross was certainly aware of the riots and the implications of the pressing need for affordable homes for the working classes.[5]

Circumventing the building ordinances, Gross developed areas outside the fire limits. These areas were becoming increasingly manageable as home sites, as public transportation systems improved and as more and more industries located outside of the central city. While horse-drawn street cars had begun in operation in Chicago as early as 1859, the first cable cars did not begin operation until 1883; the first elevated line opened in 1892. Gross shrewdly selected sites that were—or would soon be—accessible to the city by transportation lines, an advantage he emphasized in his advertising materials, along with their location outside the fire limits (fig. 1). Gross encouraged potential customers to buy before the proposed lines were actually constructed, thus being able to take advantage of the increased land values once the line was operational.

Not content to simply take advantage of existing or proposed transit systems in the location of his subdivisions, however, Gross became a director and shareholder of the Calumet Electric Railway, which served his subdivisions of Dauphin Park and Calumet Heights on the city's South Side.[6] In this role, he almost certainly influenced the routes, schedules, and fares of that line. For transit lines to be a sufficient in-

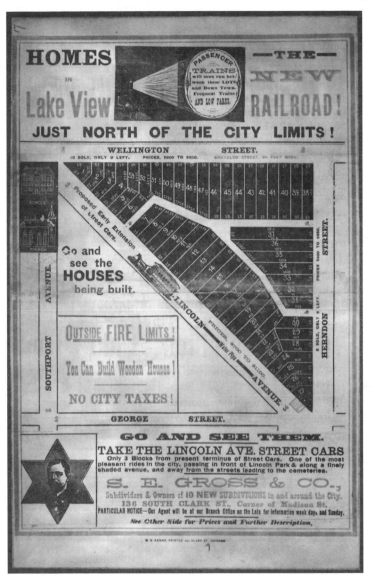

Fig. 1. S. E. Gross broadside, "Homes in Lake View," ca. 1885.
(Photo, Chicago Historical Society.)

ducement to workers to risk investing in property outside of the central city, fares had to stay within their budget limitations, and trains had to run at convenient times for commuters.

Gross also entered into a partnership with Charles T. Yerkes, the traction magnate, in 1887, to develop an addition to his Gross Park subdivision. Yerkes sued Gross in 1899 for failing to uphold his end of the bargain, which was to subdivide, improve, and sell the lots. Gross argued that Yerkes, in turn, had not performed his own duties, by neglecting "to procure the running of cars often enough to accommodate travel to and from the vicinity."[7]

In 1899 Charles Welsh was to exhort American developers to participate in "improvement in the direction of extended accommodations in the shape of suburban homes for artisans and laborers who are compelled to live in unhealthy surroundings and in overcrowded and congested quarters, and in the direction also of providing them with special facilities of transportation."[8] He touted the London suburban models of Queen's Park and Noel Park, which provided special workingmen's trains at reduced rates to enable the workers to live outside of the congested city tenements. Gross's attempts at just such an arrangement predated Welsh's article by more than a decade.

Joel Tarr, in a 1973 article, discussed late nineteenth-century writers who argued that "technology [such as improved urban transit, puts] arcadia within the reach of city dwellers who would otherwise have been denied its moral benefits." "Arcadia" was the suburban dwelling that allowed the city worker to escape the dirt, grime, and morally corrupting influences of the tenement. Tarr quotes Adna Weber's 1899 work, *The Growth of Cities in the Nineteenth Century*, which argued that improved transit systems "had to be accompanied by a shorter working day and inexpensive suburban homes if workingmen were to take advantage of an environment that combined 'the advantages of both city and country life.' "[9] Gross believed strongly in all three methods of achieving the improvement of the lives of workingmen.

Buying mass-produced materials in bulk quantities and building from standardized plans were methods by which Gross was able to keep construction costs down and homes affordable. By the mid nineteenth century, building components such as elaborate wooden moldings, windows, and doors could be mass-produced with steam-powered equipment. Thus, attractive and seemingly custom-designed homes could be built more economically than previously possible. In addition, building plans were easy to come by, published in catalogs available to consumers. Gross himself used such plans, and at least some of his house designs were taken from *Shoppell's Modern Houses*, a popular national magazine.[10] Such plans eliminated the need to hire an architect to build an aesthetically pleasing home, thus making it possible for the less well-to-do to have individualized homes.

But building a successful subdivision involved more than selecting an advantageous site and building cheap homes. The land had to be surveyed and platted; sewer, gas, and water lines (none of which were standard issue on Chicago-area property at the time) as well as streetlights had to be installed; sidewalks and roads had to be laid; and trees needed to be planted.[11] After these improvements were made—or often before—Gross set up a branch office at the subdivision and began his marketing campaign.

Once a lot was purchased, the new owner could build his own home or contract with Gross to have a house built from the more than four hundred house plans he had available. Sometimes less than a year elapsed between the time Gross purchased the land and the first homes were built. He also added major improvements to some of his subdivisions, such as schools, train stations, and meeting halls. Many of these prominently displayed his name, such as Gross Hall in Gross Park and the Grossdale Station in Grossdale. He also named many of the streets in his subdivisions for his family members and friends. Gross was proud of his ability to transform a wide expanse of "virgin soil" into a prosperous, bustling community of homes and commercial buildings. As the *Knights of Labor* put it, "Every suburban or city subdivision that Mr. Gross had managed has become a living, breathing community of prosperous citizens."[12]

What truly set Gross apart, however, was his mastery of promotion. His office churned out colorful pamphlets, catalogs, and broadsides to advertise his subdivisions. They were freely distributed to interested customers. In his pamphlet *The House That Lucy Built*, a young wife, attempting to better her family's situation, determines to buy a house. After a "lengthy conference" with a real-estate representative from Gross's office, Lucy returns home "laden with circulars and pamphlets containing instructions and designs." At the end of the tale, after Lucy has succeeded in purchasing a cottage for herself and her husband and has freed them from the tyranny of rent paying, she declares: "Every hour of our lives we render mute thanks to that large minded, public spirited man—S. E. Gross—who has rendered it possible for every man or woman to own his or her own home."[13] The pamphlet raises questions about the role of women in the decisionmaking process regarding the purchase of a home.

A recurrent theme that Gross cleverly manipulated in his advertising was the "cult of domesticity" that had become so popular by the mid nineteenth century. This middle-class movement idealized the home as the embodiment of stability, good citizenship, moral development, dedication to family, communion with nature, and protection from the vices of the city. Gross exploited these domestic images by emphasizing the superiority of home ownership in his publicity. His moralistic *Home Primer for Old and Young*, for example, contrasts the lives of two men, one a virtuous saver and the other a wastrel. The former increases his wealth and is able to buy his own home, leading to a life of complacency. The latter, who squanders his money on riotous parties and must rent an undesirable property, leads a miserable existence (fig. 2). Another advertisement, which addresses the same issue, points out that on the first of May (a traditional moving day), the homeowner could sit smugly in his cozy parlor, relaxing with his family, while the renter was forced to suffer the humiliation of moving his belongings by cart (fig. 3).[14]

The image of the homeowner and his family sitting idyllically before their fireplace—the ultimate symbol of domestic tranquillity—appears repeatedly in Gross's publications. One of his advertisements, which appeared in the Jewish newspaper *Occident*, quotes him as follows: "It is gratifying to me now to realize that as a result of my efforts thousands of comfortable homes in Chicago and its vicinity, with their happy family groups and cheerful firesides, bear witness to the realization of the first and strongest feeling of the human breast—'there is no place like home.' "[15]

In addition to his vision of domestic utopia for the working classes, Gross displayed his astute awareness of the housing needs of the immigrant population of Chicago through his advertisements in foreign languages (fig. 4). According to the *Real Estate and Building Journal*, "Thousands of emigrants who intended to stop in the city have gone beyond because they could not procure dwellings. . . . The greatest

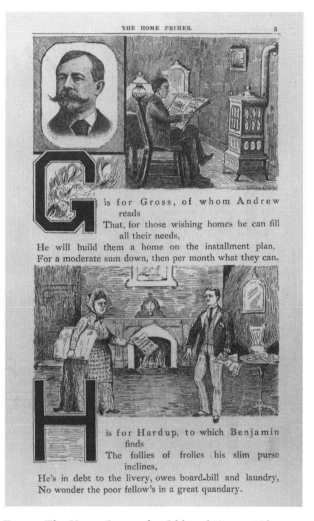

Fig. 2. *The Home Primer for Old and Young* (Chicago: S. E. Gross, 1888), p. 5. (Photo, Chicago Historical Society.)

Fig. 3. S. E. Gross, *Tenth Annual Illustrated Catalogue of S. E. Gross'
Famous City Subdivisions and Suburban Towns* (Chicago: S. E. Gross,
1891), p. 43. (Photo, Chicago Historical Society.)

need in Chicago is cheap houses for the laboring people." By recognizing their need for housing and targeting these groups through his
foreign-language advertisments, Gross appealed to yet another set of
potential buyers. For example, he published one of his catalogs in
both English and German editions. He also advertised extensively in
German-, Swedish-, and Italian-language newspapers, in addition to
papers targeted to labor unions and the Jewish population. He also
claimed that his salesmen, both in the home office and in the field,
were able to speak all languages.[16]

     Some insights into Gross's uses of advertising can be gleaned from
Theodore Dreiser's novel *Jennie Gerhardt*. One of the main characters
of the novel, Lester Kane, decides to enter the real-estate business by
going into partnership with a Samuel E. Ross—a character clearly based
on S. E. Gross. Kane trusts Ross because he has seen "his signs out on
the prairie stretches, and . . . his ads in the daily papers." To Kane this
indicates a certain reality and integrity. Citizens of Chicago may have

Fig. 4. S. E. Gross broadside, "Handsomest Brick Cottages in Chicago." (Photo, Chicago Historical Society.)

assumed the same inherent trustworthiness of Gross simply by virtue of the ubiquitousness of his advertisements. Ross described the special qualities he possessed that made him so successful—qualities that Gross himself appeared to feel that he had—"There was something in prestige, something in taste, something in psychic apprehension . . . [he was] the presiding genius."[17]

One example given of Ross's taste and genius is his selection of the name for the subdivision that he and Kane are to develop. "It was given a rather attractive title—'Inwood,' although . . . there was precious little wood anywhere around there. Ross assured [Kane that] . . . people looking for some section even partially equipped with trees, would be attracted by the name. Seeing the notable efforts in tree-planting that had been made to provide for shade in the future, they would take the will for the deed."[18] Similarly, Gross chose names such as "Under the Linden" and "Brookdale" for his subdivisions and included winding roads and tree plantings in his developments. By giving the illusion of bucolic surroundings, or "arcadia," Gross could make his areas seem more appealing to those living in the overcrowded city.

But in *Jennie Gerhardt*, as Gross may have been in reality, Ross is thwarted in his ambitions for his subdivision. It was rumored that a packing plant was considering relocating into the vicinity, and prospects for selling the land to more desirable tenants plummeted.

Ross was beside himself with rage . . . He decided, after quick deliberation, that the best thing to do would be to boom the property heavily, by means of newspaper advertising, and see if it could not be disposed of quickly before any additional damage was likely to be done to it. . . . The additional sum of $3,000 was spent in ten days to make it appear that Inwood was an ideal residence section, equipped with every modern convenience for the home-lover, and destined to be one of the most exclusive and beautiful residence sections of the city. It was 'no go' . . . from any point of view, save that of a foreign-population neighborhood, the enterprise was a failure.[19]

This fictional account brings up the question, How honest were Gross's advertisements? Did he only put on the pressure of lavish advertisements, touting the desirable traits of his subdivisions, when he was most desperate for sales? Or were these advertisements simply an extension of his genius in standing above the crowd? The last statement of the quotation gives a new twist to the consideration of Gross's advertise-

ments in foreign-language newspapers. Was he truly sympathetic to the
needs of the foreign-born working classes by targeting his *housing* to
those groups? Or was he more mercenary by targeting his *advertisements*
to those groups only when the "ideal" clients had not responded?

One of Gross's more elaborate marketing schemes was his creation
of "excursion days" to entice prospective buyers to his subdivisions. He
sponsored free trains to the sites, underscoring their accessibility to the
city. According to the reminiscences of Willis Melville of Grossdale:
"He got lots of people to come out on special trains. When they got to
the station . . . there was nothing there for miles around, except a wagon
full of beer barrels. People would have a few beers, then the band would
play lively marches and the whole group would cheerfully march out
towards [the development]. . . . Once there, they were given a real sales
pitch . . . and signed on to buy lots."[20] Through these excursions, Gross
created an image of himself as a magnanimous benefactor and nurtured
a strong feeling of community for the subdivision.

In one excursion-day advertisement, which appeared in the widely
circulated labor paper *Rights of Labor* (earlier published under the title
Knights of Labor), Gross exploited one of the philosophies behind the
Eight-Hour Day movement (fig. 5). He felt that if laborers were enabled
to work a shorter day they would have more time to commute to the
suburbs and "spend the 'time' to be gained . . . with their family under
their own roof—Independent and Happy." This sentiment echoes the
writings of Ira Steward and T. V. Powderly. Steward argued that "unless
the working classes are paid sufficient wages, they will not be able to
buy certain articles which manufacturers and merchants are so eager
to sell. Capitalists remember us as Producers, to be paid as little as
possible; but not as Consumers, to be paid enough to enable us to buy
their commodities." He included homes as commodities to which the
workers had an equal right when he wrote that "the commonest or the
most obscure laborer will live, if he chooses, in dwellings as beautiful
and as convenient as any which are now monopolized by the Wealthy
Classes."[21]

Powderly, on the other hand, had a unique insight into the advantages of the eight-hour day. He pointed out that "the adornment of the
home became an object with the man who could see his home by
daylight, and the demand for articles of home consumption and adornment increased very rapidly." While Gross seemed to be genuinely sym-

Fig. 5. Advertisement. From *Rights of Labor* (April 26, 1890). (Photo, Chicago Historical Society.)

pathetic to the plight of the workers, he also realized that reduced work hours with the same pay (which was the goal of the movement) would mean that workers would then have the time to commute to the suburbs and the desire to have more attractive homes since they would have the time to enjoy them. He also realized that if the workers' monetary situation improved, they would become additional consumers of his product—homes. In 1888 he indicated his direct support of the Eight-Hour Day movement, when he addressed a letter to workingmen that laid out his belief that it was a "favorable time for the advancement of that movement as a principle. The rapid improvements of the age, mechanical and industrial, should tend to reduce the hours of labor for the masses of the people. . . . It is a question which should interest all workers among all the people, and should be, in short, a movement by the people for the people, regardless of any political consideration whatever."[22]

Gross's popularity with the working classes took a political form when, in March 1889, the Joint Labor Party nominated him as their candidate for mayor of Chicago. The *Knights of Labor* felt that Gross was an ideal candidate, citing the fact that "nearly 8,000 working people had been given an opportunity to purchase homes, which but for him they never would have had; . . . that he is undoubtedly one of the most popular men in the city amongst the working men; that all of his work is conducted on the eight-hour principle; that he has always taken a lively interest in all affairs in which the working people are interested; . . . and also that he is a man in whom the business men of the city can and will have the very highest confidence."[23] Gross declined the nomination, according to some reports, because he did not feel that the Joint Labor Party was unified enough to be successful. According to other reports, the demands of his real-estate business were too pressing.

Even though Gross declined the nomination, his popularity with the working classes continued. In September 1889, the *Knights of Labor* carried, on its front page, the article "The Most Practical Philanthropist," namely S. E. Gross. The author claimed that Gross was a greater benefactor than one who simply showered money on the poor, "for he is helping the people to help themselves. He is teaching them self-reliance, thrift, and above all things the consummation of earthly wisdom, how to be happy." The article goes on to say that Gross's interest in the working classes went beyond a desire to provide them with homes (which of course benefited him in the end), but that he has also "always been noted as an earnest sympathizer with the working classes interesting himself in all their schemes for amelioration, advising them to join the labor organizations, and stand as a unit for their own rights."[24]

At about the time that article appeared, Gross, feeling the need for a change of scenery, took his wife on an extended trip to Europe, where he studied systems for housing the working classes in Great Britain, France, and Italy, and where he was approached by city planners eager for him to undertake developments in their areas. While there, they also visited the Exposition Universelle in Paris. Gross was disappointed that he had not known ahead of time about the exhibit of homes for the workingman at the Exposition. If he had, he would have sent a model of one of his cottages to be included. He felt that it certainly would have received an award as "the Chicago cottage contains the maximum of artistic taste and comfort in homes of this class."[25]

He was interested to see, in the exhibit, the approach taken to homes for the workingman in Europe. He found that "the grace and sentiment which usually surround the American home, however humble, were [in Europe] . . . sacrificed to the expediency of simple shelter and plainess of construction." He continued by stating that the European working-class home "seems to have placed upon it, in the method of construction, a badge which conveys to the observer an idea of poverty and a servile condition of the owner, and has not the stamp of individuality and independence of character found usually in American homes, even of the most ordinary workingman."[26]

These sentiments continue the theme that runs throughout Gross's advertisements and writings—that is, his strong belief that homes were not simply shelters from the elements, but rather they stood for something much more important. He had a very intellectual approach to houses, that went beyond his economic interest in them as products to be sold. To him, a home was a concrete, outward display of a person's drive for self-sufficiency and independence. It was a visible sign of a person's achievements and position in life, a sign that was equally valid and appropriate for the workingman as it was for the middle and upper classes. He also felt that all men should be able to afford a home of their own, and that doing so made them better citizens, for they then had a vested interest in their communities. An earlier writer had stated similar ideas as follows: "A house is the shape which a man's thoughts take when he imagines how he should like to live. Its interior is the measure of his social and domestic nature; its exterior, of his aesthetic and artistic nature. It interprets, in material form, his ideas of home, of friendship, and of comfort."[27] It is true that Gross manipulated these themes in his advertisements, but it appears from his other writings and from published interviews that he did indeed have a strong intellectual interest in the idea of "The Home."

In the 1890s and the first years of the twentieth century, Gross expanded his building activities to include more middle-class subdivisions such as Grossdale (now known as Brookfield) and Alta Vista Terrace. In 1902, at the peak of his career, he won a court case in which U. S. District Court Justice Kohlsaat ruled that Edmond Rostand's famous play *Cyrano de Bergerac* was a "piracy upon" Gross's play *The Merchant Prince of Cornville.*[28] Gross claimed that he had written the play during the building depression of the 1870s. While he won international notoriety from this case, he never became a successful playwright—in fact, his play received only one performance and was not widely read. Following the success of the court case, Gross's career began a downhill slide. In 1903 he began building three hundred houses in Chicago and West Allis, Wisconsin (near Milwaukee). A severe storm that winter delayed his building operations, however, and he was unable to meet his financial obligations. In 1904 a group of Gross's creditors, including several lumber, plumbing, and brick companies, attempted to have him declared bankrupt. He was able to fight the action by proving that his assets exceeded his liabilities by more than $1 million. Several years later, in April 1908, Gross declared bankruptcy voluntarily. The cause of his failure at the time was given as "unwise speculation," but probably was also influenced by the financial panic of 1907. While Gross's fortunes had certainly fallen from his net worth of $5 million, as estimated at the peak of his career, he was hardly destitute. At the time of his death on October 24, 1913, the estate was valued at $150,000.

While Gross may no longer be remembered for his literary activities or his flamboyant marketing techniques, he certainly left his stamp on numerous Chicago neighborhoods and suburbs. Many of the homes he built a hundred years ago can still be seen throughout the Chicago area. He left a legacy of single family homes in defined communities, convenient to public transportation, that allowed workingmen and their families to escape the cramped quarters of the central city.

[1] *Industrial Chicago* 1 (Chicago: Goodspeed Publishing Co., 1891), p. 108; S. E. Gross to Elizabeth Gross, February 13, 1868, S. E. Gross Collection, Archives and Manuscripts Department, Chicago Historical Society.

[2] "American Homes: The Difference between Europe and Chicago," *Chicago Globe*, December 22, 1889, p. 6; *Tenth Annual Illustrated Catalogue of S. E. Gross' Famous City Subdivisions and Suburban Towns* (Chicago: S. E. Gross, 1891); *Illustrated Catalogue of S. E. Gross' Lots, Houses, Cottages* (Chicago: S. E. Gross, 1889); *Report of the Social Statistics of Cities* (Washington, D.C.: Government Printing Office, 1887); Illinois Bureau of Labor Statistics, *First Biennial Report* (Springfield: By the bureau, 1880).

[3] *Fire Ordinances of the City of Chicago, Published by Order of the Board of Public Works, March 1872* (Chicago: Jameson and Morse, 1872).

[4] "North Side Stupidity," *Chicago Times*, January 14, 1872.

[5] "Hesing's Mob," *Chicago Times*, January 16, 1872; "The Fire-bugs," *Chicago Times*, January 17, 1872. For further information on the effects of the fire ordinances on working-class housing and on the ensuing protest riots, see Christine Meisner Rosen, *The Limits of Power: Great Fires and the Process of City Growth in America* (Cambridge, Eng.: Cambridge University Press, 1986), pp. 95–109.

[6] *Tenth Annual Illustrated Catalogue*, p. 27.

[7] *Charles T. Yerkes v. S. E. Gross* (1899), Circuit Court of Cook County, Ill.

[8] Charles Welsh, "Workingmen's Homes and Workingmen's Trains," *New England Magazine*, n.s. 20, no. 6 (August 1899): 765.

[9] Joel Arthur Tarr, "From City to Suburb: The 'Moral' Influence of Transportation Technology," in *American Urban History*, ed. Alexander B. Callow, Jr. (2d ed.; New York: Oxford University Press, 1973), p. 203; Adna F. Weber, *The Growth of Cities in the Nineteenth Century* (1899; reprint, Ithaca: Cornell University Press, 1967), pp. 460–64, as quoted in Tarr, "From City to Suburb," p. 208.

[10] *Illustrated Catalogue*, p. 44.

[11] For further information on the provision of infrastructure amenities by real-estate developers and by local governments, see Ann Durkin Keating, *Building Chicago: Suburban Developers and the Creation of a Divided Metropolis* (Columbus: Ohio University Press, 1988).

[12] "The Most Practical Philanthropist," *Knights of Labor*, September 7, 1889, pp. 1, 4.

[13] A. E. H., *The House That Lucy Built; or, A Model Landlord* (Chicago: Samuel E. Gross, 1886).

[14] For further information on the history and theory of the "cult of domesticity," consult Clifford E. Clark, Jr., "Domestic Architecture as an Index to Social History: The Romantic Revival and the Cult of Domesticity in America, 1840–1870," *The Journal of Interdisciplinary History* 7, no. 1 (Summer 1976); *The Home Primer for Old and Young* (Chicago: S. E. Gross, 1888); Gross, *Illustrated Catalogue* (1889), p. 43.

[15] *Occident* (Chicago), May 31, 1889.

[16] "Review of the Market," *Real Estate and Building Journal*, December 31, 1881; *Illustrirter Katalog von S. E. Gross' Bauplatzen, Hausern, Cottages* (Chicago: Samuel E. Gross, 1888); Gross, *Illustrated Catalogue*. Some of the foreign language newspapers in which Gross advertisements have been found are *Abendpost* and *Illinois Staats Zeitung* (German); *L'Italia* (Italian); *Aftonbladet Skandia* (Swedish); and *Occident* (Jewish, in English). S. E. Gross advertisment, *Knights of Labor*, September 28, 1889.

[17] Theodore Dreiser, *Jennie Gerhardt*, ed. James L. W. West III (Philadelphia: University of Pennsylvania Press, 1992), chaps. 47 and 48; and Emily Clark, "Samuel E. Gross: Dreiser's Real Estate Magnate," in James L. W. West III, ed., *Dreiser's Jennie*

Gerhardt: New Essays on the Restored Text (Philadelphia: University of Pennsylvania Press, 1995), pp. 183–93.

[18] Dreiser, *Jennie Gerhardt*, p. 333.

[19] Dreiser, *Jennie Gerhardt*, pp. 333–34.

[20] Letter from Kermit Myers, March 24, 1992, author's collection.

[21] S. E. Gross advertisement, *Rights of Labor*, April 26, 1890; Ira Steward, *The Meaning of the Eight-Hour Movement* (Boston: 1868), pp. 7, 15.

[22] T. V. Powderly, "The Plea for Eight Hours," *North American Review* 150, no. 4 (April 1890): 465. Gross's letter was published twice; first in *Frank Leslies' Illustrated Newspaper*, August 25, 1888, p. 23, and then reprinted in "Samuel E. Gross," *Knights of Labor*, February 23, 1889, p. 9.

[23] "The Joint Labor Convention," *Knights of Labor*, March 16, 1889, pp. 1, 9.

[24] "Most Practical Philanthropist," pp. 1, 4.

[25] "European versus American Homes," *Chicago Tribune*, January 19, 1890.

[26] "European versus American Homes." For another article on Gross's trip to Europe, see "American Homes," *Chicago Globe*, December 22, 1889.

[27] H. W. Beecher, "Building a House," *Star Papers* (New York, 1859), pp. 285–92, as quoted in Clark, "Domestic Architecture," p. 56.

[28] Samuel Eberly Gross v. A. M. Palmer, Richard Mansfield, and the Richard Mansfield Co., Circuit Court of the United States, Northern District of Illinois, Northern Division (1902).

Standard of Living in the Seventeenth-Century Chesapeake

An Archaeological Perspective

Dennis J. Pogue

The development of Anglo-American society in the Chesapeake region offers a case study in culture change for which considerable archaeological and documentary data are available. Living standards for all components of Chesapeake society were affected dramatically as the result of initial colonization and adaptation to the alien New World environment. For much of the seventeenth century, the Chesapeake was characterized by demographic imbalances and overall instability.

By the first years of the eighteenth century, however, Chesapeake society had achieved demographic maturity, in turn leading to the ascension of a native-born planter elite. Thus, the elements required to initiate a new phase of cultural changes were in place. This time the engine driving change was not ecological adaptation but social emulation and class conflict instead. These intertwined forces were manifested in an unprecedented boom in consumption and a corresponding change in lifestyle. For the most part, the participants were members of the gentry class, but within a few decades the consumer revolution appears to have had varying levels of impact on virtually all of Chesapeake society.

Diachronic variation in selected categories of material culture—

architectural forms, foodways (subsistence and ceramic use), and a range of household objects—is analyzed in an attempt to measure patterns in their use reflecting shifting cultural norms. An extensive body of documentary research allows the archaeological findings to be contextualized within the historical trajectory of sociodemographic development. The resulting fine-grained analyses have yielded a synthesis that stresses the volatile nature of early Chesapeake society, its dependence on tobacco as a cash crop and the resulting development of a plantation economy, and a transition to a more settled state only much later in the century.

On the other hand, archaeologists have excavated dozens of dwelling sites dating to the seventeenth century. The vast majority are isolated plantations where individual families and their bound laborers constituted the household unit. In general terms, the results of the archaeological research reinforce and complement the documentary scholarship, although significant points of contrast are evident. To date, synthetic studies have focused on architecture and the two components that make up foodways—diet and ceramic use. Reflecting well-established archaeological traditions, these studies are primarily concerned with identifying patterns in material culture that in turn may lead to inferences of broad cultural change.

In the past, the domain of standard of living has been examined almost exclusively from the perspective of the analysis of probate inventories, with little attention paid to the archaeological manifestations. In this essay, findings generated over the past two decades are synthesized to allow an archaeologically based study of how people lived in the seventeenth-century Chesapeake and how their living standards changed over time.

CHESAPEAKE COLONIZATION

Beginning as a land of opportunity for the poor and the landless of the British Isles, the Chesapeake attracted a stream of English immigrants hoping to improve their fortunes in a new world. Tobacco was selected early on as the economic foundation for the region, with the production of the crop for export to England the overriding preoccupation for all. The abundance of land and ease of its acquisition meant that those immigrants who survived, including a high percentage of those who began their careers as indentured servants, were able to establish their own plantations. Many did not survive long enough to achieve that goal, however, as disease and an alien environment combined to elevate mortality rates and lower life expectancy.[1]

For much of the seventeenth century, the makeup of the population was unbalanced. A majority of the immigrants who ventured to the tobacco colonies were young and single males who married late in life, if at all. The scarcity of women guaranteed a larger than normal proportion of unmarried men, reduced the incidence of traditional family units, and severely limited the number of offspring. When combined with high rates of mortality and morbidity, these factors retarded population increase through natural means. Finally, the imbalances reduced the societal controls normally attributed to familial interaction.[2]

By the end of the century, conditions had altered significantly. The proportion of men and women slowly had reached parity, birthrate and life expectancy both increased, and the native born finally came to outnumber immigrants. A more normal demographic profile and the prevalence of nuclear family households also meant greater stability for society as a whole. Tobacco remained the primary livelihood, but diversification into grain production as a cash crop already had begun, and fluctuations in the market and a general decline in prices paid for the "sotweed" meant that the boom period had passed forever. In its place, steadily declining profits per unit resulted in an increase in plantation size and in the supply of labor needed. This change meant decreasing opportunities for advancement for recently freed servants and others of marginal means.[3]

With the close of the century, the English labor surplus was exhausted and with it the ready pool of indentured servants upon whom Chesapeake planters had depended. Importing enslaved Africans in large numbers was the response to the scarcity of English immigrants, and by the turn of the century the numbers of enslaved surpassed those of indentured servants. The transition from indentured servitude to slavery allowed planters of means to solve their labor problem but also introduced a new, more alien element to Chesapeake society. The influx of African slaves and the resulting creation of a racially prescribed underclass has been cited as an important contributor to the rise of class consciousness that occurred at this time.[4]

By the first decades of the eighteenth century, therefore, Chesapeake society had been transformed. The social instability fostered by demographic imbalances was reduced. The more stable social structure that was established was largely the result of the rise of a dominant landed gentry. This brought about a reduction in social mobility but at the same time made such movement that much more prized. As the century progressed, Chesapeake society continued to evolve, giving up the improvisational character of the first decades of settlement and approximating more and more the traditional norms of its rural English prototype.[5]

BIRTH OF A CONSUMER SOCIETY

Numerous scholars have pointed to the development by the beginning of the second quarter of the eighteenth century of what has been described as a "consumer society." This shift has been characterized as a growing emphasis on the acquisition of consumable goods throughout all levels of Anglo-American society. The new acquisitiveness reflected desires for increased "comfort, attractiveness, and even elegance in living quarters and dress, more arrangements for individual use of space and utensils, increased emphasis on manners and social ceremony," and on "concerns to be fashionable—all summed up by the word gentility."[6]

Studies of developments in England serve as the underpinning for such interpretations. Neil McKendrick identifies "a great change in the lifestyle of the population," which he maintains was as great as that "brought about by the neolithic revolution in agriculture." McKendrick portrays this change as the transformation of man into "a consuming animal with boundless appetites to follow fashion, to emulate his betters, to seek social advance through spending, to achieve vertical mobility, through possessions." Cary Carson has taken that analysis an important step further, attributing these developments to a broader social movement, centered in Britain and northern Europe, that eventually transformed much of the world from a condition of rudimentary tool users to one of social display, or a consumer society. The cause of this profound change is identified as the breakdown of traditional means of marking status resulting from greater social mobility. The age-old need to mediate social relations in a profoundly changing social climate fostered the creation of a whole new class of status markers that were standardized yet portable.[7]

Traditionally, a man's social position "was based on his family connections, his wealth in land and labor, and the offices he held." These time-honored marks of distinction worked well in peasant communities where movement was usually confined to a relatively small area. As a consequence, possessions were valued for their functional utility, meaning that households of rich and poor alike were furnished with similar objects but with the wealthy simply owning more. All this began to change in Britain and in parts of Europe beginning in the sixteenth century. By the period of widespread migration to the transatlantic colonies, new rules for marking status were being formulated.[8]

By the last decades of the seventeenth century, a mentality of consumption was developing in America that was every bit as attuned to social display as that back home. Based on an analysis of probate inventory data from southern Maryland, Lorena Walsh concludes that "beginning about 1715 the tidewater elite began to acquire a greater array of material goods that facilitated a style of living that more clearly set them off from the ordinary folk." Evidence for this development was found in an increase in amenities such as fine ceramics, table knives and forks, books, and clocks. From inventory data compiled from four Maryland counties, Walsh and Lois Carr tabulated the occurrence of selected items considered to be amenities and plotted their frequency over time. The mean amenities index for all four counties increased significantly between 1690 and 1770.[9]

The ability to act on these new desires was fundamentally the result of generally improving economic conditions for many elements of society. The group most actively engaged in social sparring of the type represented by conspicuous consumption, however, was the comparatively wealthy native-born elite that was developing at the same time. While social distinctions may have become more rigid, as in England it remained quite possible for movement up and down the social ladder. Consumption and the quest to follow fashion became an important weapon in the struggle either to rise above or to hold on to one's station. Not surprisingly, the largest group left out of this movement—and the one whose very presence was a major cause of increased class awareness—was the growing number of enslaved Africans coming to the region.[10]

ARCHITECTURE

The result of two decades of field work, insights into Chesapeake vernacular architecture have been the single most noteworthy contribution
made by archaeologists to the study of the seventeenth-century Chesapeake. An entire class of structures for which virtually no information
previously was known has been intensively studied. This has led to attempts to reassess the development of Chesapeake architecture and to
place it within the context of a broader paradigm of colonization. The
early synthetic treatments succeeded in relating the structural components and forms that were selected to the region's socioeconomic development. In short, a particular type of relatively impermanent building,
defined by earthfast construction and other adaptations selected for
their low construction costs, developed in response to the labor-
intensive nature of the tobacco economy.[11]

During the first two decades of settlement, traditional English
building types were quickly modified for use in the Chesapeake. A distinctive type of construction that had been declining in popularity in
England for centuries was reestablished and elaborated. Built almost
completely of wood, supported by posts set into the ground, and usually
consisting of only one or two rooms, the "Virginia house" represented
a remarkable step backward for most English settlers. The main dwelling at the King's Reach site, in Calvert County, Maryland, occupied
from about 1690 to 1715, is a representative example of the mature Virginia house hall-and-parlor plan. The structure was supported by eight
posts, encompassing two main rooms and one chimney within a 30-by-
20-foot footprint, with a 10-foot-wide shed along the rear (fig. 1).[12]

Based on a comparison of inventory data from England and the
Chesapeake, James Horn maintains that "two-thirds of Maryland planters lived in dwellings of a type usually found only among the poorest
sections of English society." The syntheses of the architectural evidence
for the Chesapeake support the interpretation of earthfast housing as
an expedient viewed by their builders as adequate only because of the
extraordinary conditions encountered in settling the region. This hybrid
method of construction was selected in response to the demands of
tobacco production and had the benefit of being relatively inexpensive
and easy to build, using materials and carpentry skills that were readily
available. The selection of earthfast housing as the dominant type of

Fig. 1. Artist's rendering of the King's Reach site, Calvert County, Md. (ca. 1690–1715). (Rendering, Tim Scheirer after Chinh Hoang and Garry W. Stone; Jefferson Patterson Park and Museum.) Shown are the main dwelling and a slave quarter.

construction in the Chesapeake represents the outcome of the initial period of adaptation to the New World environment. It is no coincidence that this architectural form was in place by the late 1620s, at the same time that tobacco production was established as the region's economic mainstay.[13]

But while earthfast construction was selected at a relatively early date, experimentation in terms of house size and layout continued for several decades. In this second stage of adaptation, subtle adjustments to behavioral modes reflected ongoing changes in Chesapeake society. Having analyzed house plans derived from sixty-five sites from the period circa 1620 to 1720, Fraser Neiman identified several patterns in the variation of their layout and interior partitioning.[14]

For the period before 1640, experimentation is reflected in considerable variation in house size, in the large average number of rooms per dwelling, and in the variable placement of fireplaces and doorways. Between about 1640 and 1680, subtle shifts in dwelling size and arrangement occurred, with structure size stabilizing and direct entries predominating. By 1680 the dominant house form consisted of two main rooms, one or more end chimneys, and direct entry into the hall. Neiman relates these trends to changes in how space was used for the bulk processing of agricultural products and in the physical separation of indentured servants, and later slaves, from the planter household. Bulk processing was removed from dwellings, reducing the amount of interference with it from other household activities—with a corresponding reduction in the number of rooms required. In addition, laborers were removed to separate quarters.[15]

A well-known account by a French traveler in 1687 testifies to the widespread adoption of such housing:

Whatever their rank, & I know not why, they build only two rooms with some closets on the ground floor, & two rooms in the attic above; but they build several like this, according to their means. They build also a separate kitchen, a separate house for the Christian slaves, [and] one for the negro slaves.[16]

The developments in house form from about 1607 to 1680 appear most likely to reflect functional adaptive responses to colonization, with an initial period of experimentation followed by refinement of specific characteristics. Those characteristics were initially selected in response to particular ecological conditions, combined with the constraints resulting from imposition of the Chesapeake tobacco economy. The subsequent changes that occurred over the period from about 1680 to 1720 likely reflect a different set of stimuli, however, and are interpreted as stylistic in nature.

During the half-century after 1680—following the general selection of two-room, hall-and-parlor house plans—Chesapeake dwellings underwent significant changes. Even the wealthiest members of society continued to live in hall-and-parlor houses well into the eighteenth century, however. According to a sample of thirty-four room-by-room probate inventories for Virginia's wealthiest decedents from the period 1721 to 1730, twenty-seven lived in two-room houses, and two lived in houses consisting of one main room.[17]

But many of the houses in this period incorporated substantial stylistic additions. These included the substitution of brick for wood, with

Fig. 2. Taliaferro Site, overall view Caroline County, Va. [late seventeenth–early eighteenth century]. (Photo, Carter L. Hudgins.) The
brick foundation and brick-lined cellar are visible.

either full masonry construction or complete brick foundations instead
of posts set in the ground. The use of brick reflected a number of developments, including the improving economic position of the planter
elite, the greater permanence of such building, and the desire to emulate English traditions. Building in brick, therefore, served the dual purpose of announcing the owner's current economic standing and laying
claim to exalted social position, either actual or desired. In 1705 Robert
Beverley noted the recent trend to build in brick: "The private buildings
are of late very much improved; several Gentlemen of late having built
themselves large brick houses." Another extremely visible change was the
regularization of facades according to notions of Georgian symmetry.[18]

A recently excavated house site in Caroline County, Virginia, identified as the dwelling of John Taliaferro and dating to the late seventeenth century, exhibits a brick foundation and brick-lined cellar. The
interior arrangement of space suggests that it probably continued the
traditional plan of two, or perhaps three, rooms (fig. 2). Ocean Hall,

Fig. 3. Ocean Hall, St. Mary's County, Md., 1703. (Photo, Dennis J. Pogue.) An early dwelling of full masonry construction.

located in lower St. Mary's County, Maryland, represents the next level in brick construction. It not only boasts a full brick foundation but also complete masonry walls (fig. 3). Its date of construction has been firmly established as 1703, based on application of the technique of dendrochronology.[19]

Even more important in terms of social relations was the introduction of novel elements in the layout of houses. The most significant deviation from the dominant late seventeenth-century plan was the addition of a central passage, situated between the hall and parlor. According to both the documentary record and the limited evidence provided by extant structures, houses with central passages first began to appear with some frequency during the early years of the eighteenth century. The adoption of the central passage has been interpreted as an extension of the separation of servants from those whom they served. In the later decades of the seventeenth century, this resulted in the erection of separate servants' dwellings. Soon thereafter, the addition of the passage further separated private living spaces from intruders. As the eighteenth century wore on, houses underwent even greater seg-

mentation into public and private spaces, with new types of rooms—
such as dining rooms and withdrawing rooms—added to accommodate
more specialized uses. All of these developments were essentially stylistic in nature, serving the important purpose of marking status.[20]

A remarkable example of this new type of construction, carried
out on a grand scale by one of the wealthiest men in all of the American
colonies, is Corotoman, the home of Robert "King" Carter. Carter
erected his house about 1721; it was completely destroyed by fire in
1729. Like Ocean Hall, Corotoman was brick, but it also incorporated
a fashionable central passage. At 40 by 90 feet in dimension and two-
and-a-half stories in height, Corotoman was more than twice as large
as Ocean Hall. Carter's home also boasted such costly details as a stone-
paved basement, a semisubterranean gallery running the entire length
of one long facade, and decorative brickwork. The interior appointments were similarly ambitious, and Corotoman was widely regarded
as the "grandest mansion" in the colony. If nothing else, Corotoman
was a clear signal to Carter's fellow citizens of his claim to social prominence.[21]

SUBSISTENCE

As the result of analyzing faunal assemblages excavated from eighteen
domestic sites in Virginia and Maryland, broad patterns of changes in
subsistence practices have been identified. Henry Miller studied the
assemblages with reference to the frontier model explicitly framing his
analysis. The frontier paradigm views the trajectory of adaptation to
a new environment as entailing predictable adjustments to social and
cultural norms. The fundamental adaptations are viewed as economic
ones, modifications to what other scholars have identified as the mode
of production. The course of the selective process is enumerated as,
first, a period of simplification in face of new challenges, gradually leading to an improved adaptive "fit" and a fully adapted mode of production. The cultural trajectory is envisioned as paralleling this continuum,
with an initial period of "cultural impoverishment"—or simplification—eventually giving way to stabilization, "maturity," and cultural
elaboration. Therefore, this model assumes the fundamental correla-
tion between socioeconomic shifts and culture change.[22]

Miller interpreted the results of his study as generally supporting the frontier model and reflecting the colonization process. Evidence for "cultural impoverishment" was inferred from greatly simplified agricultural and animal husbandry practices, better suited to an uncleared woodland area than to England. A more diffuse subsistence was employed as well, with a much greater reliance on wild resources than was the case at home. Over the course of the century, stability, uniformity, and complexity in subsistence increased, which is interpreted as reflecting the transformation of the Chesapeake from a frontier to a mature society.[23]

The initial trends identified by Miller suggest functional adaptations, which were in direct response to the New World ecology. Different animal species, both wild and domestic, were selected; methods of animal husbandry were adapted; and menus changed accordingly. More subtle adjustments continued to occur over the succeeding decades, including the increase in importance of the traditional English food sources—beef and pork—and a reduction in the proportion of wild species consumed (table 1). This change is linked to improved animal husbandry practices that support the interpretation of the Chesapeake's evolution from a frontier.[24]

The third stage of development in diet, reflecting stylistic instead of functional changes, began during the first years of the eighteenth century. Pork and beef continued to be the preferred foods, but the meat was prepared differently, new sauces and spices were introduced, and variety in dishes increased. As with many other elements of material culture, adoption of these new preferences represented opportunities for social display. Anne Yentsch argues that these changes were so wide ranging as to indicate a shift from—in her terms—a "folk" to a "courtly" foodways tradition. The folk tradition represented an older, conservative mode of behavior well suited to a frontier environment, while courtly cuisine was the ascendant fashion, imported from England, that emphasized new ways of preparation and allowed for ostentatious display.[25]

CERAMICS

Patterns of changing ceramic use in the Chesapeake also indicate a period of functional adjustment, followed by stylistic elaboration. The

Table 1. Percentages of Meat from Domestic and Wild Species by
Temporal Period

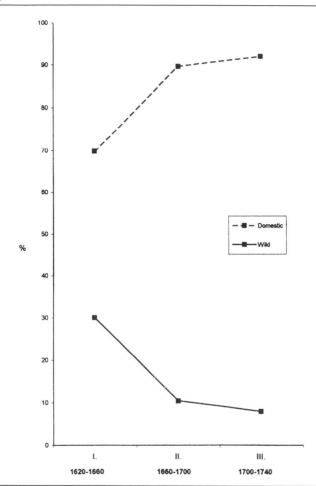

Note: Sites represented, in chronological order: The Maine, Kingsmill Tenement, St. John's, Calvert House, Bennett Farm, Chancellor's Point, Will's Cove, Drummond, Smith's Townland, Clifts, Country's House, Pettus, Utopia, Van Sweringen, Bray, John Hicks, Deacon's Tenant, and Pope's Creek. Because of their broad occupation span, several sites are represented in more than one temporal period.

following discussion is largely based on data provided by Yentsch, with the addition of several ceramic assemblages garnered from other published sources and from unpublished artifact catalogues. A total of nineteen ceramic assemblages that have been systematically categorized according to vessel types are available and have been arrayed according to functional groups: preparation and food storage, food distribution, food consumption, traditional beverages, and new beverages—primarily tewares.[26]

By the second quarter of the seventeenth century, the process of adaptation to the new Chesapeake environment was manifested in what Yentsch characterizes as a traditional, or folk, cuisine. This conservative tradition emphasized the preparation of communal, one-pot meals. In terms of ceramics, this usage is reflected archaeologically by the consistently high proportion of food preparation vessels and a correspondingly low proportion of individualized tablewares.[27]

For the ten sites spanning the period circa 1618 to 1680, food preparation wares average almost half (49.9 percent) of the total assemblages, with beverages averaging only 24.5 percent. The high percentage of preparation vessels probably reflects maintenance of a conservative foodways tradition, one that did not tax the limited resources of frontier families.[28] With the introduction of tewares and a proliferation of Staffordshire drinking vessels beginning about 1680, the number and proportion of beverage containers increase. The period circa 1680 to 1700 marks a transition in terms of the composition of ceramic assemblages, with the average percentage of preparation vessels declining to 43.6 percent and combined beverages increasing to 33 percent. From about 1700 to 1730, the proportions of food preparation vessels and beverage containers are virtually reversed from the early period, with only 21.4 percent food preparation and 55.2 percent combined beverages (table 2).

Changes in the proportions of the vessels constituting these categories show diachronic trends apparently reflecting a major shift in foodways that suggests the onset of a consumer society. Yentsch points to these data as evidence for a "trend towards . . . the presentation of individualized servings of food and drink at dining." These data largely support the findings made by James Deetz in New England, where he found an increase in the number of individualized vessels for consumption, particularly drinking vessels.[29]

Table 2. Breakdown of Ceramic Assemblages Comparing Food
Preparation and Beverage Vessels

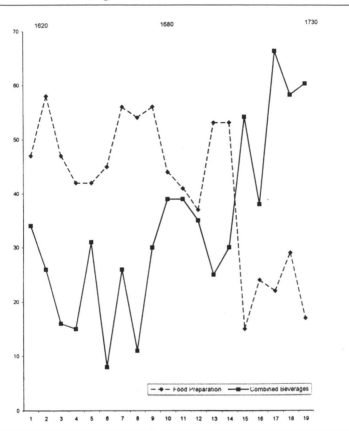

Sites represented, in chronological order: The Maine, Pasbehay, Kingsmill Tenement, Hampton, Bennett Farm, Compton, Utopia, Pettus, Clifts, 18Cv169, Van Sweringen, Drummond, King's Reach, Hicks, and Calvert. Because of their broad occupation
span, several sites are represented by multiple assemblages.

HOUSEHOLD FURNISHINGS

For the majority of the Anglo-American inhabitants of the seventeenth-century Chesapeake, the picture of their "domestic lifestyle," or "standard of living," that has emerged from more than two decades of documentary research is one of "rude sufficiency." For those at the very bottom of the social ladder, their lifestyle has been described as "remarkably, almost unimaginably, primitive." Even those fortunate few wealthiest households still generally lived in houses that, in comparison with those of their kin who remained in England, were small, dark, and drafty earthfast structures. Finally, higher social standing most often was demonstrated simply by owning more of the same generally utilitarian possessions as those found in the homes of poorer neighbors.[30]

Artifact assemblages from more than twenty sites, together spanning almost the entire first century of settlement, have been analyzed and tabulated. While in general these data support the image of a decidedly plain lifestyle, significant exceptions are indicated. Most important, this evidence suggests that the "unimaginably primitive" living conditions that have been ascribed to households in the lower economic ranks may be a somewhat exaggerated image. When taken together with dietary evidence, this information suggests that daily life for even the lowest rung of Chesapeake society may not have been as crude as is portrayed by recent documentary scholarship.[31]

Historian James Horn's comparative study of everyday rural life in England and in the Chesapeake during the second half of the seventeenth century suggests a period of cultural impoverishment in the colonies. As a result of comparing probate evidence from St. Mary's County, Maryland, and the Vale of Berkeley, Gloucestershire, Horn concluded that with few exceptions the living conditions of the Marylanders was generally much lower than in England.

Most Marylanders were found to lack such basic items as bedsteads to elevate mattresses off the floor, tables, and furniture for sitting—all items that commonly are found listed in Vale of Berkeley inventories in all wealth categories. In addition to the absence in many Maryland households of such seemingly essential objects as tables, chairs, and beds, Horn found that the items listed often were described as "old" or "worn." Such descriptors are extremely rare in the English inventories, suggesting that marginal objects continued in use in colonial households long after they would have been discarded in England. Other qualitative differences between the two communities include the composition of metal household items. In Maryland, less costly iron was by far the most common material for a variety of household utensils. In the Vale, fully 81.1 percent of the poorest households possessed at least one brass utensil and 83.8 percent had one pewter object; 98.1 percent of the households in the middle category owned brass and pewter.[32]

As a means of balancing these inventory-derived findings, a sample of household-level, archaeologically recovered artifact assemblages has been analyzed. As Chesapeake society during the colonial period overwhelmingly was made up of individual families and their bound servants and/or slave laborers residing in dispersed plantations, the household is the selected unit of inquiry for this study. To be able to consider these data quantitatively, the sample should be representative of the population as a whole. In this case, most crucially, it should span the entire period under investigation and include representatives from all wealth categories.

Even though a large number of sites have been intensively investigated, considerable limitations exist for the sample that has been assembled. The data are sufficiently broadly distributed in time to enable identification of patterns inferred as diachronically associated. The limitation of the overall sample size introduces substantial opportunity for error, however. Moreover, assessments of economic standing for the occupants of most of these sites is problematic, at best. Therefore, it has been difficult to assign assemblages to different wealth categories in any systematic fashion. Even an ordinal scale discrimination—into high, middle, and low wealth categories—is problematic and has produced a distribution heavily skewed toward the middle. Given these admitted limitations, the patterns that will be discussed here must be considered tentative.

One suggestive outcome of this exercise is the finding that the Maine site, located near Jamestown Island and the earliest of the sites included in this sample (occupied from about 1618 to 1625), had a relatively high total of ten of the twelve indexed categories represented. Included were a total of eighty-eight ceramic vessels—both finewares and coarsewares related to food storage, preparation, and consumption—fifteen table knives, and numerous spoons. Such a diversity and quantity of material culture is noteworthy given the early period and limited time span that the site was occupied. In contrast, the probable dwelling associated with these domestic objects was an insubstantial earthfast structure, comprising a single room measuring 20 by 22 feet, and a four-foot-wide shed addition.[33]

The richness of the Maine site household assemblage likely reflects the importation of relatively intact English traditions during the initial period of Chesapeake colonization. Ivor Nöel Hume also recovered similar examples of elaborate English clothing and other household accoutrements at the site of Martin's Hundred, another early settlement on the James River, which was occupied from 1619 until the 1630s. This site reflects the fragile nature of English colonization of the Chesapeake more graphically than most, as it was one of the settlements hardest hit during the Indian uprising of 1622. Features interpreted as the remnants of defensive palisades, along with large numbers of artifacts representing armor and weaponry, testify to the sometimes volatile nature of life on the Chesapeake frontier.[34]

The archaeological data produced by tabulating the selected items for the sites under investigation does, however, support the overall finding of numerous inventory studies. These suggest that, for the last half of the seventeenth century, the range of domestic materials for rich and poor alike was quite limited. The richness and diversity of materials found at the Maine and Martin's Hundred sites appears to have given way to a rather homogeneous material culture remarkable primarily for its sameness. Thus, the selective process had performed its function, producing a prescribed range of household items needed for life on the frontier. The constraints on Chesapeake society were so great that even those with means to acquire more amenities of life generally contented themselves with the same types of objects as their poorer neighbors.[35]

That this state of affairs underwent considerable change over the next several decades is suggested by a wide range of evidence, such as the architectural and foodways data and inventory studies discussed earlier. By the beginning of the eighteenth century, the rise of the Chesapeake landed gentry epitomized changing class relations that had a major impact on the social role of material culture. Consumer goods were vested with added significance as markers of social position. Such markers took on increased importance as reflections of class conflict resulting from the stratification of society among the landed elite, the growing group of middling to poor planters, and the underclass of

African American slaves. In such a society, competition and emulation became important strategies in social relations.[36]

TOWARD A CONSUMER REVOLUTION

The prevailing interpretations of colonial Chesapeake society stress the contrasts between an unstable frontier in the seventeenth century and the "golden age" of the planter elite in the eighteenth. The former was improvisational and characterized by a homogenous group of men of humble means making a new start in the New World, often by taking their first steps as indentured servants. The latter was the product of entrenched planter families whose extensive holdings included large numbers of African slaves. By extension, the historical study of the Chesapeake during the eighteenth century often has taken the form of exceedingly detailed analyses of the careers and the writings of this wealthy and privileged planter class.

The story of the development of the eighteenth-century planter society, which has taken hold of the imagination of generations of Americans, scholarly and nonacademic alike, is inextricably inter-twined with the developments of the preceding century. The trajectory of social and cultural development during the first hundred years of settlement had a direct effect on those to follow. It was not personal idiosyncrasy that led wealthy men such as Robert Carter to build large and fashionable dwellings. These structures, and the agendas of their builders, were the result of a hundred years of social development and a middle stop in the longer span of colonial history.

The complementary concepts of stylistic and functional change have been introduced in this context as a means of linking the histories of the two periods in a way that emphasizes their continuity. The various sets of evidence pertaining to the development of Anglo-American soci-ety in the Chesapeake during the course of the seventeenth century combine to support the findings of historians indicating that significant sociocultural changes occurred. Data provided by studies of architec-ture, subsistence, and ceramics provide strong archaeological evidence for shifting social and cultural norms. Initially, these changes appear most likely to reflect processes of adaptation resulting from colonization of the Chesapeake frontier. With growing social stability and general economic prosperity, Chesapeake fortunes could be turned to more frivolous, if symbolically laden, pursuits.

---

[1] This portrayal of early Chesapeake society is, by now, quite familiar as the result of a great many studies produced over the last 2 decades by the "Chesapeake School" of social historians. Just a few of those that have framed the development of this essay include: Lois Carr and Russell Menard, "Immigration and Opportunity: The Freedman in Early Colonial Maryland," in Thad Tate and David Ammerman, eds., *The Chesapeake in the Seventeenth Century: Essays on Anglo-American Society and Politics* (New York: W. W. Norton, 1979), pp. 206–42; Gloria Main, *Tobacco Colony: Life in Early Maryland, 1650–1720* (Princeton: Princeton University Press, 1982); Edmund Morgan, *American Slavery, American Freedom: The Ordeal of Colonial Virginia* (New York: W. W. Norton, 1975); and Lois Carr, Russell Menard, and Lorena Walsh, *Robert Cole's World: Agriculture and Society in Early Maryland* (Chapel Hill: University of North Carolina Press, 1991); but see David Hackett Fischer, *Albion's Seed: Four British Folkways in America* (New York: Oxford University Press, 1989), pp. 207–25, for an interpretation of seventeenth-century Virginia that stresses the social importance of a transplanted English elite beginning in midcentury.

[2] Lorena Walsh, " 'Till Death Us Do Part': Marriage and Family in Seventeenth-Century Maryland," in Tate and Ammerman, *Chesapeake in the Seventeenth Century*, pp. 126–52; Carr and Menard, "Immigration and Opportunity," pp. 206–10.

[3] Carr, Menard, and Walsh, *Robert Cole's World*, pp. 157–66; Carr and Menard, "Immigration and Opportunity," pp. 233–35; Jack Greene, *Pursuits of Happiness: The Social Development of Early Modern British Colonies and the Formation of American Culture* (Chapel Hill: University of North Carolina Press, 1988), pp. 85–87.

[4] Main, *Tobacco Colony*, pp. 25–27; Carr, Menard, and Walsh, *Robert Cole's World*, pp. 159–62; Greene, *Pursuits of Happiness*, pp. 83–85.

[5] Carr, Menard, and Walsh, *Robert Cole's World*, pp. 164–66; Allan Kulikoff, *Tobacco and Slaves: The Development of Southern Cultures in the Chesapeake, 1680–1800* (Chapel Hill: University of North Carolina Press, 1986), pp. 4–8; Greene, *Pursuits of Happiness*, pp. 81–101.

[6] Lois Carr and Lorena Walsh, "The Standard of Living in the Colonial Chesapeake," *William and Mary Quarterly*, 3d ser., vol. 45, no. 1 (1988): 135–43; Barbara Carson, "Living Habits in Seventeenth-Century Maryland" (Paper presented at the Third Hall of Records Conference, "Maryland: A Product of Two Worlds," St. Mary's City, 1984); Barbara Carson and Cary Carson, "Styles and Standards of Living in Southern Maryland, 1670–1752" (Paper presented at the annual meeting of the Southern Historical Association, Atlanta, 1976); Main, *Tobacco Colony*, pp. 247–48.

[7] Neil McKendrick, "The Consumer Revolution of Eighteenth-Century England," in Neil McKendrick, J. Brewer, and J. H. Plumb, eds., *The Birth of a Consumer Society: The Commercialization of Eighteenth-Century England* (Bloomington: Indiana University Press, 1982), pp. 9–25; Cary Carson, "The Consumer Revolution in Colonial British America: Why Demand?" in Cary Carson, Ronald Hoffman, and Peter Albert, eds., *Of Consuming Interests: The Style of Life in the Eighteenth Century* (Charlottesville: University Press of Virginia, 1994), pp. 483–697.

[8] Carson, "Consumer Revolution," p. 523.

[9] Lorena Walsh, "Urban Amenities and Rural Sufficiency: Living Standards and

Consumer Behavior in the Colonial Chesapeake, 1643–1777," *Journal of Economic History* 43 (1983): 109–17; Carr and Walsh, "Standard of Living," pp. 137–38.

[10] Carson, "Consumer Revolution," pp. 483–697; David Jordan, "Political Stability and the Emergence of a Native Elite in Maryland," in Tate and Ammerman, *Chesapeake in the Seventeenth Century*, pp. 266–69.

[11] Fraser Neiman, "Domestic Architecture at the Clifts Plantation: The Social Context of Early Virginia Building," in Dell Upton and John Vlach, eds., *Common Places: Readings in American Vernacular Architecture* (Athens: University of Georgia Press, 1986), pp. 292–314; Cary Carson, Norman Barka, William Kelso, Garry Stone, and Dell Upton, "Impermanent Architecture in the Southern American Colonies," *Winterthur Portfolio* 16, nos. 2/3 (Summer/Autumn 1981): 135–96.

[12] Dennis Pogue, *King's Reach and Seventeenth-Century Plantation Life* (Annapolis: Maryland Historical and Cultural Publications, 1990).

[13] James Horn, "Adapting to a New World: A Comparative Study of Local Society in England and Maryland, 1650–1700," in Lois Carr, Philip Morgan, and Jean Russo, eds., *Colonial Chesapeake Society* (Chapel Hill: University of North Carolina Press, 1988), p. 154; Neiman, "Domestic Architecture," pp. 303–306; Carson et al., "Impermanent Architecture," pp. 141–55.

[14] Fraser Neiman, "Temporal Patterning in House Plans from the Seventeenth-Century Chesapeake," in Theodore Reinhart and Dennis Pogue, eds., *The Archaeology of Seventeenth-Century Virginia* (Richmond: Dietz Press, 1993), pp. 251–83.

[15] Neiman, "Temporal Patterning," pp. 261–70.

[16] Durand de Dauphine, *A Huguenot Exile in Virginia; or, Voyages of a Frenchman Exiled for His Religion, with a Description of Virginia and Maryland*, trans. and ed. Gilbert Chinard (New York: Press of the Pioneers, 1934), pp. 119–20.

[17] Dell Upton, "Vernacular Domestic Architecture in Eighteenth-Century Virginia," in Upton and Vlach, *Common Places*, p. 317.

[18] Robert Beverley, *The History and Present State of Virginia*, ed. Louis B. Wright (Chapel Hill: University of North Carolina Press, 1947), p. 289.

[19] Dendrochronology entails taking bore samples from wooden structural members and comparing their growth rings with a master sequence of patterns of annual growth that has been developed for the region. Mark Edwards, "Dating Buildings by Tree Ring Analysis," in *Three Centuries of Maryland Architecture* (Annapolis: Maryland Historical Trust, 1982), p. 26.

[20] Upton, "Vernacular Domestic Architecture," pp. 321–23; Neiman, "Temporal Patterning," pp. 267–70.

[21] Carter Hudgins, "Patrician Culture, Public Ritual, and Political Authority in Virginia, 1680–1740" (Ph.D. diss., College of William and Mary, 1984), pp. 248–56.

[22] Henry Miller, "Colonization and Subsistence Change on the Seventeenth-Century Chesapeake Frontier" (Ph.D. diss., Michigan State University, 1984), p. 372; Eric Wolf, *Europe and the People without History* (Berkeley: University of California Press, 1982).

[23] Miller, "Colonization and Subsistence," pp. 16–17.

[24] Miller, "Colonization and Subsistence," pp. 372–76, table 1 after Miller's table 21, p. 294.

[25] Anne Yentsch, "Chesapeake Artefacts and Their Cultural Context: Pottery and the Food Domain," *Post-Medieval Archaeology* 25 (1991): 25–72; Anne Yentsch, "Minimum Vessel Lists as Evidence of Change in Folk and Courtly Traditions of Food Use," *Historical Archaeology* 24, no. 3 (1990): 24–53.

[26] Yentsch, "Chesapeake Artefacts," pp. 35–60; Dennis Pogue, "Standard of Living in the Seventeenth-Century Chesapeake: Patterns of Variability among Artifact

Assemblages," in Reinhart and Pogue, *Archaeology of Seventeenth-Century Virginia*, pp. 371–99.

[27] Yentsch, "Minimum Vessel Lists," p. 34.

[28] Yentsch, "Chesapeake Artefacts," p. 43.

[29] Yentsch, "Minimum Vessel Lists," p. 35; James Deetz, *In Small Things Forgotten: The Archaeology of Early American Life* (New York: Anchor Press, 1977), p. 57.

[30] Lorena Walsh, "A Culture of 'Rude Sufficiency': Life Styles in Maryland's Western Shore between 1658 and 1720" (Paper presented at the Annual Meeting of the Society for Historical Archaeology, Nashville, 1979); Carson and Carson, "Styles and Standards," pp. 6, 13; Horn, "Adapting to a New World," pp. 152–54.

[31] Henry Miller, "An Archaeological Perspective on the Evolution of Diet in the Colonial Chesapeake, 1620–1745," in Carr, Morgan, and Russo, *Colonial Chesapeake Society*, p. 195; Carr and Walsh, "Standard of Living," p. 135.

[32] Horn, "Adapting to a New World," pp. 152–64.

[33] Alain Outlaw, *Governor's Land: Archaeology of Early Seventeenth-Century Settlements* (Charlottesville: University Press of Virginia, 1990), pp. 14–15, 53–54, 100.

[34] Ivor Nöel Hume, *Martin's Hundred* (New York: Alfred A. Knopf, 1982).

[35] Carson and Carson, "Styles and Standards," pp. 5, 13.

[36] Greene, *Pursuits of Happiness*, p. 93; Carson, "Consumer Revolution," pp. 483–697.

The Evolution of the House in Early Virginia

Jan K. Gilliam

In 1775 Dr. Samuel Johnson, the great lexicographer, defined *house* as "a place wherein a man lives; a place of human abode." His definition of *home* was subtly different—"his own house; the private dwelling." Home connoted something more personal—the relationship of the inhabitant to the structure in which he lived. It was in the eighteenth century that the Virginia gentry house evolved into a home in the sense of moving from a place where people sought shelter from the elements, through the stage of house as social proclamation of rank, status, and wealth, to a place where people found shelter from others, a domestic place of comfort shared with family and close friends (fig. 1). The living structure housed fewer inhabitants than previously, and use of the house changed and adapted as prevailing attitudes toward self, peers, and children changed. By the third quarter of the eighteenth century, architects Robert and James Adam could include in their text, "The parade, the convenience, and social pleasures of life, being better understood, are more strictly attended to in the arrangement and disposition of apartments."[1] This was particularly true for the Virginia gentry as the nature of their lifestyle meant that their houses served both public and private functions. This evolution occurred primarily among the gentry—the

This essay is based on research begun by the author and Betty Leviner, curator of exhibition buildings at Colonial Williamsburg, while working on *Furnishing Williamsburg's Historic Buildings*. The author wishes to thank Leviner for her support while working on this project and for her helpful comments and careful editing of this paper.

Fig. 1. "The Story of Pamela, Plate 12," London, Eng., 1745. Line engraving; H. 12½", W. 16". (Colonial Williamsburg Foundation.)

upper level of society who could afford to make changes in their lifestyles. Most Virginians were of the middle and lower ranks who were less likely or unable to build new homes. Separate spaces within a house, made necessary by new rituals and ideas of privacy, also seemed beyond their means or needs.

Virginia colonists' concepts of the house and how it functioned in their lives was different from our notions today. Colonists were born, grew up, were married, took ill, died, and had their funerals in their homes. Family members were much more aware of the life passages of others since they occurred at frequent intervals in the domestic setting. John Mason, the son of statesman George Mason, writing years after his mother's death, recalled the times spent with her during her illness, memories that also brought vividly to mind the "Furniture and Structure of her Room." Even though he was only seven years old when she died, he remembered being with her on her bed when she was sick, sharing her prescribed milk punch, and receiving her final blessings and advice just before she died. Both her illness and death occurred at home in the first floor chamber where family members could not help but be constantly aware of, and influenced by, her presence.[2]

Illness of one or more family members affected the entire household—from the servant who attended the sick to the family who worried over the patient, and to the one ill, who might be confined to one room for an extended period of time. Diarists of the period frequently recorded the illnesses of friends, neighbors, and family members. Everyone was affected in some way by sickness. William Byrd II had to cope with the illness of his first-born son Parke, which lingered for about three weeks during which time his daughter Evelyn also got sick. The children fluctuated between improving health and relapse into sickness, causing much anxiety for the parents. When Ben Carter fell ill, Mrs. Carter insisted on moving him to the main house so she could be near him and ensure his constant care. Parents had reason to be anxious since children often died in the first few years of life. Byrd lost his son Parke before the boy was a year old. Mrs. Carter lost six children during her lifetime, several of whom were only a few days old.[3]

Adults also suffered illnesses that often confined them to one room of the house until they were well. Mrs. Carter, becoming ill February 21, retired to her chamber and did not emerge again until March 2, when she felt well enough to dine with the family. At the same time, the Carters' housekeeper kept to her room because of pains. As mentioned earlier, Mrs. Mason spent much of her illness confined to her chamber. Old age also required a special place in the household. Seventy-year-old Anne Matthews of York County, crippled with rheumatism, wrote to John Norton that she had to give up keeping her own house and move in with family, where she was "helpt from the Bed to Chair Confind to one Room."[4]

These frequent encounters with illness meant adjustments to daily life and the running of the household. The sick were kept at home since there was no alternative place to send them. While a doctor might visit the patient, it was left to the family and servants to minister to the sick on a daily basis. This might require new sleeping arrangements for parents, spouses, servants, or siblings. It might cause a change in the way the house functioned as well as affect the interaction among family members.

Other elements that affected the domestic lives of the colonists were the celebrations of rites associated with the church—christenings, weddings, and funerals—which often took place in the home. Frances Baylor Hill, a young girl who kept a journal for the year 1797, attended many of these events at the homes of friends. In March she saw two weddings take place in one evening in the same house followed by dancing and supper. In September she and her mother went to visit with her sister who had just had a baby. The new mother fell ill and soon died. In one day the child was christened and the mother buried. While the events are related by one girl, she refers to the many other people who were present at these events. These visitors, whether family or friends, stayed at the house, some for just the day while others remained for several days.[5] Guests had to be put up in the house, fed, and entertained. The events, whether joyful or sorrowful, drew people together in the domestic setting.

Daily life consisted of more than simply visiting and the occasional celebration of special events. Mundane activities were carried out every day in the house. William Byrd's daily routine consisted of reading and exercise in the morning. He might also have written, whether for pleasure or business, and kept up with his many correspondents. For the ladies there were meals and housekeeping to oversee, but there was also time to read, write letters, and sew. Frances Baylor Hill's diary is a testimony to the energy and activity of a young Virginia lady. She often visited with neighbors, but she also stayed at home to read and to knit, quilt, sew, iron, and cook. Some children attended school, which was held in the house or in a building nearby. Mrs. Nelson of Yorktown provided her children with religious training every morning in her chamber. The Carter children were taught academic subjects by their tutor but also engaged in dancing lessons held for a few days at a time at a planter's house. The Carter girls learned and practiced music with their father, Robert Carter.[6]

With family members each engaged in their own activities, the house was a busy place. Children, visitors, and parents all moved about and interacted in the familiar domestic setting. Although the home was the site of family events, the family also played host to the outside world. Hospitality was a requirement of eighteenth-century society. Lack of it provoked extreme indignation and social censure. John Mason wrote: "the Habit was Families who were connected or on Friendly terms to visit and spend several Days or weeks at the respective mansions of each other." Throughout the century, travelers and diarists frequently recorded examples of Virginians' hospitality and "full tables and open doors."[7]

The diaries of Hill and Fithian, tutor to Robert Carter's children, include many entries referring to the times when they visited others' homes or when visitors came to call at their houses. Hill frequently went out to visit, sometimes staying overnight and at other times remaining just for dinner or the afternoon. One January dinner was attended by many friends including ten children. On the other hand, in April, after having spent a few days visiting friends, Hill arrived home to find her mother by herself and very lonesome. Sometimes she returned to find an unexpected number of people there, ready to dine and be entertained. Fithian was a less eager traveler, but nonetheless made an effort to go about the neighborhood and to accept some of the frequent invitations he received to dine out.[8] Meals, whether breakfast, dinner, or supper, attracted visitors—some for social reasons and at others for business.

Visitors might drop by at any time just to chat or in response to a casual invitation to dine or to visit. Other, more planned activities, drew guests from all over. Special events such as a dancing school, a ball, a wedding, or a funeral could draw guests and keep them at the house for several days. A house saw a constant flow of guests coming and going. These visitors had to be fed, entertained, and boarded for as long as they chose to stay. Some overnight visits were unplanned but rather forced on the guest by weather. Putting up so many people, planned or unplanned, caused adjustments in the house. When the dancing school was held at Nomini Hall, Fithian breakfasted with a few adults as well as eighteen young men and women. All these guests had stayed overnight. Because the Carters were "thronged with company," Fithian had to share his accommodations with two of the young men. Because of the nature of the house and furnishings, it was possible to move things about and accommodate all the people. While this did not happen every day, it was frequent enough to occur several times in a year.[9]

Houses did not start out as the large plantation homes easily able to accommodate all of these functions. They had much more humble beginnings. In the seventeenth century, Englishmen arrived in Virginia hoping to acquire great riches and then return to England to live in style. Many of those who came, though, if they survived the harsh condi-

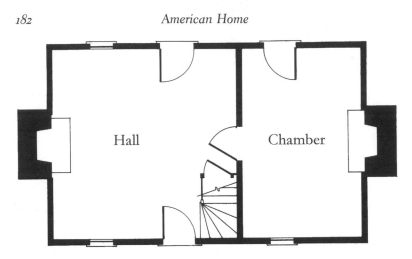

Fig. 2. Floor plan of a hall/chamber house. (Colonial Williamsburg Foundation.)

tions, did not gain immediate wealth but instead settled down to create a new life for themselves in a new colony. One of the necessities of life in the developing colony was to find shelter whether one intended to stay only a few months or several years. The first structures built for this purpose generally were simple wooden buildings often constructed on posts stuck in the ground rather than on more permanent-type foundations. These dwellings typically consisted of one or maybe two rooms on the first floor—the hall and the chamber, or parlor, as the bed/sitting area might be called—and a half story above (fig. 2). The hall was the principal room in the house opening directly to the outside. Here most of the activities of the family took place, including entertaining, cooking, eating, and sleeping. The room contained simple furnishings that could be used for a variety of functions.[10] A single table provided a flat surface where one could work, prepare a meal, eat, and play games. The chamber, if the family were wealthy enough to afford a second room, provided a space away from all the activity in the hall.

As the colony developed, society began to take shape. For several decades, Englishmen, most without families or wives, had arrived in Virginia. Some came as indentured servants who attached themselves to a master until they could branch off on their own. Although women and families did come to the colony in limited numbers, men outnum-

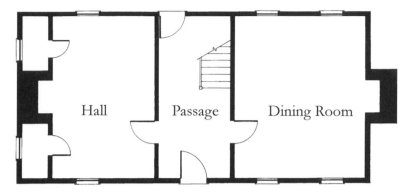

Fig. 3. Floor plan of a hall/passage/parlor house. (Colonial Williamsburg Foundation.) Although not shown here, the chamber was a room to the back of the dining room and only accessible through that space. The chamber could be a small room taking away some of the dining room space or an entirely new addition to the back.

bered women for much of the early period. The high mortality rate also affected the demographics of society. These factors made it more difficult for Virginians than for their Northern counterparts to settle into family life, and smaller impermanent living quarters gave way only slowly to more permanent houses. As the community stabilized and grew, Virginians began to build permanent dwellings either in one of the few established towns or as the center of a large plantation. As they settled in, the colony's well to do inhabitants found ways to control and order their society as well as their own lives. The houses they began to build or rebuild reflected this need for ordering.[11]

The common house plan of hall/chamber became separated by a center passage (fig. 3). With this division, the passage now opened directly to the outside, meaning the hall no longer received everyone or accommodated every activity. It became the formal point at which the outside world interacted with those inside. By the second quarter of the eighteenth century, the bed and most personal items were removed from the hall, further emphasizing its new role as the center of formal, social interaction. The chamber as the most private space slid around to the back of the house leaving room for an intermediate space called the dining room. Although termed *dining room*, it was not necessarily for this function alone but rather became the setting for many of the less formal activities previously encountered in the hall. With the addition of the intervening passage, which effectively shielded access to all other rooms, the planter could maintain control of circulation within the house. Even though this layout of rooms became the common plan, room usage continued to evolve as the needs and desires of the owners changed during the century.[12] As the house plan evolved, additional rooms were added to the second floor.

By midcentury the hall was the "center of the family's social landscape," as Dell Upton has phrased it. Entrance to this socially superior room was selective. Here the owner could make a visual statement about his social status and wealth and could regulate those with whom he chose to share this space. It was about this time too that the hall became more commonly called the *parlor*. The room contained some of the most elaborate furnishings and architectural detailing, which signified its status as the best room in the house. During the second half of the century, the parlor lost some of its preeminence to the increasingly important dining room.[13]

The passage was a subordinate space that was socially neutral. Visitors would enter the passage and from there be judged whether they were worthy to penetrate further into the planter's home or whether that was as far as they would be allowed. The passage, however, was found to be a particularly comfortable room in the summer because of the cross ventilation provided by doors at either end opening to the outside. Here one could also relax away from the formal atmosphere of the hall. Although perhaps used as a room only seasonally at first, the passage, especially with the addition of heat, could be lived in year round. Eventually the passage was a recognized room in itself. As in other areas of the house, the decoration and furnishings chosen for the space reflected this change by becoming more variable and numerous, and they became a further statement of the owner's status.[14]

The dining room, often located across the passage from the hall, was at first considered as a secondary room of the house. It was the room that became the center for all the informal activities inappropriate for the now formal hall. However, as dining grew in importance, so too did the room. The eighteenth century saw the act of consuming food grow into a social ritual performed by the gentry. In dining the gentry created an event that differentiated themselves from the rest of colonial society.[15] It was not just that they could serve more elaborate dishes or more exotic foods, that they could serve them off a whole panoply of fancy dining wares, and that they had the leisure time to sit while several courses were served but also that they knew how to conduct themselves at such affairs. The setting, food, and behavior created a significant gap between the lower classes and the gentry that the latter strived to maintain.

Previously, meals had been eaten from shared vessels from one pot attended by family and servants alike. By the end of the seventeenth century, servants and serving spaces were being relocated from the house to separate buildings. This physical separation of servants and their work further defined room usage within the house and the relationships of servants and masters.[16] With the exodus of servants, the expansion of rooms, and the growth in wealth, the gentry set about refining meals, especially dinner, into social events for themselves and their peers only.

Dining became an important part of the famed hospitality of the region. Since the dining room was now the setting for a special activity attended by a select group, the style and quality of the furnishings became more important. This room provided an opportunity to show off silver, ceramics, and glassware associated with dining, an area in which specialized pieces and forms had proliferated as meals became more elaborate. Eventually, as the importance of the meal grew, the dining room outstripped the parlor as the largest room in the house and occasionally even matched it in elegance. In some cases the rooms actually changed places so that the largest room featured dining (fig. 4). Other houses saw the additions of small dining rooms that accommodated informal meals and equipped the family with a more intimate space for socializing.[17]

This triad of public spaces—dining room, passage, and parlor— was complemented by the private space of the chamber. Here the family could retreat from the outside world to find some modicum of privacy. Many houses had a bedchamber on the first floor that could be the best chamber slept in by the master and mistress. In the larger houses additional chambers existed on the second floor for guests and other family members. In some instances, especially as the century progressed, the first floor was given over entirely to public and semipublic rooms with all chambers being above stairs. Even with this layout there

Fig. 4. Dining room, Peyton Randolph House, Williamsburg, Va. (Colonial Williamsburg Foundation.)

was still a definite hierarchy of rooms from the best chamber with a well-furnished highpost bed to much smaller rooms that might contain only a lowpost bed or two and a table. At Nomini Hall the four second-floor rooms were all designated chambers, one for Mr. and Mrs. Carter, one for the "young Ladies," and two for "occasional company." While the chamber might be primarily for sleeping and dressing, it also served as the mistress's space wherein she might entertain friends, oversee the household, and gather with family. A niece of Mrs. Nelson's wrote a charming piece about "a table and its history" in which she shares memories with an old-fashioned table owned by Mrs. Nelson. She reminds the table of the times when "one or two of her [Mrs. Nelson] young female friends [was] sitting with her, while you [the table] held the candle, tea things, work or Book, whichever she required." Mrs. Nelson also used her room each morning for catechizing her children and, once they had been dismissed, she stayed to engage in her own private devotions.[18]

Even though these rooms had acquired their own spheres of influence, their uses were not as rigid as the names might imply. The largest room in the house, whether it was the parlor or dining room, might accommodate a variety of activities if the number of guests demanded it. During winter, if a fire was burning brightly in one room, there was no need to waste fuel to heat another just for the sake of eating in the dining room. On New Year's Day Robert "King" Carter, suffering with gout, hobbled into the parlor, where he "sat most of the day" playing cards and eating. If because of illness or work one could not move about so freely, then the activities could come to him. Governor Gooch's bedchamber in the Governor's Palace in Williamsburg became the site of a meeting with a committee of burgesses when the ill governor could not appear at the Capitol.[19]

Many of these new houses were built on the Georgian plan of symmetry, which generally meant that there were two rooms on each side of the passage. There was a hall/parlor, a dining room, and a chamber; the function of the fourth room varied. In some gentry houses it was the study—a place for the master of the house to conduct business. He might also entertain friends in this more intimate setting in the same way that the mistress of the house might use her chamber. Sometimes the fourth room was a second dining room used only by the family when they were not entertaining more formally. In the case of Gunston Hall, John Mason referred to the room as the small dining room used by the family, while a larger, formal room for company was at the other, public, end of the house. However, the room became George Mason's study when he was involved in work and politics. He might shut himself away in the study or library leaving the family to make use of the other dining room so as not to disturb him. By 1775 Nomini Hall's first floor consisted of the dining room where the family usually sat, a second dining room for the children, a study or library for Mr. Carter, and a ballroom. Other uses were found for this fourth room as the needs of the owner dictated. Often the terms *back chamber* or *back room* were used, reflecting the unspecified nature of this space or the lack of any particular function associated with it. While the locations of these rooms varied as each house was built to an owner's specifications and needs, the names and basic uses of the rooms remained fairly consistent.[20]

By the second half of the eighteenth century, colonial builders used this Georgian vocabulary but adapted it to suit the needs of Virginia society, especially as it affected the control of social relations. Every time friends or family entered a house, the setting would be familiar because it was mirrored in their own houses. This evolution and expansion of space and privacy was mostly confined to the upper class. Many of the middling and lower-class families lived in smaller houses, some in the two-room structures prevalent earlier in the century. By the nineteenth century many of these Virginians still lived in one or two rooms, although they had begun to acquire more furnishings and individual goods.[21] While room specialization and privacy developed in the main house on gentry plantations, these ideas still remained foreign to those who lived on the outside—namely, the slaves, who lived in communal settings with very few dining amenities or private sleeping rooms.

Once a gentleman had made a decision about the layout of rooms in his dwelling, each interior space needed further refinement to make its purpose clear. "As Distress was the Parent of it [Architecture], so Convenience was the first Object it regarded: Magnificence and Decoration were the Result of long Refinement, and designed to flatter the Ostentation of the Owners." Architectural embellishments within each space established a hierarchy and helped to articulate a room's importance and use. Moldings, mantels, and fireplaces varied in elaboration and symbolism depending on the room in which they were found. When Robert Carter ordered wallpaper for three "parlors" in his house, he wanted good paper for one room, better paper for another, and the best paper for the third room.[22] Wallpaper alone, however, did not make the room complete.

Furnishings of all types further defined the spaces. With increased wealth and proliferation of objects available to consumers, owners could choose furnishings that served to make statements about the owner's status as well as the status of an individual room. Like the architectural embellishments of a room, the furniture placed in the spaces also had a hierarchy. The best chairs, those that were of better wood, more ornately carved, or of the latest fashion, were found in the best room, whether that was the parlor or dining room. Cheaper, less-fashionable, or plain chairs were relegated to less public rooms such as a bedchamber. Inventories of the period show this arrangement not only by listing pieces as "old" or "old fashioned" but also by assigning cash values to the pieces. These values help today's readers to know that chairs listed at more than £1 each will be very different from those costing only 5 shillings each. They will be in different settings within the house, the former in the dining room (see fig. 4), the latter in a back bedchamber.[23]

Virginia's eighteenth-century town dwellers spent more of their income on household furnishings than did the plantation owners. Townspeople not only came in closer contact with their peers, as well as stores and tradesmen offering a variety of goods, but they also socialized in well-furnished surroundings. Here there might be more pressure and desire to stay abreast of fashion and keep up or even outdo their neighbors.[24] In many letters and orders, the words "genteel," "handsome," and "fashionable" occur frequently. Yet goods were not solely for display. Virginians expressed a desire that goods be useful as well as elegant.

Many of the wealthier Virginians had agents in London with whom they kept accounts and from whom they ordered goods to be used in their houses in the colony. Everything could be ordered for the house, from the nails and hinges used in the construction of the house to the fireplace mantels and wallpaper used to embellish the interior. All furnishings, from the most elaborately carved chairs to the cheapest cooking pot, could also be purchased by invoice and sent over. John Page, Jr., later governor of Virginia, in a letter to John Norton, his agent in London, complained of his debts, which were the result of a poor crop and "the necessary Expences of an encreasing Family joined to the Commencement of Housekeeping in a large House." His "large house" was the Gloucester County mansion Rosewell, which he inherited.[25] Other York County residents who had dealings with the merchant company of John Norton and Sons sent lengthy invoices detailing the kinds and numbers of goods they wanted for their houses and families. Setting up and maintaining a large Virginia plantation did not come cheap, but Virginians were willing to spend their money (often going into debt) to acquire the goods they most wanted for their homes.

There were, of course, risks and disadvantages to ordering goods from such a distance. Virginians had to trust that their written requests would provide enough information so that the agents knew exactly what to purchase and send. Norton's son, John Hatley, had the advantage of being able to rely on his mother to purchase some of his goods in London and then ship them to Virginia. On one occasion, however, in her letter, she berates John Hatley, "If you would be more Explicit in your orders it will be more Satisfactory & the only way to be well serv'd." She then cites instances of his lack of specificity when ordering. For example, he ordered blankets without listing either the quantity or the sort. Once written for, it took time for goods to arrive, and one could never be sure that what would one day appear at the docks was exactly what had been ordered. Several letters to John Norton from his Virginia clients complain that the tradesmen frequented by Norton were sending over poor quality goods but charging first quality prices. Robert Carter Nicholas, as well as other correspondents, confirmed that "several Articles in my last Invoice Mrs. Nicholas assures me are charged higher than they could be bought in the Stores of Williamsburg, dear as they are." Peter Lyons wrote, "I know they [the tradesmen] think anything good enough for Virginia, but they should be informed better, and be made to know that the people in Virginia have a good taste and know when they are imposed on, as well if not better than most of their Gentry or Quality in England, and that when they send to London it is to get the best Goods in their kind not so much regarding price as quality."[26] Virginians wanted to furnish their homes and dress their families in the styles of London and not be looked upon as inferior.

There was clearly a great problem with buying goods sight unseen. Martha Jacquelin expressed her disappointment in her purchase of firetools, which arrived a year after she placed the order. They turned out to be too heavy for her to lift, so she had to send them back. Another problem was concern over the condition in which the goods arrived. Lyons, in the same letter that he discussed the poor quality of goods shipped, included in his invoice "one peice of Cambrick not to exceed nine Shillings per yard the peice that came this Year at six Shillings and three-pence was very coarse full of Holes and unfit for use." Improper packaging and unforeseen conditions during the long ocean voyage could cause damage to even high quality goods. William Reynolds opened a package of china newly arrived from London and found that the breakage was more than five percent.[27] All these concerns were the risks of buying directly from England.

Another option for acquiring goods was to buy from the local stores and tradesmen. These were patronized by a wide range of Virginians, from slaves and servants who had no alternative sources to those who could afford to order direct from England. The stores offered a great variety of goods, most imported from London. Goods were also shipped from the northern colonies into Virginia. *Virginia Gazette* advertisements of the period list the wide variety of items that could be purchased. One of the selling points of these advertisements was that goods,

Fig. 5. Parlor, George Wythe House, Williamsburg, Va. (Colonial Williamsburg Foundation.)

as well as tradespeople themselves, were direct or lately from London. Another source of furnishings was the family. Just as today, items were inherited and sold secondhand. The furnishings in a house would be a combination of new, old, and used pieces rather than being all of one period.

Access to these sources meant that the houses in which the colonists lived could be as simple or as elaborate as the owners could afford or chose to make them. Despite the variety of sources, rooms tended to be furnished with a basic group of objects appropriate to the primary use of the room. A parlor generally had a fashionable set of twelve chairs, a variety of table forms such as a card table or tea table, perhaps a looking glass, and some smaller accessories (fig. 5). The dining room was similarly furnished with a set of chairs, one or two dining tables, a side table, and the dining equipment (see fig. 4). Each bedchamber contained one or two beds, a dressing table and glass, a few chairs, and perhaps a clothespress or chest of drawers (fig. 6). This is just a general outline of the kinds of basic forms found in the rooms. Each owner

Fig. 6. Bedchamber, George Wythe House, Williamsburg, Va. (Colonial Williamsburg Foundation.)

chose what was best for his use. Since the use of the rooms varied, the pieces were moved from room to room as needed.

Each room took on a different look as the owners chose the styles, colors, and textiles for furnishings. They might buy new furniture for some rooms but not others. They might redecorate and remodel certain areas to suit their changing tastes and to stay in fashion. In 1762 Robert Carter ordered wallpaper for three rooms as well as the staircase and passage. Each room had a different color scheme, one crimson, one white with green leaves, and one blue with yellow flowers. This would have made a dramatic impression on anyone visiting him in his Williamsburg house located next door to the Governor's Palace. Several years later Carter and his family had moved to his plantation seat, Nomini Hall, because the house on Palace street was "not sufficiently roomy for our family." However, he did mention perhaps building an addition to their house in town so he might join his friends in Williamsburg again.[28]

Owners personalized their houses by making selections from the vast array of goods available and by decorating with such items as family portraits and silver as well as quilts and linens stitched by the women in the household. While written evidence of some of these more personal items is scarce, some of the less fragile objects have survived often because they were important pieces to the family. These tangible things along with written and graphic records provide a way to reconstruct the living arrangements of the past.

The interest and money lavished on their houses reflected not only personal taste, but also the gentry's desire for gentility and cultivation. Cultivation included personal refinement of grace, manners, and accomplishments. Such cultivated people met in select companies where each could display this learned behavior. A suitable environment prepared in the best taste was the obvious meeting place in which to mingle with one's peers. Janet Shaw, a woman traveling in the Carolina backcountry, expressed the importance of these refinements when she was entertained at an unfinished plantation: "Though the house was no house, yet the master and the furniture made you ample amends."[29] The houses provided the backdrop and the furnishings the setting for this refinement. The *Builder's Dictionary* expressed these sentiments under the heading Decorum or Decor—"Decency is particularly used in Architecture for the suitableness of a Building, and the several Parts and Ornaments thereof, to the Station and Occasion." Decorum was "to signify the observing a due Respect between the Inhabitant and Habitation." The house and its furnishings became a necessary extension of one's identity as a gentleman. Carter Hudgins identified Robert "King" Carter with his house—"Just as Carter's multiple roles in government overlapped with his role as planter, so the function and appearance of his house mixed the conventions of public buildings with those of private residence."[30]

As rooms divided and specific modes of entertainment and needs arose, the numbers and types of furnishings increased. Just as several years ago *computer desk* and *printer stand* were not official furniture terms, so too, in the seventeenth century, tea table was not a recognized furniture form. As activities became formalized and items were identified as unique to that event, tradesmen and manufacturers responded by developing specialized pieces that soon became standard equipment. As participants in these rituals, the gentry associated themselves with these events and the accompanying paraphernalia and the status inherent in them. Further into the eighteenth century, it became more common to list these pieces by name in inventories. A table was not only walnut or mahogany but might be a tea, card, backgammon, dressing, or dining table. These were not just names used at random; each piece had a specific, recognized form and size. Many of the furniture directories, such as Thomas Chippendale's, not only pictured these pieces but also included notes detailing in which rooms specific pieces should be properly placed. People began identifying with the objects in a way that they could not earlier in the period.[31] Despite this growing specificity, furnishings remained somewhat multipurpose as did the rooms in which they were placed.

Furniture was still portable and compact. Pieces were made to fit snugly against the wall out of the way, leaving the center of the room unencumbered by furniture not in use. Only the furniture required for a particular activity was pulled away from the wall and arranged about the room as the event or time of day dictated. The remaining pieces stayed tucked away until the activity changed and they were needed. Pieces were not only moved about within a room but also could be carried to other rooms of the house if needed or even to the outside if desired. Many of the Windsor chairs so common in late eighteenth-century passages were lightweight, painted green, and ideal for outdoor seating furniture. Furniture was moved about, too, according to the season. Carpets might be taken up in the summer and fireboards or flowers might replace the andirons in the fireplaces. Window curtains might be put up only in the wintertime to guard against drafts. This portability and adaptability allowed the owners to use their houses to their best advantage for any situation.[32] With the number of guests varying from day to day and the situation of the family changing whether due to illness or death or birth, this flexibility in furnishings would be particularly useful.

The houses in which the gentry lived were an integral part of their identity as members of this upper segment of society. In the Preface to the *Builder's Dictionary* is the statement: "Every Structure is raised to answer some particular End."[33] These gentry houses supplied the visual statement about who their owners were and what their status in the community was. This statement could be easily read and understood by colonial society whether the observer was part of the gentry or not. But this was the public side of the house. There was also the private side, which was far more intimate and transformed the house into a home. In this setting parents and children interacted with one another and with family and friends on a daily basis. It was here that the children learned from their parents' examples their place in society. But just as the evolution of spaces and furnishings changed as lifestyles changed during the eighteenth century, future generations would also see change in the way they viewed and used their homes. The eighteenth century was just one chapter in the evolution of the home.

---

[1] Samuel Johnson, *A Dictionary of the English Language* (1755; reprint, New York, 1979); Robert Adam, *The Works in Architecture of Robert and James Adam*, ed. Robert Oresko (New York: St. Martin's Press, 1975), p. 56.

[2] John Mason, "The Recollections of John Mason" (Gunston Hall Archives, Lorton, Va., typescript by Terry Dunn from the original manuscript), pp. 9–10.

[3] Louis B. Wright and Marion Tinling, eds., *The Secret Diary of William Byrd of Westover, 1709–1712* (Richmond: Dietz Press, 1941), pp. 177–87; Hunter Dickinson Farish, ed., *The Journal and Letters of Philip Vickers Fithian, 1773–1774: A Plantation Tutor of the Old Dominion* (Williamsburg, Va.: Colonial Williamsburg Fndn., 1957), p. 181.

[4] Farish, *Journal of Fithian*, pp. 67–69; Frances Norton Mason, ed., *John Norton and Sons, Merchants of London and Virginia* (Richmond: Dietz Press, 1937), p. 139.

[5] William K. Bottorff and Roy C. Flannagan, eds., "The Diary of Frances Baylor Hill of 'Hillsborough' King and Queen County, Virginia (1797)," *Early American Literature Newsletter* 2, no. 3 (Winter 1967): 20, 42–43.

[6] Wright and Tinling, *Diary of William Byrd*; Bottorff and Flannagan, "Diary of Frances Baylor Hill"; Farish, *Journal of Fithian*; Lavinia DeNood, "Furnishing Plan for the Nelson House of the Colonial National Historical Park, Yorktown, Virginia" (1976, typescript, Colonial Williamsburg Fndn.), p. 67.

[7] Mason, "Recollections," p. 16; Edward Kimber, "Observations in Several Voyages and Travels in America," *London Magazine* (1746), quoted in *William and Mary Quarterly* 15, no. 3 (January 1907): 146.

[8] Bottorff and Flannagan, "Diary of Frances Baylor Hill," pp. 20, 23, 31; Farish, *Journal of Fithian*.

[9] Farish, *Journal of Fithian*, pp. 33, 35. For further discussion of Virginians' use of their homes, see Rhys Isaac, *The Transformation of Virginia, 1740–1790* (Chapel Hill: University of North Carolina Press, 1982), pp. 58–87.

[10] Dell Upton, "Vernacular Architecture in Eighteenth-Century Virginia," *Winterthur Portfolio* 17, nos. 2/3 (Summer/Autumn 1982): 96–97.

[11] Cary Carson and Lorena Walsh, "The Material Life of the Early American Housewife" (Paper presented at Women in Early America conference, November 5–7, 1981, Williamsburg, Va.), p. 24; Upton, "Vernacular Architecture," p. 102.

[12] Upton, "Vernacular Architecture," pp. 102–4.

[13] Upton, "Vernacular Architecture," p. 104; Mark R. Wenger, "The Central Passage in Virginia: Evolution of Eighteenth-Century Living Space," in Camille Wells, ed., *Perspectives in Vernacular Architecture II* (Columbia: University of Missouri Press, 1986), pp. 138, 140, 142.

[14] Wenger, "Central Passage," pp. 140–49.

[15] Upton, "Vernacular Architecture," pp. 103–4. For a complete discussion of the evolution of the dining room, see Mark R. Wenger, "The Dining Room in Early Virginia," in Thomas Carter and Bernard L. Herman, eds., *Perspectives of Vernacular Architecture III* (Columbia: University of Missouri Press, 1989), pp. 149–59.

[16] Wenger, "Dining Room," p. 152; Carson and Walsh, "Material Life," pp. 26, 30.

[17] Wenger, "Dining Room," pp. 154–59.

[18] Upton, "Vernacular Architecture," pp. 103–4; Farish, *Journal of Fithian*, p. 80. On Mrs. Nelson's table, see DeNood, *Furnishing the Nelson House*, pp. 67, 69.

[19] Robert "King" Carter letterbook, January 1, 1727/8, Christ Church, Lancaster Co., Va. (transcript); Graham Hood, *The Governor's Palace in Williamsburg: A Cultural Study* (Williamsburg, Va.: Colonial Williamsburg Fndn., 1991), p. 208.

[20] Upton, "Vernacular Architecture," pp. 98, 103, 108; Mason, "Recollections," pp. 12–13; Farish, *Journal of Fithian*, p. 80.

[21] Upton, "Vernacular Architecture," p. 118; Carson and Walsh, "Material Life," p. 25; Isaac, *Transformation of Virginia*, p. 305.

[22] *The Builder's Dictionary; or, Gentleman and Architect's Companion*, 2 vols. (London, 1734; reprint, Washington, D.C.: Association for Preservation Technology, 1981), 1: preface; Robert Carter to Thomas Bladon, February 16, 1762, Robert Carter letterbook, Colonial Williamsburg Archives, Williamsburg, Va. (microfilm, Colonial Williamsburg Fndn.).

[23] On furniture hierarchy and assigned values, see Peyton Randolph inventory in *Inventories of Four Eighteenth-Century Houses in the Historic Area of Williamsburg* (Williamsburg, Va.: Colonial Williamsburg Fndn., 1974), pp. 24–26.

[24] Carson and Walsh, "Material Life," pp. 44, 48–49.

[25] Mason, *John Norton and Sons*, p. 94.

[26] Mason, *John Norton and Sons*, pp. 168, 184, 188–89, 364.

[27] Mason, *John Norton and Sons*, pp. 144, 175, 189.

[28] Carter to Bladon, February 16, 1762, and Carter to Peyton Randolph, January 23, 1773, both in Robert Carter letterbook, vol. 1 (1772–74), Duke University Library, Manuscripts Division (transcription, Colonial Williamsburg Library).

[29] Richard L. Bushman, "American High-Style and Vernacular Cultures," in Jack P. Greene and J. R. Pole, eds., *Colonial British America: Essays in the New History of the Early Modern Era* (Baltimore: Johns Hopkins University Press, 1984), p. 358; for other comments on refinement, see Isaac, *Transformation of Virginia*, p. 303; Carson and Walsh, "Material Life," p. 45.

[30] *Builder's Dictionary*, vol. 1, s.v. "Decorum"; Carter L. Hudgins, "Patrician Culture, Public Ritual, and Political Authority in Virginia, 1680–1740" (Ph.D. diss., College of William and Mary, 1984), p. 253.

[31] Carson and Walsh, "Material Life," pp. 31, 33, 41, 44, 46.

[32] Jan K. Gilliam and Betty C. Leviner, *Furnishing Williamsburg's Historic Buildings* (Williamsburg, Va.: Colonial Williamsburg Fndn., 1991), pp. 4–5, 12–13, 63.

[33] *Builder's Dictionary*, 1: preface.

"In the Middle of This Poverty Some Cups and a Teapot"

The Furnishing of Slave Quarters at Colonial Williamsburg

Martha B. Katz-Hyman

The dynamic presentation and interpretation of slavery and the slave system in eighteenth-century Williamsburg and its environs is a relatively recent addition to the interpretive program of the Colonial Williamsburg Foundation. In 1982 a committee of educational staff and administrators recommended the development of interpretations and programs reflecting the lives of slaves in eighteenth-century Wil-

The author thanks Dennis O'Toole, Graham Hood, Rex Ellis, and John Sands for their leadership and inspiration; Harold Gill, Ann Smart Martin, Patricia Samford, Linda Baumgarten, Patricia Gibbs, Willie Graham, and Michael Nicolls, who generously shared the fruits of their research; Cary Carson, Kevin Kelly, Ed Chappell, and Vanessa Patrick, for their incisive questions and healthy skepticism; the Colonial Williamsburg interpreters who make these spaces come alive; Alicia Tucker, who did much of the basic research for this project and who wrote a report that was the origin of this paper; the author's colleagues in the Department of Collections; Jay Gaynor, for his friendship, support, encouragement, and constructive criticism; and the author's family.

The author also thanks the Special Collections Division, Georgetown University Library, Washington, D.C., for permission to quote from the daybook of James Carroll, which is part of the archives of the Maryland Province of the Society of Jesus; the Special Collections Library of Duke University, Durham, North Carolina, for permission to quote

liamsburg, and in 1985 five buildings in Colonial Williamsburg's Historic Area were designated as "black presence" sites. Soon after, the
decision was made to also reconstruct the slave quarter at Carter's
Grove. Responsibility for the furnishing of all of these sites was assigned
to Colonial Williamsburg's Collections Division.[1]

At the beginning of this effort, the curators were aware of a small
body of information about slaves' material possessions. They knew, for
example, that slaves received clothing, blankets, and food on a regular
basis and that their housing was generally provided by their masters.
Some surviving written descriptions of the interiors of late eighteenth-
century slave quarters suggested other goods in living spaces, such as
cooking equipment, tobacco pipes, and tools. And archaeological discoveries pointed to the use of ceramics in slave quarters. But in general,
rather than providing answers, the information available led to even
more questions: Did the documentation accurately and completely reflect the material environment of slaves? Did slaves have only the bare
essentials for living, or did they have some of the amenities that were
usually obtained by whites throughout the colony? Other than being
given goods by their masters, were there other ways in which slaves
acquired their material goods? What were these ways? What did slaves
do with these goods? How did they arrange the possessions they did
have? After nearly two hundred years of Virginia slavery, did blacks
maintain any African traditions, and if so, how were such traditions
reflected in slaves' material goods? Without answers to these and similar
questions, it appeared that furnishings at each site would be limited to
basic clothing and bedding, with some ceramics and other goods as
documented in the sources available at the time.

The five sites chosen for initial furnishing represented specific
types of urban slave spaces, including upper- and middling-class homes,
a commercial establishment, a trade shop, and a generic "ad hoc"
space. The use of scenarios required that historically plausible groups
of inhabitants be determined for each site, along with a range of activities and social relationships appropriate for each location. Once these

---

from the Francis Porteus Corbin Papers; the Library of Virginia, for permission to quote
from the manuscript diary of Col. Francis Taylor; and AT&T, who funded the writing
of Alicia Tucker's original report in 1988 and the furnishing of black presence sites as
part of a grant for the strengthening of black programming at Colonial Williamsburg.

scenarios were determined, the furnishings were specifically formulated for each space. The curators drew up lists of furnishings for each space based upon primary and secondary sources that dealt with slave material culture as well as a general knowledge of rural and lower class urban furnishings of eighteenth-century Tidewater Virginia. Thus it was a relatively straightforward task to obtain the needed objects (primarily reproductions) and install them at the designated sites based on the agreed-upon scenarios and the limited information available. Although a general knowledge of eighteenth-century room arrangement and object use was applied to the furnishing process, modifications, especially those reflecting slave material culture, were anticipated as more information became available. The sites were opened to the public in March 1988.

As the furnishing of these spaces was completed, work began on furnishing the Carter's Grove Slave Quarter, which was designed to reflect a rural slave site. Residents for each of the proposed living spaces at the quarter were defined by Colonial Williamsburg Foundation historians. They selected the names, ages, relationships, and occupations of the various people who might have inhabited such a site, including young, single field hands, an African-born elder, a skilled carpenter and his family, a trusted foreman, and a female-led household. Within this group there was a hierarchy, just as there was in the wider community. Some slaves lived with very few material goods. Others had access to a great many—obtained through their own skills, through contact with fellow slaves and whites, and through other opportunities to exercise their personal initiative.

Once the residents were selected, the curators then conceived of a furnishings plan for the quarter. Although much of the plan was accepted by the Carter's Grove Slave Quarter planning team with little difficulty, some aspects were questioned. Some team members felt that the plan included too many goods for slaves at this rural site. The curators insisted that slaves had access to a greater range of goods than had been previously supposed, while other committee members maintained that except for very unusual cases, most slaves lived in very meager circumstances with minimal amounts of clothing and only basic food, shelter, and material possessions.

To resolve these differences of opinion, a concerted effort was made to examine all available evidence on the subject. During this process of compiling and analyzing the references collected by curators, architectural historians, research historians, historic trades staff, and others, the curators discovered that there was much more information available about eighteenth-century Tidewater black material culture than previously realized. Many documents routinely used by curators as sources for furnishing the exhibition buildings in the Historic Area also contained bits and pieces of information about slaves and slave material culture, but prior to this project, most of it had never been gathered in one place. Once assembled, it turned out to be surprisingly voluminous.

The first documents examined were probate inventories. In eighteenth-century Virginia, only moveable property was listed in a probate inventory—that is, furniture, clothing, cooking equipment, dining equipment, and the like. Slaves were considered moveable property and thus were included in probate inventory listings. The portions of these inventories related to slave-occupied areas usually included only the equipment used to work the property (tools, agricultural or trade equipment, etc.), sometimes the blankets and corn reserved for future distribution to the slaves, and cooking equipment and other furnishings provided for the overseer or master but never the clothing, food, ceramics, and blankets slaves already had. Taken at face value, the inventories seemed to indicate that masters provided a bare minimum for their slaves and that, indeed, slaves lived in the most meager of circumstances with the most basic of provisions: clothing, blankets, and a diet of corn. Consequently, only these few objects could be exhibited at slave sites.

A more thorough analysis of the probate inventories revealed that the objects listed at slave quarters fell into three distinct categories: 1) furnishings either provided for the overseer as part of his agreement with the plantation owner or used by the master during a stay at a particular quarter; 2) tools and equipment provided by the master and necessary for the quarter's operation; and 3) food and clothing intended for slaves but which had not yet been distributed. None of the personal goods known from other sources to have been at slave quarters appeared in these inventories in the expected quantities.

The inventory of Landon Carter, for example, listed 181 slaves at his residence at Sabine Hall and a total of 202 slaves at his other properties. Neither bedding, food, nor clothing for the slaves were listed in any of the inventories. Yet Carter consistently wrote in his diary of the clothing and food that he gave his slaves. One of them, Betty, cut out fifty suits of clothing in November 1763 for other slaves. The next year, in November 1764, Carter purchased seventy pairs of shoes for slaves. On September 19, 1770, he killed a "beef" for his slaves, and in an entry for May 15, 1776, he noted that he gave his slaves enough cloth for two suits each year.[2]

Such evidence argued strongly for the contention that, although slaves were legally the property of their owners and technically could not own property themselves, for all practical purposes 1) slaves' personal goods were considered by both blacks and whites to belong to the slaves and therefore not subject to inventory, or 2) white owners felt that the items owned by their slaves were of no value and therefore did not include them in probate inventories, or 3) slaves' personal items were included in the value listed for the slave.[3] Therefore, while probate inventories could be used to determine the types and quantities of goods owners kept at their quarters, they were not reliable as the primary guides for furnishing the Carter's Grove Slave Quarter with slaves' *personal* goods.

Similarly, other types of legal documents included few specific references to slaves' personal property. A handful of wills list slaves as legatees: for example, the 1779 will of Patrick Mackey of Norfolk County, Virginia, left "My Blue Rug [a bedcovering], Old Sheets and Old Bed . . . to my Negro Wench Pegg."[4] Criminal trial proceedings were likely to deal with stolen goods rather than with goods legitimately obtained.

Letters prove to have a wealth of information about slaves and their material world. In a letter written February 10, 1773, Thomas Everard ordered "4 Strong Great Coats for Negros 2 for men about the House and 2 for Lads Postillions" from merchant John Norton in London. Joseph Ball, a Virginian living in London in the 1740s, wrote often to his nephew and plantation administrator, Joseph Chinn, with detailed instructions regarding the slaves on his plantation. In February 1744, he specified that each adult slave "must have a Good Suit of the Welch Plains [a type of fabric] made as it should be, not too Scanty nor bob-tail'd. And Each must have Two Shirts, or Shifts, of the ozenbrigs." George Washington was just as concerned with his slaves' clothing, for in 1788 he asked Clement Biddle in Philadelphia to purchase "German and British Oznaburgs of the best quality, suitable for making Negroes shirts and shifts."[5]

Similarly, period diaries give some insight into the lives of slaves.

For example, Frances Baylor Hill of "Hillsborough" in King and Queen County, Virginia, wrote in her diary in June 1797 that she and her mother "went over the river to see Phill who was very ill when we got over he died in about an hour, his pour wife was greatly distress'd I never was sorry'r for a negro in my life." Some journals also record payments made to slaves for goods and services. Philip Vickers Fithian, tutor to the children of Robert Carter of Nomoni Hall in Westmoreland County, noted in January 1774 that he "gave *Martha* who makes my Bed, for a Christmas Box, a *Bit*, . . . I gave to John also, who waits at Table & calls me to Supper a *Bit*." Francis Taylor, an Orange County, Virginia, planter, noted in his diary many monetary transactions in which he bought chickens and produce from his slaves and paid them for extra work.[6]

Travelers to the New World, especially those who visited Virginia and other southern states in the years right after the American Revolution, did not hesitate to express their views on slaves and slavery. These descriptions often emphasize the repugnant nature of slavery and in doing so, include information about the material lives of slaves. French traveler Ferdinand-Marie Bayard visited Virginia in 1791. In describing the interior of one slave quarter house, he wrote:

A box-like frame made of boards hardly roughed down, upheld by stakes constituted the nuptial couch. Some wheat straw and corn-stalks, on which was spread a very short-napped woolen blanket that was burned in several places, completed the wretched pallet of the enslaved couple. . . . An old pot, tilted on some pieces of brick was still white with *Homany*. A few rags soaked in water, were hanging in one of the corners of the fireplace. An old pipe, very short and a knife blade, which were sticking in the wall were the only effects that I found in the dwelling.[7]

Examining the account books of both merchants and craftsmen revealed the types of goods purchased in Tidewater Virginia for slaves' use. Purchases of shoes, stockings, livery, hats, blankets, and tools for the use of slaves are commonly found in these account books, and the frequent use of the same descriptive terms for these goods—"Negro shoes," "plaid hose for Negroes," "Negro cotton"—indicates that these were common items whose definition was well understood by residents of the region. For example, the account books of William Allason, a merchant in Falmouth, Virginia, reveal numerous sales of all kinds of goods for the use of slaves: hoes, shoes, oznaburg, and plaid stockings to name just a few items. Likewise, plantation account books record purchases for the slaves, such as Robert Carter's purchase of shoes for the "people" at Old Ordinary Quarter in November 1773.[8]

It is one of the anomalies of eighteenth-century Tidewater Virginia slavery that even though slaves were regarded as property and bought and sold like livestock, they were also active participants in the region's market economy. The pages of these same account books also record payments made directly to slaves for goods and services and record credit purchases slaves made for themselves. It is impossible to know the details of cash sales to slaves because the records of such sales were usually not associated with the name of a particular individual, but those slaves who ran credit accounts—and there were more than just a handful—purchased a variety of goods. Between 1760 and 1768, Colchester, Virginia, merchants Glassford and Company kept a running account with Jack, a slave who belonged to Mr. Linton's estate in Colchester. Jack obtained, among other things, textiles, liquor, knives, cooking equipment, and tools in exchange for his work as a carter and carpenter. Another slave named Jack, also a carpenter, purchased an iron pot from William Allason in 1776.[9] Account books, therefore, were a good source of data about the types of goods purchased by both owner and slaves for use at a slave quarter.

Two potentially valuable sources of information turned out to be of limited help in understanding the material culture of eighteenth-century Tidewater Virginia slaves—slave narratives and period illustrations. Eighteenth-century slave narratives are rare and deal primarily with the experience of slavery in an episodic way (that is, there is little description of clothing, food, or possessions). Although they were very valuable for learning about experiences of enslaved Africans, they contributed little to our knowledge of eighteenth-century slaves' material lives.

Considerable time was spent attempting to locate prints, paintings, and other visual records of eighteenth-century Virginia slave life. There are many eighteenth-century visual representations, both English and American, of individual slaves but almost no period visual sources that illustrate the environment in which slaves lived and worked, the material goods they used in their everyday lives, or how these objects were arranged within a particular living or working area.

By contrast, advertisements for runaways constitute one of the best sources for information about slaves and the goods they used. Most advertisements specify the time and place of escape, the slave's physical appearance, the clothing worn at the time of the escape, any skills the slave had, and any items the slave might have taken. A probable destination (if known) and the reward offered for the slave's return are also included. It is apparent from a close reading of these advertisements that slaves wore a variety of clothing, from the basic "uniform" of field hands to the much more elaborate wardrobe worn by household and personal servants. References in these advertisements to slaves "clothed in the usual manner of labouring Negroes" or to "the usual negro dress" suggest that there was a general standard for slave clothing. The more elaborate clothes listed in the advertisements ("a pair of shoes with buckles"; "new brown cloth waistcoat, lappelled, lined with white taminy, and yellow gilt buttons"; "white linen shirts . . . and osnabrug trousers") indicate that slaves could obtain a greater variety of clothing.[10]

Because so many of these advertisements list slaves' skills, they became important sources for determining what tools may have been at a slave quarter. In March 1770, Joshua Jones placed the following advertisement in the *Virginia Gazette*: "RUN away from the subscriber, In York county, about the 11th or 12th of November last, a very black Negro man named BEN . . . by trade a carpenter, and understands something of the coopers business. . . . He took with him sundry carpenters and coopers tools. I expect he will endeavour to pass for a freeman, as he can read tolerably well."[11] That Ben was a carpenter and cooper means that there probably were tools for making at least hogsheads, tubs, and other barrels; pails; and other such items at the slave quarter where he lived and presumably worked. Listing reading and writing among his skills suggests that there may have been writing implements or a book or two at the quarter as well. Thus, a close inspection of such advertisements provides clues to material goods not previously thought to have been at a slave quarter.

The final source of information about eighteenth-century Tidewater Virginia slave material culture is archaeological recovery. The types of artifacts recovered by archaeologists are limited to those things that are durable or that the ground will more or less preserve: metal objects, ceramics, and bones and seeds. These things are precisely the articles for which documentary references are limited and inconclusive. For example, documentary evidence consistently refers to slaves eating some form of corn (usually hominy) and pork, usually together, with perhaps some chicken or fish. The archaeological excavation of sites associated with slave quarters reveals the remains of beef, fish, chickens, and pigs, as well as the seeds of a variety of vegetables and fruit, indicating a more varied diet for some slaves than the written evidence would indicate. Similarly, documentary sources say little about what slaves used as eating utensils and dishes, but the archaeological evidence from most slave sites reveals that they used a variety of ceramic types and forms and utensils for food preparation and consumption. How these forms were acquired is not revealed archaeologically, but the ceramic remains (most of which are of imported English and Chinese wares) point to an environment in which they were commonly used.[12]

Finally, the accounts of eighteenth-century travelers to Africa offer insights into cultural traditions that may have persisted in America. For instance, in 1830 the executors of Capt. Hugh Crow of Liverpool, England, published the memoirs of his travels to the west coast of Africa, and in particular Bonny, the imperial capitol of the Ibo, the area from which many of Virginia's slaves were taken. In these memoirs Captain Crow noted, "Most of the hard articles such as lead and iron bars, chests of beads, and marcelas (a kind of coin), they bury under the floors of their houses. Much valuable property is secreted in that way."[13] Here is evidence that the root cellars found archaeologically at so many eighteenth-century slave sites may in fact be an African cultural tradition that was brought to the New World and survived.

Contrary to initial expectations, this close examination of primary sources revealed that slaves in Tidewater Virginia in the period 1750 to 1790 lived in a variety of circumstances, ranging from situations where they had only the bare necessities to situations where they lived with goods that might be considered luxuries. They had access to these goods in a variety of ways.

The "issued goods" that masters provided for their slaves—basic clothing, simple food and, cooking utensils—were given to slaves on a more or less regular schedule. For example, in 1732, William Hugh Grove, an Englishman, visited Virginia and noted that "[the slaves] are allowed a peck of Indian Corn per Week." Joseph Ball, writing from England to Joseph Chinn in 1743/44, specified that "[t]he old Ewes and Rams, before they are too old, must be kill'd, & given to the Negroes; and they at the Quarters must have part." In 1767 Landon Carter wrote: "Note: we took out this day 16 Bushels of eared Corn from the M[angorike] Corn house to make the peoples' allowance." This continued to be the practice into the nineteenth century. Martha Ogle Forman, who lived in Cecil County, Maryland, noted in 1842 in her diary that "Mr. Nowland gave out the people's meat, he gave each a hog's head and made out the rest of the allowance with beef."[14] Masters issued clothing every fall and spring to their slaves, including shirts, shifts, breeches, stockings, shoes, and hats. For example, in a series of lease agreements for his various properties, Robert Carter specified that

each male Negro 9 years old, and upwards to have one Waistcoat and breeches, one pair of Woolen Hose[,] one pair of Summer Breeches, two oznabrings shirts, one Blankett, and one pair of Shoes each, Each Female Negro 8 years old and upwards to have one Jackcoat and Petticoat[,] one pair of Woolen Hose, two oznaburg shifts, one blankett, one summer Petticoat, one one [sic] pair of Shoes each, of the younger Negroes to have one Woollen frock, the males one shirt the females one shift, the summer Breeches and Petticoats & Shirts & Shifts for Children to be furnished the first Monday in June, the other cloathing & Blanketts to be furnished the first Monday in December.

Johann David Schöpf, a German traveler through the Upper South in the years right after the Revolution, noted in North Carolina that "well-disposed masters clothe their negroes once a year, and give them a suit of coarse woollen cloth, two rough shirts, and a pair of shoes." Wool blankets were distributed to each slave every year or every other year.[15] As noted earlier, once these goods were issued, they were usually considered the property of the slave.

In addition to these essentials, masters supplied slaves with tools, implements, and even special clothing required to do their jobs: plows, hoes, rakes, shovels; hammers, anvils, axes, saws, planes, and chisels; pots, andirons, pot hooks; spinning wheels and looms; livery and special footwear. These tools and special equipment, all of which might be called "supplies," remained the property of the master and were expected to remain at the quarter, even if their users were sold to another owner.[16]

Besides these "issued" and "supplied" items, masters sometimes gave their slaves outmoded or worn clothing and other goods as gifts. Joseph Ball instructed Joseph Chinn in 1749 as follows: "The old Cloths must be disposed of, as follows: The Grey Coat Wastecoat & breeches, with brass buttons, and the hat to poor Will: The stuff shirt to Mingo: and the Dimmity Coat & breeches and the knife in the pocket to Harrison: and Aron's Old Livery with one pair of the Leather breeches and one of the Linen frocks to Moses: and the other frock and rags & [illeg.] as you think fit."[17]

But issues, supplies, and hand-me-downs from masters were not the only goods slaves obtained. Nearly all slaves had some skill, whether as a field hand, a basketmaker, a carpenter, a blacksmith, a cook, or a spinner. With these skills, many were able to make the things that they needed or desired for daily life, ranging from the simple—mended clothing or gourds for drinking vessels and bowls—to the complex—sleeping platforms, stools, or even musical instruments for their own entertainment.

Other slaves relied on their skills as farmers and foragers to increase the amount of food available to them both for their own tables and as a marketable commodity. Much of this food was grown by slaves at their quarters. The description by Edward Kimber, an English novelist who traveled through Maryland in 1745 and 1746, of a slave quarter as "a Number of Huts or Hovels, built some Distance from the Mansion-House; where the Negroes reside with their wives and Families and cultivate at vacant times the little Spots allow'd" implies that he saw many such quarters. Francis Taylor wrote in his diary in May 1795 that his "Negroes [were] planting for themselves." Other observers noted that slaves raised poultry and caught fish. Traveler Thomas Anburey described a planter near Charlottesville who, instead of providing his slaves with the usual rations, "grant[ed] his negroes an acre of ground, and all Saturday afternoon to raise grain and poultry for themselves." Using their chicken, eggs, produce, and foraged foodstuffs, slaves bartered to obtain goods. This bartering usually took place between slave and master. Landon Carter wrote in 1777: "My Poor Slaves raise fowls, and eggs in order to exchange with their Master now and then." Francis Taylor often traded with slaves by means of barter: in August 1788 he "bought some Grass seed of Col Taliaferro's Jack for Pr breeches"; in March 1790, "Reu Taylor's Sam brought some Timothy seed for which I [Francis Taylor] gave him a Jacket"; five years later in July 1795, Taylor "bought 1 doz chickens of Col Willis's Phil he had a pair Breeches & to pay me 1/6 worth more." And in an interesting exchange in August 1798, Taylor gave "old Joe a quart whisky for a peck onions."[18]

Slaves also bought and sold goods on the open market. Food products were the most common items that slaves sold. James Mercer, writing in 1779 to a friend in Loudoun County, wrote, "I know allready that Chickens or other fresh meat cant be had but in exchange & Bacon to spare will allow me a preference with the Country people or rather Negroes who are the general Chicken merchants." Besides bartering with his slaves, Francis Taylor also purchased such items as carp, oysters, cabbages, and potatoes for his own table, paying his slaves in cash.[19]

Slaves earned money through selling products of their skilled labor. Robert Carter observed in 1731 that his slaves "surely must depend on a great deal of their Time in making Pails & Piggins & Churns for Merchandizing. Manuel tells me the smith does a great many jobs for neighbours." Jack, the slave who belonged to the estate of Mr. Linton near Colchester, Virginia, earned credit of more than £100 from Glassford and Company over the course of nine years (1760–69) for mending bridges, building furniture, and other miscellaneous carpentry work, as well as for selling poultry. In 1768 William Allason paid John Fitzhugh's "Negro Harry" for "puting up Shelves in Kitchen & making Stairs &c." And in 1796 Francis Taylor paid his half-brother's slave, Tom, for "2 days work hooping nest ware & repairs of Porch etc."[20]

Some slaves also earned money through tips. In 1768 John Frere of London wrote his cousin, John Hatley Norton, in Yorktown and asked him to send any plant or animal fossils that might be found in the area. Frere wrote, "if such Things are to be found, the Negroes I suppose for a small Gratuity wou'd bring them to you."[21]

With the money that slaves earned they were able to buy goods of their own choosing, and the goods they bought were as varied as the goods available. In 1737 "Negro Jack" bought fabric, scissors, thread, hose, and penknives from Thomas Partridge. "Negro Jack," who made furniture and other wooden articles for Glassford and Company, bought a wide range of goods, from rum and fabric to a wineglass and a plane iron between 1760 and 1769. Robert Carter noted in his diary in 1785 that he "paid old Nat a dollar he wanted, he wanted to buy Brandy to bury his Granddaughter Lucy, but I refused to sell; telling him he might lay out his Annuity as he pleased."[22]

Another way in which slaves obtained goods was by theft. Virginia established a special court in each county to try these cases, and it is in the records of these courts that we learn what slaves stole: primarily money, tools, fabric, and food. In 1747 two of Landon Carter's slaves, Manuell and Ralph, were indicted for breaking into Carter's mansion and stealing "two hundred and thirty three Ells of Dreheda Canvas . . . Four Torinton Rugs . . . Four suits of Cotton Cloath . . . Ten yards of Half Thicks . . . Four Sides of Leather . . . Five files . . . [and] Two Dozen Hose." Goods stolen in such quantities were undoubtedly intended for resale. George Washington, in 1793, acknowledged such trade when he tried to prevent his former carpenter's daughter from going into business as he feared "her shop wd. be no more than a receptacle for stolen produce by the Negroes." He knew that without this source of cheap goods, poor whites "would be unable to live upon the miserable land they occupy." The goods taken by these slaves in Richmond County may have been stolen to barter or sell, but other goods were stolen to assist in escaping, as reported by the owner of Sam, "a bright Mulatto Man Slave," who took with him "his Bedding, a new spotted Rug which he had stolen, and several Yards of mixed coloured Broadcloth, cut from a whole Piece that he had stolen, the remainder of which he distributed amongst the Sloop [Tryal]'s Crew to bribe them to Secrecy."[23]

But knowing how slaves obtained their goods, and even what these goods were, did not answer the questions surrounding the actual placement of these objects in the spaces themselves: How did people use these things? Where did people sit? Where did they store their possessions? How "new" or "old" did these things look? How cluttered or neat were these spaces? Did these spaces look the same as spaces occupied by poor whites? In short, how did these spaces look two hundred years ago?

There was no easy answer. The descriptions of slave quarters found in written sources were helpful but inconclusive. The following observation of Julian Niemcewicz, a close friend of Polish general and patriot Tadeusz Kosciuszko, written during a visit with George Washington at Mount Vernon in 1798, illustrates the problem:

We entered one of the huts of the Blacks, for one can not call them by the name of houses. They are more miserable than the most miserable of the cottages of our peasants. The husband and wife sleep on a mean pallet, the children on the ground; a very bad fireplace, some utensils for cooking, but in the middle of this poverty some cups and a teapot . . . A very small garden planted with vegetables was close by, with 5 or 6 hens, each one leading ten to fifteen chickens. It is the only comfort that is permitted them; for they may not keep ducks, geese, or pigs. They sell the poultry in Alexandria and procure for themselves a few amenities.[24]

How is this to be understood? Was what Niemcewicz calls a "hut" and what is now called a "hut" the same thing? What is a "mean pallet?" Does the fact that Niemcewicz describes the children as sleeping "on the ground" mean that the husband and wife slept off the ground in a bed of some kind? What were the "utensils for cooking," and what kind of "cups and a teapot" did Niemcewicz see? He obviously was told, either by Washington or one of his overseers, that the slaves sold their chickens in Alexandria, but what kind of "amenities" did they purchase? What would a slave consider an "amenity?" In short, was it possible to translate this description into an actual room setting?

Despite the fact that most of the contemporary descriptions of slave quarters were as limited in detail as Niemcewicz's (recall Ferdinand-Marie Bayard's, earlier), the information related in them was translated as best as possible into actual room settings. Furthermore, given the decision to represent a range of living groups, occupations, and status among the imaginary inhabitants at the Carter's Grove quarter, the furnishings were consciously chosen to represent this range.

Specific details from the various descriptions or revealed by archaeology were incorporated together to create scenarios in the quarter: Niemcewicz's "very bad fireplace, some utensils for cooking" [and] "a few cups and a teapot"; Bayard's "old pot, tilted on some pieces of brick," "rags soaked in water," and an "old pipe, very short and a knife blade . . . sticking in the wall"; and Joseph Ball's favored slave, Aron Jameson's "small Iron pot & hooks and Rack to hang it on, an Iron skillet, a copper sauce pan, an old Bridle & Saddle, a Cheese a Narrow ax . . . a Violin and some spare strings [and] a small spit" are all part of the furnishings at Carter's Grove.[25] Each of the designated living areas for each scenario is furnished in a different way. The young field hands, who sleep in the same space with the hoes, plows, grain, and rakes, have the most basic of goods and sleep on straw, covered by simple blankets. At the other end of the slave-quarter living scale, the foreman, who lives with his family in a separate house, slightly removed from the other two buildings, has a free-standing bed, a table, a variety of ceramics, and a kit of cooking equipment that can handle almost any requirement. All of them were slaves, but they lived in material settings that differed considerably; it is important to remember that while some slaves had no choice but to make do with almost nothing, the legal and physical condition of slavery did not necessarily mean that all slaves lived in abject physical misery.

There are some things about the furnishings as they were chosen and installed, both at Carter's Grove and within Colonial Williamsburg's Historic Area, that are pure conjecture. Lacking detailed descriptions either verbal or visual, all of the furnishings at the slave quarter, as in the Historic Area, were installed using a general knowledge of eighteenth-century room arrangement. The arrangements of specific items in specific rooms were determined by how the spaces might be best utilized or most logically arranged to make the most of heat from the fireplace, to accommodate crowded rooms, or to store treasured possessions, and they were governed as much by curatorial logic as by specific references.

The objects installed in each space are reproductions of English or colonial goods that were available during the eighteenth century and to which slaves had access. But there is almost no written evidence regarding how, if at all, African traditions influenced the selection of goods when choices were available or the arrangement of those goods — although recent archaeological excavations at "Utopia" on the site of the eighteenth-century Kingsmill Plantation, "Rich Neck," the Ludwell plantation near Williamsburg, and the African Burial Ground in New York City indicate that African traditions and customs in decoration and burial were maintained over several generations. Besides this recent archaeological material, we can hypothesize that locally made ceramics; raised sleeping areas of different types, mentioned by many eighteenth-century travelers to West Africa; and the root cellars or pits found by archaeologists throughout Virginia and the Carolinas in association with slave quarters may be West African cultural traditions that persisted through the eighteenth and nineteenth centuries.[26] Through the research of Linda Baumgarten and others, slaves' basic clothing and its appearance is known, but it is not understood how slaves modified their issued clothing in order to make it more personal or how African traditions influenced any modifications that were made. Answers to questions of how and to what extent African traditions influenced slaves' material lives will come only with further research.

Through the reconstruction and furnishing of the slave quarter at

Carter's Grove and the furnishing of various spaces in the Historic Area, Colonial Williamsburg now interprets this painful yet important subject in settings that help visitors realize that there was indeed "another half" in Williamsburg—the half of Williamsburg's population that was black and enslaved—and that this is how they may have lived. Some visitors, on seeing these spaces, think that the people who lived in them did not live that badly, especially considering the fact that many of Virginia's free white population lived in much the same material circumstances although they did not have their shelter, food, and clothing provided for them. However, the following observation of Isaac Weld, an English traveler in Virginia in 1795–96, is worth considering:

let the condition of a slave be made ever so comfortable, as long as he is conscious of being the property of another man, who has it in his power to dispose of him according to the dictates of caprice; as long as he hears people around him talking of the blessings of liberty, and considers that he is in a state of bondage, it is not to be supposed that he can feel equally happy with the freeman. It is immaterial under what form slavery presents itself: whenever it appears, there is ample cause of humanity to weep at the sight, and to lament that men can be found so forgetful of their own situations, as to live regardless of the feelings of their fellow creatures.[27]

Slavery, no matter how beneficent its perpetrators, is still slavery—and it would be many long years until it was eliminated. The furnishings seen today in the slave-occupied settings in the Historic Area and at the Carter's Grove Slave Quarter are the backdrops against which Colonial Williamsburg's interpreters help the visitors experience another aspect of eighteenth-century life. Although it is an aspect that may cause pain and give offense, and it is one that some interpreters find difficult to discuss, Colonial Williamsburg has made a concerted effort to confront the issue in a variety of ways, of which the furnishing of slave quarters is only one. Through the interpretation of this aspect of eighteenth-century life, visitors may better understand contemporary American society and the problems that confront us today.

---

[1] This paper is derived from a research report written for the Colonial Williamsburg Foundation titled " 'In the Middle of This Poverty Some Cups and a Teapot': The Material Culture of Slavery in Eighteenth-Century Virginia and the Furnishing of Slave Quar-

ters at Colonial Williamsburg." The initial version of this report was written in 1989 by Alicia Tucker, Colonial Williamsburg Foundation intern; Jay Gaynor, curator of mechanical arts; and the author of this essay. For a more detailed discussion of the history of the interpretation of slavery at Colonial Williamsburg, see Rex M. Ellis, *Presenting the Past: Education, Interpretation, and the Teaching of Black History at Colonial Williamsburg* (Ph.D. diss., College of William and Mary, 1989). Carter's Grove plantation, owned by Colonial Williamsburg, is located on the James River approximately 5 miles southeast of the city of Williamsburg. The site includes the mansion, which was built by Carter Burwell in 1754, renovated by Mr. and Mrs. Archibald M. McCrae beginning in 1928, and is now restored to its 1930s splendor; an eighteenth-century reconstructed slave quarter; the Winthrop Rockefeller Archaeology Museum; and the partially reconstructed 1619 Wolstenholme Towne.

[2] "An Inventory of the Estate of Landon Carter, Esq. Dec'd. Taken Feb. 1779," Landon Carter Papers, Sabine Hall Collection, Alderman Library, University of Virginia, Charlottesville; Landon Carter, *The Diary of Colonel Landon Carter of Sabine Hall, 1752–1778*, 2 vols., ed. Jack P. Greene (Richmond: Virginia Historical Society, 1987), 1:242, 281, 494; 2:1040.

[3] Although the probate inventories were, of course, not produced by the deceased slave owner, the men who created these inventories often were themselves slave owners, and their attitudes on this subject could be argued to be reflective of the attitudes of most Tidewater Virginia slave owners.

[4] Will Book No. 2 (1772–78), Norfolk County Courthouse, Va., p. 131 (microfilm M-1365-21, Colonial Williamsburg Fndn.).

[5] Thomas Everard, Williamsburg, to John Norton and Sons, London, February 10, 1773, in Frances Norton Mason, ed., *John Norton and Sons: Merchants of London and Virginia; Being the Papers from their Counting House for the Years 1750 to 1795* (Richmond: Dietz Press, 1937), pp. 300–301; Joseph Ball, London, England, to Joseph Chinn, Virginia, Ball Letterbook, 1743–59, February 18, 1743/44, Library of Congress, Washington, D.C. (microfilm M-21, Colonial Williamsburg Fndn.). George Washington to Clement Biddle, April 4, 1788, in George Washington, *The Writings of George Washington from the Original Manuscript Sources*, 39 vols., ed. John C. Fitzpatrick (Washington, D.C.: U.S. Government Printing Office, 1931–44), 29:458.

[6] Frances Baylor Hill, "The Diary of Frances Baylor Hill of Hillsborough[,] King and Queen County Virginia [1797]," ed. William K. Bottorff and Roy C. Flannagan, *Early American Literature Newsletter* 2, no. 3 (Winter 1967): 33; Philip Vickers Fithian, *Journal and Letters of Philip Vickers Fithian: A Plantation Tutor of the Old Dominion* (Charlottesville: University Press of Virginia, 1957), p. 54; Francis Taylor diary, 1786–99, Library of Virginia, Richmond (microfilm M-1759, Colonial Williamsburg Fndn.).

[7] Ferdinand-Marie Bayard, *Travels of a Frenchman in Maryland and Virginia with a Description of Baltimore and Philadelphia in 1791*, trans. and ed. Ben C. McCary (Williamsburg, Va.: Ben C. McCary, 1950), p. 13.

[8] William Allason Papers, 1757–1804, Falmouth [Va.] Store, Ledger G, September 1768–October 1769, Library of Virginia, Richmond (microfilm M-1144-8, Colonial Williamsburg Fndn.); Robert Carter III, Nomini Hall Waste Book, 1773–83, September 18, 1773 (Special Collections, microfilm M-50, Colonial Williamsburg Fndn.). The use, by slave owners, of the term *people* for enslaved African Americans was common throughout the Chesapeake in the eighteenth and early nineteenth centuries.

[9] The account began in 1760 and ended in 1769. John Glassford and Company Papers, Records for Virginia, Colchester [Va.] Store (hereafter Glassford papers), Ledgers A–B, D–I, November 9, 1760–August 26, 1769, Library of Congress, Washington, D.C. (microfilm M-1442-8-11, Colonial Williamsburg Fndn.); William Allason daybook,

June 11, 1773–June 18, 1777, Allason papers, Falmouth [Va.] Store (microfilm M-1144-4, Colonial Williamsburg Fndn.).

[10] *Virginia Gazette* (Purdie and Dixon), March 8, 1770, November 8, 1770, May 7, 1767, December 13, 1770, and *Virginia Gazette* (Hunter), July 15, 1752, all in Lathan A. Windley, *Runaway Slave Advertisements: A Documentary History from 1730s to 1790*, vol. 1, *Virginia and North Carolina* (Westport, Conn.: Greenwood Press, 1983), respectively, pp. 78, 88, 52, 88, and 28. On slave clothing, see Linda Baumgarten, " 'Clothes for the People': Slave Clothing in Early Virginia," *Journal of Early Southern Decorative Arts* 14, no. 2 (November 1988): 27–70, and Linda Baumgarten, "Plains, Plaid, and Cotton: Woolens for Slave Clothing," *Ars Textrina* 15 (July 1991): 203–22, for thorough documentation of the types of clothing worn by slaves, seasonal variations in this clothing, special types of clothing worn by slaves (such as livery), variations in clothing between house slaves and field hands, and the lengths to which owners went to make sure that this clothing was serviceable but obtained at the best price.

[11] *Virginia Gazette* (Purdie and Dixon), March 22, 1770, in Windley, *Runaway Slave Advertisements*, 1:78–79.

[12] J. F. D. Smythe, an English traveler, described the midday meal of a Virginia slave as "hominy and salt, and if his master be a man of humanity, he has a little fat, skimmed milk, rusty bacon, or salt herring to relish his hominny or hoe-cake" (J. F. D. Smythe, *A Tour in the United States of America . . .* [London, 1784], 1:44). William Kelso, *Kingsmill Plantations, 1619–1800: Archaeology of Country Life in Virginia* (Orlando, Fla.: Academic Press, 1984), p. 183; Anna Gruber, "The Archaeology of Mr. Jefferson's Slaves" (Master's thesis, University of Delaware, 1990), p. 103. Even some forms of colono-Indian ware (also called colonoware), the low-fired earthenware pottery produced (in Virginia) either by Native Americans or by African Americans, were influenced by English and Chinese imported goods. The form of the colonoware teapot illustrated in Edward D. C. Campbell, Jr., with Kym S. Rice, eds., *Before Freedom Came: African Life in the Antebellum South* (Charlottesville: University Press of Virginia, 1991), p. 69, pl. 15, for example, indicates that its maker was familiar with Anglo-American wares of the same period. For a more extensive discussion of colonoware in Virginia, see Leland Ferguson, *Uncommon Ground: Archaeology and Early African America, 1650–1800* (Washington, D.C.: Smithsonian Institution Press, 1992), pp. 44–55.

[13] Hugh Crow (edited by the executors), *Memoirs of the Late Captain Hugh Crow of Liverpool, Comprising a Narrative of His Life Together with Descriptive Sketches of the Western Coast of Africa, Particularly of Bonny* (Liverpool, Eng.: G. and J. Robinson, 1830; reprint, London: Frank Cass, 1970), p. 251.

[14] William Hugh Grove, "Virginia in 1732: The Travel Journal of William Hugh Grove," ed. Gregory A. Stiverson and Patrick H. Butler III, *Virginia Magazine of History and Biography* 85, no. 1 (January 1977): 32; Ball to Chinn, Ball letterbook, February 18, 1743/44; Carter, *Diary*, 1:334; Martha Ogle Forman, *Plantation Life at Rose Hill: The Diaries of Martha Ogle Forman, 1814–1845*, ed. W. Emerson Wilson (Wilmington: Historical Society of Delaware, 1976), p. 424.

[15] See the copies of the agreements between Carter and the various lessors of his plantations for the years 1789–90 (dated December 31, 1788), specifying how much clothing each slave was to receive each season and when it was to be distributed; Robert Carter, "2nd Book of Miscellanies, 1787–1790," Robert Carter Papers, 1759–1805, Library of Congress, Washington, D.C. (microfilm M1439-2, Colonial Williamsburg Fndn.). Johann David Schöpf, *Travels in the Confederation, 1783–1784*, trans. and ed. Alfred J. Morrison (Philadelphia, 1911; reprint, New York: Burt Franklin, 1968), p. 147. George Washington corresponded with his plantation overseers for months about blankets, blanket prices, differences in materials, and which slave would get which type of blanket; see the follow-

ing correspondence in Washington, *Writings*: Washington to Clement Biddle, May 15, 1783, vol. 26, pp. 435–36; Washington to Biddle, June 11, 1783, vol. 27, p. 6; Washington to Philip Marsteller, July 25, 1787, vol. 29, p. 254; Washington to George Augustine Washington, September 2, 1787, vol. 29, pp. 268–69.

[16] The Francis Porteous Corbin Papers contain inventories listing quarters owned by Edmund Jenings in York and King William counties in 1712. Each inventory records the names of resident slaves and the overseer; clothing, bedding, tool, and utensil allotments; livestock; and buildings at each quarter. Note that the listings specified clothing that was given to each slave, not the clothing the slave already had. At Ripon Hall Plantation, no bedding was given out that year, and neither is what *was* there listed; the inventory notes "The Bedding at present will do—but 'tis Necessary it be recruited by the next Winter" (Francis Porteous Corbin Papers, 1662–1734, William R. Perkins Library, Duke University, Durham, N.C. [microfilm M36-3, Colonial Williamsburg Fndn.]). More than 75 years later, the lease agreements between Robert Carter of Nomini Hall and his various lessors not only specified the responsibilities and rights of each party but also listed the slaves on each quarter with their respective values (both replacement and hire), the various buildings on the property and their values, and, for most of these properties, an inventory of the agricultural equipment on each plantation with their values; Carter, "2nd Book of Miscellanies."

[17] Will Book No. 2 (1772–78), Norfolk County Courthouse, Va., p. 131 (microfilm M-1365-21, Colonial Williamsburg Fndn.).

[18] "Eighteenth-Century Maryland as Portrayed in the 'Itinerant Observations' of Edward Kimber," *Maryland Historical Magazine* 51 (1956): 327; Taylor diary, May 9, 1795; August 17, 1788; March 14, 1790; July 12, 1795; and August 13, 1798; Thomas Anburey, *Travels through the Interior Parts of America*, 2 vols. (London: William Lane, 1789; reprint, New York: New York Times, 1969), 2:331–32; Carter, *Diary*, 2:1095–96.

[19] James Mercer to Battaile Muse at Col. Peyton's, Loudoun Co., Va., April 3, 1779. Battaile Muse Papers, William R. Perkins Library, Duke University, Durham, N.C.; Taylor diary.

[20] Robert Carter to Benjamin Grayson, July 13, 1731, Robert Carter letterbook (University of Virginia), quoted in Philip D. Morgan, "The Development of Slave Culture in Eighteenth-Century Chesapeake America" (Ph.D. diss., University College, London, 1977), p. 222. Ledgers A–B, D–I, Glassford papers (microfilm M-1442-8-11, Colonial Williamsburg Fndn.); Cash Sales, 1764–89, July 18, 1768, Allason papers (microfilm M-1144-9, Colonial Williamsburg Fndn.); Taylor diary, September 2, 1796.

[21] Mason, *John Norton and Sons*, pp. 43–44.

[22] Thomas Partridge ledger, 1735–40, November–December 1737, and January [1738], fol. 43, Frederick Hall Plantation Books, 1727–1863, Hanover, Louisa, and York Counties, Va., Southern Historical Collection, University of North Carolina Library, Chapel Hill (microfilm M-24-4, Colonial Williamsburg Fndn.); Glassford papers, Ledger H 1767, October 1767–June 28, 1768, fol. 103 (microfilm M-1442-10, Colonial Williamsburg Fndn.); Robert W. Carter diaries, February 20, 1785, quoted in Morgan, "Development of Slave Culture," p. 385.

[23] Carter diary, February 20, 1785, quoted in Morgan, "Development of Slave Culture," p. 237. George Washington to William Pearce, November 16, 1794, and December 22, 1793, in Washington, *Writings*, 34:24; 33:203–4; *Virginia Gazette* (Purdie and Dixon), March 7, 1771, in Windley, *Runaway Slave Advertisements*, 1:191–92.

[24] Julian Ursyn Niemcewicz, "Under Their Vine and Fig Tree: Travels through America in 1797–1799, 1805 with Some Further Account of Life in New Jersey," trans. and ed. Metchie J. E. Budka, *Collections of the New Jersey Historical Society at Newark* 14 (Elizabeth, N.J.: Glassmann Publishing Co., 1965), pp. 100–101.

²⁵ Niemcewicz, "Travels through America," pp. 100–101; Bayard, *Travels*, p. 13; Ball to Chinn, Ball letterbook, April 23, 1754.

²⁶ Eighteenth-century English author and traveler Thomas Astley, compiling reports from other travelers in a general description of Guinea and Benin, described West Africans who had "an Estrade, or Sopha, on which they lay Mats, . . . for a Foot Height, about six long, and as much broad, which serve for Beds, which they surround with Pagnes [small pieces of cloth used as loincloths] sewed together, or printed Linen, like Curtains," as well as other people whose sleeping area consisted of "a Bank of Earth, raised about two Feet from the Floor, which, having a Mat laid thereon, serves them for a Bed" (Thomas Astley, comp., *A New General Collection of Voyages and Travels* . . . , vol. 2 [London, 1745; reprint, London: Frank Cass, 1968], pp. 523, 527). On root cellars, see Crow, *Memoirs*.

²⁷ Isaac Weld, *Travels through the States of North America, and the Provinces of Upper and Lower Canada, During the Years 1795, 1796, and 1797* (4th ed., London: John Stockdale, 1807; reprint, Johnson Reprint Corp., 1968), p. 149.

"They Are Very Handy"
Kitchen Furnishings, 1875–1920

Olive Blair Graffam

On a cold January day in 1875, with succotash cooking on the stove, Arvada Nichols Metcalf described her new home in Buchanan, Michigan, in a letter to her sister, Estella. Arvada and her new husband rented a four-room apartment on the first floor of an eight-room house. Her vivid description of the kitchen and pantry is used in its entirety because it is a case study in material culture. Writing that the bare kitchen floor "when clean looks quite well," Arvada continued:

We have a nice stove in the room. On one side a wood box papered with paper like that on the wall of our sitting room in Crown Point. Behind it is a paper tacked up to keep the wall clean. Over it the clock shelf with clock, ink bottle, pen holder, Glycerine bottle, clock key and spring key on it. Behind the door is hat rack with two overcoats, three hats and my waterproof hanging on it. Next is a picture, then a window. In front of the window stands the table full size with red spread over it and on it stands the lamp on mat, sewing basket and box, daily paper and plate of apples. These are all lifted off three times a day and set back. After the window, in the corner is a picture, then a window then my little match barrels and looking glass and comb case, then the outside door. Then a picture and then the buttery door.

The author thanks Alice Schmidt for sharing family history and the recollections of her mother, Floy Leonard Hankins, and is grateful to Rodris Roth for her ongoing and generous support.

Arvada's letter revealed the extensive use of the buttery or pantry:

There are four shelves in the buttery on which are my dishes & the flour barrel
stands by the end of the shelves with cloth over that Ma gave me and my shirt
board on which I lay the tablecloth. Next is a window. On the casing hangs
my sack of clothespins. At one end I have one of my big boxes set with two
water pails on it, dipper, cup and soap dish and wash dish. Behind it is a paper
tacked up and over it a towel. Next is the door behind which my big apron
hangs and the broom stands. On the other side of the door is another box that
stands on the side and has a shelf in. I set all my iron ware in there and on
top I wash dishes, have never done any work on my new table yet. Behind the
box is a paper tacked and in the center hangs the dish pan and one side the
wiping cloth and on the other my three kettle covers, one above the other.
Inside of the box hangs the dish cloth and rag and on the outside at the end
hang the face rag and lamp rag and stick. Now I have got round to the shelves
where I started. Under the shelves set the washboard (I have a new one), the
little keg of soap and the market basket. Next is a door to go in the hall to go
upstairs. In there I keep dirty clothes, a tub and a trunk. Between that door
and the stove sets that little papered box Ma gave me. I set my crock on there
when I bake pan cakes. The day I wash I set the water pails on the other box
and wash on that box in front of the window. I expect you will think that is
awful to wash in the buttery but I do. It is the handiest place in the house and
the room is plenty large. Down cellar we have everything. Nothing freezes down
there. It is handy to have a cellar. Now I believe I have told you all. The things
in the kitchen and the buttery are so they are very handy.[1]

The specificity of twenty-four-year-old Arvada Metcalf's letter indicates she organized and managed her household furnishings. Arvada
was "space-conscious." In a letter written in 1874, she described a parlor,
"And if you haven't on too large hoops, you can stand in the center of
the room and turn around without touching anything."[2]

Arvada's kitchen and pantry probably occupied a large portion of
the first-floor apartment. The dimensions of Arvada's kitchen and pantry
remain unknown, but it is possible to visualize the kitchen and furnishings from her vivid description and suggest her arrangements with an
architectural sketch (fig. 1). Clearly she tried to manipulate the space
with convenience in mind.

Convenience may or may not have been foremost in the minds
of American builders, architects, carpenters, and house-plan writers
who have arranged household space for more than three hundred years.
In the evolutionary process of moving from multiuse to specialized

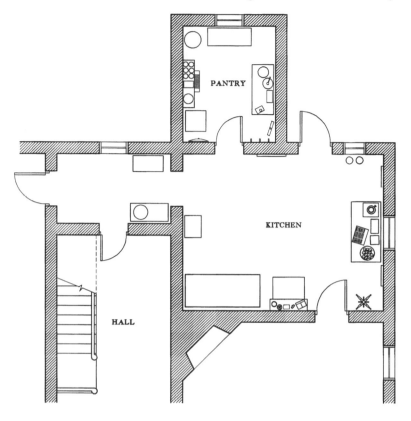

METCALF HOUSE ~ 1875

Fig. 1. Earl H. Graffam, Jr., kitchen arrangements as described in Arvada Nichols Metcalf's January 14, 1875, letter. (Drawing, Earl H. Graffam, Jr., 1997.)

space, the kitchen was planned as a workspace concealed at the back of the house or in the basement. Gwendolyn Wright notes that throughout the nineteenth century, few builders ever saw the kitchen as more than a large workroom. The result was usually a square or rectangular kitchen with or without auxiliary spaces occupying almost 25 percent of the first floor.[3]

Nineteenth-century women experienced the limitations of household space in kitchens that were overwhelmed by size and inconvenience. Popular magazines and farm journals contained house plans and articles about kitchen furnishings that reinforced awareness of their plight. Like many of her contemporaries, Arvada was a subscriber and reader. In 1874 she wrote to Estella, "Are you going to take The Fireside this year? We are not nor The Christian Union. We want to take Harpers and Scribners."[4]

Gail Winkler writes that Louis Godey began to publish architectural drawings in the *Lady's Book* as early as 1846. Godey used designs by John Claudius Loudon, John B. Papworth, and others without compunction because international copyright laws were not in effect in America. In 1850 Godey introduced American architectural plans. He was the first to combine architectural details and advice to housewives in response to subscriber interest in household planning.[5]

Sally McMurry studied nineteenth-century farmhouse designs by affluent northern farmers and farmers' wives published primarily in northern agricultural journals from 1830 until 1900. Although these planners were not typical American farmers, McMurry's study reveals how early women realized the limitations of household space and sought remedies for architectural shortcomings. One designer proposed to move the kitchen from the back of the house facing the barnyard and outbuildings to a more desirable location with a view of the public road. In the last quarter of the nineteenth century, farm journal writers joined others in discussions about convenient kitchen arrangements.[6]

It is safe to assume Arvada and her sister, Estella, had read Catharine Beecher's prescription for everything in its place in a proper kitchen. In 1869 Beecher and her sister Harriet Beecher Stowe wrote *The American Woman's Home*, an expanded version of Beecher's *Treatise on Domestic Economy for Use of Young Ladies at Home and at School*. *Treatise on Domestic Economy* was published in 1841 with succeeding editions until 1856 and became a textbook in schools and young ladies' seminaries.[7]

Siegfried Gidieon describes Beecher as a prophetic writer who understood the concepts of workplace organization. Her post–Civil War ideas preceded and were independent of household mechanization.[8] Beecher viewed the manipulation of space to accommodate the housewife as part of the organizational process.

In *American Woman's Home*, the chief consideration of the featured Christian home is convenience. Beecher meant her home to be suburban or rural, but her principles of residential design and interior layout are universally adaptable. The two-story house with basement is illustrated and described in detail. The kitchen is located on the first floor, confirming her belief that "a kitchen should always, if possible, be entirely above-ground, and well lighted." Sliding glass doors separate the kitchen from the stove room. The refrigerator or built-in ice-closet is located in the basement, the traditional storage area for perishables.[9]

The organized, built-in spaces that surround the sink and the food preparation center are the most remarkable aspect of the kitchen plan. The dry food stuffs, cooking utensils, supplies, and cleaning areas are brought together in a planned and orderly fashion to fulfill Beecher's requirement of "all conveniences in the kitchen and cellar, and a place appointed for each article." Individual pumps for well water and rain water beside the sink complete the labor-saving installations for cleaning.[10] Only the stove remained apart.

Symbolically, the cookstove also stands alone as the dominant kitchen furnishing. Susan Strasser labels the cast-iron stove as the major nineteenth-century technological change in household cooking, which was the principal task of housewives. The tending of the stove and the household cooking and baking required a constancy hard to imagine. The stove was seldom cool. In an oral history interview, Jane White of Owen County, Indiana, observed that her mother "got breakfast on the old woodburning stove and she would start her dinner . . . she would put them on right after breakfast, and, of course, for supper, why she would start right after dinner about preparing supper." Baking was a separate activity from everyday cooking. With or without servants, most women did their own baking. At the age of ninety-three, Grace Hawkins recalled: "I'd have to fix five or six lunches. Well, you had to have something for them to eat. Sometimes on wash days, when I didn't have enough time, I'd slice down icebox butterscotch cooky dough and bake that. But I baked every day of the year. How'd I do all that?"[11]

The cookstove or range, which burned wood and coal, dominated the kitchen space because of size; the ventilation process necessitated proximity to a fireplace or chimney. The larger range was modeled on the fireplace in which iron plates were extended across the hearth to enclose a space for an oven and a separate space for hot water. Later the fire grate was also enclosed, and the range was further developed with a series of sophisticated improvements. By the end of the nineteenth century, the term *range* was also applied to the smaller, freestanding cookstove. The average width of the range was at least twice that of the stove. Despite its greater convenience, the range, which was installed into a chimney or new brickwork, proved too costly for the average householder.[12]

Cooking space requirements did not end with mere measurements of the stove. Measurements in trade literature generally included the size of the covers or lids, the dimensions of the oven, and occasionally the length of the fire box. Stove pipes, woodboxes or coal scuttles, pokers, ash buckets, shovels, and various other accessories added to the space requirements for the stove. Trade catalogues such as Perry and Company's *Oriental Stove Works* contained illustrations of different models with and without extensions or improvements. An 1868 Perry and Company catalogue included an illustration of their "Improved Dictator Cooking Stove with Extension Top" (fig. 2). The company boasted the stove combined "all the modern improvements that are desirable." Despite added girth or height, the water reservoir attached to the cookstove surface and the tall narrow hot-water heater piped to the kitchen range were easily among the most popular of nineteenth-century home improvements.[13] A constant supply of hot water brought a much-needed convenience to the kitchen.

Arvada's sister, Estella Nichols Leonard, lived in Plymouth, Indiana, the hometown of the Nichols and Leonard families. After her marriage, Estella first lived in an apartment above W. W. Hill's Bakery, where her husband, William Eugene, worked. Later, as their family grew, they moved to a nine-room house.

Floy Leonard Hankins, born May 18, 1889, was the fifth of Estella's six children. In a taped interview with her daughter Alice Schmidt, Floy described her childhood home. The first-floor space of the two-story house was divided into six rooms: parlor, front bedroom, living or sitting room, large bedroom, dining room, and kitchen. Floy Hankins remembered the kitchen as "square" with one built-in cupboard in the corner. "In another corner was the 'famous table,'" she recalled, which held the bucket of drinking water. The brass bands on the wooden bucket were polished every Saturday, when everything was cleaned, "including the kids." The pump at the sink was for cistern water, intended for

Fig. 2. Improved Dictator Cooking Stove with Extension Top. From Perry and Co., *Oriental Stove Works* (Albany: By the company, 1868), p. 15. (Winterthur Library.)

washing. The iron sink always held a basin. Here faces and hands were washed and hair combed every morning. A mirror hung above the sink; below were cupboards, which held the heavy iron utensils. A stairway to the cellar occupied another corner, with a protective rail around the stairs. The big cookstove and its accompanying woodbox dominated the room. Floy's job as a young girl was to keep the woodbox filled. A gasoline stove also occupied kitchen space and was used in summer. Floy noted that although most gasoline stoves were "table-top affairs," theirs was a "two-decker" with an oven below. Both stoves "took up a lot of room," she said.[14]

The family never used the kitchen as social space. When asked if the family spent most of the time in the kitchen, Floy exclaimed, "Oh, no, in the sitting room!" The Leonard family only ate in the kitchen in the winter, at an oval table formerly in the dining room.

The kitchen was remodeled and enlarged about 1896. In one of Floy's most charming recollections, she told of the remodeling that resulted in an uneven ceiling. The remodelers installed a pole for support. This unique feature always intrigued visiting playmates. Her next-door neighbor, the young son of the high school principal, declared, "When I grow up, I'm going to have a hundred poles in my kitchen."[15]

Floy remembered the family kitchen and its furnishings as it appeared more than twenty years after Arvada's letter of 1875. Floy was born almost fourteen years later and never knew her aunt, who died in 1879. Although Floy's childhood recollection is not as detailed as her Aunt Arvada's letter, some late nineteenth-century change can be detected. The stove and woodbox took precedence in both accounts, their stationary position in the kitchen taken for granted. Floy's account of the gasoline stove used in summer denotes an interim solution to the intolerable heat produced by the woodburning stove. The auxiliary stove provided a temporary improvement but increased the shortage of space.

Arvada used the pantry extensively for washing dishes, laundering clothes, and personal hygiene. A single source probably provided the water kept in the pantry for multipurpose use. Estella's kitchen was equipped with an iron sink and a pump that provided cistern water for all washing needs, while family drinking water from another source was kept in a bucket on the table. Arvada used boxes, tables, shelves, and nails or hooks for storage. Estella's kitchen was equipped with at least one built-in cupboard. Both households were dependent on cellar storage.

Arvada's letter implies that she and her husband probably ate in the kitchen, where the Leonard family took only winter meals. Floy's emphatic statements about kitchen usage demonstrate the changing perception of kitchen from a multipurpose room to specialized space. By no means was this view of the kitchen universal. Lizabeth A. Cohen in her study of urban working-class families from 1885 to 1915 concluded that even with a parlor, these families preferred a larger kitchen space for socializing. Cohen says this choice was both a rejection of middle-class values and an affirmation of traditions brought from American rural roots or ethnic heritage.[16]

Disparities in lifestyle, income, and cultural advantages prevent the designation "typical American home," yet the very commonality of kitchen objects eases some restrictions imposed by class, ethnic, urban, rural, or regional distinctions. Trade literature, magazine and newspaper advertising, and contemporary literature are replete with descriptions of kitchen furnishings.

Miss Parloa's Kitchen Companion is firm about kitchen size and furnishings.[17] Maria Parloa, one of the first teachers at the Boston Cooking School, was a pioneer in the early cooking school movement that blossomed after home economics courses were installed at land grant universities. Her book is typical of 1880s and 1890s household advice literature.

Written in 1887, *Kitchen Companion* stipulates the kitchen should be large enough to accommodate range, sink, dresser, table, and chairs with minimum walking. In the chapter "An Ideal Kitchen," a diagram illustrates satisfactory arrangements for kitchen furnishings (fig. 3). The large freestanding dresser, which had long occupied American kitchens, remains virtually unchanged except for sliding glass doors. The sink, with its grooved drain board, rests on iron legs. The sink is flanked by a hinged table and a movable table with two drawers that measures precisely two and one-half feet by three and one-half feet. A settle table stands against the wall opposite the sink. One small zinc-covered table faces the range to receive hot dishes. Parloa confirmed the range to be the most important furnishing. Space determined whether a portable cookstove or set range was used: the range may only be approached from the front; the cookstove is accessible from all sides.[18]

A pantry about eight feet by twelve feet provides storage for all household equipment. It is furnished with tables and a variety of racks and shelves. Various pots and pans, spoons, cups, and pastry boards

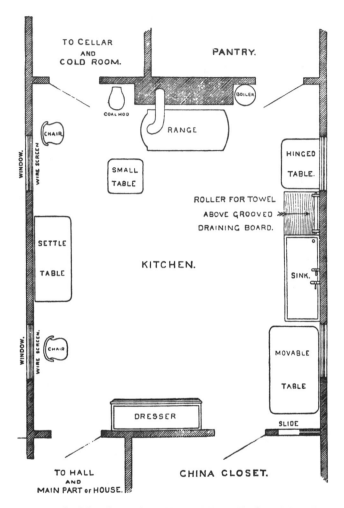

Fig. 3. Ideal kitchen plan. From Maria Parloa, *Miss Parloa's Kitchen Companion: A Guide for All Who Would Be Good Housekeepers* (Boston: Estes and Lauriat, 1887), p. 13. (Winterthur Library.)

hang from brass hooks. Some prepared foods and fresh fruit are kept here, while other auxiliary storage spaces hold canned and dried goods. Perishable fruit, vegetables, and meat are kept in the cellar. The adjacent china closet contains a sink for washing good china and glassware.[19] Although Parloa gave her kitchen thoughtful consideration, the numerous additional work spaces clearly do not save steps.

Excessive floor space did not solve the storage problems caused by quantities of required foodstuffs or household utensils. Because most late nineteenth-century homes included a pantry, built-in kitchen storage was scarce. Contemporary photographs invariably show vertical space consumed by numerous shelves (fig. 4). Kitchen utensils, dishcloths, and drinking vessels hang from hooks in hopeful convenience, much as in Arvada's pantry.

Unlike other household furnishings, many kitchen objects were stationary. The stove, sink, and pump generally remained in place to-

Fig. 4. Housemaid in kitchen of Fowler house, Danvers, Mass., ca. 1890. (Society for the Preservation of New England Antiquities, Boston.)

gether with the multiple shelves and occasional kitchen cupboard. The location of the stove or range was usually dependent on the chimney, while water pipes determined the location of pump and sink. House-keepers seldom moved the table, chairs, dresser, or chest because of their relationship to existing windows and doors.

Throughout the four decades surveyed, the most common portable object remained Floy's "famous" kitchen table. On its surface, dishes were washed, bread was made, the baby was bathed, meals were served, letters were written, and fabric was cut. In 1887, the year Parloa wrote her discourse, Miller and Company of West Farmington, Ohio, offered a finished maple table with poplar top; its dimensions, twenty-seven by forty-one inches, almost precisely fit the Parloa requirement.[20]

The portable pie safe and icebox/refrigerator at various times occu-pied the kitchen, cellar, pantry, back porch, or dining room. Since the mid nineteenth century, one or both were commonly found in the American home. The function of the pie safe was food storage. Beecher recommended cold meats, cream, and other perishables be kept in "a safe or moveable closet with sides of wire or perforated tin" located in the cellar, adding that ants could be discouraged by placing the safe legs in containers of water. Parloa dispersed her perishables, designating space in the cellar for the cold storage of meats, pickles, fruit, and vege-tables. Cooked food went to a wall closet in the pantry, while a refrigera-tor or icebox occupied a corner of her pantry. An advertisement for the Baldwin refrigerator is included in her cookbook.[21]

Refrigerators were a godsend but often were messy and smelly. The ice man usually left a trail of water and muddy prints, prompting various solutions, such as placing the refrigerator in a closet that opened on the porch. Manufacturers offered refrigerators in various sizes and styles. For example, the 1894 Challenge Iceberg Refrigerators trade catalogue featured a model with or without sideboard attachment. The hand-carved sideboard addition was twenty-seven inches high and sported a beveled "French" mirror.[22]

One of the most popular innovations to bring together far-flung objects was the Hoosier cabinet. The Hoosier Manufacturing Company boasted their Cabinet No. 14 was "as near the ideal thing in the way of a kitchen cabinet as will ever be made." The cabinet, made of oak with solid brass knobs and catches, measured sixty-seven inches in height and forty inches in width with an overall depth of thirty inches.

The flour bin at the top of the cabinet held fifty pounds of flour, which was sifted when dispensed. The sugar bin was on the opposite side. Tea and coffee canisters and six spice cans lined the door. The tabletop measured twenty-eight by forty inches with more usable space than the average table, said Hoosier, because cooking supplies were stored in the cabinet. One of the three drawers was lined for cornmeal.[23]

The Hoosier boasted the portability of the table, pie safe, and refrigerator. A satisfied customer from North Dakota wrote, "In the winter of 1902 when coal was so high and scarce, we moved our range and Hoosier Kitchen Cabinet into the dining room and closed up the kitchen."[24]

Hoosier billed Cabinet No. 14 as "The Great Step-Saver," coming right to the point about the misuse of kitchen space: "You go from range to pantry, from pantry to kitchen table in an endless chain of wearying footsteps every time you prepare a meal. In this respect, if you don't own a Hoosier Kitchen Cabinet, you are not better off than your great grandmother was." Hoosier illustrated the step-saving theme with diagrams (fig. 5). The footprints tell the story better than words. This particular idea is still used by kitchen planners today, who sometimes instruct clients to coat their shoes with flour and observe the traffic pattern through the kitchen. The Hoosier catalogue touches on an early twentieth-century philosophy about space. Not only will objects be grouped together, but "each article has its own special place, just where it is easiest to get at."[25]

The Hoosier not only saved steps but brought order and organization to small kitchen furnishings and supplies in an attractive manner. In 1887 Helen Campbell bemoaned the fact that the parlor and other public areas "consume all the money, and the kitchen fares as it can, being finished with odds and ends, and lacking in every real essential." The idea of the kitchen as a catch-all continued, and, approximately twenty years later, Gustav Stickley wrote, "Even in a small house the tendency too often is to make the kitchen the dump heap of the whole household."[26]

The writings of designers, planners, home economists, and efficiency and management experts bridged the gap into the twentieth century. Robert Wiebe writes that a new middle class with burgeoning ranks of professionals in law, medicine, home economics, and social work spurred on progressive reform in the United States at the begin-

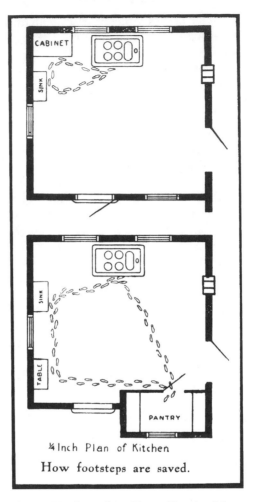

CABINET

SINK

PANTRY

SINK

TABLE

¼ Inch Plan of Kitchen

How footsteps are saved.

Fig. 5. Kitchen plan. From Hoosier Manufacturing Co., *Hoosier Kitchen Cabinets* (New Castle, Ind.: By the company,
[1905]), p. 9. (Trade Literature Collection,
Smithsonian Institution Libraries.)

ning of the new century. Home economists were interested in more than domesticity and viewed the family as society's most important unit, awaiting enrichment by scientific principles. Many realized these principles were applicable to all facets of home management and planning. Home economics departments could be found at approximately thirty colleges. The eastern cooking schools added teacher training to their programs. Women attended cooking classes, listened to lectures on household management, and read the appropriate magazines.[27]

Homemaker magazines catered to the middle-class housewife; *House Beautiful* (1896) was the earliest and best known. Published in Chicago, its pages were filled with articles on interiors, photographs of homes, features on specific rooms, and a general philosophy of what women must know and practice in the home. The popular *Good Housekeeping Magazine* and *Ladies' Home Journal* were not homemaker magazines but dealt with personal topics, fiction, and home concerns. *Ladies' Home Journal*, however, had a strong influence on domestic architecture. The magazine's early appeals to architects to submit residential schemes for publication met with indifference, but the first design published was well received. In 1901 a series of designs by Frank Lloyd Wright began. Thousands of *Ladies' Home Journal* plans were ordered. James Marston Fitch credits Wright as the first American architect to fully understand the aesthetic implications of the revolution in the American home created by industry. This revolution, however, had its roots in the diverse writings of foresighted women professionals. "Architects would probably have gone on building miserable kitchens forever had the domestic-science classes not taught women themselves," wrote Anna Leach in 1899.[28]

Contemporary articles suggested the availability of household help determined the size of the kitchen. House planners inevitably proposed a large kitchen for a household with servants and often designated an area adjacent to the kitchen for the maid's room. Nina C. Kinney offered two plans for updating the kitchen of 1901 in the *American Kitchen Magazine*; one with a maid in mind, the other for a family with no household help. For the servantless home, the solution was a small room combining kitchen and dining areas. Both plans included built-ins, double sinks, refrigerators serviced by outside delivery, good lighting, and a separate baking space.[29]

Although the majority of households did not employ full-time

household help, the servant issue was an ongoing topic in advice literature and popular magazines. Advertising exploited the subject. The
Hoover trade literature proclaimed, "The Hoosier System is an insurance against servant troubles. It means a neat kitchen, and a servant
appreciates that. She has to spend most of her time there."[30]

The servant class was shrinking, and factory work was preferable
to housework. These verses reprinted in *House Beautiful* in 1908 express
the situation:

> Mamie's in the factory,
> Annie's in the store,
> Bridget will not worry
> With housework any more.
> Mollie's in a sweat-shop,
> Kate's a manicure,
> No one scrubs or washes,
> Wages are no lure.
> Maggie's an apprentice,
> Flossie's making mats,
> And that is why we're living,
> Most all of us, in flats.
>
> Puck[31]

The debate about kitchen size raged. Gwendolyn Wright states the
kitchen now received more emphasis than the parlor in many builders'
pattern books. The average kitchen was roughly 120 feet square. The
quest for efficiency focused on a small and sanitary kitchen, but many
rejected this view. They clung to nineteenth-century memories: "My
grandmother's kitchen is a cherished memory picture. The stove, the
sink, and work table were simply incidentals. . . . The room was big
and square, and it was a long way from the dark couch corner over to
the tall clock ticking away the slow minutes of the winter afternoon."[32]

The size issue took on a scientific flavor that permeated magazine
articles. In "Scientifically Designed Kitchens," George Walsh theo-
rized, "We have erred in the past in both ways by building too small
or too large kitchens." Charles E. White, Jr., an architect, chose practi-
cality as his theme in "Planning a Vital Department: The Kitchen
Where Science Should Over-Rule Art." White conceded that "the
modern, successful kitchen . . . is largely a matter of application of
ideas gleaned from women." He added these must be refined "by the

inventive genius of the architect." White proposed that the methods of efficiency engineers coupled with analysis and design should be applied in the simplest manner. Writing in 1916, Harriette Taber Richardson prescribed a kitchen composed of many work centers. Richardson emphasized these centers should be placed "so that their positions will give equal service in any type of kitchen. . . . A place for everything is not enough, the places must be related."[33]

Household advisers did not neglect kitchen furnishings. *Ladies' Home Journal* published Parloa's 1905 basic list of kitchen furnishings priced at twenty-eight dollars with a second list for the housekeeper who could invest sixty-five dollars. Parloa assumed all modern houses and apartments were furnished with a range and set tubs, but she advised saving a reserve of twenty-five dollars for a range. In her basic list, the kitchen furniture is sparse: only a table with a drawer, two chairs, and an ice chest. Milk-pans, stewpans, bread and cake pans, and a roaster are listed with a variety of cooking, serving, and eating utensils. Stoneware dishes for baking are included with serviceable earthenware bowls. Tinware for storage, woodenware, a steamer, and the ever-present dipper appear with a coffeepot and coal hod. Strainers, measuring cups, the popular egg-beater, and a host of other small furnishings are not forgotten.[34]

In the organization of utensils, a domestic struggle of sorts was waged for vertical space. Mrs. M., one of several readers commenting in the column "My New House," published in *House Beautiful* in 1914, exclaimed, "In my kitchen you will see a thousand hooks—more or less—so that everything may be hung up out of the way and yet be within easy reach." On the same page, an opposing philosophy appeared, "Let the walls be clear and clean."[35]

Again Harriette Taber Richardson tried to be systematic, "Actual measurement of the utensils is more than necessary to provide useful shelf room," she noted. Richardson summarized the problems of kitchen arrangements and commented on the housewife's dilemma. The architect controlled the stationary features of the kitchen: the chimney, water pipes, windows, doors, and often the arrangements of the stove, sink, and shelves. The housewife struggled with the placement of furnishings and coped with an assortment of utensils.[36]

Industry supplied the latest mass-produced furnishings. Advertising showcased the products with department stores and mail-order houses as distributors. In Chicago, Marshall Field was typical of the large department stores that created "model rooms" and displayed the latest gadgets and appliances. In 1872 Montgomery Ward began a mail-order business in Chicago, an important transportation center. Sears, Roebuck, and Company moved from Minneapolis to Chicago in 1887. Reaching a diverse audience, the mail-order catalogue was often the only magazine found in isolated homes.[37]

In 1913 a study of an early rural Minnesota township of about three thousand people revealed the percentages of mechanical innovations introduced in homes: "oil stoves, fifty-seven; furnace, fifteen; hard-coal stoves, forty-four; soft-coal heaters, thirty-one; washing machines, thirty-three; washing machines run by engine, ten; drinking water in house, eleven." For the housewife, toil was unremitting. "In only ten percent of the places was a hired girl kept. Sixty-nine percent of the families were without any girl help of sixteen years of age or over." Only 27 percent of the homes contained periodicals such as *Ladies' Home Journal*.[38]

In an article written for the *Department of Agriculture Farmers' Bulletin*, Anna Barrows used the 1910 census figures of six million farms to estimate that at least eight million farm women, including female helpers and servants, labored in the kitchen. She concluded their lives could be simplified and enriched by improving the arrangement of kitchen furnishings. The key was usage.[39]

When Barrows stated a kitchen used only for cooking required less space, she meant that storage and meal service were the two functions that required a larger kitchen. The storage problem was simplified if the farm was located near a shopping area, where food staples and other necessities were convenient. Regardless of location, however, more space was required if family or hired hands ate in the kitchen.[40]

The placement of stove, sink, and work table determined kitchen convenience, Barrows concluded, because the focus of kitchen labor is food preparation, service, and cleanup. Acknowledging that much is precluded by plumbing and the chimney, she offered before-and-after plans. Her solution drew the work centers together, linked them at center with the portable kitchen table, and placed them as near the dining room and pantry as possible.[41]

Barrows did not discuss electricity in the farmhouse. The electrical appliances displayed at the 1893 World's Columbian Exposition remained novelties in the early twentieth century. Availability and acceptance were not immediate. "Electricity is making its way into the kitchen through the parlor and dining-room," wrote Anna Leach in 1899, pointing to the electric teakettle, coffeepot, and chafing dish. In 1911 Helen Louise Johnson railed in *Good Housekeeping*, "Why is it that when a lecture on fireless cookers is given six hundred women will venture out in the rain to hear it; and when electrical devices are talked about on a pleasant day less than two hundred will attend?"[42]

The ubiquitous fireless cooker was one of the most popular kitchen furnishings in the 1900s and 1910s. The fireless was an insulated box lined with metal into which preheated soapstone or metal disks were placed to receive containers of partially cooked food. The cooker was a time-saver and a godsend in overheated kitchens. Advertising and articles, such as "Canning with the Fireless" and "Achievements of the Fireless Cooker" published in *Good Housekeeping* in August 1909, touted the benefits of fireless cooking.[43] Women gladly incorporated this convenient object into their kitchen space.

The kitchen of the Woodrow Wilson House documents early twentieth-century spatial arrangements. Location, wealth, and years distance the house from the homes of Arvada and Estella. The Woodrow Wilson House, a property of the National Trust located at 2340 S Street, N.W., in Washington, D.C., is an urban town house designed by Waddy Butler Wood in 1915 for Washington businessman Henry Parker Fairbanks. At the end of his second term in 1921, President Woodrow Wilson and his wife purchased the house, where he died in 1924. Mrs. Wilson remained in the house until her death in 1961. In a house designed to be staffed by servants, domestic duties were assumed for years by Isaac and Mary Scott, who lived at the residence, and by day-servants who were hired as needed.[44]

Although various improvements were made, the spacious kitchen and many furnishings remain intact (fig. 6). The room is a rare cultural artifact because most turn-of-the-century kitchens were gutted and modernized. The kitchen is located at ground level. The centerpiece is the coal and gas range topped by an impressive hood. This French range probably was distributed by a Washington dealer. In 1904 the *Architectural Record* reported that a French range "with its black steel sides and nickel plated trimmings is a handsome piece of kitchen furniture. At one end, it will have a section devoted to cooking with gas. At the proper

Fig. 6. Kitchen, Woodrow Wilson House, Washington, D.C. (Woodrow Wilson House/National Trust, Washington, D.C.)

height, a projecting curved hood will collect most of the smoke . . . and allow it to be drawn into a vent flue in the chimney."[45]

The combination of fuels is a reminder of the long-lasting doubts about cooking with gas. The earliest patent relating to American gas stoves was given in 1855, but not until the 1880s were gas stoves sold in appreciable numbers. This combination range offered cooler cooking in summer, with coal burning capabilities as needed, and consumed less space than Floy's gasoline and cast-iron cooking stoves of the 1890s. A Hermatic fireless cooker owned by Mrs. Wilson stands beside the stove.[46]

The original architectural drawings make clear the location of range and sinks. The vegetable sink is located across from its companion, fitted with wooden drain board. The small kitchenware that hangs above the sink is a reminder of the controversy over vertical usage. A large pantry lined with shelves provides kitchen storage. A McCray ice-box made in Kendallville, Indiana, and an early General Electric refrig-erator remain in the room. The stationary zinc-top table stands before the stove to receive hot dishes. The hinged table, which appeared in Parloa's 1887 sketch, is replicated here almost thirty years later. A dumb-waiter carried food from the kitchen at ground level to the butler's pan-try and the dining room one floor above. Designed by a prominent architect as a modern and efficient kitchen, the room reveals how little had changed in forty years. The observer has the haunting impression of having just walked into Miss Parloa's kitchen and yearns to ask Mary Scott if things were "handy."

At the outset of the twentieth century, furnishings remained in-compatible with their kitchen space. Despite an outpouring of residen-tial designs, household advice, and advertising, the kitchen was a room of wasted space and unnecessary steps. In the first twenty years of the new century, many changes were proposed for the American home, but the actuality of change was uneven. It would be another ten years or more before many of the efficient and scientific proposals would be realized; some would never be fulfilled. There were great disparities among the kitchens of the wealthy upper class, middle-class progres-sives, the urban working class, and farmers.

Thousands of words were written about convenient kitchens, but change was slow. Prescriptive writers were unrealistic in expecting an immediate alteration of workplace reality. Architects played constant catch-up to prescribed changes, and kitchen planners and manufactur-ers also struggled in the conquest of space. Kitchen furnishings re-mained low on the household priority scale. A new sofa or organ in the parlor usually took precedence over a cupboard needed to alleviate kitchen clutter.

Arvada's letter revealed an awareness of household space and an effort to make her kitchen furnishings "handy." Decades later, Floy could recall the space of Estella's "square" kitchen and the arrange-ments of the stove, sink, and the kitchen table. Women accepted and adapted as best they could, but the question remained, "Where do I put it?"

The prime users of the kitchen were women, and their influence on kitchen design was considerable. The roots of modern kitchen plan-ning lay in the nineteenth century and provided the foundation for

early twentieth-century reformers whose names became household
words.

[1] Arvada Nichols Metcalf to Estella Nichols Leonard, January 14, 1875, private
collection.

[2] Metcalf to Leonard, February 4, 1874, private collection.

[3] Clifford Edward Clark, Jr., *The American Family Home, 1800–1960* (Chapel Hill:
University of North Carolina Press, 1986), pp. 15, 42–45; Gwendolyn Wright, *Moralism
and the Model Home: Domestic Architecture and Cultural Conflict in Chicago, 1873–1913*
(Chicago: University of Chicago Press, 1980), pp. 37–38.

[4] Metcalf to Leonard, March 1874, private collection.

[5] Gail Caskey Winkler, "Influence of Godey's *Lady's Book* on the American Woman
and Her Home: Contributions to a National Culture, 1830–1877" (Ph.D. diss., University
of Wisconsin, Madison, 1988), pp. 148–51, 155–58, 387.

[6] Sally McMurry, *Families and Farmhouses in Nineteenth-Century America: Vernacular Design and Social Change* (New York: Oxford University Press, 1988), pp. 3–5, 25–
29, 114–16.

[7] Catharine E. Beecher and Harriet Beecher Stowe, *The American Woman's Home*
with an intro. by Joseph Van Why (1869; reprint, Hartford, Conn.: Stowe-Day Fndn.,
1975).

[8] Siegfried Giedion, *Mechanization Takes Command: A Contribution to Anonymous
History* (New York: Oxford University Press, 1948), pp. 513–19.

[9] Beecher and Stowe, *American Woman's Home*, pp. 371, 23–25, 32, 38–39.

[10] Beecher and Stowe, *American Woman's Home*, pp. 228, 35.

[11] Susan Strasser, *Never Done: A History of American Housework* (New York: Pantheon Books, 1982), pp. 47–49; Jane White, interview in Eleanor Arnold, ed., *Feeding Our
Families: Hoosier Homemakers through the Years, An Oral History Project* (Indianapolis:
Indiana Extension Homemakers Assoc., 1983), p. 82; Harvey Green with the assistance
of Mary-Ellen Perry, *The Light of the Home: An Intimate View of the Lives of Women
in Victorian America* (New York: Pantheon Books, 1983), p. 60; Grace Hawkins interview
in Arnold, *Feeding Our Families*, p. 84.

[12] Harvey Green, *Light of the Home*, p. 61; Loris S. Russell, *Handy Things to Have
around the House* (Toronto: McGraw Hill Ryerson, 1979), pp. 30–33; Priscilla J. Brewer,
" 'We Have Got a Very Good Cooking Stove': Advertising, Design, and Consumer Response to the Cookstove, 1815–1880," *Winterthur Portfolio* 25, no. 1 (Spring 1990): 44.

[13] Perry and Co., *Oriental Stove Works* (Albany: By the company, 1868), pp. 3, 15,
Winterthur Library; Brewer, "We Have Got a Very Good Cooking Stove," pp. 47–49;
Green, *Light of the Home*, pp. 61–62.

[14] Floy Leonard Hankins, interview with Alice Schmidt, spring 1984, private
collection.

[15] Hankins interview.

[16] Lizabeth A. Cohen, "Embellishing a Life of Labor: An Interpretation of the Material Culture of American Working-Class Homes, 1885–1915," *Journal of American Culture*
3, no. 4 (Winter 1980): 756–72.

[17] Maria Parloa, *Miss Parloa's Kitchen Companion: A Guide for All Who Would Be
Good Housekeepers* (Boston: Estes and Lauriat, 1887), p. 9.

[18] Parloa, *Kitchen Companion*, pp. 10–14, 16–17.

[19] Parloa, *Kitchen Companion*, pp. 17–25.

[20] Miller and Co., *Twenty-Eighth Semi-Annual Catalogue and Price List* (West Farmington, Ohio; 1887, Trade Literature Collection, Smithsonian Institution Libraries.

[21] Beecher and Stowe, *American Woman's Home*, p. 376; Parloa, *Kitchen Companion*, pp. 18, 23–25; see also Baldwin Manufacturing Co. advertisement on unnumbered page at back of book.

[22] Alice Kellogg, *Home Furnishing, Practical and Artistic* (New York: Frederick and Stokes, 1905), p. 76; Challenge Corn Planter Co., *Ninth Annual Illustrated Catalogue and Price List of the Challenge Iceberg Refrigerators, Sideboard, and Ice Chests* (Grand Haven, Mich.: By the company, 1894), pp. 24–25, Trade Literature Collection, Smithsonian Institution Libraries.

[23] Hoosier Manufacturing Co., *Hoosier Kitchen Cabinets* (New Castle, Ind.: By the company, [1905]), pp. 16, 21, 22–24, Trade Literature Collection, Smithsonian Institution Libraries.

[24] *Hoosier Kitchen Cabinets*, p. 29.

[25] *Hoosier Kitchen Cabinets*, pp. 21, 8, 9.

[26] Helen Campbell, "A Comfortable House," *Cosmopolitan* 3, no. 3 (May 1887): 196; Gustav Stickley, *Craftsman Homes* (1909; reprint, New York: Dover Publications, 1979), p. 142.

[27] Robert H. Wiebe, *The Search for Order, 1877–1920* (New York: Hill and Wang, 1967), pp. 111–21; Emma Seifrit Weigley, "It Might Have Been Euthenics: The Lake Placid Conferences and the Home Economics Movement," *American Quarterly* 26, no. 1 (March 1974): 79, 80–83.

[28] Gwendolyn Wright, *Building the Dream: A Social History of Housing in America* (New York: Pantheon Books, 1981), pp. 164–67; James Marston Fitch, *Architecture and the Esthetics of Plenty* (New York: Columbia University Press, 1961), pp. 81–84; Anna Leach, "Science in the Model Kitchen," *Cosmopolitan* 27, no. 1 (May 1899): 96.

[29] Nina C. Kinney, "Two Kitchens," *American Kitchen Magazine* 14, no. 6 (March 1901): 210–15.

[30] *Hoosier Kitchen Cabinets*, p. 8.

[31] *House Beautiful* 23, no. 4 (March 1908): 32.

[32] Wright, *Building the Dream*, pp. 169–70; Mabel Wood Johnson, "A Plea for the Large Kitchen," *Boston Cooking School Magazine* 6, no. 6 (January 1902): 246–47.

[33] George F. Walsh, "Scientifically Designed Kitchens," *House Beautiful* 30, no. 6 (November 1911): 183; Charles E. White, Jr., "Planning a Vital Department: The Kitchen Where Science Should Over-Rule Art," *House Beautiful* 33, no. 1 (December 1912): 27–28; Harriette Taber Richardson, "Kitchen Units: Do Working Centers Help to Solve the Problem of Convenience?" *House Beautiful* 39, no. 2 (January 1916): 58, xiii.

[34] Maria Parloa, "How to Furnish a Kitchen," *Ladies' Home Journal* 22, no. 11 (October 1905): 30.

[35] Elizabeth C. Moore, "My New House," *House Beautiful* 36, no. 3 (August 1914): 96; L. D. Stearns, "The Kitchen," *House Beautiful* 36, no. 3 (August 1914): 96.

[36] Richardson, "Kitchen Units," pp. 59, xiii.

[37] Earl Lifshey, *The Housewares Story: A History of the American Housewares Industry* (Chicago: National Housewares Manufacturers Assoc., 1973), pp. 90–94.

[38] Carl W. Thompson and G. P. Warber, "A Rural Township in Minnesota, 1913," in David J. Rothman and Sheila M. Rothman, eds., *Sources of the American Social Tradition, Volume II, 1865 to Present* (New York: Basic Books, 1975), pp. 83, 84, 85.

[39] Anna Barrows, "The Farm Kitchen as a Workshop," *Department of Agriculture Farmers' Bulletin* 607 (Washington, D.C.: U.S. Government Printing Office, 1914), p. 1.

[40] Barrows, "Farm Kitchen," pp. 4–5.

[41] Barrows, "Farm Kitchen," pp. 10–15.

[42] Leach, "Science in the Model Kitchen," p. 102; Helen Louise Johnson, "Why Not Use Electricity?" *Good Housekeeping* 52, no. 4 (April 1911): 471.

[43] Edith Emery, "Canning with the Fireless," *Good Housekeeping* 49, no. 2 (August 1909): 210; Bertha Bellows Streeter, "Achievements of the Fireless Cooker," *Good Housekeeping* 49, no. 2 (August 1909): 211.

[44] Frank J. Aucella, assistant director, Woodrow Wilson House, Washington, D.C., interview with author, August 5, 1992.

[45] *Boyd's Directory of the District of Columbia*, Washington, D.C., 1912, p. 547; "The Planning and Furnishing of the Kitchen in the Modern Residence," *Architectural Record* 16, no. 4 (October 1904): 384–92.

[46] Russell, *Handy Things*, pp. 34–37; Aucella interview.

The Wealth of a Rebellion That Was

The Material Culture and Domestic Space of Bacon's Rebellion in Virginia, 1677

John H. Sprinkle, Jr.

In 1677 Mr. Thomas Hansford, a prominent resident of York County, Virginia, lived with his wife, children, and six servants on a "most commodious seat of land . . . with a very good dwelling house, 2 new tobacco houses of 40 foot each, and a good orchard." This seventy-five-acre farmstead was one portion of Hansford's fifteen-hundred-acre landholdings spread among four plantations. Roaming about this real estate were a total of sixty-three cattle, swine, and horses.[1]

Hansford's home included a hall and parlor, with chambers above each, and a detached kitchen. In Hansford's hall were eleven leather chairs, a table, stool, couch, and cupboard. The parlor contained two feather beds with bolsters, rugs, and blankets. The hall and parlor chambers held three additional feather beds, one with a "suit of curtains fringed and trimmed with silk." Among Hansford's personal belongings were twelve pieces of silver plate, including a tankard, a bowl, six spoons, and two fish cups. Bonded for £200 in 1677, Hansford's estate was sold at auction for almost thirty thousand pounds of tobacco in

The author thanks James P. Whittenburg and Esther C. White for their comments during the preparation of this study.

1679. In sum, Hansford appears to have been a relatively successful tobacco planter living in one of the most settled and stable portions of the Virginia colony during the late seventeenth century.[2]

Hansford was also a rebel. In fact, he was "a most egregious rebel: accounted next under [Nathaniel] Bacon the chief" participant in the violent revolt known as Bacon's Rebellion. A series of raids between Native American and English settlements in 1675 eventually triggered a widespread uprising among the English Virginians in 1676. Fearing governmental inaction, Nathaniel Bacon, a relative newcomer to the colony, illegally assumed command of a strong militia force and directed attacks on several Native American groups. After being indicted as rebels by Gov. William Berkeley, the Baconians marched on James-town, forced the established government into exile, and then set fire to the colonial capital. With the inopportune death of Bacon that fall, the malicious rebellion soon faltered. Governor Berkeley rallied the Loyal-ist forces and reestablished his royal government by January 1677. Hans-ford and at least twenty other Baconians were later executed, and Gover-nor Berkeley was removed from office by a royal commission sent by Charles II to investigate the revolt.[3]

To their Loyalist contemporaries, the Baconians comprised the "vulgar and most ignorant people" in Virginia who were "unsatisfied" and "impatient" with Governor Berkeley's attempts to control Anglo-Indian conflict on the colony's frontier. Across the colony, "the ruder sort" of Virginians were led into rebellion against the Loyalists by "the darling of the people," Nathaniel Bacon, and approximately one hun-dred principal rebels. This Baconian leadership was described in 1677 as "free men that had but lately crept out of the condition of servants." Viewed by the Loyalists as traitors and rebels, the Baconians saw them-selves as defenders of their lives, fortunes, and colony against Indian aggression and governmental neglect.[4]

Unexpectedly exploding across the Old Dominion during the mid-1670s, Bacon's Rebellion has been variously interpreted as a precursor to the American Revolution, a sectional conflict between core and pe-ripheral English settlements, a threshold in the formation of a slave-based colonial society, and a class-based civil war. The Baconians are traditionally defined as a group of economically and socially frustrated frontier settlers who, faced with declining opportunity in the colony, chose to rebel against the established colonial government. Historians have generally followed the characterization of the Baconians as a "rabble crue" comprising "only the rascality and meanest of the people . . . there being hardly two amongst them . . . who have estates or are person of reputation and indeed very few who can either write or read." Given traditional interpretations of the revolt—that the Baconians were primarily frustrated servants, slaves, and ex-indentured servants led by a single elite Virginian—Hansford's comfortable material surroundings are in stark contrast to his participation in Bacon's Rebellion. In short, Hansford was too well-off to be a rebel.[5]

The detailed record of Hansford's estate was gathered during 1677 in the aftermath of the Baconian uprising. Because of the treasonous rebellion, the estates of twenty-three principal Baconians were attained by an act of the colony's general court. Attainder is the legal process by which all the possessions of a person convicted of treason are forfeited to the Crown. The rebel estates were "only to be inventoried" and "security taken" against embezzlement until the king signaled his "further pleasure." Although collection of the attainder inventories was supervised by two prominent Loyalists, the rebel estates were appraised at the local level by "the most knowing and rational of [a rebel's] neighbors."[6]

The Baconian inventories are significant because of the data they contain and for the manner in which the information was recorded. Unlike most seventeenth-century probate inventories from the Chesapeake region, the Baconian attainder inventories list both the rebels' personal estate and their real estate. They contain intriguing descriptions of the quality of landholdings, housing, and farm improvements that are absent in other inventories. Although individual items were not given monetary valuations, bonds offered as security for several estates ranged from £40 to £500. United not by the legal process of probate but by their involvement in rebellion, the Baconians appear to present a more comprehensive view of late seventeenth-century Chesapeake farmsteads. In short, the Baconian inventories provide a unique opportunity to appraise the material world and domestic space of these rebels.[7]

Land was the primary focus of wealth in the seventeenth-century Chesapeake. The principal Baconians lived in eight counties within the James-York Peninsula and along Virginia's Southside. With three thousand acres of "good," "indifferent," and "poor" land spread across five plantations, Anthony Arnold owned the largest and most diverse parcels among the Baconians. The smallest total landholding was William West's 160 acres of "ordinary land." Individual farms ranged in size from Hansford's 75-acre York County farmstead to plantations with as many as 1,500 acres. At least two Baconians held leases on farmland. Although one-third of the rebels apparently held no real estate, the average Baconian controlled about 1,000 acres of land. By comparison, the average acreage in Middlesex County, Virginia, in 1677 was approximately 660 acres. Thus, the major Baconians had above-average landholdings when compared with their Chesapeake neighbors.[8]

Although none of the Baconian plantations equaled the permanence of Berkeley Loyalist Arthur Allen's "Bacon's Castle" in Surry County, descriptions of the Baconian "dwelling plantations" varied from James Crews's "very good plantation with a formal dwelling house with brick chimneys [and] four fires" to John Whitson's fifteen-hundred-acre farm with a "small old dwelling house." Most of the housing was of wooden, earthfast construction: only Bacon lived in a "small new brick house." William Rookings lived in a "new framed dwelling house covered with shingles," while William Scarburgh had died before his "new framed dwelling house" could be completed. Four of the Baconians had "new" additions to their existing homes. Most of the Baconian housing was in at least "good" condition in the judgment of the appraisers. Out of twelve specific dwelling descriptions, only Whitson's home was termed as being small and old. Thomas Whaley's plantation contained a "35 foot dwelling house." Housing age, size, and condition were important status indicators in a region of impermanent architecture.[9]

Hansford lived in a typical Chesapeake region dwelling house that comprised two rooms on the ground floor with chambers above both rooms. It was probably similar to the house detailed in a 1679 Henrico County building contract between Loyalist Thomas Chamberlaine and carpenter James Gates: a frame structure forty feet long by twenty feet wide, clapboard covered, with the upper and lower floors divided into two rooms each. The dwelling, which cost twelve hundred pounds of tobacco and took seven months to build, had ground-laid sills, no cellar, and two chimneys. As revealed by several archaeological investigations of earthfast housing, the twenty by forty foot dimension was common for "Virginia" houses in the Chesapeake. These homes were, however, "very pleasant inside, with convenient windows and openings."[10]

The Loyalist appraisers described Hansford's two rooms as a hall and a parlor. Seven of the Baconian inventories referenced a "hall" as the principal room in the house. Only two "parlors" are recorded, but other rooms may have served the same function, such as Bacon's "brick house," which certainly contained his most formal rooms. While halls functioned as the primary domestic space, parlors were relatively private spaces within the Chesapeake home and were found in only the wealthiest households. Hansford's home was of such quality that it was taken over by the York County Court for its monthly meetings after the rebellion.[11]

Above, below, and adjoining the Baconian's hall and parlor were an assortment of recorded inner rooms, garrets, and chambers. Thomas Hall and William Scarburgh's homes contained a "room above stairs." William Hunt's "new hall" had a "room adjoining," as did Robert Jones's kitchen. These informally defined spaces were probably additions to the original structure and provided extra sheltered space for the full range of household activities. Although several of the inventories are room-by-room descriptions, details about interior architectural appointments are limited to references to white chambers, shingled rooms, window curtains, and brick fireplaces.[12]

A transatlantic perspective on housing standards among the leading Baconians in the Chesapeake follows from comparison with contemporary English dwellings. As James Horn has documented, most Virginians and Marylanders experienced a substantial decrease in housing quality when they emigrated to the colonies. English houses were also more durable and of a better quality than the impermanent architecture of earthfast housing of Virginia and Maryland. Whereas in England the average middling farmer's house would contain five to seven rooms, in the Chesapeake the typical house had only two rooms.[13]

In the colonies, the limitation of domestic space may be explained by the scarcity of skilled labor in a tobacco economy. In the late seventeenth century, William Fitzhugh advised against building larger dwellings in the Chesapeake because carpentry cost three times as much and took three times as long as was typical in London. A decade after Bacon's Rebellion, a French visitor noted that "whatever their rank, and I know not why, they build only two rooms with some closets on the ground floor, and two rooms in the attic above." "According to their means," planters built several of these two-room–plan dwellings as well as detached kitchens and separate houses for English servants, black slaves, and the tobacco crop. Earthfast housing was so common that "when you come to the home of a person of some means, you think you are entering a fairly large village."[14]

Most Baconian housing was clearly superior to the Chesapeake norm with regard to quality and size. Nine of the inventoried Baconians lived in houses with three or more rooms. Of these, five occupied dwellings comparable in size to average English homes. William Hunt's house contained a total of at least eight rooms. Baconian houselots were generally described as having "much good and new framed housing." William Carter and James Crews lived in "formal" dwellings with brick fireplaces and chimney stacks. In all, based upon the number of identified rooms, two out of three Baconians lived in above-average housing. Although the Baconians probably experienced a decline in their standard of living upon migration to the Virginia colony, their material world, in terms of housing quality, appears to have been substantially better than that of other settlers.[15]

Housing was not the only concern of the Baconian appraisers. Plantation outbuildings, especially tobacco barns, were considered an important part of an estate's value. Baconian plantations contained "very much other very good wooden buildings" or "other housing" in "large and good condition." Thomas Whaley had three tobacco houses measuring twenty, thirty, and fifty feet in length. Besides "tobacco houses," a variety of outbuildings "suitable to the plantation" were recorded within the houselots of the Baconian farmsteads. Found on at least seven estates, "kitchens" were the most common structure mentioned. James Crews's kitchen even had a brick chimney. Three "quarters" were recorded as being for the housing of servants and slaves. Dairy-related structures, such as a milkhouse or a buttery, were not unusual. Five grist mills were noted. One plantation contained an "office," while William Rooking's farm included a "store for merchants at the landing" along the James River. Together with William Hunt's kitchen, buttery, and milk house was a "smith's shop, well furnished with good bellows, forges and nine hammers." In general, Baconian real estate represented substantial investments in the process of "farm-building," which was the "central activity" of the Chesapeake agricultural system.[16]

Living in the quarters, garrets, and adjoining rooms of the twenty-

Table 1. Baconian Servants and Slaves

	English		Black		Indians			Total		
	M[a]	F	M	F	M	F	Unknown	M	F	T[b]
Arnold	1	—	—	—	—	—	—	1	—	1
Bacon	1	—	4	2	5	1	—	10	3	13
Carter	—	—	1	1	—	—	—	1	1	2
Chisman	—	1	4	3	—	—	—	4	4	8
Cookson	—	—	—	—	—	—	—	—	—	—
Crews	—	1	1	1	1	1	1	2	3	6
Drummond	4	1	2	1	—	—	1	6	2	9
Grove	1	—	—	—	—	—	—	1	—	1
Hansford	3	1	—	—	—	—	2	3	1	6
Hall	4	1	—	—	—	—	?	4	1	5
Hunt	3	—	8	7	—	—	2	11	7	20
Isles	2	—	—	—	—	—	—	2	—	2
Jones	3	—	—	—	—	—	—	3	—	3
Page	1	—	—	—	—	—	—	1	—	1
Rookings	—	—	2	3	—	—	—	2	3	5
Scarburgh	—	—	—	—	—	—	—	—	—	—
Stokes	—	—	—	—	—	—	—	—	—	—
Turner	1	—	—	—	—	—	?	1	—	1
West	—	—	—	—	—	—	—	—	—	—
Whaley	—	—	—	—	—	—	—	—	—	—
Whitson	1	—	—	—	—	—	—	1	—	1
Wilsford	—	—	—	—	—	—	—	—	—	—
Young	—	—	—	—	—	—	—	—	—	—
Totals	25	5	22	18	6	2	6+	53	25	84

Source: "Proceedings and Reports of the Commissioners for Enquiring into Virginian Affairs and Settling Virginian Grievances, 1677," Survey Report 749 (850), Colonial Office 5/1371, Public Record Office, pp. 220–50.
[a] M = male; F = female.
[b] T = total of males and females combined.

three Baconian plantations were a total of eighty-four English indentured servants, black slaves, and Native Americans of uncertain legal status (table 1). Two thirds of the inventories noted the presence of encumbered laborers, with a total of thirty English servants and forty black slaves recorded. More than twice as many male laborers were enumerated as female, although the proportion of men to women was more balanced among the slave population, where three family groups were in evidence. Roaming across the improved and unimproved landscape of the Baconian plantations were more than 750 head of livestock (table 2). Cattle, swine, horses, and sheep averaged thirty-four animals per household. Thus, with numerous family members, servants, and livestock, the Baconian farmsteads were crowded and active places.[17]

Table 2. Baconian Livestock

	Swine	Horses	Cattle	Total
Arnold	48	3	12	63
Bacon	24	11	14	49
Carter	6	6	32	44
Chisman	11	6	33	50
Cookson	—	1	4	5
Crews	13	1	24	38
Drummond	—	5	—	5
Grove	12	3	10	25
Hansford	12	3	48	63
Hall	16	8	28	52
Hunt	11	4	42	57
Isles	13	4	38	55
Jones	20	4	28	52
Page	8	2	25	35
Rookings	—	1	7	8
Scarburgh	10	1	17	28
Stokes	—	5	16	21
Turner	9	3	6	18
West	20	1	9	30
Whaley	6	6	18	30
Whitson	—	2	—	2
Wilsford	5	3	7	15
Young	—	—	16	16
Totals	244	83	434	761

Source: "Proceedings and Reports of the Commissioners for Enquiring into Virginian Affairs and Settling Virginian Grievances, 1677," Survey Report 749 (850), Colonial Office 5/1371, Public Record Office, pp. 220–50.

Note: In addition to their swine, horses, and cattle, John Isles and Nathaniel Bacon owned 9 sheep and 24 sheep, respectively.

The homes of the rebels contained an impressive array of personal possessions, both practical necessities and luxury goods. James Crews slept on a "very good English square bedstead, colored and sized with good [fabric] and red [valance] framed with large feather bed and a red worsted rug." William Drummond's feather bed included a bolster, white blankets, four pillows, a large colored rug, and a bedstead "hung about with yellow bayse." In all, the twenty-three Baconians owned thirty-seven beds, most of which were described as "new feather beds."[18]

Most personal possessions were simply listed as being within a particular room, but linens and silver plate were often separated for special accounting. In silver plate, the Baconians owned at least 80 spoons, 6 tankards, 5 porringers, 4 tumblers, and 15 silver cups. William Carter's plate included a large tankard, a scalloped sugar dish, 4 small dishes, a saltcellar, a small tumbler, and 11 spoons. John Iles's linens included 6 canvas shirts, 2 fine pillowcases, 1 old diaper tablecloth, 6 diaper napkins, 2 small canvas tablecloths, 2 fine towels, and 1 damask towel. For sale in Crews's store were "fine," "narrow," and "broad damask" material; stockings for girls, boys, and men; yarn, ribbon, and 12 pairs of shoes.[19]

The Baconian inventories yield more information about the participants than a simple list of their material possessions. Through study of the material world, interdisciplinary researchers have documented a relatively low standard of living for most colonists in seventeenth-century Chesapeake. Poor living conditions, combined with the likelihood of early adult mortality, contributed to the development of a "mentalité of transience" among colonial settlers. Some historians believe that it was a general societal frustration with the political, economic, and material world in the late seventeenth century that led to uprisings such as Bacon's Rebellion. Analysis of the domestic space and material possessions of the major Baconians can be used to place the individuals within an appropriate social and historical context.[20]

Researchers concerned with the relationship between the material standards of living and the stability of colonial culture have developed an "amenities index" with which to study growing consumerism. Table 3 is a comparison of the amenities index values calculated by Lois Carr and Lorena Walsh for rural Anne Arundel County, Maryland, with those from the Baconian estates. Neither the Anne Arundel County nor the Baconian inventories contained examples of table forks, wigs, or

Table 3. Amenities Index Comparison

Household Item	Anne Arundel Co. £95 to 225[a] (%)	Baconian £220[b] (%)
Coarse earthenware	53	14
Bed or table linen	87	95
Table knives	27	0
Table forks	0	0
Fine earthenware	7	14
Spices or signs thereof	27	54
Religious books	60	22
Secular books	0	18
Wigs	0	0
Watches or clocks	0	0
Pictures	7	4
Silver plate	13	36

Source: "Proceedings and Reports of the Commissioners for Enquiring into Virginian Affairs and Settling Virginian Grievances, 1677," Survey Report 749 (850), Colonial Office 5/1371, Public Record Office, pp. 220–50. Lois Green Carr and Lorena S. Walsh, "The Standard of Living in the Colonial Chesapeake," *William and Mary Quarterly*, 3d ser., vol. 45, no. 1 (January 1988): 135–59.

Note: The average bond value for the Baconian estates (£220) was compared to a similar range of estate values for the Maryland data.

[a] N = 103.

[b] N = 23.

timepieces. These household items became commonplace during the early eighteenth century. Relative to that of the Baconians, the Anne Arundel County data yielded greater percentages of table knives, coarse earthenware, religious books, and pictures. However, the Baconian households had more linens, fine earthenware, spices, secular books, and silver plate than those in the Maryland sample. The point here is not to suggest that the Virginia Baconians lived in greater luxury than a comparable group of Marylanders. Rather, it is to demonstrate that, measured against Chesapeake standards, the Baconians' households were quite comfortably appointed with both practical and luxury items.[21]

With spices to flavor their food, linens on their tables and beds, books for entertainment and education, and silver vessels to demonstrate their success, Baconians clearly had the economic ability to possess many of the amenities that made life in seventeenth-century Chesapeake more bearable. Charted against the Anne Arundel County data, the Baconian home was relatively well furnished. The Baconians' personal possessions were the material cultural signposts that distinguished them from their less-successful neighbors. As defined by Carr and Walsh, many of the Baconian leadership had taken the first steps toward "gentility."[22]

Extensive historical analysis of the principal Baconians suggests that the leaders of the rebellion were relatively well established within the colony. These Baconians had diversified their livelihood as tobacco planters to include practical trades such as smithing and milling, as well as operating merchant stores. Measured in terms of estate value, acres of farmland, and control of servant and slave labor, most of the leading Baconians appear to have had substantial economic success.[23]

Holdings in land, labor, and livestock can be used to calculate an "economic means index" (EMI) through which to gauge an individual's relative economic success along the Tobacco Coast (table 4). Based on a late eighteenth-century standard and although limited in its application to merchants and other nonfarmers, the EMI is a sound method to compare relative wealth among the Baconians. On average, the Baconians controlled one-tenth of the land, labor, and livestock found among the richest Virginians during the late eighteenth century. With a range of 3.5 to 18.0, the Baconian EMI appears to compare favorably to the results from other late eighteenth-century households.[24]

Using statistical and other more qualitative measures, the inventoried Baconians fall into three roughly equal groups that may represent the colonial elite, county elite, and middling farmer social and economic categories. Robert Jones represents middling farmers among the Baconians. His estate included a leased plantation "with good housing and well seated." Jones farmed this land with the help of three English servants who tended his twenty-eight cattle, twenty swine, and four horses. Among his personal possessions were a new brass mortar and pestle, a saltceller, tablecloths, napkins, and a feather bed with bedstead, cords, bolster, blankets, and a red rug. Robert Jones also had influential friends among the Loyalists: sentenced to die, he was allowed to leave the colony instead.[25]

Table 4. Baconian Economic Means Index (EMI)

Name	Land	Labor	Stock	Horses	EMI
Arnold	33.33	0.71	7.5	9.38	12.73
Bacon	19.44	9.28	8.75	34.38	17.96
Carter	22.99	1.4	20.0	18.75	15.79
Chisman	2.77	5.71	20.63	18.75	11.96
Cookson	—	—	2.5	6.25	4.38
Crews	6.01	2.14	15.0	3.12	6.57
Drummond	—	6.42	—	15.63	11.25
Grove	—	0.71	6.25	9.38	5.45
Hansford	16.84	4.28	30.0	9.38	15.12
Hall	—	3.57	17.5	25.0	15.36
Hunt	—	14.28	26.25	12.5	17.68
Isles	—	1.43	23.75	12.5	12.56
Jones	—	2.14	17.5	12.5	10.71
Page/Pope	—	0.71	16.63	6.25	7.86
Rookings	6.67	3.57	4.38	3.12	4.43
Scarburgh	2.0	—	10.63	3.12	5.25
Stokes	—	—	10.0	15.62	12.81
Turner	—	0.71	3.75	9.38	4.61
West	1.78	—	5.63	3.12	3.51
Whaley	—	—	11.25	18.75	15.0
Whitson	16.67	0.71	—	6.25	7.88
Wilsford	4.45	—	4.38	9.38	6.07
Young	4.45	—	10.0	—	7.22
Average	11.45	3.57	12.94	10.23	10.09

Source: "Proceedings and Reports of the Commissioners for Enquiring into Virginian Affairs and Settling Virginian Grievances, 1677," Survey Report 749 (850), Colonial Office 5/1371, Public Record Office, pp. 220–50. Eric G. Ackerman, "Economic Means Index: A Measure of Social Status in the Chesapeake, 1690–1815," *Historical Archaeology* 25, no. 1 (1991): 26–36.

William Chisman is a clear example of the county-level elites among the Baconians. A justice on the York County court, Chisman was also Thomas Hansford's brother-in-law. His two-hundred-fifty-acre farm was populated by one English servant, four black male slaves, and three black female slaves. Fifty head of livestock roamed his land. His house contained two feather beds, one described as new, a variety of table linens, a fair quantity of nutmeg, cloves, and ginger, and fifteen silver spoons.[26]

Not surprisingly, Bacon was typical of the colonial elite Baconians. He held title to at least 1,730 acres of farmland while living at Curles plantation, which included a dwelling, kitchen, milk house, quarter, and smith's shop. His laborers included thirteen individuals: one English servant, six black slaves, and six Native American laborers. The chief rebel slept on a large, good feather bed with bolster, two pillows, a pair of blankets, and a large woolen rug. Bacon was an educated man, and his rooms contained a large bible, a trunk of "well bound volumes," another parcel of books, and three large pictures, "figures of good works and size." As a member of the Governor's Council, Bacon was clearly a member of the Virginia elite.[27]

Yet the documents appear to tell only half the story of the Baconian farmsteads. Ongoing archaeological investigations conducted by Virginia Commonwealth University at Bacon's plantation on the James River have expanded our understanding of the chief rebel's homestead. Described as a "small new brick house," excavations have revealed that the building boasted a ceramic tile roof, casement windows, and a molded brick water table. Among the "much other very good wooden buildings" on the Baconian farmstead was an extensive system of defensive trenches and underground bunkers built during the rebellion. These earthworks, along with the presence of glass windows and limestone fireplace mantel decorations were unrecorded in the estate's inventory. Thus, the full character of the seventeenth-century household can only be described through the integration of historical and archaeological investigations.[28]

Analysis of available records suggests that the principal Baconians represented a broad cross section of individuals within the Virginia colony, and therefore exhibited a diversity of characteristics that probably describes the general nature of the colony's inhabitants. Like the rest of the Virginia population, most of the Baconians were immigrants, many were literate, and several were well educated. Many Baconians were married and had families. Only two Baconians could be documented as former indentured servants. In fact, despite their characterization as "the ruder sort," Baconians seem to have drawn their leadership from the "middling sort" or better. Inventory descriptions of the farms, homes, and personal possession of the principal Baconians confirms their status as well-seated settlers.[29]

The contrast between the description of Baconians as a "giddy-headed multitude" and the reality of their material, social, and economic status as middling farmers and elite planters is important for understanding the motivations that underlay the causes of the rebellion. Although indentured servants and former servants certainly participated in the revolt, the inventories clearly indicate that it was led by a cadre of elite Virginians who were supported by many other middling and yeomen farmers. Thomas Hansford was indeed a rebel, but he was certainly not (as depicted by the Loyalists) one of the "vulgar and most ignorant people" living on the frontier whose frustration and failure with the status quo in Virginia forced him into rebellion. Viewing the principal Baconians as accomplished Chesapeake planters rather than "the lowest of the people" should foster new interpretations of the rebellion as well as provide additional evidence for a regional standard of living.[30] As detailed in the attainder inventories, the homes of the leading rebel participants provide a more accurate picture of the social characteristics of the Baconians than the caustic descriptions of the Loyalists in the aftermath of Bacon's Rebellion.

---

[1] Descriptions of Hansford's and other Baconian estates are contained in: "Proceedings and Reports of the Commissioners for Enquiring into Virginian Affairs and Settling Virginian Grievances, 1677," Survey Report 749 (850), Colonial Office 5/1371, Public Record Office, pp. 217–51 (hereafter cited as Colonial Office records). For an abstract of these records, see John Davenport Neville, *Bacon's Rebellion: Abstracts of Materials in the Colonial Records Project* (Richmond: Jamestown Fndn., 1976), pp. 134–48.

[2] Colonial Office records, p. 243.

[3] For a summary of Bacon's Rebellion, see Warren M. Billings, John E. Selby, and Thad W. Tate, *Colonial Virginia: A History* (White Plains, N.Y.: KTO Press, 1986), pp. 77–96.

[4] Sir Herbert Jeffreys, Sir John Berry, and Francis Moryson, "A True Narrative of the Rise, Progresse, and Cessation of the Late Rebellion in Virginia, Most Humbly and Impartially Reported by His Majesties Commissioners Appointed to Enquire into the Affaires of the Said Colony," in Charles McLean Andrews, ed., *Narratives of the Insurrections, 1675–1690* (New York: Scribner, 1915), pp. 106–11, 113, 116, 118, 131.

[5] Edmund S. Morgan, *American Slavery, American Freedom: The Ordeal of Colonial Virginia* (New York: W. W. Norton, 1975), p. 258. Other major historical studies of Bacon's Rebellion include: Thomas Jefferson Wertenbaker, *Torchbearer of the Revolution: The Story of Bacon's Rebellion and Its Leader* (Princeton: Princeton University Press, 1940); Wilcomb Washburn, *The Governor and the Rebel* (New York: W. W. Norton, 1957); and Steven Saunders Webb, *1676: The End of American Independence* (Cambridge: Harvard University Press, 1985). See also Warren M. Billings, "The Causes of Bacon's

Rebellion: Some Suggestions," *Virginia Magazine of History and Biography* 78 (1970): 409–35.

[6] *The Compact Edition of the Oxford English Dictionary* (New York: Oxford University Press, 1971), s.v. "attainder"; Colonial Office records, p. 220.

[7] Lorena Walsh, "Questions and Sources for Exploring the Standard of Living," *William and Mary Quarterly*, 3d ser., vol. 45, no. 1 (January 1988): 116–23; Gloria L. Main, "Probate Records as a Source for Early American History," *William and Mary Quarterly*, 3d ser., vol. 32, no. 1 (January 1975): 89–99; and Anna L. Hawley, "The Meaning of Absence: Household Inventories in Surry County, Virginia, 1690–1715," in Peter Benes, ed., *Early American Probate Inventories*, Annual Proceedings of the Dublin Seminar for New England Folklife 12 (Boston: Boston University, 1989), pp. 23–31. Unfortunately, the lands, housing, goods, servants, or livestock enumerated were not appraised in tobacco or other currency. Deeds, Orders, and Wills, Vol. 6, York County, Va., Records, p. 123.

[8] Colonial Office records, p. 248. Darrett B. Rutman and Anita H. Rutman, *A Place in Time: Explicatus* (New York: W. W. Norton, 1984), p. 124. In 1668 the average landholding was about 900 acres. Nine years after the rebellion it had fallen to only 417 acres. The average for 1677 (660 acres) was calculated by finding the midpoint between 900 and 417 acres (that is 657 acres). The average landholding by the executed Baconians was calculated by taking the figures given in the attainder inventories; Colonial Office records, pp. 220–50.

[9] Colonial Office records, pp. 227, 249. Cary Carson et al., "Impermanent Architecture in the Southern American Colonies," *Winterthur Portfolio* 16, no. 3 (Summer 1981): 135–96.

[10] Philip Alexander Bruce, *Economic History of Virginia in the Seventeenth Century* (1835; reprint, New York: Macmillan, 1895), p. 151. Warren M. Billings, ed., *The Old Dominion in the Seventeenth Century: A Documentary History of Virginia, 1606–1689* (Chapel Hill: University of North Carolina Press, 1975), p. 306. See also William M. Kelso, *Kingsmill Plantations, 1619–1800: Archaeology of Country Life in Colonial Virginia* (New York: Academic Press, 1984); Frazer D. Nieman, *The "Manor House" before Stratford (Discovering the Clifts Plantation)* (Stratford, Va.: Robert E. Lee Memorial Fndn., 1980); and Dennis J. Pogue, *King's Reach and Seventeenth-Century Plantation Life*, Jefferson-Patterson Park and Museum Archaeological Studies No. 1 (Annapolis: Maryland Historical and Cultural Publications, 1990).

[11] James P. P. Horn, " 'The Bare Necessities': Standards of Living in England and the Chesapeake, 1650–1700," *Historical Archaeology* 22, no. 2 (1988): 78.

[12] White chambers probably refer to plastered rooms. One visitor noted, "Those who have some means, cover them [the dwellings] inside with a coating of mortar in which they use oyster-shells for lime; it is as white as snow" (Billings, *Old Dominion*, p. 306).

[13] Horn, "Bare Necessities," pp. 74–91.

[14] Bruce, *Economic History*, pp. 149–50; Billings, *Old Dominion*, p. 306.

[15] Archaeological investigations over the last 2 decades have given physical expression to the verbal description of housing and living conditions in the seventeenth century. Carson, "Impermanent Architecture." Only 5 Baconians lived in typical Chesapeake housing. Anthony Arnold owned a "Virginia house," and John Whitson's home was described as "small and old" (Colonial Office records, pp. 220–50).

[16] On the important role of farmbuilding in the Chesapeake region, see Carson, "Impermanent Architecture," pp. 135–96; and Lorena Walsh, Russell B. Menard, and Lois Green Carr, *Robert Cole's World: Agriculture and Society in Early Maryland* (Chapel Hill: University of North Carolina Press, 1991). Hansford's housing was called "all new." Tobacco houses varied in quality from John Whitson's "old" house to Thomas Young's "very good tobacco house" (Colonial Office records, pp. 220–50).

[17] Rutman and Rutman, *Explicatus*, p. 123. In Middlesex County, the average number of servants and slaves in 1668 was 5.1 persons, and in 1687 it was 3.8 persons. The standard deviation for servants and slaves in 1668 was 9.0 individuals: for 1687, it was 12.5.

[18] Colonial Office records, pp. 220–50.

[19] Colonial Office records, pp. 220–50.

[20] Walsh, "Questions and Sources," p. 123; Horn, "Bare Necessities," p. 89; Darret B. Rutman and Anita H. Rutman, *A Place in Time: Middlesex County, Virginia, 1650–1750* (New York: W. W. Norton, 1984), pp. 82–86.

[21] Lois Green Carr and Lorena S. Walsh, "The Standard of Living in the Colonial Chesapeake," *William and Mary Quarterly*, 3d ser., vol. 45, no. 1 (January 1988): 135–59.

[22] Carr and Walsh, "Standard of Living," p. 137.

[23] John H. Sprinkle, Jr., "Loyalists and Baconians: The Participants in Bacon's Rebellion in Virginia, 1676–1677" (Ph.D. diss., College of William and Mary, 1992).

[24] The EMI for the estate of Thomas Pettus, a wealthy James City Co. planter, was calculated as 19.7 for 1691; Eric G. Ackerman, "Economic Means Index: A Measure of Social Status in the Chesapeake, 1690–1815," *Historical Archaeology* 25, no. 1 (1991): 26–36. Values for livestock, labor, and landholding are relative to the estates of the 100 richest men in late eighteenth-century Virginia as described in Jackson Turner Main, "The One Hundred," *William and Mary Quarterly*, 3d ser., vol. 11, no. 3 (July 1954): 354–84. The EMI is calculated with the following formulas: Land = (number of acres x 100)/9000; Labor = (number of servants and slaves x 100)/140; Livestock = (number of animals x 100)/160; Horses = (number of animals x 100)/32; EMI = (Land + Labor + Livestock + horses)/N; N = number of variables with data.

[25] Colonial Office records, pp. 223–24.

[26] Colonial Office records, pp. 238–39.

[27] Colonial Office records, pp. 227–30.

[28] L. Daniel Mouer, "Digging a Rebel's Homestead," *Archaeology* 44, no. 4 (July/August 1991): 54–57. Excavations at the Curles plantation have been conducted for 9 seasons.

[29] Sprinkle, "Loyalists and Baconians."

[30] Morgan, *American Slavery*, pp. 261–62.

Safety and Danger in a Puritan Home

Life in the Hull-Sewall House, 1676–1717

Marion Nelson Winship

In the town of Boston, on the twenty-eighth of February 1676, Samuel Sewall, an ambitious and aspiring twenty-three-year-old, was married to Hannah Hull, just turned twenty, the only surviving child of John Hull, a successful Boston merchant, and his wife, Judith. The wedding took place in John Hull's house, in a room that Sewall would later describe as "that we [now] call the Old Hall; t'was then all in one, a very large room."[1] In this house, later modified and enlarged to suit their growing family and prospects, Samuel and Hannah Sewall would live together for the forty-one years of their marriage until Hannah's death in 1717; Samuel Sewall would live there until his own death in 1729.

Today nothing remains of the physical neighborhood in which the Sewalls lived their long married life. The Hull-Sewall house stood on the High Street of the town of Boston. Jordan Marsh Department Store now covers the site. Along the route that the Sewalls so often trod between home and meetinghouse, there is a Burger King. On nice days, the sidewalks are crowded with street vendors plying souvenirs of

The author is grateful to Robert Blair St. George and Katherine C. Grier for their criticism and encouragement. An early version of this essay was awarded second prize in the 1993 Colonial Essay Contest sponsored by the Colonial Society of Pennsylvania and the Philadelphia Center for Early American Studies.

Boston's "Freedom Trail." Samuel Sewall is named on the historical marker in front of the "Old South Meetinghouse," but it is the
eighteenth-century replacement to the building the Sewalls knew.
And the Sewalls would scarcely recognize the graveyard they once
knew tragically well. At the "Old Granary Burying Ground," tourists
snap one another's pictures in front of the gravestones. The tomb that
bears Samuel Sewall's name was erected by nineteenth-century descendants.

Of the Sewalls' house, nothing material remains, but traces of the
house do survive in the diary that Sewall kept from the year of their
marriage until his death. In the diary, Sewall discussed the public issues
that concerned him as a merchant and judge. Like other Puritan men,
he used his diary to record the signs of God's Providence that he encountered while traversing the town about his daily business. (The diary, as a result, often reads like a catalogue of every accident and afflic-
tion in Boston!) Sewall was particularly struck by the juxtapositions of
health and sickness, of life and death: the "very extraordinarily suddain"
death—to take a typical example—of one Major Richards who "was
abroad on the Sabbath, din'd very well on Monday," scolded a servant,
fell into a fit, and died.[2]

Sewall also recorded the most striking events at home, which
makes his diary an extraordinary window into the life of a Puritan family. Abbott Lowell Cummings made wonderful use of the architectural
clues embedded in these domestic references.[3] Here I enlist them to a
different cause: to ask what the house and home meant to this Puritan
husband and wife.

Tracking the home life of Samuel and Hannah Sewall, I soon
realized, with some trepidation, that my findings lay at odds with an
influential recent essay. In "The Mental World of Samuel Sewall,"
David D. Hall observed, as I have, a distinctive quality of the diary:
Sewall seemed so often and so utterly taken by surprise. He was startled
by loud noises, struck by sudden deaths; his world seemed full of melan-
choly coincidences. Hall argues that the central motivation of Sewall's
life was his yearning for security, protection, and (in the religious sense)
assurance. While this yearning could never be satisfied, it could be
"lessened or resolved through ritual practice," ranging from daily family
prayer to driving a good-luck nail into an unfinished house to setting
protective stone cherubim on his front gateposts. And so, when Sewall

returned from his judicial circuit to record in his diary, "Find all well. Laus Deo," Hall concludes: "Sewall moved from darkness into light as he entered the house that he shared with Hannah's mother. Here he was on safe ground; here peace and quiet reigned: 'Laus Deo.' "[4]

Hall's Samuel Sewall came *home* to safety, peace, and quiet. But that interpretation entirely misses what Sewall himself could never ignore, the ongoing family life in his household. His diary shows, if only obliquely, that he was always aware of the family cycles of pregnancy, birth, suckling, and weaning and that he enjoyed the commotion of healthy, growing children. Above all, the diary bears powerful witness to Sewall's awareness that this domestic fabric might at any time be rent by sudden illness and death.

The Sewalls lost ten of their fourteen children before Hannah's own death. Samuel had no more control over these deaths at home than over the hundreds of others that he recorded in his diary. When seven-month-old Stephen suddenly took ill and died the next evening, Sewall noted that he had been a hearty baby with "two teeth cut, no convulsions." Sewall was on court business in Salem in 1696 when someone brought him the "amazing news" that his wife had given birth to a stillborn son. He was haunted by these catastrophes: staying at an inn while on circuit, he woke in alarm to hear someone approaching on horseback. It must be a messenger come to give him bad news from home, Sewall thought, and he recalled his sorrowful all-night journey home after hearing of the stillbirth six years before. *This* time, he recorded in his diary, God dismissed him from the "burden of that sorrowful surprise" and "laid it," instead, on another traveler. And so, whenever Sewall noted his homecoming with the phrases "Find all well. Laus Deo," he expressed his fervent thanks—indeed his surprise—since he was keenly aware that his homecoming might have been otherwise.[5]

For Samuel Sewall, the physical house itself offered no security. By the 1690s, the house built by Hannah's grandfather was too small for a household of at least four adults and five young children. But the Sewalls were impelled to build a new addition only after the old kitchen chimney "blazed out very sorely at top, appeared to be very foul" and caught the shingles on fire: the old house had become dangerous. The new brick house, however, also threatened disaster. Hannah had resisted the building project because she was pregnant and "loath to ly in at another place." Her husband uncharacteristically agonized, "What we shall now doe, I know not." During the construction, Samuel reminded himself again and again of the perils of the enterprise. A daughter was born and died. When the new roof was raised, Samuel gave thanks that there was "no hurt done." Climbing about an upstairs chamber of the unfinished house, he slipped and only escaped "great danger" by hurling himself across the joists. And he recorded one of the coincidences that always struck him so: Samson Waters, a man like Samuel himself, "just building a great House, Roof up," suddenly died.[6]

When the new house was nearly complete, Governor Bradstreet and the minister Cotton Mather were dining with the Sewalls in the "new kitchen" when a violent hailstorm broke almost five hundred squares of glass in the front windows. As neighbors "gazed upon the house to see its ruins," Mather prayed with the family. God had broken the brittle part of the Sewall house, the minister observed, and he prayed that the assembled company would all be ready for the time when their clay tabernacles should also be broken. "Twas a sorrowful thing for me to see the hous so far undon before twas finished," Sewall mourned, even as he acknowledged the truth of the minister's words. Completed, the substantial brick house would bring no more security. "A Mouse had like to have burnt up my House, and what was in it," Samuel wrote of a near-disastrous fire in their chamber-closet. The protective cherubim on the gateposts could not withstand a "prodigious" wind. Sewall forced himself, through his diary, to recognize again and again that, in God's eyes, any earthly house was "brittle."[7]

The most grievous surprises of Samuel Sewall's life happened at home, and they centered on the room most often mentioned in the diary. The chamber is the key to the meaning of the home life of this Puritan family. In many of its functions, the chamber was simply the hall once-removed. As in the hall, marriages took place, and prayer meetings were held. The "private" prayer meetings and fasts were actually social occasions, which involved sending out invitations and providing "Biskets, and Beer, Cider, Wine." Social life on the largest scale took place in the hall, though as many as a dozen people could be accommodated around "the Great Oval Table" in the chamber.[8] The chamber is the most-often-mentioned room in the diary, however, for uses that did not overlap with those of the hall: the central functions of family life.

Samuel recorded the births of the Sewalls' children as crises in the chamber. When Hannah went into labor, she would wake him into action to stir up the fire and go for the midwives. Unless the women called him into the chamber, it seems, he remained praying and worrying in the hall or kitchen. After a successful delivery, while the women dined on "rost Beef and Minc'd Pyes, good Cheese and Tarts," Samuel went out to post a prayer at the meetinghouse. The chamber was so often a sickroom that to be "Fain to keep the Chamber" was synonymous in the diary with illness.[9]

When Hannah was dangerously ill in 1676, Samuel anxiously chronicled every development in the chamber and took his turn watching Hannah there. During the crisis, he slept in the kitchen chamber; he would report his own return to the chamber as a turning point of his wife's recovery. Most often, though, the room was associated in Samuel's diary not with recovery and health but with sickness, death, and the fear of death. When the Sewalls heard after midnight that their married daughter was near death, "All the family were Alarm'd, and gather'd into our Bed-Chamber." While a son who was a minister prayed with the family, Sewall rushed to his daughter's home to send for ministers and to pray with her himself. Returning home later after the daughter's death, he recorded, "When I enter'd my Wife's Bed-Chamber, a dolefull Cry was lifted up." Hannah's own death would one day produce a "flood of Tears in our Bed-Chamber."[10]

It was in the chamber that Sewall often learned of family trouble or disaster. The death of beloved Mother Hull took place in her own chamber, but Samuel connected the disaster with the chamber he and Hannah shared. He recorded in remorseful retrospect that after family prayers that night "at prayer with my wife in the Chamber, [I] was wofully drowsy and stupid." Then, "About one at night, Jane [a servant] comes up with an unusual Gate, and gives us an account of Mother's illness." Similarly: "In the night after 12, Susan [a servant] comes, and knocks at our chamber door, and said she could not sleep, was afraid she should dye. Which amaz'd my wife and me. We let her in, blew up the Fire, Wrap't her warm, and went to bed again."[11] In this large household there would always be sudden crises, of course. In Sewall's diary they are associated with specific references to the chamber.

The bed and the cradle, central furnishings of the chamber, also received Sewall's detailed mention in the context of untoward events: "This night Little Hull hath a Convulsion Fit, as he lay with me in

Bed." When he recorded one of the most detailed material references in the diary, Samuel was worried about Hannah, who, after a dangerous pregnancy, had just given birth to their last child: "My wife gets onto the pallet bed in her Cloaths and there keeps, while linnen curtains are put up within the Serge; and she is refreshed by it." The cradle, probably an old one inherited from the Hulls, was only mentioned when an infant was ill. The first Sewall infant, John, was "asleep in the Cradle, and suddenly started, trembled, his fingers contracted, his eyes starting and being distorted." When later infants also had convulsions, Sewall did not detail the symptoms, but he continued to mention the cradle. When their last child was born, six years after the previous pregnancy had ended in miscarriage, the Sewalls no doubt had already passed on the old cradle to a married child. Sewall recorded the purchase of a "wicker Cradle for Judith of Tho. Hunt; which Cost Sixteen Shillings." Both the material detail and the mention of money are extremely rare in the diary: Sewall's worry over the birth of this last child provoked his particular notice.[12]

The Sewall house, and particularly the chamber, seem overwhelmingly "dolefull" and dangerous because that, overwhelmingly, is how they are mentioned in the diary. But the Sewalls were not grim Puritans who fit the famous H. L. Mencken stereotype. Even in the diary, we catch glimpses of Samuel and Hannah enjoying their home and the fine things in it; and we can see this even more clearly in Samuel's correspondence with English merchants from whom he purchased some of the good things of life. These letters offer a useful balance to the self-conscious worrying of the diary, but, in the end, they affirm its message. Ordering blocks of freestone for the quoins of the new house, for example, Sewall also worried over the propriety of the purchase, complaining that "the costliness of them bespeaks a Grandure far beyond my estate, and which I have purposely avoided."[13]

Similarly, the Sewalls' enthusiastic interest in fine furnishings for themselves and their home was never quite a simple pleasure. Samuel would not order expensive silk for himself "out of a particular dislike I had to the wearing of so much in this poor country." Hannah desired "a piece of good Serviceable Silk for our Daughter." Cloth for daughters' dresses must carry a seemly design "of Herbs or Leaves; not of Animals, or artificial things." When Hannah, through her husband, asked for white fustian for bedcurtains, a woolen counterpane, and a half dozen chair covers, it was so that "she may set her two Little daughters on work and keep them out of idleness."[14]

Sewall recorded in loving detail the young couple's first attempts at entertaining, as when Governor Bradstreet and his lady "drank a glass or two of wine, eat some fruit, took a pipe of Tobacco in the new Hall, and wish'd me joy of the house." When a cousin admired his new painted shutters and "in pleasancy said he thought he had been got into Paradise," Sewall enjoyed the joke.[15] But more often he used the diary not simply to record these pleasant feelings but to remind himself of their danger.

Sewall was proud to "invite all the Magistrates" and their wives to their home for a fast—a social occasion where ministers were invited to preach and pray. He was so pleased with the effect of his invitations that he copied the entire text into the diary. But the diary entry of the next day shows the danger of this simple pride and pleasure. Sewall had been to Roxbury Meeting, where he invited some important men to the fast. Exhilarated by this social success, he forgot his usual homecoming apprehensions, and so he was truly shocked at what awaited him there: "When I come home I find Hullie extream ill having two Convulsion Fits, one of them very long. The Child is much changed."[16] In Sewall's diary entry, innocent pleasure becomes the first heedless half of a doleful coincidence. This episode tells us why the everyday prides and pleasures of home life are so seldom recorded in the diary. The business of the diary was to recall the precariousness of such pleasures.

The day after fire broke out in the upper chamber-closet, Sewall tried to write an account of the incident in his diary. He listed every item that had contributed to the family's safety, including a floor that, "being well-plaister'd between the Joysts," was not burnt through, some "Stubborn Woolen" window curtains that "refus'd to burn," and his own quick thinking. On the other side of the scale, he noted every circumstance that had put the family in peril: the closet was full of inflammables—boxes of papers, wafers for wax seals, and even gunpowder. Sewall concluded that there was no human accounting for the family's deliverance: "Thus with great Indulgence GOD saved our House and Substance, and the Company's Paper." This was the lesson he repeated to Hannah: "As I lay down in my Bed, I said to my Wife, that the Goodness of God appeared, in that we had a Chamber, a Bed, and

Company."[17] And as he recorded each step of this mental struggle in the diary, the lesson was repeated.

Pride and pleasure of home, the joys and sorrows of family life—Sewall used his diary to remind himself that these, like everything else he recorded there, were part of God's unaccountable Providence. But what were the meanings of home and home life for Hannah Sewall? How did they connect to her faith? How might her apprehensions have shaped and been shaped by what historian David Hall called "the mental world of Samuel Sewall?" To address these questions, we will, of course, take note when Samuel mentions her ("As I lay down in my Bed, I said to my Wife . . ."), but we must also press the diary a difficult step further—to see if it will yield the texture of Hannah's life in the house.

Although Hannah presided over precisely the events that caused Samuel to mention the chamber so frequently—birth, sickness, and death—she remains at best a shadow in her husband's diary. Samuel recorded the events of the Sewall chamber just as he did the events of his greater Boston world. He recorded births but not pregnancies, weaning but not nursing, turning points of an illness or recovery but not its duration, and deaths. To recover the ongoing life in the chamber from these diary entries, I plotted the duration of pregnancies, lactation, and, where clues allowed it, the whole course of each family illness. And, in any case, much of the texture of family life simply cannot be tabulated. A table that presents all this information, I can report from experience, will be a technical and visual disaster. Since we know the family birthdates, we can imagine the normal noise, laughter, and activity of healthy children of appropriate ages. We can also add the daily work in the large Sewall household, hardly glimpsed in Samuel's diary, in which Hannah must have spent most of her waking hours.[18] This life in the chamber might be envisioned as a fabric in which the woof is time. The strands of the warp are the ongoing life processes. The threads of the woof mark dates and events—the stuff of Samuel Sewall's diary entries. At certain points, dark threads identify the sudden deaths and the most grievous surprises. Viewing the Sewalls' home life in this way shows how much Samuel chose to leave out of his diary. Highlighting how much more constantly Hannah kept in the chamber, it also suggests some ways in which her "mental world" might differ from her husband's.

I do not mean, however, to create two separate gendered spheres of meaning for the Hull-Sewall house. Because of the episodic nature of diary keeping, neither Samuel's nor Hannah's continuous daily affection for the family is expressed, though presumably both parents in this caring family felt it and acted upon it. Nor does the scarcity of diary evidence prove that Samuel took no part in the ongoing life of the chamber. Occasionally, at least, he shared in watching over sick children. When baby Sarah had a "convulsion fit," Sewall reported, he and Hannah took her into bed with them. When Hannah was pregnant and then occupied with the weak newborn Henry, it was Samuel who took little Hull into his bed. As two-year-old Sarah neared the end of her life, Samuel and Hannah seemed equally involved — and neither was exactly a constant and laborious nurse confined to the sickroom. Samuel recorded, "This day I remove poor little Sarah into my bedchamber, where about break of day Dec 23 she gives up the ghost in Nurse Cowell's arms." At the end, he recorded with remorse, "Neither I nor my wife were by." Because Hannah was pregnant and feeling ill, Samuel was "lodg[ing] with her in the new Hall."[19]

By considering the ongoing processes of home life combined with Sewall's experience outside the home, we can best approximate how the house figured in his mental world. Recognizing the thickness of the fabric of life in the Sewall household for both husband and wife clarifies the choices Samuel made in his diary. The shock of his returning home to find Hull ill came from Samuel's intimate nights in the chamber with his beloved "Hullie" as well as from his distance from it. Nevertheless, although he was daily aware of the "sickly painfull Life" of his daughter Sarah, Samuel seldom mentioned her. He noted her birth, one day of convulsions, and her final illness and death.[20] He chose, in other words, to record the sudden strokes of God's Providence rather than to give a daily account.

If we cannot understand the mental world of Samuel Sewall by ignoring his home life, neither can we understand the world of Hannah Sewall by defining it as some vital but inchoate flow in the chamber. Hannah, the only child of old-style Puritan parents, also had been raised "to the Word," and she participated daily in Word-centered rituals. The sudden death of a healthy infant must have been a sorrowful surprise to her as well as to her husband. She also joined Samuel dining out, going to meeting, and making excursions whenever her health, the health of her children, and her reproductive cycle permitted. She probably made her own separate social rounds as well. Hannah, as well as her husband, was sometimes in another room or even away from home when a child took ill.[21] Nevertheless, the biological facts of Hannah's life most often kept her at home and made her experience quite different from her husband's.

Hannah's apprehensions were shaped more by the warp of continuous domestic life than the woof of sudden happenings. When the chamber-closet caught fire, for example, Hannah "complain'd of smoak," while Samuel immediately "took the Alarm." Hannah assumed an everyday annoyance. In contrast, Samuel's daily encounters with the sudden strokes of Providence around Boston made *him* apprehend a calamity. If Hannah had kept a diary, it might also be full of catastrophes, but the smoking fires would outnumber the burning houses, and toothaches would outnumber mortal illnesses.[22]

Two other "houses" featured importantly in Sewall's diary—the meetinghouse and the family burial vault. In both, Sewall's patterns of ritual, to return to Hall's terms, are tellingly more powerful and effective than at home. In the end, however, these extensions of the house echoed the same meanings and provided Samuel with the same awful reminders of God's unaccountable Providence.

In the meetinghouse Samuel could enlist the blessing of the community for the safety of his family. When someone was seriously ill at home or when someone had recovered from illness, Samuel (but never Hannah) sent a special prayer to the meetinghouse. At home, during childbirth, virtually ousted from the chamber, Samuel could do little but keep busy—the seventeenth-century equivalent of being sent out to boil water. The physical well-being of mother and child within the chamber were completely beyond his control. But he could "save" the child by taking it from the chamber to "hold it up" before God in the meetinghouse. On these important occasions (always detailed in the diary), Hannah was still, always, confined to her bed. In fact, in spite of indications that women early became the majority in New England churches, the actual attendance at meeting often must have been heavily male. In the "rawness and uncertainty" of winter Sabbaths and at the many other times dictated by their pregnancies or by children's needs, women stayed at home.[23]

Samuel *seemed* more powerful in the meetinghouse, but the life-

and-death events at home were so intertwined with the rituals there that ultimately, as the following powerful nightmare illustrates, he felt the same alarm in both houses. While confined to a ship for England in 1688, Samuel dreamed that Hannah was "brought to bed" while he found himself "by inadvertancy Got up into the uppermost Gallery" so that he "knew not how to get down to hold up the child."[24] Samuel's nightmare room was simultaneously a chamber and a meetinghouse with its gallery. This dream was a nightmare because in it, Samuel, naturally fairly helpless in the chamber, was deprived of the ritual power that he counted on practicing in the meetinghouse.

Like the meetinghouse the family burial vault was an extension of the chamber in which Samuel was more at home than his wife. After family funerals he recorded each detail in the diary, listing important guests with particular satisfaction. In the vault even housekeeping was Samuel's province. He could add a new step, repair a door, collect and rebury scattered bones, and arrange and rearrange the family coffins. In preparation for his infant Sarah's funeral, for example, he "went at noon to see in what order things were set" and found the task "an awfull yet pleasing Treat." In the "dark house," at least, Samuel could take account of God's Providence, but, in the end, the purpose of the account, like the purpose of his diary, was the reminder: "The Lord knows who shall be brought hether next."[25]

Just as Hannah left the house much less often than her husband and attended meeting less often, she never tended to the burial vault. That she was usually too ill or too pregnant even to attend family funerals suggests forcefully how religious experience might have been different for women. On December 24, 1685, for example, during the funeral of her infant son Henry, Hannah lay in the chamber with women and children for company (including little Hull who had been having the convulsions that would kill him six months later). What were Hannah's thoughts during this funeral? When Samuel returned—with the older children and the midwife and nurse who had carried the corpse—he would tell Hannah about the funeral. In this case, she would hear that the attendance had been most gratifying but also that flooding had displaced the baby's coffin to a makeshift burial. Perhaps Hannah's and Samuel's apprehensions would become mediated and even somewhat transformed as they talked together (Samuel's diary, however, offers no evidence to support this hopeful presentism). The diary does suggest that family prayer, conducted by Samuel in the chamber, served as communication and commiseration at such times.[26] Although Hannah's thoughts during these prayers are lost to history, the differences in Hannah's and Samuel's experience suggest distinct perceptions of safety and danger and of life and death.

For Samuel Sewall, neither the house nor even its extensions—the meetinghouse and the family vault—could ever be "safe ground." In the chamber, at the heart of his house, he found safety simultaneously most desirable and—by any of his efforts—least attainable. For that reason, home life was central to Samuel's religious life and, although it may not appear so on first reading, central to his diary. Samuel's pleasure in the house and his experience of the fabric of everyday home life only heightened his alarm at its fragility. For fifty-three years, he recorded every death and surprising event in Boston, including those at home, to remind himself of that fragility.

The meaning of home life for Hannah Sewall remains elusive in her husband's diary, although by reconstructing the ongoing biological processes of the house, we get a glimpse of the daily home life to which she was often confined. Her experience undoubtedly led her to an apprehension of God's signs that differed from her husband's, but there is no reason to suppose that she had a separate understanding of the purpose of those signs, which was to prepare herself and those she loved for their "Long Home."[27]

The poet Anne Bradstreet (first wife of the Governor Bradstreet whom the young Sewall was once so proud to invite to his new house) reminded herself of that central purpose through her poems. She recalled the pleasures of her home, burned down in 1666:

> Here stood that trunk, and there that chest,
> There lay the store I counted best.
> My pleasant things in ashes lie,
> And them behold no more shall I.
> Under thy roof no guest shall sit,
> Nor at thy table eat a bit,
> No pleasant tale shall e'er be told'
> Nor things recounted done of old.
> No candle e'er shall shine in thee,
> Nor bridegroom's voice e'er heard shall be.

Then, as Samuel continually reminded himself to do through his diary and as Hannah no doubt reminded herself in her own (undocumented

and, in large part, undocumentable) ways, Bradstreet set aside the happy
memories and forswore her pleasant inventory:

> Thou hast an house on high erect,
> Framed by that mighty Architect,
> With glory richly furnished,
> Stands permanent though this be fled.
> It's purchased and paid for too
> By Him who hath enough to do.
> A price so vast as is unknown
> Yet by His gift is made thine own;
> There's wealth enough, I need no more,
> Farewell my pelf, farewell my store
> The world no longer let me love,
> My hope and treasure lies above.[28]

---

[1] M. Halsey Thomas, ed., *The Diary of Samuel Sewall, 1674–1729*, 2 vols. (New York: Farrar, Straus, and Giroux, 1973), 1:15. Nathaniel Hawthorne would thoroughly transform this occasion in a short story, "The Pine Tree Shillings"; see Nathaniel Hawthorne, *Wonder-book and Tanglewood Tales, and Grandfather's Chair* (New York, 1892), pp. 458–64.

[2] On Puritan diary writing and diarists, see Alan Macfarlane, *The Family Life of Ralph Josselin, A Seventeenth-Century Clergyman: An Essay in Historical Anthropology* (New York: W. W. Norton, 1970), pp. 3–11; Richard S. Dunn, "John Winthrop Writes His Journal," *William and Mary Quarterly*, 3d ser., vol. 41, no. 2 (April 1984): 185–212; Edmund S. Morgan, ed., "The Diary of Michael Wigglesworth," *Colonial Society of Massachusetts Publications* 35 (1942–46): 426–44; and Cotton Mather, *The Diary of Cotton Mather, 1681–1724*, 2 vols., Collections of the Massachusetts Historical Society, 7th ser., vols. 7–8 (Boston: By the society, 1911–12). Of particular interest as the diary of Hannah Sewall's father, is Sacvan Bercovitch, ed., *The Diaries of John Hull*, vol. 7 of *Puritan Personal Writings: Diaries* (New York: AMS Press, 1983); Thomas, *Diary of Samuel Sewall*, 1:318.

[3] Abbott Lowell Cummings, "Notes on Furnishing the Seventeenth-Century House," *Old-Time New England* 46, no. 3 (January–March 1956): 57–67; Abbott Lowell Cummings, *The Framed Houses of Massachusetts Bay, 1625–1725* (Cambridge: Harvard University Press, 1979); Abbott Lowell Cummings, "The Beginnings of Provincial Renaissance Architecture in Boston, 1690–1725," *Journal of the Society of Architectural Historians* 42, no. 1 (1983): 43–53.

[4] David D. Hall, *Worlds of Wonder, Days of Judgment: Popular Religious Belief in Early New England* (Cambridge: Harvard University Press, 1990), pp. 213–38, quotations on pp. 231, 217.

[5] Thomas, *Diary of Samuel Sewall*, 1:145, 350, 474, 470.

[6] Thomas, *Diary of Samuel Sewall*, 1:307–8, 312, 314, 318. Besides Hannah's widowed mother, the household often included a nurse, a young servant or 2, and a female relative who helped with housework and child care. By the 1690s, the Sewalls had enlarged the house at least twice. When they married, it had been a wooden, shingle-roofed house with a "Little Hall," a "Great Hall," at least 2 chambers, a garret, a kitchen,

and a kitchen chamber (Thomas, *Diary of Samuel Sewall*, 1:24, 25, 36, 41, 42, 63, 340; 2:621, 835).

[7] Thomas, *Diary of Samuel Sewall*, 1:330; 2:1026. The Sewalls guessed that a mouse had caused this fire by rolling a candle from the chamber hearth into a closet; *The Letterbook of Samuel Sewall*, 2 vols., Collections of the Massachusetts Historical Society, 6th ser. (Boston: By the society, 1886), 1:389.

[8] Thomas, *Diary of Samuel Sewall*, 1:63, 79, 97, 141, 174; 2:861; 1:609. The old house contained at least 2 chambers; the building of 1693 added 4 more. Samuel and Hannah sometimes moved between chambers in the new house and the old and also sometimes slept separately. Unless otherwise indicated, I take Samuel's references to the chamber to mean the room in which he and Hannah were currently sleeping.

[9] Thomas, *Diary of Samuel Sewall*, 1:41, 312, 324, 459, 609; 2:845.

[10] Thomas, *Diary of Samuel Sewall*, 1:24, 2:645; Sewall to Jeremiah Dummer, January 25, 1717/18, *Letterbook of Samuel Sewall*, 2:83.

[11] Thomas, *Diary of Samuel Sewall*, 1:334; 2:731.

[12] Thomas, *Diary of Samuel Sewall*, 1:43–44, 68, 89, 90, 460; for an alternative view of Sewall's "notice" of material objects, see Mary Adams Hilmer, "The Other Diary of Samuel Sewall," *New England Quarterly* 55, no. 3 (September 1982): 354–67.

[13] H. L. Mencken defined Puritanism as "the haunting fear that someone, somewhere, may be happy" (H. L. Mencken, *The Vintage Mencken* [New York: Vintage Books, 1955], p. 233). Sewall to John Ive, February 19, 1691/2 and October 24, 1693, in *Letterbook of Samuel Sewall*, 1:128–30 and 137–38. For a discussion of Sewall's ambivalence about new architectural fashions, see Cummings, "Beginnings of Provincial Renaissance Architecture," p. 49.

[14] See the following correspondence in *Letterbook of Samuel Sewall:* Sewall to John Ive, October 24, 1693, August 25, 1709, and August 16, 1706, 1:137–38, 384, 338; Sewall to Daniel Allen, March 28, 1687, and Sewall to Edward Hull, March 28, 1687, 1:43–44.

[15] Thomas, *Diary of Samuel Sewall*, 1:339.

[16] That the Sewalls' social life was so bound up with prayer may help to explain a "very unusual dream" he recorded in 1686: "Our Saviour . . . Came to Boston and abode here sometime, and moreover . . . He Lodged in that time at Father Hull's." Samuel made no judgment on the ingenuous pride of his dreaming self, who wished he had shown more respect to Father Hull "since Christ chose when in Town, to take up His Quarters at his House" and who admired the "Wisdom of Christ in coming hither and spending some of His short Life here" (Thomas, *Diary of Samuel Sewall*, 1:63, 91).

[17] Thomas, *Diary of Samuel Sewall*, 2:621–22. Sewall served as a secretary-treasurer for the Company for Propagating the Gospel in New England and kept its books in the closet just below the fire; George Parker Winship, "Samuel Sewall and the New England Company," *Proceedings of the Massachusetts Historical Society* 67 (1941–44): 72–73.

[18] For a detailed reconstruction of the life cycle of a Puritan family, see Alan Macfarlane, *The Diary of Ralph Josselin, 1616–1683* (London: Oxford University Press, 1976), pp. 81–125. On early New England women as wives and mothers, see Laurel Thatcher Ulrich, *Good Wives: Image and Reality in the Lives of Women in Northern New England, 1650–1750* (New York: Oxford University Press, 1982), pp. 87–163; the thick domestic fabric described here was, in effect, Hannah's diary; it also explains why so few women kept diaries. For an ingenious reconstruction of domestic work, see Ulrich, *Good Wives*, pp. 11–86; and, for a rare diary of a New England "good wife," see Laurel Thatcher Ulrich, *A Midwife's Tale: The Life of Martha Ballard, Based on Her Diary, 1785–1812* (New York: Vintage Books, 1991). For the challenge of recovering a woman's life from her husband's diary, see Virginia Bernhard, "Cotton Mather's 'Most Unhappy Wife': Re-

flections on the Uses of Historical Evidence," *New England Quarterly* 60, no. 3 (September 1987): 341–62.

[19] Thomas, *Diary of Samuel Sewall*, 1:89, 337, 363–64.

[20] Sewall to Israel Chauncey, January 9, 1696/7, in *Letterbook of Samuel Sewall*, 1:181. For a provocative discussion of the centrality of marriage and family life to Puritan men, drawn from 2 early diaries, see Ann M. Little, "Men on Top?: The Farmer, the Minister, and Marriage in Early New England," *Pennsylvania History* 64 (Special Supplemental Issue, Summer 1997): 123–50.

[21] Thomas, *Diary of Samuel Sewall*, 1:100, 363–64.

[22] Thomas, *Diary of Samuel Sewall*, 2:621. In a letter, Sewall similarly wrote that Hannah, who was "very impatient of Smoak," woke him to complain that "there was so much Smoke in the Chamber, she could not bear it" (Sewall to Jeremiah Dummer, February 13, 1709/10, *Letterbook of Samuel Sewall*, 1:389). See, for example, the comparison of the Maine diaries of Martha Ballard and Henry Sewall in Ulrich, *Midwife's Tale*, pp. 30–32, 92–93, 111–12.

[23] Thomas, *Diary of Samuel Sewall*, 1:152.

[24] Thomas, *Diary of Samuel Sewall*, 1:186.

[25] Thomas, *Diary of Samuel Sewall*, 2:696; 1:364, 389.

[26] Thomas, *Diary of Samuel Sewall*, 1:88. For a provocative discussion of the spiritual power of Puritan men, see Ann Kibbey, "Mutations of the Supernatural: Witchcraft, Remarkable Providences, and the Power of Puritan Men," *American Quarterly* 34, no. 2 (Spring 1982): 125–48.

[27] Sewall used the phrase "Long Home," in Sewall to John Storke, October 30, 1717, *Letterbook of Samuel Sewall*, 2:77.

[28] Jeannine Hensley, ed., *The Works of Anne Bradstreet* (Cambridge: Harvard University Press, 1967), pp. 292–93.

Race, Realism, and the Documentation of the Rural Home during America's Great Depression

James C. Curtis

For more than a half century, the eighty thousand photographs of the Farm Security Administration (FSA) have served as a source of primary historical evidence about American rural life during the Great Depression. The photographic project was initiated under the auspices of the Resettlement Administration in 1935, relocated under the Farm Security Administration in 1937, and finally transferred to the Office of War Information in 1942. Hailed as the nation's premier documentary collection, the FSA file (now at the Library of Congress) has often been treated as a repository of revealed truth. Part of this aura of realism is a by-product of a historic faith in the veracity of all photographs. As Susan Sontag astutely observed, Americans regard photographs not as "statements about the world, so much as pieces of it." I have argued that FSA photographs are not literal "slices of life" but rather cultural constructs, reflecting the preconceptions, preferences, and prejudices of their makers and the depression audience for which they were intended.[1] This essay examines the depiction of home and family in FSA photography with specific emphasis on the issue of race.

My methodology closely resembles that of an archaeologist or social historian. The FSA photographic file is a relatively undisturbed
body of evidence similar to a pristine excavation site or a newly discovered cache of probate inventories. Unlike their artistic and journalistic
colleagues, FSA photographers did not have the freedom to select the
images they deemed most appropriate for the picture file. As government employees they were required to surrender all their photographs
to project headquarters in Washington, D.C. Occasionally, strong-
willed individuals such as Dorothea Lange were able to obtain dupli-
cate prints for their own use, but the file itself remained under the
control of project director Roy Stryker. He insisted that his photographers produce as many images as possible and used the growing bulk
of the file to counter criticism that government photography was a bu-
reaucratic boondoggle. To charges that FSA photography was pure pro-
paganda, Stryker responded that the aim of his unit was historical investigation and public education. A burgeoning collection of photographs
buttressed this defense.

Although the FSA file was reorganized after World War II and the
pictures divided into more than one thousand subject categories, the
original arrangement (by photographer and assignment) is preserved in
a 1943–44 microfilm version of the eighty thousand captioned prints.
The contextual information offered by this arrangement, which resembles archaeological deposition, is critical to understanding the motives
and strategies employed by project photographers. Previous FSA scholarship tends to ignore the photographs as a primary form of evidence,
preferring instead to concentrate on the correspondence of Stryker and
the interviews with project photographers. Although Stryker's letters often reveal his attitudes toward the file and contain occasional instructions to his staff, they rarely reveal information on individual images or
photographic series. Conducted decades after the fieldwork was completed, oral history interviews are even more problematic. Photographers were asked repeatedly about their famous images but rarely about
companion photographs that never appeared in print. FSA photographers routinely took series of photographs and not single pictures. Subsequently, these companion images, when examined in the context of
the original assignments, reveal meanings lost in even the most famous
FSA photographs. The series often indicates the preconceptions, strategies, and aesthetic agendas that project photographers brought to their

work. It also can reveal what individual photographers chose to include and what they decided to leave out of a final image.

Commissioned to create a comprehensive portrait of rural life during the Great Depression, the FSA photographic project used the powerful symbols of home and family to generate support for government relief efforts. Project administrators sought to present rural folk as needy but not helpless victims of the depression. Dorothea Lange's *Migrant Mother* (1936) typified the FSA's presentation of agrarian suffering and sacrifice (fig. 1). With Arthur Rothstein's photographs of the Dust Bowl

Fig. 1. Dorothea Lange, *Migrant Mother*, 1936. (Farm Security Administration Collection, Library of Congress.)

and Walker Evans's extended series on Alabama sharecroppers, these celebrated pictures presented rural folk as bearers and protectors of agrarian traditions. This apotheosis culminated in 1940 with the publication of Sherwood Anderson's *Home Town*—a book illustrated with more than one hundred FSA images that underscore the author's belief that rural values provided an antidote to the malaise of urban America.[2]

In creating this celebratory portrait, government photographers excluded African Americans, who constituted a substantial percentage of the rural labor force. Black sharecroppers and migrant workers appeared in the FSA file with great regularity—but as negative not positive symbols.[3] African American families, homes, and material possessions fell under the relentless gaze of imagemakers who stripped away the marks of civilization in a quest for the primitive.

The concept of the primitive, although deeply rooted in American culture, defied a single definition. The primitivism that FSA photographers ascribed to African Americans was a negation of the enobling, Edenic vision popularized during the colonial era. In its most traditional form, the primitive invoked "dreams of a paradise on earth," where the excesses of civilized society would disappear as people lived "in nature according to nature." Primitivism's promoters argued that this model environment fostered "sexual innocence, equality of status and peaceful simplicity." Moreover, the inhabitants possessed "vigorous minds, unsullied by the complexity and sophistication of modern civilization." During the 1930s, regionalist artists as well as FSA photographers located such virtues among the white yeomanry. They did so at the expense of African Americans who became the embodiment of a primitivism divorced from enlightenment ideals, nineteenth-century romanticism, and twentieth-century attachments to the simple life.[4]

In the spring of 1937, the FSA dispatched its youngest photographer, twenty-two-year-old Arthur Rothstein, to Gee's Bend, Alabama— a community of black tenant farmers. Although the FSA had been active in Gee's Bend for almost two years and already had helped the hard-pressed residents turn a profit, Rothstein was instructed to treat this community not as a New Deal project but as a "primitive setup." Contemporary reports characterized Gee's Bend as a "tribal like settlement" and maintained that the African-American residents were "far away from civilization in their habits and manner of living."[5] Pursuing his assignment, Rothstein produced an extended series of more than

Fig. 2. Arthur Rothstein, large family at Gee's Bend, Ala., 1937. (Farm Security Administration Collection, Library of Congress.)

fifty photographs. A number of these images inverted the familiar FSA symbol of the small, independent, rural family.

By far the most famous photograph to emerge from Rothstein's Alabama sojourn is the image of a male figure standing in front of a group of sixteen women and children (fig. 2). In the original caption for this picture, Rothstein identified his subjects as "descendants of former slaves . . . living under primitive conditions on the plantation."[6] Rothstein's terse statement and his deliberate placement of people implied that this was a large nuclear family and that the male in the foreground was the father of all the children shown.

As composed and captioned, this photograph departs dramatically from such FSA classics as *Migrant Mother,* in which Lange deliberately excluded subjects so that her image conformed to middle-class expectations on family size (see fig. 1). Such photographic eugenics occurred frequently in FSA depictions of white tenant farmers but rarely in the presentation of black families. For example, a 1940 photograph taken in Caswell County, North Carolina, Marion Post Wolcott presented an African American family of nine seated on the porch of their home. In an apparent attempt to demonstrate the emotional as well as financial benefits of government relief, Wolcott showed her subjects laughing, an emotion banished during most FSA picture-taking sessions. The image came perilously close to Hollywood caricatures and to the century-old Sambo stereotype of southern blacks as carefree, childlike, and happy-go-lucky individuals.[7]

Rothstein's depiction of Gee's Bend's families as sprawling, uncontrolled units bears the mark of long-standing stereotypes of black sexuality and promiscuity. Since the nineteenth century, whites in the North and the South had reacted to the presence of African Americans with a combination of fear and fascination. According to one recent scholar, the African American was "regarded as a savage" and was "thought to be a creature under the domination of his passions, especially his sexuality." The black community was often referred to as " 'New Liberia,' or 'New Guinea' or 'Little Africa.' " Rothstein was prepared to find such patterns of behavior at Gee's Bend. Private and government reports made mention of large families, and some alluded to a high rate of illegitimacy at Gee's Bend.[8] The young photographer added to these allegations by using his camera to count children and to call attention to what he presumed were unwed mothers. He made little attempt to locate the community's young black males, and by excluding them from his series, he further reinforced the impression that children at Gee's Bend were born either into large families or out of wedlock.

The photographer's preconceived notions of primitivism encompassed the material world as well. In his letter of instructions to Rothstein, Stryker provided a graphic description of housing conditions at Gee's Bend. Rothstein was forewarned that the African American tenant farmers lived in ramshackle "cabins of mud and stakes which they hew themselves." To Rothstein's surprise, only a few chimnies were constructed of mud and sticks. The houses and outbuildings in Gee's Bend were of notched-log construction consistent with building types employed by whites and blacks throughout the South. Such details as riven shingles and carefully applied siding gave every indication of skill and craftsmanship decidedly at odds with the photographer's preconceptions. Once exposed to the actual buildings and the ample evidence of the community's architectural competence, Rothstein had

the opportunity to modify his views—to present local residents as resourceful individuals capable of managing the design, construction, and
furnishings of their dwellings.[9] Such a portrait, however, would have
detracted from government plans to provide Gee's Bend with modern
housing. Rothstein's assignment was to record the "before pictures,"
leaving to later reporters the task of illustrating the impact of govern-
ment-sponsored construction. Rothstein did create a few close-ups of
mud and stick chimneys and one portrait of a resident wielding what
the photographer called a crude wooden implement. In fact the tenant
was using a "fro" to split shingles in the traditional manner. Except for
these singular images, Rothstein avoided architecture at Gee's Bend.
He used the substantial log buildings as a primitive backdrop for his
portraits of family units. Yet to the informed eye, the log buildings provide mute testimony to the resourcefulness and skill of these black tenant farmers.

The buildings of Gee's Bend bear a striking resemblance to the
log homes of Pie Town, New Mexico, that Rothstein's colleague Russell
Lee recorded three years later. Lee, however, used the architecture of
this tiny white community to signify the positive values of the pioneer
not the negative associations of the primitive. Lee's trip to this isolated
New Mexico village was part of a systematic effort to identify and preserve America's small-town heritage. Stryker embarked on this campaign at the suggestion of Robert Lynd, coauthor of *Middletown* (1929).
Lynd encouraged Stryker to find photographic proof that ideals associated with home, family, and community survived in the countryside.
Lynd's research suggested that these values had been sorely compro-
mised by "Middletown's" headlong rush toward materialism. In the
small town shooting scripts that he subsequently prepared for his photographers, Stryker made no mention of African Americans. Instead he
followed Lynd's example and conceived of representative communities
as having little or no black population.[10] Even in southern towns with
a substantial percentage of African American residents, Stryker's photographers presented the communities as white preserves.

Lee's portrait of Pie Town as America's "last frontier" was also
inspired by Lewis Mumford's *Technics and Civilization.*[11] Lee presented
Pie Town's homesteaders as avid students of nature who quickly mas-
tered the elements of wood technology in their construction of log
houses, hand tools, and workshops in the wilderness. Pie Town's archi-

Fig. 3. Russell Lee, log building under construction, Pie Town, N.M., 1940. (Farm Security Administration Collection, Library of Congress.)

tectural competence was more imaginary than real. Although Lee showed various stages in the construction of a log home, his captions for the series contain information that undercuts the image of homesteaders as skilled and resourceful architects. One photographed log building was a rented structure being relocated on the property of an absentee landlord (fig. 3). The builder was not a homesteader but a hired hand, too poor to purchase this or any of the other log structures he had erected for the families of Pie Town.

As Rothstein misinterpreted architecture so he misread the interior furnishings and decoration of Gee's Bend's log buildings. Like his FSA colleagues, Rothstein was struck by the practice of covering walls with decorative paper and newsprint (fig. 4). He used these interiors as ironic backgrounds without understanding their customary significance. What appeared to Rothstein as a primitive form of decoration and insulation was in fact an established custom in both black and white households. Freshly hung paper was one mark of a well-kept home; there were even prescriptions for the most appropriate designs or illustrative material for individual rooms of the house. The newsprint on the wall and the scalloped paper decoration of the mantel covering seen in figure 4 indicate a design competence of no less significance than Gee's Bend's tradition

Fig. 4. Arthur Rothstein, interior of tenant cabin, Gee's Bend, Ala., 1937. (Farm Security Administration Collection, Library of Congress.)

of log building. This photograph also attests, although inadvertently, to another area of competence; Rothstein undoubtedly composed this image to feature the FSA's introduction of sewing machines to Gee's Bend. A later report claimed that this technological improvement enabled "the girls and ladies of the community . . . to make simple dresses and other articles of wear." The report implied that women at Gee's Bend lacked any familiarity with needlework and that only when "taught by the Home Economics teacher to use patterns" were they capable of providing for their own wants.[12] Yet the object being produced in the photograph is not a simple piece of clothing but a complicated quilt. Rothstein's caption makes only slight mention of this time-honored craft. In FSA photographs of white families, the quilt often signified the maintenance and transmission of regional and familial traditions.

The most intriguing image in the Gee's Bend series is an interior

Fig. 5. Arthur Rothstein, interior of plantation house, Gee's Bend, Ala., 1937. (Farm Security Administration Collection, Library of Congress.)

photograph of the former plantation house (fig. 5). Upon his arrival, Rothstein learned that this dwelling had been occupied by black tenants since 1907, when the last member of the Pettway family died and the plantation passed to absentee owners. The decaying southern mansion had become a staple of FSA photography perhaps because the project was founded in the same year that Margaret Mitchell's runaway best-seller *Gone with the Wind* (1935) renewed the nation's romance with the Old South. But if Walker Evans's pictures of abandoned Louisiana plantations evoked the nostalgia of Mitchell's epic, Rothstein's photo-graph of a black foreman and his family seated in the Pettway plantation parlor recalled the film *Birth of a Nation* (1915), in which D. W. Griffith depicted an aggressive black culture displacing southern white society.

Rothstein designed this photograph to suggest that such displace-ment led to social disarray. He seated his subjects around the hearth, long emblematic of middle-class family unity. Yet the makeshift condi-tion and haphazard arrangement of furniture stand in sharp contrast to traditional parlor portraits where material objects attested to power, affluence, and status. Missing a back slat, bound together with bailing wire, this foreman's chair is a fragile replica of the proverbial seat of paternal authority. Surrounding the fireplace are wall decorations that recall the years when whites still occupied the plantation. Standing in the center of the mantelpiece, wedged in between two framed prints, is a photograph of a white male, perhaps the last of the Pettway occupants. How convenient that the clock above bears the name "Regulator" and that its base is shaped like an arrow that points directly at this small photograph. Long-standing racial stereotypes maintained that white slave owners and their descendants provided a necessary regulation and discipline missing from African American culture. Indeed, an unpublished government report on Gee's Bend maintained that before the arrival of the FSA in 1935, the tenant farmers were "illiterate, unorganized, indolent, and [had been] a drain on [previous] relief organizations." But what of the emancipation print in the left background of the photograph showing Lincoln freeing the slaves? Was Rothstein inserting a subtle tribute to African American progress since the Civil War? Perhaps, but the Lincoln reference can also be interpreted as praise for presidential benefactors past and present. It is worth noting that Franklin Roosevelt actively promoted the Lincoln legend in his political strategies of the late 1930s.[13]

Although the intent of Rothstein's parlor portrait seems clear, the content of this image raises several questions. Why would this African American family possess these mementos? Why would they arrange them in such a symbolic fashion? Where were their own memorabilia? There are several possible explanations for the retention of these white artifacts in the plantation house. The foreman and his family may have preserved the hearth decorations as a tribute to the Pettway family or perhaps as a sign of the passing of power from plantation owner to tenant manager. On the other hand, the foreman's family may have confined themselves to other rooms of the house, reserving the parlor as a display area where government officials would be free to arrange objects for publicity purposes. The fact that one of the framed prints is sideways lends support to this theory. This would not have been the first FSA photograph in which objects were arranged for or by the photographer to communicate predetermined messages.[14]

Alternately, these may not be white objects at all. The artifacts may belong to the foreman and his family, who displayed them to make their own statement. For example, the picture of Theodore Roosevelt posted to the left of the fireplace refers to martial exploits during the Spanish-American War and his famous charge up San Juan Hill. Black troops participated in this battle as they did during World War I. Indeed, the foreman wears what appear to be military issue puttees. Is he calling attention to his family's martial heritage? Or is he suggesting that his position as plantation foreman involves paramilitary powers? If deliberate, the foreman's presentation of self and home was also intentionally subtle, no doubt in deference to long-standing white fears of black militancy.

Less than six months after Rothstein completed his assignment, some of his photographs appeared in print, not to illustrate a government report but to accompany John Temple Graves's article in *New York Times Magazine* titled "The Big World at Last Reaches Gee's Bend." In recounting his visit to Gee's Bend, Graves made frequent references to primitivism. Like Rothstein he drew parallels between this isolated village and the tribal societies of Africa. He described the typical authority figure at Gee's Bend as a black tenant farmer who "without benefit of nose ring or paint" presented himself as "the chieftain of a primitive tribe." For Graves, Gee's Bend was an exotic locale where "the drums of Africa [and] the banjos of antebellum times . . . are tokened there on the plateau above the curving river where half a hundred little cabins surround a great cotton patch."[15]

Although he employed the tribal metaphor, Graves's view of the primitive differed markedly from that of Rothstein. The journalist presented the residents of Gee's Bend as competent individuals, not dependent wards of the government. His portrayal of the black tenants was reminiscent of descriptions of American Indians as noble savages being overwhelmed by an insensitive majoritarian culture. Graves characterized Gee's Bend as "crude, backward [and] poor" but maintained that the residents shared a proud tradition of self-reliance, and "given half a chance" they might continue to be "happy and productive, self-serving and self-governing." His essay presented the FSA's relief effort as a mixed blessing. Two years of federal assistance had put the community on the road toward economic health, but Graves was quick to add that the sharecroppers played a major role in this recovery. By maintaining an optimistic attitude, following government prescriptions, handling relief monies in a responsible manner, and making timely payments on government loans, the black tenant farmers retained a large measure of autonomy. Graves shared the residents' anxiety about the long-term effects of federal intervention. He wondered whether "the well-intentioned plans of the government for rehabilitation of these picturesque and normally happy, independent people" would "make a regiment of them, put them in standardized houses, bring them into contact with a world that will spoil and dissipate them, rob them of self-reliance, individuality, peace."[16]

Graves's musings about the dangers of government paternalism help explain his selection of photographs for his article. He included none of Rothstein's images of large families—not that Graves overlooked the family unit. Quite the contrary, he presented familial cohesion as a stablizing influence and bedrock of Gee's Bend's tradition of self-reliance. Graves made clear that large family units were extended and multigenerational. For example, he provided a verbal portrait of the family assembled in Rothstein's courtyard scene (see fig. 2). Graves's depiction is at odds with both the composition and the caption for Rothstein's photograph. Where the photographer labeled this group "a large family" and composed the picture so that the lone male figure appeared to be the biological parent of all the children shown, Graves identified the man as "sixty-five-year-old Patrick Bendoff, who lives with his wife and many children and grandchildren." The author went on to say that Bendoff occupied the "best cabin" in a family compound that included separate dwellings for his married children plus "seven additional one room buildings." According to Graves, Bendoff was in the habit of making "a distinguished occasion of it when he welcomes visitors under the big Chinaberry tree that flourishes in this clean front yard." Little did Bendoff realize that in assembling his kinfolk to pose for Rothstein, he would be subjecting them to scrutiny about illegitimacy, promiscuity, and loose family morals. By contrast, Graves presented Bendoff as "a moral man" who might provide temporary housing for sons and daughters "who, without having attained marital status, are parents." But in such instances, Bendoff expected "to see each of these married to the other party as soon as economic conditions permit."[17]

Graves's positive depiction of Gee's Bend extended to architecture as well as family life. Because his visit followed Rothstein's departure by only a few months, Graves observed the same extant structures and new construction that Rothstein had used to shape his photographic report. Yet the author's verbal description has a distinctly romantic tone missing in the captions for Rothstein's photographs and in the compositions as well. Although "the cabins are shabby and poor," Graves wrote, "the logs that wall them are hand-hewn." So were the roof shingles that had "weathered to a gray so silvery and soft that Eastern architects would sell themselves down the river for a sight of them." Graves made several references to the pool of skilled carpenters at Gee's Bend. "When there was a marriage, the men of the community would build a cabin for the new couple as a gift," he wrote, adding that this token was all the more precious because it was "of work rather than money." The community's architectural competence was evident in public as well as private structures. Graves observed the men of Gee's Bend "building a new church, exchanging their service at a neighboring sawmill for some special lumber." Meanwhile the women "obtained money for nails and other incidentals through the sale of eggs."[18] Because Rothstein paid little attention to traditional architecture and chose instead to characterize such exchanges as indexes of a primitive economy, he conveyed the impression that the residents of Gee's Bend were in desperate need of new dwellings and the government supervision to build them.

Graves's respect for the customs and traditions of the black tenant farmers was tempered by his nostalgia for the Old South. Although he described the former plantation house as "a ghost, paintless and in unsightly repair," he waxed eloquent about "the beautifully proportioned rooms, the high ceilings, the fine detail of cornice, woodwork and plaster." These elements were reminiscent of the bygone era—"of a day that was." Continuing in the same vein, Graves described the black foreman and his family living amid the ruins of white civilization "surrounded by the faded relics and fine woodwork" of former "masters gone with the wind." But Graves reassured his readers that the black occupation of the plantation house was not cause for alarm for the foreman was still "the white man's Negro." Although charged with the responsibility for collecting rents from outlying tenants, the foreman's main duties were ceremonial—"to play host to white visitors—take them around the Bend, take them through the house, answer questions." Graves chose a distant shot of the plantation exterior to illustrate this portion of his essay. Considering his affinity for subtlety and nuance, it is not surprising that he rejected Rothstein's parlor photograph (see fig. 5). The image was too direct, too confrontational in tone and composition.[19]

In the closing paragraphs of his article, Graves argued forcibly that the primitivism of the community was worth protecting. "No one can visit Gee's Bend without an appreciation of the racial virtues preserved there," he observed, noting that these qualities tended "to disappear in more civilized quarters where the ambition of the Negro is to become only a carbon copy of the white man." To illustrate his conviction, Graves included several of Rothstein's close-up pictures of women and children. Rothstein never intended these images as commentaries on individual character; his captions say nothing about matters of racial integrity or intelligence. Graves stripped away the original captions and used the photographs to drive home his preservationist's plea. He presented the community as "a storehouse of original racial qualities, a laboratory in which the most excellent characteristics of the people may be isolated for example's sake." In essence, Graves argued that Gee's Bend was already a model environment whose residents had little to learn from the government. Federal intervention might create cooperative enterprises such as cotton gins and cane and grist mills, but the tenants needed no tutelage in the practice of a "cooperative plan." After all, Graves concluded, they had been cooperating all their lives, not out of a devotion to efficiency or economy but because of their strong kinship network and "because they all like and trust one another."[20]

Graves was not the last visitor to report on the FSA's project at Gee's Bend. In the spring of 1939, Stryker sent another staff member, Marion Post Wolcott, to make the FSA final photographic record of the community. Predictably, Wolcott's "after pictures" cast the government project in a light distinctly different from Rothstein's 1937 pictorial presentation. Perhaps to reassure viewers that the federal government had solved the major social ills featured in Rothstein's "before pictures," Wolcott studiously avoided the subjects of illegitimacy and familial instability. In her extended series of more than one hundred images, she took no pictures of large family groups. Instead she fashioned photographs of small tenant families carefully posed near their new government houses. Wolcott made the case for government improvement by widening her angle of vision to include the original log residences as well (fig. 6).

Seemingly a simple contrast between the old and the new—the

Fig. 6. Marion Post Wolcott, old and new tenant
houses, Gee's Bend, Ala., 1939. (Farm Security Administration Collection, Library of Congress.)

primitive and the modern—Wolcott's photograph is a complex document that raises numerous questions about the government's goals and
the community's response to outside intervention. Why, for instance,
did the log buildings remain standing next to the government replace-
ments? In 1936 and 1937, during the first phases of the project, the
retention of old homesteads made sense. Families could live in their
ancestral dwellings while waiting to move into the new buildings. But
once construction was complete, why were the log structures not torn
down or at least converted to use as outbuildings?

Part of the answer to these questions lies in a government report
issued shortly before Wolcott's visit in spring 1939. This document indicates that new house construction was a relatively low priority at Gee's
Bend. The FSA's first goal was to promote agricultural diversification
and thereby reduce the community's dependence on cotton production. To this end, the FSA constructed barns and other essential outbuildings for the promotion of livestock and the development of such
crops as corn, hay, peanuts, and peas. The tenants were also encouraged
to develop subsistence gardens; FSA funds subsidized construction of
protective fencing and drilling of new wells. The report mentioned the
government's desire to have the tenants occupy new houses but the
construction timetable indicated that these dwellings would not be

completed for at least two years and that at the end of the project no more than 50 percent of participating families would have new residences.[21]

The symbolic significance of the new homes outweighed their economic importance. Wolcott used the new buildings to demonstrate that government standardization was pushing back the barriers of primitivism. In her captions she stressed that local residents participated in the construction process, that they were partners with the government. Yet there were severe restrictions in this partnership. The black tenants had no choice of house plans and limited options in matters of exterior decoration. They were instructed to paint their homes either white or gray. A scholar from the Tuskeegee Institute who conducted field research in Gee's Bend several years after Wolcott's departure questioned this regimentation. Why, he wondered, were all families expected to live in such uniformly small houses? With "two main rooms, a small room and a kitchen," the new dwellings were clearly inadequate for tenant families with more than two or three children. Yet the government insisted on uniformity even though there was "little or no objective justification for such a policy."[22]

While inadequate for the space needs of the average tenant family at Gee's Bend, the new houses called attention to the government's social programs. The small, spartan structures, carefully situated next to the old log buildings suggested that Gee's Bend had turned away from a primitive past marked by unchecked population growth and was adopting the modern standard of family planning. What better way to illustrate that progress than by showing the rough hewn cabin giving way to the freshly painted frame house?

But the presence of the log building in this photograph can be read much differently, not as a sign of acceptance but rather of resistance to government designs and requirements. Indeed, during his visit in 1937, Graves recorded the complaints of several villagers that the new houses lacked such customary features as dogtrots (breezeways) and lean-to kitchens.[23] One tenant farmer, identified by Graves as a leader of the community, indicated his desire to live in his log house even when his new residence was completed. In an apparent attempt to overcome such objections, the FSA stipulated that in addition to receiving construction materials, the tenants would be paid five cents per hour for building their homes. They were promised an additional ten cents per hour to be paid as a credit when the project was complete. The residential re-building of Gee's Bend was therefore part of a larger effort to stimulate the economy by introduction of wage labor and by an unusual pro-gram of enforced savings. Although these monetary incentives may have ensured eventual completion of government housing, they did not guarantee that the villagers would use the new homes as their sole residences.

From government housing, Wolcott turned her attention to the new health clinic and school, where she continued to illustrate modern-ization's triumph over primitivism. As a prelude to her coverage of the clinic, Wolcott took a portrait of an elderly midwife seated in front of her traditional log home. Wolcott's caption implied that midwifery was a practice more akin to folk custom than medicine; the health clinic would therefore bring modern services to Gee's Bend. But her interior shots show no delivery room, nursery, nor any medical equipment per-taining to childbirth. Nor does the report of the project's home econo-mist mention infant mortality as a major health concern. Quite the contrary, this document records thirty-five live births and no stillbirths or infant deaths in the two years prior to Wolcott's visit. Apparently all the births took place in the tenants' homes. Community residents may well have continued to use the midwife to assist in these deliveries. The tenacity of folk medicine and customary practices of birthing may explain the pairing of two seemingly unrelated observations in the home economist's medical report. While proudly proclaiming that "we could not hope for better health," she noted "we have many superstitions and practices in the Bend." Not surprisingly, Wolcott made no attempt to record home medical care; photographs of the project nurse making house calls would have undercut the image of the clinic as the primary caregiving institution in the community. Instead, Wolcott took a series of photographs of a white physician conducting examinations at the clinic. The home economist's report indicates that this doctor lived at considerable distance from Gee's Bend and that the only resident health care professional was an African American nurse. Wolcott's photo-graphs reduce the nurse's role to that of lecturer on such innocuous topics as the proper method of making a sickbed.[24]

Contrary to her appearance in these photographs, the African American nurse was the primary provider of government health care at Gee's Bend. Overworked and underpaid, she won little recognition for her extraordinary efforts. The white project manager had even with-held her paycheck on the grounds that she was deliquent in paying rent on her government lodging. After the nurse produced receipts proving that she had made timely payments, the manager grudgingly released her pay. The nurse also had been the target of verbal abuse by a local storekeeper. She related these incidents to a visiting social worker who was in Gee's Bend at the same time Wolcott was completing her photographic survey.[25] It seems unlikely that Wolcott would have altered the thrust of her documentation even if she had been apprised of these incidents. Her task was to depict progress at Gee's Bend. She certainly was not going to record evidence of government indifference to or complicity in racial discrimination.

In her photographs of educational programs, Wolcott once again employed architecture as a primary symbol of progress. She designed a series of exterior shots to show that the old one-room log schoolhouse had been superseded by a spacious new building. Wolcott took a half dozen photographs of children on the playground learning new games under the supervision of a government instructor. Interior photographs praised a curriculum heavy on vocational education in secretarial skills, shop, and home economics. A closer examination of these images reveals the limits of government modernization. The playground consisted of a large tract of undeveloped dirt and was entirely bereft of recreational equipment. The schoolhouse had no electricity and was heated by an old-fashioned woodstove. Schoolbooks seemed in short supply. Finally, in a puzzling sequence of photographs, Wolcott showed students in the school's cooperative garden being instructed in the use of agricultural implements. The tools in these photographs were throwbacks to the days of slavery. What could the government teach the child of a tenant farmer about the proper use of a hoe?

Images of new classrooms and attentive students supported the government's claim that the tenant farmers welcomed educational reform. But while young people willingly posed for Wolcott, some village elders remained suspicious of the FSA's intent. The most serious resistance came from the two Baptist congregations that had been active in the community for decades. In their extended analysis of Gee's Bend, Wolcott and Rothstein produced but three photographs of these churches. Curiously, these images dealt not with religion or worship but with the use of the church as a temporary school. The most memorable was a

1937 Rothstein photograph of an elementary class being held in the church. A visiting teacher writes on a makeshift blackboard that is placed in front of the pulpit.

Rothstein intended this image as testimony to government initiative and flexibility. Rather than await completion of the new school, project managers had pressed the church into service. The image conveys the added message that the church hierarchy sanctioned the government's plans. Quite the opposite was true. The congregation objected to this violation of sacred space and the displacement of the altar by educational objects. The FSA eventually overcame these objections but only after extended negotiations. Religious resistance to educational reform did not cease with the completion of the new schoolhouse. The congregations continued to criticize various aspects of the curriculum, particularly the FSA's insistence that physical education would provide an outlet for the excessive sexual energy of the community's adolescents. When the FSA tried to promote baseball and basketball, the minister denounced such play as sinful. These were not the objections of a solitary eccentric. One visitor to Gee's Bend observed that "practically every aspect of the lives of these people seems centered about the church."[26] The list of religiously proscribed activities extended far beyond America's pastime to include adultery, dancing, fighting, cursing, card playing, drunkenness, and gambling.

The vitality of religion at Gee's Bend constituted a real problem for those commissioned to report on the government's battle against primitivism. Although strict and fundamentalist, the Baptist churches clearly were not purveyors of primitive religion. Indeed, one of the most important details in Rothstein's photograph is the credo "ONE LORD, ONE FAITH AND ONE BAPTISM." As these words announced essential Christian belief, they also attested to the importance of language in religious ritual and thereby subtly undermined Rothstein's presentation of the government as the sole adversary of illiteracy.

When Wolcott reached Gee's Bend, she decided to ignore religion. Instead, she portrayed the tenants as eager converts to the FSA's agricultural cooperatives. The cooperative store, the grist mill, and cotton gin: these were the institutions that would point the way toward modernization and self-sufficiency. Wolcott covered them in detail. In one sequence she showed tenant farmers congregating outside the grist mill, their wagons loaded with corn. She then entered the mill to show the corn being ground and the meal loaded into sacks for the tenants' return trip. Wolcott completed the sequence with a shot of a homeward-bound tenant driving his wagon down a dirt road, alongside of which ran a new drainage ditch. This image was intended to summarize the entire cooperative endeavor and to symbolize the government's belief that Gee's Bend was on the road to economic recovery and self-sufficiency.

But amid all of these positive symbols, there is one negative image. As she sat outside the cooperative store taking pictures of the tenants socializing and loading their wagons, Wolcott noticed one of the drivers sound asleep on top of his cargo. She moved in for a close-up. In creating this picture, Wolcott indulged the age-old stereotype of African Americans as lackadaisical workers and indolent individuals.

Wolcott's photographs at Gee's Bend suggest the limits of her vision and that of her sponsors as well. In her report on Gee's Bend, she showed government programs in action and charted the course of economic recovery. Like her FSA colleagues, she depicted African Americans as worthy recipients of federal assistance and eager students of modern agrarian methods. But she stopped short of portraying them as exemplars of agrarian independence, familial cohesion, or rural self-sufficiency.

A similar myopia mars John Collier's 1940 photograph of a black foreman and his family in a New Jersey migrant camp (fig. 7). Like Wolcott's pictures of the school and health clinic at Gee's Bend, this image was designed to show that government-run facilities provided black laborers with an improved standard of living and helped educate them in matters of hygiene and domestic economy. Collier's hitherto unpublished image bears a strong resemblance to Russell Lee's famous composition of a Texas farm couple taken the previous year (fig. 8). Both photographs responded to Stryker's call for pictures of Americans "at home in the evening listening to the radio." Stryker believed such images could demonstrate that the rural home was still a center of family life, whereas in *Middletown* modern entertainment disrupted domestic solidarity. Stryker's imperative explains an otherwise incongruous contrast in the Texas photograph between details of poverty (torn and tattered clothing) and signs of luxury (the floor-length radio). Lee placed the large console at the center of this image not to suggest that these relief recipients were given to extravagant expenditure of govern-

Fig. 7. John Collier, interior of migrant camp, N.J., 1940. (Farm Security Administration Collection, Library of Congress.)

ment money but to demonstrate that the radio promoted unity and an informed citizenry.

In Collier's photograph the radio also appears at the center of family life. Unlike Lee's subjects, this family has put on freshly laundered clothes for the occasion. This is not a large family like the ones presented at Gee's Bend. The artifacts in this spare interior—especially the traditional oil lamp, the curtains, and the makeshift clothes closet— attest to cleanliness and order. Yet one object negates the impression of neatness, discipline, and hard work. There is an empty whiskey bottle on the baseboard, located so that it divides the family. A small detail? A mere happenstance? Perhaps, but the object is on direct axis with the camera, and Collier chose a depth of field that brought the label into sharp focus. Moreover, the other pictures from this migrant camp demonstrate that Collier exercised complete control over his subject matter.

Collier's image is but one of many FSA photographs that call attention to instabilities in African American domestic life. Instead of concentrating on thrift and sober industry, qualities of life often highlighted in portraits of white families, Stryker's photographers often would take

Fig. 8. Russell Lee, interior of tenant home, Hidalgo County, Tex., 1939. (Farm Security Administration Collection, Library of Congress.)

pictures of black laborers gambling on payday, purchasing liquor at the company store, or engaging in various forms of late-night revelry. Such is the context for Wolcott's famous portrait of a Florida "juke joint" (fig. 9). This is not to say that white subjects never danced before an FSA camera. Indeed, one of Lee's most memorable Pie Town photographs is entitled *Jigger at a Square Dance* (fig. 10). But this display took place inside a log home, before an appreciative audience of women who had spent the afternoon working on a quilt and had then hoisted the quilting frame to the ceiling to make way for the dance. Lee's pictures of these activities heeded Stryker's call for images showing that in rural America the home stood at the center of family and community life. By contrast, the juke joint had achieved notoriety as a site where black migrant workers spent their meager wages on frenzied entertainment.[27] By concentrating on such activities outside the home, Wolcott and her FSA colleagues implied that black sharecroppers

Fig. 9. Marion Post Wolcott, "Juke Joint," Belle Glade, Fla., 1940. (Farm Security Administration Collection, Library of Congress.)

lacked a stable home life and that only under the supervision of government social workers would they be able to develop constructive habits of thrift and self-discipline.

The preconceptions and prejudices evident in the foregoing photographs of African Americans are all the more complicated because they were born of good intentions. To promote reform of economic ills that had plagued rural America since the 1920s, Stryker and his staff painstakingly constructed portraits of poor white tenants as innocent victims of the Great Depression and as decent, deserving citizens. Given a helping hand, these sturdy yeomen would quickly rebuild their homes and provide for their own wants. Their ingrained independence would prevent them from becoming permanent wards of the government. Such flattering portraits would admit no major character flaws or social defects, certainly not those of bigotry or racial discrimination.

Fig. 10. Russell Lee, "Jigger at a Square Dance," Pie Town, N.M., 1940. (Farm Security Administration Collection, Library of Congress.)

And so Stryker and his photographers circumvented the subject of race whenever possible. But this avoidance constituted a covert form of discrimination. In portraying white tenant farmers as disciples of democracy and progress, FSA photographers left little or no room for a complementary picture of African Americans. The virtues of the white yeoman became the defects of the black primitive. For sexual innocence, industry, and ingenuity, the FSA substituted sexual promiscuity, indolence, and incompetence. In sum, FSA photographers, like apologists of a bygone age, developed their positive images from negatives more than a century old.

¹ The literature on the FSA photographic project is vast and most easily approached through Penelope Dixon, *Photographers of the Farm Security Administration: An Annotated Bibliography, 1930–1980* (New York: Garland Publishers, 1983). Of the many recent works to interpret FSA photographs, Maren Stange, *Symbols of Ideal Life: Social Documentary Photography in America, 1890–1950* (New York: Cambridge University Press, 1988) places the greatest emphasis on the ideological goals of the project, while Carl Fleischhauer and Beverly Brannan, eds., *Documenting America, 1935–1943* (Berkeley and Los Angeles: University of California Press, 1989) contains images pertinent to this study, as well as suggestive essays by Lawrence Levine and Alan Trachtenberg. Susan Sontag, *On Photography* (New York: Farrar, Straus, and Giroux, 1977), p. 4. James C. Curtis, *Mind's Eye, Mind's Truth: FSA Photography Reconsidered* (Philadelphia: Temple University Press, 1989).

² Sherwood Anderson, *Home Town* (New York: Alliance Book Corp., 1940).

³ For an examination of FSA photography that enumerates and identifies images of African Americans, see Nicholas Natanson, *The Black Image in the New Deal: The Politics of FSA Photography* (Knoxville: University of Tennessee Press, 1992). Natanson estimates that there are more than 6,000 photographs of African Americans in the FSA file.

⁴ Robert F. Berkhofer, Jr., *The White Man's Indian: Images of the American Indian from Columbus to the Present* (New York: Alfred A. Knopf, 1978), p. 72. Primitivism's place in American culture in the late nineteenth century is ably defined in T. J. Jackson Lears, *No Place of Grace: Anti-Modernism and the Transformation of American Culture, 1880–1920* (New York: Random House, 1981). For the concept of the primitive in American folk art, see John Vlach, *Plain Painters: Making Sense of American Folk Art* (Washington, D.C.: Smithsonian Institution Press, 1988). Although it does not address primitivism directly, David Shi, *The Simple Life: Plain Living and High Thinking in American Culture* (New York: Oxford University Press, 1985), traces the history of related ideas from the colonial era to their full flowering in the "back to the land" experiments of the twentieth century.

⁵ Roy Stryker to Arthur Rothstein, February 18, 1937, Roy Stryker Collection, Photographic Archive, University of Louisville, Ky. (hereafter cited as RSC). Resettlement Administration report, May 21, 1937, as quoted in Fleischhauer and Brannan, *Documenting America*, p. 147.

⁶ Arthur Rothstein, caption for Gee's Bend photograph, negative 25232, FSA Photographic Collection, Library of Congress (hereafter cited as FSA/LC).

⁷ The characteristics of the Sambo stereotype were first discussed at length by Stanley Elkins in 1960 in his controversial *Slavery: A Problem in American Institutional Life* (rev. ed., Chicago: University of Chicago Press, 1977). On the controversy surrounding this work, see Ann J. Lane, *Debate over Slavery: Stanley Elkins and His Critics* (Urbana: University of Illinois Press, 1971). See also Winthrop Jordan, *White over Black: American Attitudes toward the Negro, 1550–1812* (Chapel Hill: University of North Carolina Press, 1968). For the role of science in the perpetuation of this complex of attitudes, see Stephen Jay Gould, *The Mismeasure of Man* (New York: W. W. Norton, 1981). John W. Dower, *War without Mercy: Race and Power in the Pacific War* (New York: Pantheon Books, 1986), provides both a historical context for and an interpretation of racial attitudes on the eve of World War II. On Hollywood's depiction of African Americans, see Thomas Cripps, *Slow Fade to Black: The Negro in American Film, 1900–1942* (New York: Oxford University Press, 1977).

⁸ Ronald T. Takaki, *Iron Cages: Race and Culture in Nineteenth-Century America* (New York: Alfred A. Knopf, 1979), p. 114. In addition to the 1937 Resettlement Administration report previously cited, there are several other unpublished documents pertaining to Gee's Bend; they include the 1937 and 1939 reports of FSA home economist W. K.

Idlett, that of an official visitor, Constance E. H. Daniel (1939), and an unpublished, undated academic paper by Nathaniel S. Colley, a scholar from the Tuskeegee Institute. Typescripts of these documents are in the Migratory Labor Collection, Archive of Folk Culture, Library of Congress (hereafter cited as MLC).

⁹ Stryker to Rothstein, February 18, 1937, RSC. Although built upon sociolinguistic concepts developed by other scholars, Henry Glassie, *Folk Housing in Middle Virginia: A Structural Analysis of Historic Artifacts* (Knoxville: University of Tennessee Press, 1975), remains the essential starting point for an examination of the concepts of competence and performance in vernacular architecture. See also Catherine Bishir, *Architects and Builders in North Carolina: A History of the Practice of Building* (Chapel Hill: University of North Carolina Press, 1990).

¹⁰ The standard work on log buildings is Terry Jordan, *American Log Buildings* (Chapel Hill: University of North Carolina Press, 1985). Robert S. Lynd and Helen Merrell Lynd, *Middletown: A Study in Modern American Culture* (New York: Harcourt Brace, 1929), p. 8. For an analysis of Stryker's relationship with Lynd, the development of the small town shooting scripts, and Lee's series on Pie Town, see Curtis, *Mind's Eye, Mind's Truth*, pp. 93–122.

¹¹ Lewis Mumford, *Technics and Civilization* (New York: Harcourt Brace, 1934).

¹² On the tradition of covering walls with paper, see Charles Martin, *Hollybush: Folk Building and Social Change in an Appalachian Community* (Knoxville: University of Tennessee Press, 1984). Nathaniel S. Colley, "Customs, Attitudes, and Folkways of Gee's Bend" (MLC, undated typescript), p. 7.

¹³ "Report on Gee's Bend" (MLC, 1939[?], typescript), p. 1. On the popularity of Abraham Lincoln among Roosevelt's advisers, see Alfred Haworth Jones, *Roosevelt's Image Brokers: Poets, Playwrights, and the Use of the Lincoln Symbol* (Port Washington, N.Y.: Kennikat Press, 1974).

¹⁴ On Walker Evans's rearrangement of objects and interiors in Hale County, Ala., see Curtis, *Mind's Eye, Mind's Truth*, pp. 23–44.

¹⁵ John Temple Graves II, "The Big World at Last Reaches Gee's Bend," *New York Times Magazine* (August 22, 1937), pp. 12–15. Gee's Bend was the subject of several journalistic accounts, particularly, Beverly Smith, "Molasses and Sowbelly," *American Magazine* 124, no. 1 (July 1937): 156–57, 164–67; and Renwick C. Kennedy, "Life at Gee's Bend," *Christian Century* (September 1, 1937), pp. 1072–75.

¹⁶ Graves, "Big World Reaches Gee's Bend," pp. 12, 13, 15.

¹⁷ Graves, "Big World Reaches Gee's Bend," p. 15.

¹⁸ Graves, "Big World Reaches Gee's Bend," pp. 12, 13, 15.

¹⁹ Graves, "Big World Reaches Gee's Bend," pp. 12, 15.

²⁰ Graves, "Big World Reaches Gee's Bend," p. 15.

²¹ Idlett, "Gee's Bend Farms" (MLC, 1939, typescript), pp. 3–4.

²² Colley, "Customs, Attitudes, and Folkways," p. 6.

²³ Graves, "Big World Reaches Gee's Bend," p. 15.

²⁴ W. K. Idlett, "Gee's Bend Farms," pp. 2–3. In addition, see Wolcott's photographs of the health clinic: negative nos. 51580D and 51583D, FSA/LC.

²⁵ Constance E. H. Daniel, "Report on a visit made April 17–21, 1939, to Gee's Bend" (MLC, 1939, typescript), pp. 8–9, 11–12.

²⁶ Colley, "Customs, Attitudes, and Folkways," p. 8.

²⁷ The previous fall, Wolcott took pictures of late-night drinking and gambling in a Clarksdale, Miss., juke joint: negative nos. 52487D and 52497D. For a scholarly study that puts "jookin' " and the "Juke Joint" in the perspective of African American culture, see Katrina Hazzard-Gordon, *Jookin': The Rise of Social Dance Formation in African-American Culture* (Philadelphia: Temple University Press, 1990).

Scrapbook Houses

A Late Nineteenth-Century Children's View
of the American Home

Rodris Roth

In the hands of children, scrapbooks became houses. Pictures of furniture and furnishings were collected and cut out, then arranged in room settings, and, finally, pasted in place on the pages of albums. Of the twenty-five examples located, including four from the Smithsonian collections, most date from about 1880 to 1910 (fig. 1). The scrapbooks come from the northeastern and Mid-Atlantic United States and were made by, or for, girls about six to twelve years old from middle-class families. The twenty-five albums form the basis of this study and, except for three in private collections, constitute the accompanying list, "Some Scrapbook Houses in Public Collections" (appendix). Each album is cited within this essay by its corresponding appendix number.[1]

Documentation varies from album to album. Occasionally there is an inscription by the maker or original owner, a date or datable material, or a family history. Sometimes documentation is lacking altogether. A house in a scrapbook could be made by anyone, without regard to the person's age, gender, locality, race, or religion. The pastime was,

The author is indebted both to the institutions that have collected the albums and, especially, to their staff who supplied information about the albums, brought them to her attention, and made them available for study, namely Thomas Beckman, Robert I. Goeler, Jane Hirschkowitz, E. Richard McKinstry, Rosemary B. Philips, Nicolas Ricketts, Monica Simpson, Deborah Smith, and Beatrice Taylor.

Fig. 1. Four scrapbook houses. A "Parlor" is shown in the open album made for Edith W. Washburn by her nurse, Miss Scanison, Thomaston, Maine, 1892 (appendix, no. 10). Paper, paste, ink, paint, leather; L. 13¾". (Other albums are appendix, no. 11 *left*, no. 12 *right*, and no. 13 *foreground*.) (Smithsonian Institution.)

in a word, democratic. The only requirement was access to paper and pencil, scissors, and paste. Nevertheless, the albums reveal that their makers were well acquainted with, if not part of, the dominant culture in the United States. In the albums, the prevailing taste of the period in home interiors was the norm. The decor of real and scrapbook houses matched.[2]

Some albums are still inhabited by movable paper doll families, while others are peopled by permanent occupants, pasted in place on the page. These "scrapbook houses," or paper doll houses, as they are better known, vary in size, shape, and appearance, ranging from store-bought albums to homemade volumes to reused old ledgers. The techniques and materials used in the construction of the rooms depicted also vary, but certain features dominate. The rooms usually are treated consistently throughout an album. For instance, they may have wallpaper backgrounds, have people permanently pasted in place, be rendered entirely in paint, or be framed by curtains. In some scrapbooks the scale of the furniture is consistent, while in others the appropriateness of the object not its size is what matters. Nor is correct perspective of concern to some makers of paper doll houses. Additionally, a scrapbook-house room can either spread across a pair of facing pages or fill a single sheet.[3]

In one type of album the pages are covered with wallpaper. Figure 1 includes an example of this type, with the interior identified by the word "parlor" written in pencil on the edge of its left page. From Thomaston, Maine, and about fourteen inches high, the seventeen-room scrapbook house in which this parlor is located was constructed in a ledger first used in 1842 (appendix, no. 10). When reused a half century later, it was inscribed: "Miss Scanison, (my nurse) made / this when I was sick / in 1892. / I am always going / to keep it to remember / her by. / (Edith E. Washburn)." In the wallpapered-type interior, often the floor portion of the page is "carpeted" with one wallpaper pattern while the wall portions are papered with different patterns, perhaps from the actual house in which the child making the album lived.

Another category is that in which the occupants are permanent. An example is an album of twenty-some rooms made about 1890 by a Mystic, Connecticut, mother for her children (appendix, no. 13). Besides cutout furnishings, there are cutout people collected from printed sources. In this category, wallpaper is seldom used. Instead, the rooms are assembled directly on the album's blank pages. Pasted in place, the people enjoy one another's company or go about their daily chores. Sometimes the rooms incorporate drawn and painted elements in addition to printed ones. For instance, on the porch or piazza of the Mystic, Connecticut, album, sections of the railing and a column are drawn in and, along with the printed cutouts, are tinted with watercolors. The selection and placement of figures presents a lively scene.

Representative of the painted-album category is a dining room and adjacent area with a fireplace, perhaps for after-dinner coffee, from a scrapbook made in Lebanon, Pennsylvania, around 1905 (fig. 2) (appendix, no. 17). The interior is executed with ink, graphite, and watercolors as are each of the other five rooms in the big book, which measures nearly twenty-five inches long by thirty-two inches wide when open.

Fig. 2. Dining room in a scrapbook house made by Christine Ruth and Martha Ross, Lebanon, Pa., ca. 1905 (appendix, no. 17). Paper, paste, ink, paint, cloth; L. 24¾". (Strong Museum, Rochester, N.Y.)

The exuberant artists of the remarkably modish album were two little girls, Christine Ruth and her friend Martha Ross. They made the paper doll family, too. Although the interior is a painted one, the viewpoint is the same as in other types of houses. We are standing directly in front of, and looking straight at, one side of a room. In scrapbook houses, cupboards, chests, and cabinets are usually firmly attached to the page, but sometimes they are made to open by lifting a door or drawer flap to "store" clothes or dishes. The buffet, at the left, with its display of silver hollowware on the counter and crystal punch set above is unusual in being a movable piece.

The curtained setting forms yet another category as seen in a bedroom from an early twentieth-century scrapbook that contains more than thirty rooms, plus outdoor areas (fig. 3) (appendix, no. 19). On the first page are painted a door, shrubs, two windows, and a lantern. It is a facade, of sorts. A quaintly lettered, printed sign reads "Kenilworth / Inn" and above one window is the date "1903 A.D." The curtains framing the bedroom are tissue paper, and the tiebacks are paper trim. In some rooms crepe paper is used instead of tissue paper for the curtains. Rather than a stage set, the scheme may represent a view through a curtained

Fig. 3. Bedroom in a scrapbook house, United States, ca. 1900–1920 (appendix, no. 19). Paper, paste, ink, paint, cloth, leather; L. 14¼". (Joseph Downs Collection of Manuscripts and Printed Ephemera, Winterthur Library.)

window or a portiered doorway. Or, it may derive from the artistic convention of the draped background in portrait paintings. Whatever the intent, the result is dramatic. Noteworthy as well is the use of a view of an interior as an alternative to arranging a room from cutout furnishings. Sometimes, as in this bedroom, the view is extended or supplemented by a few appropriate pieces, such as furniture cut from printed sources and a looking glass made of silver paper in a crepe-paper frame.

While each album is an individual project with its own style, each also belonged to the broad group of "scrapbook houses" and, within that, to one of its subgroups, such as the wallpapered type, the permanently peopled type, the painted type, and the curtained type. The numerous albums and their similarity suggest a common origin, one or more of the children's or family magazines that proliferated in the later part of the nineteenth century. Examined were juvenile periodicals such as *St. Nicholas* and *Youth's Companion* and big-circulation women's and home periodicals such as *Ladies' Home Journal* and *Harper's Bazaar*. Other periodicals scanned included *Delinator, Godey's Lady's Book, Good Housekeeping*, and *McCalls*.[4]

In the family magazines there are articles about playthings to make and picture books to assemble. In the children's magazines there are stories and poems about paper dolls. Accompanying pictures show paper dolls as well as children cutting out paper dolls and playing with them, even housing them, but not in scrapbooks. The illustration for "The Story of The Paper Dollies" from the September 1883 issue of *St. Nicholas* shows two young mistresses of scrapbook houses and the comfortable and pleasant surroundings in which they lived. Such settings are replicated in the scrapbooks, such as the playroom in a six-room album (appendix, no. 15). The cover is stamped in gold letters "PAPER DOLLS HOUSE / EMILIE P. HICKEY." The picture from *St. Nicholas* also helps identify sources of the printed cutouts and provenances, so to speak, of the occupants of the scrapbooks. At the center of the playroom are the figures of Mabel and Kate from the picture. Carefully cut out, the two girls are placed in front of the fireplace and among their companions in a permanently peopled–type album.[5]

The picture confirms assumptions that the directing hand of older siblings and, especially, parents was ever present. The middle class firmly subscribed to a belief in the guidance and supervision of children. It took many forms. One might be providing juvenile periodicals, such as *St. Nicholas*, the highly acclaimed and widely revered nationally distributed monthly. Magazines were appreciated whether received by subscription, exchanged among friends, or passed on by wealthier relatives. Not every family had the financial means or chose to subscribe, but many did, which is a gauge of the increasing affluence of the middle class. It is also a measure of their respect and desire for culture and learning—and their indulgence of their children. Some families could afford not only to buy magazines but also to cut them up, eventually. Surely, the periodicals were read and reread many times and shared with playmates and neighbors as well before succumbing to scissors. Use of old magazines along with old ledgers and account books reminds us that frugality was still a virtue.[6]

Did the idea for the scrapbook house originate in the popular periodicals of the 1880s or 1890s? No articles predating 1900 have been located, but the authors of some of the early twentieth-century articles do refer to paper doll houses as a pastime of their childhood or as old-fashioned. Writing in 1906, one unnamed author remarked, "These paper doll houses are rather old, perhaps out of fashion among little girls. It may be the mothers have forgotten to tell the modern children about them! As a child, they were the delight of many a stormy day with me." The author's—and mothers'—childhood would have been a decade or more earlier. The timing coincides with the 1880s and 1890s dating of most of the albums and the timing of their introduction to a wider audience.[7]

Yet scrapbook houses appeared in this country even earlier than the late nineteenth century, that is, before the above-mentioned generation. As a general rule, cutout printed pictures in albums are probably from outdated publications. It seems safe to assume that a scrapbook house, therefore, postdates the latest cutout in it by a few years. Three examples that appear to date from the 1860s or 1870s are known. Two in private collections are constructed of furnishings and people cut from printed materials of those decades. These albums may have been made many years afterward, incorporating old material. Yet, they, like the albums made around the turn of the century, have every appearance of being put together about the same date as the cutout printed artifacts and figures in them, that is the 1860s or 1870s. Further, the third album is inscribed with the date 1861. Marian B. Howard, a serious collector of paper dolls and the author of numerous articles and books, described it in 1966: "Quite the most interesting early scrapbook paper doll house it has been my privilege to examine was made in an account book of vertical format. . . . Dated 1861, the book is inscribed 'To Mary Lee, Her Very Own Paper Doll Book, from Lt. Winfield Scott.'" The album contains a facade or "house front with its entrance door, a picket fence," and walk, and "21 furnished rooms" including a dining room, kitchen, bedroom, bathing room, and picture gallery.[8]

Despite the date of these albums, the earliest article about scrapbook houses found was in the September 1902 *Ladies' Home Journal*. The author, Marion Dudley Richards, recalls her childhood "Fun with Paper Dolls," as she titled the article. Instead of commercial paper dolls, she preferred the ones she cut from magazine pictures. "I could have a mother, a father, a daughter, a son, a baby, a nurse, a cook, a butler, a gardener, or anything I desired," she wrote. The houses she made at first were "in the shelves of my mother's wardrobe with regular doll-house furniture" or "on the floor, with half-open books for partitions and wooden blocks and rolls of cloth or paper for furniture." As she grew older she improved the accommodations of her paper dolls: "I took to making houses in books."[9]

Richards explains how to start the project: "These book houses any one can make, with a slight effort, for any little girl. Fifty or seventy-five cents will buy a large book or album for the purpose, though my first efforts were expended on old report books." The next step was to obtain "catalogues of furniture, lamps, ice-chests, stoves or any other illustrations that may be cut out and pasted into a book to make it look like a room." As for the rooms, Richards takes us on a tour. Here is how she described the scrapbook house in 1902:

The first page of the book may be left for pictures of the lawn, and the second makes a good piazza, upon which to place rattan chairs and tables, with a door and windows, if possible, in the background. The next two pages facing each other may be arranged like two sides of a hall, with the doors and windows showing; with the hat tree, the umbrella rack, chairs, tables, stairs, doorway into the parlor—preferably without cutting a hole in the page—pictures or anything that seems appropriate.

The next two pages may be the parlor or the reception-room, arranged in the same way with the necessary furnishing, and space may be devoted, in like manner, according to the thickness of the book, quantity of materials and ideas of the child, to the library or music-room, the dining-room, kitchen, cellar, and so on. A conservatory may be added, or a "den"; and a study or office if the child wants the father to be a doctor.

Upstairs the number of bedrooms must be regulated according to the requirements of the paper family, with pages allowed for a guest-room or two, a sewing-room, sitting-room and bathroom, servants' rooms, playroom and nursery.[10]

Scrapbook houses were an ideal medium to introduce girls to their future roles as wives, mothers, and homemakers. Once built, the paper doll house had to be furnished, which involved considerable searching and selecting of proper and tasteful objects. The placement and arrangement of furnishings were factors to be considered too. The house in a scrapbook, just as much as an actual one, had to be run and maintained properly. All this activity required time and patience, thought and decision, to say nothing of dexterity and neatness, whatever one's age. Richards, in the final words of advice, makes clear the value of a paper doll house: If the child's "mother, sister or friend who develop her interest in these" paper dolls and their book houses, "will guide her selection and assist in the careful cutting out, there is nothing better nor more instructive for a little girl."[11]

Two years later, in 1904, *Harper's Bazaar* carried an illustrated four-page article titled "Homes for Paper Dolls." The author, Emily Hoffman, offered advice similar to Richards's. Making a home for paper dolls, she remarked, "will keep the little girl busy and happy, and do away with that well-known rainy-day wail of nursery ennui, 'Mamma, I don't know what to do.'" The supplies needed were "a blank book, some old magazines, a pair of scissors, and a pot of mucilage." The advertisements at the back of magazines were recommended to the child so that the paper dolls, Hoffman declared, "can enjoy all the comforts of home and fairly revel in luxuries." This activity was, in a word, shopping, or at least a form of it. Imitating one's parents and guided by them, the child duplicated many activities of the adult world in putting together an album.[12]

Being a consumer and contractor for a paper doll house involved planning, locating a site, and selecting materials; surveying printed sources; arranging and rearranging the furnishings; and combining colors, patterns, and textures. It required familiarity with a range of social and domestic activities, an awareness of the fine and applied arts, and certainly an acquaintance with household management including overseeing staff—of the "occupied" albums, almost all had a maid, and many had a cook and other help.

"One of the advantages of making a paper-doll home," as Hoffman astutely remarked, "is that it cannot be accomplished at one sitting; the little girl must hunt for what she wants and learn to make the most of her material." And hunt she did. There was a world of paper goods in which to shop and select each and every item of furnishing. Indeed, the same paper flood that deluged the nation with magazines—that in part fostered the scrapbook projects—also carried with it other ingredients for albums, such as papers, trims, and stickers and scraps. In addition, it brought waves of commercial paper toys, both imported and domestic.[13]

In the United States, paper dolls were produced and marketed in some quantity by the middle of the nineteenth century. Also available were three-dimensional paper doll furniture and paper doll houses. Paper dolls, while flat, seem to have lived in a three-dimensional world aside from the scrapbook house. Although three dimensional and flat paper doll houses were in use simultaneously by the 1860s, the flat or scrapbook houses seem to have been exclusively homemade and remained so at least until the end of the century. In their paper game and toy catalogue for 1896–97, Milton Bradley Company of Springfield, Massachusetts, offered "A Home for Paper Dolls." It came in three sizes of six, ten, and fourteen rooms, the latter with two lawns. The toy was described as consisting of "sheets of cardboard on which are printed interior views of the various rooms in the house. The owner of the unoccupied 'house' furnishes each room by cutting out pictures of furniture and people from catalogues, illustrated papers, fashion books, etc, and pasting them on the sheets, thus making pictures showing the rooms completely furnished." The example illustrated in the catalogue was "an exact representation of a nursery actually furnished by a little girl." As is evident from the scrapbook houses, there was an abundant supply of cutout printed furnishings. It may even have reached surplus proportions. Besides pasting the cutout furnishings in the different rooms, according to Milton Bradley, "The little girls take as much pleasure in exchanging especially desirable pictures of which they happen to have an overstock as do the boys in trading rare stamps for their stamp albums." Surely the game company was responding to a prevailing pastime and the plenitude of printed materials. Although the printed sheets eliminated the need to decorate the room, shopping for furnishings, cutting them out, and then placing each piece properly gave the young owner more than enough to do. In this instance, Milton Bradley's paper doll home appears to be derived from the scrapbook house. It also is related to the cut-and-paste toys.[14]

Paper pasting games and cutout books, brightly colored and mass produced via chromolithography, abounded in the later nineteenth century. Mostly of European origin, they included house interiors. An English product featured on one page a picture of three children with a dollhouse and on another page illustrations of the furnishings and occupants to be cut out and put in the dollhouse's parlor, kitchen, sitting room, and bedroom. A French example included a view of a young girl's room with her doll in it. The missing furnishings and doll's clothing as well as the child herself had to be selected from an accompanying page, cut out, and pasted in the appropriate spaces. Paper pasting games of German origin were popular too. A kitchen scene required cutting and then placing pots, pans, and utensils; buckets, baskets, and pails; a stove, shelves, racks, and a cupboard with doors that folded back to reveal the provisions; china tableware; and more utensils. Although these cutout toys do not seem to be the direct prototypes for the album houses, bits and pieces from them found their way into scrapbook rooms.[15]

The kitchen in a forty-room album acquired in Boston is furnished with a number of items from the German kitchen just described (appendix, no. 18). Included are the open-shelf cupboard, the closed-door cabinet, and the racks of utensils and pots and pans. Many of the same fittings are seen in another kitchen, this one in the twenty-room scrapbook house from Mystic, Connecticut (fig. 4) (appendix, no. 13); its porch was described earlier. Parenthetically, this is a permanently peopled–type album as is the Boston album (appendix, no. 18). When the doors of the cupboard in the Mystic kitchen are opened, they reveal the contents that, like the other chromolithographed items in the room, are identical to those in the German paper toy.

The kitchen staff in this album suggests some of the other sources culled to construct a scrapbook house. The woman standing at the upper right is from an advertisement for Ivory Soap. In fact, she is holding the product in her hand. The older woman, sitting at the lower left, her hands raised—perhaps in disbelief that "the Ivory Soap floats"—is from an advertisement of a competitor, Pearline, a packaged soap.[16]

While some paper doll houses may be well staffed and even luxurious, they all seem surprisingly ordinary. One would think a scrapbook house could take any shape or form desired. It could be a storybook mansion, fairy-tale castle, or sleek time machine on a faraway planet. It need be limited only by one's imagination. With scrapbook houses, the fantasy may have been in the realm of size, that is, the number and kinds of rooms and the quantity of things, as well as in the richness of the fittings. The number of rooms in scrapbook houses ranges from as few as six to as many as forty. In some instances the interiors are named. In most instances a room's use is obvious from the furnishings, but occasionally guesswork is required. The more ambitious albums include: an art gallery, ballroom, billiard room, and breakfast room; a

Fig. 4. Kitchen in a scrapbook house made by Harriet Green Brown for her children, Mystic, Conn., ca. 1890 (appendix, no. 13). Paper, paste, ink, paint; L. 12½″. (Smithsonian Institution.)

conservatory, dressing room, exercise room, game room, and guest chamber; an office, schoolroom, theater, and, in one dwelling, even a wine cellar. The service side of the house is recorded in the albums as well, with pantry, laundry, and servants' quarters. There are outdoor areas, too, with lawns, gardens, and parks and, in a single instance, a tennis court.

There was a male presence in the scrapbook houses. The albums were peopled by paper doll families with fathers, sons, brothers, uncles, and cousins. There were also male servants. Some rooms were decidedly masculine, at least in the eyes of the album makers at the turn of the century. The larger palatial scrapbook house often had a game room such as the one in an album of the wallpapered-type with twenty-five

Fig. 5. Game room in a scrapbook house made by Louise Hovey, United States, ca. 1890s (appendix, no. 12). Paper, paste, ink, paint, leather; L. 17". (Smithsonian Institution.)

interiors (fig. 5) (appendix, no. 12). An ornamental note is the trophy at the center, composed of tennis rackets, fencing foils, and a baseball glove. Like this game room, boys' bedrooms in scrapbook houses often harbored sporting equipment, weight-lifting machines, Indian clubs, dumbbells, and home exercisers. Although girls and women joined in, such activities were associated with boys and men. For instance, in the picture of fencing practice, located beneath the trophy, the participants are male and the spectator is female.

With its "upstairs and downstairs" rooms, the scrapbook house affords us an unusual opportunity to go anywhere in the house we choose, to open doors, look in cupboards, observe the occupants, and wander from room to room. The young mistress of a scrapbook house may have explored the rooms in the same manner when playing with her paper dolls. Describing her two childhood albums, Anita Carolyn Blair wrote: "In going through a trunk I found 2 old books called Paper Doll Houses. As one turns the pages the house, garden & various . . . rooms of a residence [are represented] & one moved the paper dolls about in them as in a dolls house" (appendix, nos. 3, 4). Paper dolls were put in the scrapbook houses for safekeeping, a practice that encouraged neatness and responsibility. The writers on children's activities and projects were quick to emphasize the point. "The object," of an album, explained one author, "is to keep the paper dolls from being scattered all over the house and getting torn and lost."[17]

A final paper doll house is of the wallpapered-type and is made in a tall, narrow ledger (appendix, no. 11). Many of the furnishings are of wallpaper or other kinds of papers, not printed pictures from magazines and catalogues. The chairs, tables, beds, and bureaus and other furniture are shapes cut out of colored and decorated paper. Albums so furnished form another subgroup, the decorated-paper furnishing type. Originally used for accounts in 1854, the ledger was "remodeled," probably in the 1880s. A penciled note on the first page reads "Made by / Grace Curtis Stevens / in Marlboro, Mass. / Born 1871." A cross-section of a three-story house, with two rooms per floor, is arranged across facing pages (fig. 6) (appendix, no. 11). It is the single instance of this format in the ledger. Each of the twenty other rooms in the book is individually rendered. The diminutive scale of the furnishings is unusual, too. It may have suggested the cross-section format as a means of accommodating the tiny pieces. The rooms are, from left to right and bottom to top, the kitchen and dining room on the first floor, the parlor and sitting room on the second floor, and two bedrooms on the third floor. The mere opening of the scrapbook grants access behind the facade of this house or any other. What mischief the young owners and makers of these dwellings may have been up to, what domestic tragedies may have darkened the pages, what festive occasions lightened them, and what stories were acted out in the rooms can only be surmised.

In July 1910, *Harper's Bazaar* carried an article titled "A Doll's House." Though devoted mainly to that subject, there were a few paragraphs about how to make paper doll houses. It could be done in "a large new blank-book, . . . in one of father's old account-books, or even in a discarded telephone-book." Among materials recommended by the author, Carolyn Sherwin Bailey, were wallpaper to cover the pages, and "advertising pictures of magazines" for furnishings. In her parting words on the subject, Bailey summed up scrapbook houses: "Two pages should be used for each room, and if the furniture is cut very carefully, the result will be a book-house of which any little girl may be proud."[18]

Clearly there were many girls who could make this claim. And so could their mothers and sisters, who surely were the consultants if not

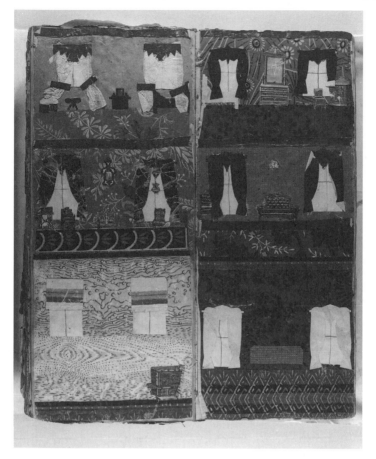

Fig. 6. A paper doll's paper doll house in a scrapbook house, made by Grace Curtis Stevens, Marlboro, Mass., ca. 1880s (appendix, no. 11). Paper, paste, ink, paint, leather; L. 16½″. (Smithsonian Institution.)

the guiding hands in most projects. Another possible participant was the art student. Four of the albums were made by students associated with either an industrial design school, an art institute, or a society of decorative art. This category raises the possibility that scrapbook houses may have been school assignments. In addition, three other albums of a standard manufactured variety, having the same dimensions and same coarse cloth coverings, are embellished in the same manner on the cover with a distinctive scheme of three wax "seals" holding a leather tying thong. Further, each album features a facade on the first page although the techniques used in assembling the rooms differ from album to album. More than a coincidence would seem to account for these matching books. A commercial venture may be the source. Perhaps the albums, with accompanying directions for constructing a house, were magazine premiums, mail order items, or shop purchases.[19]

In the end, one wonders if scrapbook houses were as much the wishes, desires, and fantasies of the mothers and older sisters as of the children. By the later nineteenth century, "household art" was women's domain. The scrapbooks may be but another manifestation of this trend.

The albums opened many more avenues than anticipated. Further study is needed to understand and interpret these material records of the past. They are, among, other things, documents of childhood activities, domestic settings, household arrangements, mass marketing, and middle-class life. Nevertheless, it seems safe to say that the number of completed albums, most showing evidence of use, suggest that in a society with rising expectations and achievable goals, the children could and did participate, via scrapbook houses. And, of course, scrapbook houses are a delight in and of themselves.

POSTSCRIPT 1996

When this essay was presented in 1992, I surmised that an article existed predating 1900 with directions for constructing a paper doll house. I had searched for but did not find one. Recently, an example was located. "The Paper-doll's House" by Jessie E. Ringwalt appeared in *Godey's Ladies' Book and Magazine* of August 1880. Accompanying it were four line drawings of a front door, hall chair, staircase, and furnished room spread over two facing pages of an album. In this article the model for the scrapbook house appeared fully developed. The author recommended using a blank book for the dwelling. On the first page was to be the front door or, a "further improvement," the facade or "whole front of the house . . . in a red brick, or . . . stone." The rooms were to follow in sequence—hall and staircase, drawing room or parlor, dining room, schoolroom or study, playroom, sleeping apartments, bathroom, and kitchen—"as if the house was being viewed by a guest." Prior to furnishing the rooms, the maker of the scrapbook was advised that "it is customary to first arrange, on the outer edge of each page, a graceful drapery, representing a window-curtain" of paper, lace, or net. Appropriate objects and where to obtain them were discussed. They might be pictures from "advertising sheets and newspapers" or "shapes cut to resemble them in tinted," embossed, or gilt papers. Next the furnishings were arranged and "then pasted across the foot of the pages." Slits could be cut in or by the furniture and the paper dolls inserted so as to stand or sit in the rooms. Another suggestion was to cut open the doors in sideboards and cupboards to provide storage for dishes, linens, and clothing. Finally, an idea was offered by Ringwalt that perhaps explains what, at first glance, looks like a cross-section of a dwelling in an album of otherwise separate rooms (see fig. 6). She wrote, "The very heart of this doll-house is found in its own doll-house. In the play-room is placed a tiny dwelling cut in tinted paper." Surely, the multiroom dwelling in figure 6 is for the paper dolls' paper dolls. The finishing touch to an album, it is a summary in minutiae of paper doll or scrapbook houses.[20]

---

[1] Of the 25 scrapbook houses located, 3 were privately owned and 22 were in 7 public U.S. institutions of 27 surveyed around the country. For the 3 albums in private collections, see note 8. The other 22 albums constitute the appendix and are referred to by their list number in the following summary. Dates were inscribed in 5 albums: 1892 (nos. 1, 10), 1893 (no. 2), 1903 (no. 19), and 1919 (no. 5). A few examples appear to date as early as the 1860s or 1870s—the 3 in private collections—and one as late as 1919 (no. 5), but most of the scrapbooks I have seen were made around the turn of the twentieth century. Except for one from Chicago, the scrapbooks are associated with the northeastern United States, that is, New England and the Mid-Atlantic region, either by documentation, place of acquisition, or internal evidence. Localities include the following documented by inscriptions or family history: Connecticut (no. 13), Delaware (no. 5), Illinois (no. 4), Maine (no. 10), Maryland (no. 3), Massachusetts (no. 11), and Pennsylvania (nos. 1, 2, 17); by place

of acquisition: Massachusetts (no. 18) and Vermont (no. 16); and by internal evidence: Massachusetts (no. 20) and Mid-Atlantic states (no. 19).

[2] Owner's names, all girls, were inscribed in 11 scrapbooks (see appendix): Anita (nos. 3, 4), Christine (no. 17), Deborah (no. 5), Edith (no. 10), Emilie (no. 15), Grace (no. 11), Lizah[?] (no. 16), Louise (no. 12), Martha (no. 17), and Mary (nos. 1, 2). In 2 instances, according to the accompanying histories, the owners were also the albums' makers (nos. 12, 17). Other identified makers were mothers (nos. 5, 13), a nurse (no. 10), and art students (nos. 1, 2, 3, and 4), 2 of whom were cousins of the child owning the books. Old ledgers were used in at least 5 instances (nos. 1, 10, 11, 18, and 21). For a view of period interiors recorded in photographs, see William Seale, *The Tasteful Interlude: American Interiors through the Camera's Eye, 1860–1917* (1975; 2d ed. rev. and enl., Nashville: American Association for State and Local History, 1981). For the prescriptive literature about interior decoration, see Martha Crahill McClaugherty, "Household Art: Creating the Aesthetic House, 1868–1893," *Winterthur Portfolio* 18, no. 1 (Spring 1983): 1–16.

[3] Almost the only available source on the subject is Flora Gill Jacobs, *A History of Dolls' Houses* (New York: Charles Scribner's Sons, 1965), chap. 16, "Houses for Paper Dolls," pp. 248–57. Four illustrations of "German cut-out books" and data about them accompany the chapter and are identified by Jacobs as a marketplace, counting room, drawing room, and nursery. They have pasted-in people. The cited source for the German cut-out books is Karl Grober, *Children's Toys of Bygone Days* (orig. German ed., 1927; English ed., London: B. T. Batsford., 1928), pp. 36–37, figs. 145–48. In the eighteenth century, according to Grober, "German engravers . . . brought out a series of pictures meant only for cutting out." These paper toys were cut out and "stuck onto large sheets of pasteboard, and the background was then painted in. Thus each child could make its own picture-book. . . . The Bavarian National Museum in Munich possesses two such picture-books, dating from the end of the eighteenth century" (Grober, *Children's Toys*, pp. 36–37). Whether these albums are the prototype of scrapbook houses has not been determined. Jacobs mentions an "illustrated 38-page monograph entitled *Homes for Paper Dolls and Kindred Paper Toys* was brought out by Marian B. Howard of Miami, Florida," in 1953 (Jacobs, *History of Dolls' Houses*, p. 257). I have been unable to locate a copy of this publication.

[4] For brief histories of the periodicals and their significance, see Frank Luther Mott, *History of American Magazines*, 5 vols. (Cambridge: Harvard University Press, 1938–68), under the headings: juvenile periodicals, women's activities, and the individual magazine names. R. Gordon Kelly reviews the history of children's magazines and the scholarly and interpretative study of them; R. Gordon Kelly, ed., *Children's Periodicals of the United States* (Westport, Conn.: Greenwood Press, 1984), pp. ix–xvi; see also the specific entries for *St. Nicholas* and *The Youth's Companion*.

[5] Examples of magazine articles in family magazines that feature children's projects include: Frederica Kunze, "Home-Made Toys," *Ladies Home Journal* (April 1887): 5, with illustrations and instructions for making dolls, cradles, and animals; Fannie L. Faucher, "What Josie Did," in "Mother's Corner," *Ladies' Home Journal* (April 1889): 7, with chair, sofa, and table patterns for children to make cardboard doll furniture for themselves or for "birthday or holiday presents"; Elisabeth Robinson Sorit, "Children in the Country," *Ladies' Home Journal* (August 1893): 18, with suggestions or "Resources for Rainy Days," such as "dressing a doll or making a scrap-book for a children's hospital or to send in the next missionary box"; and "Mother's Corner," *McCalls* (June 1895): 155, with directions for making "An Education Scrap Book," with pictures of "noted people of the day." Examples of stories, poems, and pictures of paper dolls in children's magazines include: Gertrude Huntington, "A Tragedy in the Garret," *St. Nicholas* (April 1882): 464–67, an illustrated short story about "two little girls" and their paper dolls, "cut

from fashion journals," who live with 3-dimensional pasteboard furniture in rooms formed by "old books . . . stood up on end"; and Pauline King, "Paper-Doll Poems," *St. Nicholas* (June 1896): 693, about the adventures of 2 paper dolls and their dog.

[6] Eighty-eight-year-old Mabel Bobbitt of Shelby County, Ill., recalled sharing the cost of a subscription to *Youth's Companion*, in an interview in the 1980s. She was one of 4 children in the family in the late 1890s when an aunt "paid a dollar a year and my father had to pay the other 75¢ to get" the magazine (Eleanor Arnold, ed., *Girlhood Days* [Bloomington: Indiana University Press, 1987], p. 48).

[7] "A Paper Doll House," in "A Mother," *Modern Priscilla* (January 1906): 20, was brought to my attention by Rosemary B. Philips, librarian, Chester County Historical Society. Marion Dudley Richards, "Fun with Paper Dolls," *Ladies' Home Journal* (September 1902): 41, also dates the scrapbooks to her childhood. Miss Anita Carolyn Blair, who offered the 2 paper dollhouses (nos. 3, 4) of her childhood in the 1890s to the Chicago Historical Society, remarked that "they might be of interest as an example of a little girl's toys of the period. No children seem to know today what they are nor do they play with paper dolls" (Blair to Paul M. Angle, Chicago Historical Society, April 10, 1958, Decorative and Industrial Arts Collection, Chicago Historical Society).

[8] I examined one privately owned album when it was brought to the Smithsonian for identification in 1987. Two pages of another were kindly brought to my attention by Diana Korzenik; they were illustrated in her book, *Drawn to Art: A Nineteenth-Century American Dream* (Hanover, N.H.: University Press of New England, 1985); Korezenik to author, October 6, 1992. Marian B. Howard, "Paper Doll Houses Delight Young of All Ages," in United Federation of Doll Clubs, *Seventeenth Convention Program* (Chicago: By the federation, 1966), p. 24. The album's owner was not disclosed, and its whereabouts and that of the Howard collection are unknown. The Lee and Scott family association remains to be explored as does the identity of Lt. Winfield Scott vis-a-vis the renowned American military officer (1786–1866) of that same name.

[9] Richards, "Fun with Paper Dolls," p. 41. Other articles with instructions for constructing a paper doll house in a scrapbook include, in chronological order, the following after Richards's piece of 1902: Emily Hoffman, "Homes for Paper Dolls," *Harper's Bazaar* (January 1904): 84–87; "A Paper Doll House," *Modern Priscilla* (January 1906): 20; Carolyn Sherwin Bailey, "A Doll's House," *Harper's Bazaar* (July 1910): 474.

[10] Richards, "Fun with Paper Dolls," p. 41.

[11] Richards, "Fun with Paper Dolls," p. 41.

[12] Hoffman, "Homes for Paper Dolls," pp. 84, 86.

[13] Hoffman, "Homes for Paper Dolls," p. 87.

[14] Anne Tolstoi Wallach, *Paper Dolls* (New York: Van Nostrand Reinhold Co., 1982), pp. 12–31, provides a brief survey of paper dolls in the nineteenth century. Blair Whitton, *Paper Toys of the World* (Cumberland, Md.: Hobby House Press, 1986), pp. 114, 118, fig. 156A, describes and pictures Milton Bradley's "A Home for Paper Dolls"; for other examples of furniture for paper dolls, see pp. 131–34.

[15] For the English dollhouse, see Jacobs, *History of Dolls' Houses*, p. 252. For the French girl's room, see Mary Hillier, *Dolls and Doll-makers* (New York: G. P. Putnam's Sons, 1968), facing p. 194, figs. 210, 211, p. 194. For the German kitchen, see Eva Stille, *Doll Kitchens 1800–1890* (orig. German ed., 1985; English ed., West Chester, Pa.: Schiffer Publishing, 1988), p. 44.

[16] The Ivory Soap advertisement in the kitchen is of unknown date, but another, "To Preserve the Softness," in the laundry was copyrighted 1886 and appeared in *Ladies' Home Journal* (December 1887): 32. The Pearline advertisement, "Does it Hurt Clothes?" appeared in *Godey's Lady's Book* (April 1890): ii; it may have appeared elsewhere earlier.

[17] Blair to Angle, Chicago Historical Society, April 10, 1958. Richards, "Fun with Paper Dolls," p. 41.

[18] Bailey, "Doll's House," p. 474.

[19] The scrapbook houses made by art students are appendix, nos. 1, 2, 3, and 4. The 3 matching albums are nos. 5, 14, and 19. Besides the similarities noted, the 3 albums match with respect to another feature as well: the word "SCRAPS" and a few decorative motifs appear on the covers but in a different style on each.

[20] Deborah A. Smith, "Consuming Passions: Scrapbooks and American Play," *The Ephemera Journal* 6 (1993): 73; Smith cites and quotes from the article in *Godey's*, pp. 160–62. In discussing "scraphouse" albums, she illustrates 3 rooms—a bathroom, drawing room, and parlor, or perhaps living hall (figs. 16–18, pp. 73–74)—in a scrapbook that, I learned from correspondence with the Strong Museum, was their album 90.2559, which is no. 18 in the accompanying appendix. I am grateful to Helena Wright for bringing this article to my attention. Two other references for making a paper doll house were recently brought to my attention by Beverly Gordon and Neville Thompson, respectively, for which I am appreciative: Carolyn Wells, "A Paper Doll's House," *The Puritan* 9 (1901): 273–75, and *The Good Housekeeping Discovery Book No. 1* (New York: Phelps Publishing Co., 1905), pp. 78–79. Of the albums that have come to my notice recently, one acquired by the Smithsonian Institution's National Museum of American Art is the subject of an illustrated article kindly forwarded by author and curator Lynda Roscoe Hartigan: see Lynda Roscoe Hartigan, "The House That Collage Built," *American Art* 7, no. 2 (Summer 1993): 88–91.

Appendix

Some Scrapbook Houses in Public Collections

CHESTER COUNTY HISTORICAL SOCIETY

No. 1. L.1991.12.7. Ledger. Made for Mary Sharpe Hemphill, West Chester, Pa., by a cousin, a student at the Pennsylvania Museum and School of Industrial Design, Philadelphia, November 12, 1892. Gift of Dorothy A. Bryan.

No. 2. L.1991.12.7. Album. Made for Mary Sharpe Hemphill, West Chester, Pa., by a cousin, a student at the Pennsylvania Museum and School of Industrial Design, Philadelphia, August 23, 1893. Gift of Dorothy A. Bryan.

CHICAGO HISTORICAL SOCIETY

No. 3. 1958.156. Album. Made for Anita Carolyn Blair, Chicago. According to the donor, made by the Decorative Arts Society of Baltimore, ca. 1895, as a gift from her mother and father. Gift of Anita Carolyn Blair. (Portions reproduced in Barbara Chancy Ferguson, *The Paper Doll: A Collector's Guide with Prices* [Des Moines, Iowa: Wallace-Homestead Book Co., 1982], pp. 54–55, 61.)

No. 4. 1958.157. Album. Made for Anita Carolyn Blair, Chicago. According to the donor, made by Miss Jenks, a student at the Art Institute of Chicago. Gift of Anita Carolyn Blair. (Portions reproduced in Barbara Chaney Ferguson, *The Paper Doll: A Collector's Guide with Prices* [Des Moines, Iowa: Wallace-Homestead Book Co., 1982], p. 54.)

HISTORICAL SOCIETY OF DELAWARE

No. 5. 1990.24. Album. Made for ten-year-old Deborah G. H. Turnbull by her mother, Deborah Halsey Turnbull Scott, Wilmington, Del., Christmas 1919.

MUSEUM OF THE CITY OF NEW YORK

No. 6. 55.81.68. Album, ca. 1870s. (Eight rooms reproduced in *Toys and Games: Imaginative Playthings from America's Past* [Alexandria, Va.: Time-Life Books, 1991], pp. 42–43.)

No. 7. Unnumbered. Album. Art nouveau–style rooms, ca. 1890s.

No. 8. Unnumbered. Album, ca. 1890s. Gift of Miss Hilda Strauss.

No. 9. Unnumbered. Album, ca. 1870s. Gift of Mrs. William B. Harding.

SMITHSONIAN INSTITUTION, NATIONAL MUSEUM OF AMERICAN HISTORY

No. 10. 58.23. Ledger. Made for Edith E. Washburn by her nurse, Miss Scanison, Thomaston, Maine, 1892. Gift of Miss Helen R. Newcombe and Miss Elisabeth W. Newcombe (see fig. 1).

No. 11. 59.71. Ledger. Made by Grace Curtis Stevens, Marlboro, Mass., ca. 1880s. Gift of Dr. and Mrs. Arthur M. Greenwood (see fig. 6).

No. 12. 61.293. Album. Made by Louise Hovey, ca. 1890s. Gift of Lispenard Seabury Crocker (see fig. 5).

No. 13. 301846.1. Album. Made for her children by Harriet Green Brown, Mystic, Conn., ca. 1890. Gift of Mrs. Raymond Johnson and Mrs. Harold Sim (see fig. 4).

STRONG MUSEUM

No. 14. 78.7248. Album, 1920–40.

No. 15. 78.7253. Album. Made for Emilie P. Hickey, ca. 1885. (Playroom has cutout figures from *St. Nicholas* [September 1883]: 873, and is reproduced in Harvey Green, *The Light of the Home* [New York: Pantheon Books, 1983], p. 50.)

No. 16. 80.214. Album. Made for Lizah[?] Thomas, Vermont[?], 1870–90.

No. 17. 88.9. Album. Made by Christine Ruth and Martha Ross, Lebanon, Pa., ca. 1905 (see fig. 2).

No. 18. 90.2559. Ledger. Massachusetts[?], ca. 1890. (Bathroom includes a figure from an advertisement for Ivory Soap, copyrighted 1886, *Ladies' Home Journal* [February 1888]: 20.)

WINTERTHUR MUSEUM, GARDEN, AND LIBRARY

No. 19. Folio 36. Album. Facade marked "Kenilworth/Inn," and "1903" (see fig. 3).

No. 20. Doc. 13. Album. Labeled of Merrill and Mackintire, Books and Stationary, Salem, Mass., and marked: "PAT. MAY 22, 1883."

No. 21. 80x21. Ledger, ca. 1880. (Library includes a picture of a table by Clowes and Gates Manufacturing Co., Worcester, Mass., patented June 19, 1877.)

No. 22. 85x21. Ledger.